LAROUSSE
Dictionary of
WINES
of the World

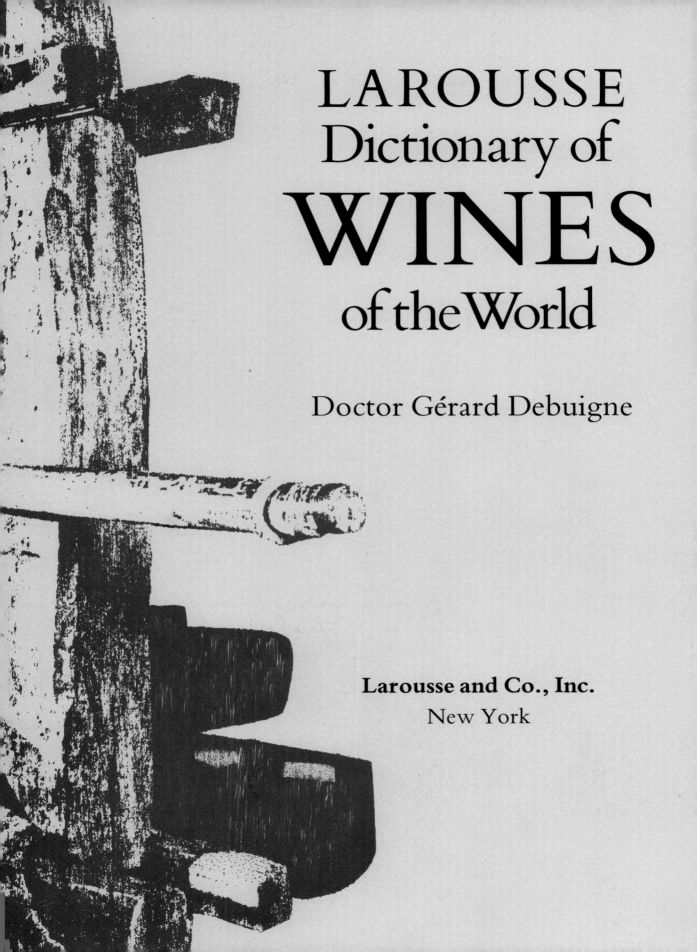

LAROUSSE
Dictionary of
WINES
of the World

Doctor Gérard Debuigne

Larousse and Co., Inc.
New York

Drinking horn (Germany, 15th Century). Musée de Cluny. Phot M.

FOREWORD

Since Genesis, wine has always existed side by side with man and played a role in the events of his life: communion wine, votive wine, wine of honour. . . .

Olivier de Serres, in his *Théâtre d'Agriculture,* wrote in 1600: 'After bread comes wine, the second element given by the Creator for the preservation of life and the first celebration of his excellence'. A gift from heaven certainly, but from a heaven which is far from always merciful! Wine is also a product of man's endeavour and – above all – a work of art.

Today, the art of the vigneron is not only based on tradition but has become a true science, tempered by an intelligent, empirical instinct. The *Larousse Dictionary of Wines of the World* permits the man of today, always pressed for time, to learn rapidly and without long research the successive phases of the creation and life of wine; the different vinicultural regions and the 'races' of wines; the indispensable technical details of vinification and legislation affecting wine as well as the vocabulary used by wine-lovers.

Many subjects are now so complex that it can be almost impossible to know everything about any one. This is the case with wine. There is no living person who could hope to embrace all the knowledge related to it. This book does not pretend to treat such a vast and profound subject in depth but, by putting within everyone's reach all the essential facts, it will engender a respect and love for this noble and mysterious juice of the grape.

September at the château of Saumur from Les Très Riches Heures du Duc de Berry. *Musée Condé, Chantilly.* Phot. Giraudon.

A

abondance Abondance is the wine liberally diluted with water that is sometimes given to children in French schools.

acescence Also known as *piqûre,* this disease is caused by acetic bacteria which attack all fermented liquids, notably wine, making them sour and acid.

acid (malic) An element found mostly in unripe grapes which gives them a characteristic sour★ taste. The quantity of malic acid decreases as the fruit ripens because of the part it plays in the respiratory processes of the plant. These processes accelerate when the temperature rises, which is why grapes contain little malic acid in hot years and too much in cold years.

Under the influence of certain bacteria, malic acid decomposes during malo-lactic fermentation★. This results in a reduction in the overall acidity of the wine.

acid (sorbic) The use of this acid, in the form of potassium sorbate, is officially limited to a maximum of 200 mg per litre. It is used as a partial substitute for sulphur dioxide★ as a sterilising agent and deoxidant. Sorbic acid is especially useful in the treatment of sweet wines when sulphur dioxide has to be used to prevent refermentation★. Sulphur dioxide sometimes produces a noticeable smell and taste in the wine, an undesirable effect that can be greatly reduced by the substitution of a quantity of sorbic acid. However, as sorbic acid is effective only as a fungicide and an inhibitor of yeasts and ineffective against bacteria, it must always be used in conjunction with sulphur dioxide.

Sorbic acid also has several drawbacks.

If the acid solution is not fresh it can impair the taste of the wine; bacteria may attack it and cause it to decompose which results in a very disagreeable taste comparable to that of geranium stalks; and lastly, resistant yeasts sometimes develop at the bottom of the bottle and form unpleasant lumps of deposit. Sorbic acid should, therefore, only be used immediately before bottling on wine that has been stabilised and is completely free of bacteria.

acidification The process of adding tartaric acid to must, or citric acid to wine, when a very hot and sunny year has produced a wine deficient in acidity. Without this corrective measure the wine would lack balance and freshness and would not keep well. Acidification is not a chemical process, it is simply the correction of a deficiency in substances which are normally constituent parts of the wine. Citric and tartaric acid are both natural products.

acidity (fixed) The combination of all the organic acids normally contained in the fruit and also present in the wine, e.g. malic acid★, tartaric acid and lactic acid.

acidity (real) This is expressed by chemists as pH, which, without going into technical details, can be said to represent the intensity of a wine's acidity. Some acids have a more active acidity than others, which is why wines with the same total acidity★ can have different pH ratings. For acid solutions pH is graded from 7 to 0, 7 being absolute neutrality and 0 absolute acidity. The lower a wine's pH, the higher its acidity. According to a French oenologist named Jaulmes, wines have a pH of between 2·7 and 3·9. The first figure would represent a very acid wine and the second, a very neutral and flat one.

acidity (total)   The total or overall acidity of a wine is composed of all the free and combined acid substances present in it, i.e. its volatile acidity★ and its fixed acidity★. The health and longevity of wine depend on its acid content as do the qualities known as freshness and nerve★, or crispness. Acidity itself depends on the condition of the grapes. In cold years they are still relatively unripe at harvest time and the resulting wine has too much acid, tasting tart and green★. In some cases deacidification★ is legally permitted as a corrective measure for excessive acidity. In hot years, on the other hand, overripe grapes make wine with a low acid content which has to be corrected by acidification★. A well-balanced, reasonably long-lived wine should have a total acidity of 4–5 g per litre.

Two wines with the same overall acid content can taste completely different owing to the different nature of their constituent acids. If tartaric acid predominates, for example, the wine will have a rough taste. This, however, disappears quite quickly as, with the advent of cold weather, the tartaric acid is changed into insoluble potassium bitartrate.

acidity (volatile)   Volatile acids are those which can be separated from the wine by distillation. Wine normally contains only a small quantity, from 0·3–0·4 g per litre. Any increase in this proportion is evidence of microbial adulteration, which is why French law statutorily prohibits the sale of wines showing 0·9 g of volatile acidity in the vineyard and 1 g in the shops. The principal constituent element of volatile acidity is acetic acid (or vinegar) which can make wine practically undrinkable. It begins by tasting piquant, or sharp, and later becomes distinctly sour★. Volatile acidity always increases with age and produces a piqué wine. There is no remedy, especially as dépiquage, chemical correction of the sourness, is strictly forbidden by law. When the volatile acidity of a wine is strong enough (about 0·7 g) to be noticeable in taste, the wine is said to be feverish, and later sour and piqué.

Africa   As vines can only be grown in a temperate climate, the only parts of this vast continent that produce wine are the temperate zones of the north (Morocco★, Algeria★ and Tunisia★) and the south (South Africa★).

age of the vine   This has a very great influence on the quality of wine. A plant takes three years to produce its first grapes and from ten to twelve years to make a respectable wine. The greatest wines have always been made from vines between twenty and forty years old. Vignerons say: 'You need old vines for great wines'.

aggressive   An aggressive wine 'attacks' the taste buds, either with an excessive acidity caused by unripe grapes or with an excess of tannin due to a prolonged fermentation period.

Ahr   A small river in western Germany which joins the Rhine from the west just north of Coblenz. The vineyards perched on the steep hillsides of the river valley are planted almost entirely with the Pinot Noir of Burgundy, locally known as Spätburgunder. They are the most northerly vineyards in Europe. Their pale red wines, which are delicious and have a fine bouquet, are the best red wines of Germany (which produces very few). The wines are rarely exported, and are best drunk slightly chilled in their native region around the towns of Ahrweiler, Neuenahr and Walporzheim.

aigre   A disorder giving wine a sour taste

Electric pH meter for measuring the acidity of wines. Ecole Nationale d'Agriculture de Montpellier. Phot. M.

8

caused by the *Mycoderma aceti*★ bacteria which turn wine into vinegar. It occurs most frequently in barrels which are not filled properly and in which the wine lost by evaporation is not replaced with sufficient care or regularity – leaving the bacteria the air they need for their development. Acetic bacteria are even more liable to develop when the temperature exceeds 30°C and this accounts for the frequency with which the malady occurs during the summer months.

A sour taste in a wine is immediately noticeable. When a proportion of the acetic acid combines with alcohol it produces a sharp taste, which is even more unpleasant. The correction of this fault is forbidden by French law, as is the sale of such wine.

Ain-Bessem-Bouira Algerian wines grown south-east of Algiers on limestone or schistose soil at an altitude of about 500 m. The red wines are very full-bodied (at least 13° alcohol), bright and supple, with a pleasant, well-rounded flavour. The rosés, which are also fairly alcoholic, are a pretty bright pink, almost cherry-red, colour and are fruity and easy on the palate. Ain-Bessem-Bouira wines were once classified VDQS★.

Ain-el-Hadjar A small Algerian vineyard in the department of Oran whose wines were once VDQS★. They are grown high up on the plateaus, at altitudes of between 600 and 1200 m. The wines, which can be red, rosé or white, are generally of good quality and keep well in bottle. The reds are very full-bodied (13·8°) and well balanced, with a delicate bouquet and mellowness. The equally full-bodied whites and rosés are fragrant and fruity.

Aix-en-Provence (Coteaux d') The wines produced around the ancient city of Aix qualify for the VDQS★ label. They are made from the classic grapes of Provence★, i.e. Grenache, Carignan, Cinsault and Mourvèdre for the red and the rosé, and Clairette, Ugni and Muscat for the white. They are pleasant, fruity, full-bodied wines.

Alameda A county in northern California★ east of San Francisco Bay. The main vineyards are situated in the Livermore Valley, around the town of Livermore. The fine gravelly soil seems ideally suited to fine white European grapes such as Sauvignon, Sémillon, Pinot Blanc and Chardonnay. The region's output is almost entirely white, and its wines are among the best in California. The best-known vineyards are Concannon, Cresta Blanca and Wente Brothers.

alcohol The alcohol content of a wine is formed during fermentation of the must. The natural grape sugar is converted by yeasts into roughly equal amounts of alcohol and carbon dioxide★. The alcoholic strength of the wine is usually between 8 and 14°, sometimes 15°. Normal fermentation cannot produce a strength of more than 15°, consequently a wine with more than 15° of alcohol (i.e. 15% by volume) has invariably been fortified in some way with extra alcohol. Wines which have been subject to mutage★ can have an alcoholic strength of 18–22°. One degree of alcohol is produced by roughly 17 g of sugar per litre for white wine and 18 g for red. Thus a 10° wine will have been made from juice containing 170 g of sugar per litre if white, 180 g if red.

Alcohol sustains other constituent elements of the wine and also contributes greatly to its longevity. A wine rich in alcohol is more agreeable to the palate, although ultimately more tiring to the drinker. Unfortunately, alcoholic strength was once, in the public mind, synonymous with quality, and until quite recently the degree of alcohol was a popular criterion of excellence. Nowadays, the wine-buying public is more discerning and generally prefers lighter, less full-bodied wines.

The alcohol content of a wine depends on various factors: the species of grape; the nature of the soil (wine grown on limestone, for example, is generally richer in alcohol than wine grown on pebbly, siliceous soil); the climate (a hot, dry climate tends to produce wines with more body); and lastly the vintage (wines grown in a hot year usually have a relatively high alcohol content). The alcohol should never dominate the taste of the wine, but should always blend perfectly with the other elements. Chaptalisation★ can therefore be a very risky operation. The addition of

sugar to the grape juice in order to increase the wine's alcohol content may disturb the natural balance between its various elements and result in a harsh, unbalanced and mediocre wine. Wines rich in alcohol are characterised by the English words vinous★, heády★, full-bodied★, generous★ and spirituous. (Their French equivalents are *vineux, capiteux, corsé, généreux* and *spiritueux*.)

ALCOHOL (TOTAL)   The expressions total alcohol, acquired alcohol and potential alcohol are sometimes used in reference to vins blanc liquoreux (sweet white wines). The total alcohol is the sum of the acquired alcohol and the potential alcohol. Thus Sauternes★, for example, has an official minimum alcohol content of 13°, of which at least 12·5° is acquired alcohol. This means that Sauternes must have at least 12·5° of real alcohol, the remaining 0·5° being 'potential' alcohol, i.e. sugar. As

same name. It is a member of the Muscat★ family, a fact evident in both its bouquet and its taste. The best wine is produced on the island of Elba, particularly around the town of Portoferraio, whose name it sometimes bears. It is a smooth dessert wine that has a wide reputation. It is not unlike a port, although it is lighter in body and possesses a fine aroma of Muscat.

Algeria   All the vineyards of this former French colony were planted by French colonisers who settled in the country from 1842 onwards. As phylloxera★ ravaged the vineyards in the south of France, planting was begun on a massive scale in Algeria, on both hills and plains. Today, the principal varieties of grape are Carignan, Cinsault, Grenache, Cabernet, Morastel, Mourvèdre and Pinot for red wines, and Faranah, Clairette, Ugni Blanc and Aligoté for white.

Until recently Algerian wines were used

Vineyards of the Mitidja, Algeria. Phot. OFALAC and Ministry of Information, Algiers.

it takes 17 g of sugar per litre to produce one degree of alcohol, the extra 0·5° would be obtained by adding 8·5 g of sugar to each litre of grape juice (a quantity which is, in fact, often exceeded).

Likewise, 11° of Monbazillac's★ official 13° total alcohol content must be acquired alcohol with the remaining 2° of potential alcohol being produced by 34 g of sugar per litre. Quarts-de-Chaume★ must have 13° of total alcohol, of which 12° is acquired alcohol, etc.

Aleatico   An Italian grape which produces a red, usually sweet, wine of the

as the basis of French vins de coupage★, or blended wines. Made as they were from common, extremely prolific vines, they were for a long time merely mass-produced vins ordinaires (table wines). However, several wines grown in the mountain regions gradually improved in quality until they finally qualified for the important VDQS★ label. This was the result of more than a century's work by pioneers from the Languedoc, Jura and Burgundy regions of France, who gradually adapted their grapes and methods of vinification to the soil and climate of Africa.

Vineyards of the Mitidja, Algeria. Phot. OFALAC and Ministry of Information, Algiers.

The red wines, always full and generous, were sometimes remarkably good, with a pronounced bouquet and a certain quality. They had the additional advantage of maturing quickly. Some of the white wines, although they were not well known, were light and fruity but lacked vigour.

Algerian wines have not been officially entitled to the VDQS label since the country's independence in 1962, as French wine laws can no longer be enforced. Algeria is now expected to define the quality of its own wines in accordance with the standards established by the international wine laws.

Besides table wines, Algeria, since 1880, has produced mistelles★ (wines used in the preparation of apéritifs), and has been France's chief supplier since 1910. The country also manufactures vins de liqueur★, or fortified wines, of its own. Some of them, such as those made from Muscat grapes on the hills of Harrach and the estate of the Trappist order at Staouéli, are excellent.

Since its independence, the young Algerian State has tried to maintain the wine production which was previously so important to the country. However, in the area of Algiers and Tizi-Ouzou where viticulture remains one of the most important agricultural activities, numerous vines, particularly the Mitidja, have been abandoned due to the inexperience of the new proprietors. This region produces well-balanced reds which are often fruity. The region of El Asnam (Orleansville) produces vigorous, highly-coloured wine. The best are still from the Côtes du Zaccar★. Wines from the regions of Médéa★ and Ain-Bessem-Bouira★ also have a very fine reputation. The old department of Oran which produces more than two-thirds of the Algerian harvest has some of the best Algerian wines. The region of Mostaganem★ makes fine, fruity wines on the chalky slopes of the Haut-Dahra★ and robust wines on the plain. South of the Béni-Chougran mountains, Mascara★ and Coteaux de Mascara are well-known names of wines from the vineyards of Ain-el-Hadjar★ and the Mountains of Tessalah. Finally, the region around Tlemcen★ produces some fine wine, especially Coteaux de Tlemcen.

Exportation is the only outlet for production as the Moslem population does not drink wine, according to the rule of the Koran. About 90–100% of Algerian wine has always been exported, the majority of it to France.

alliaceous Having the smell and taste of onion or garlic. This develops when sulphur dioxide★ which is used as an antiseptic combines, under certain conditions, with the alcohol of the wine.

Aloxe-Corton This commune at the foot of what is locally known as 'la Montagne' is the starting point of the really great crus of the Côte de Beaune*. The Aloxe-Corton appellation officially includes some vineyards in the Ladoix-Serrigny and Pernand-Vergelesses* communes. The red and white wines are equally well known.

In great years the red wines are for many wine-lovers the most revered of all Côte de Beaunes, and are certainly the ones which age best. They are magnificent Burgundies, firm, well balanced and potent with a full, well-rounded bouquet that has a slight flavour of kirsch.

The white wines are very full-bodied and have great vitality. They are a marvellous golden colour and have a faint aroma of cinnamon. The whites rank with the best Meursaults*, and according to some admirers often even surpass them.

The crus are Corton (red and white) and Corton-Charlemagne (white only). Wines labelled simply with the communal appellation Aloxe-Corton are, although excellent, less distinguished and full-bodied; they mature more quickly, but also age sooner. (See Index.)

Alsace The vineyards of Alsace rise in terraces on the slopes between the Vosges mountains and the Rhine valley. Stretching from Wasselonne, near Strasbourg, in the north to Thann, near Mulhouse, in the south, they cover an area just over 100 km long and from one to five km wide. Facing east, south and south-east, they perch picturesquely on hillsides whose altitude varies from 200–450 m, sheltered from the cold, humid, north-westerly winds by the Vosges mountains. There are about 100 viticultural communes, two-thirds of which are in the Haut-Rhin department and the remaining third in the Bas-Rhin. The most famous are Ammerschwihr, Barr, Eguisheim, Riquewihr, Kaysersberg, Mittelwihr and Ribeauvillé.

The distinctive feature of these eminent vineyards is their originality. The varied composition of the soil (gneiss and granite, pink sandstone, clay and limestone, alluvium, sand and gravel), the diversity of the micro-climates, and the variety of the vines give them a character all of their own. One feature peculiar to the wines of Alsace, and almost unique among French

wines, is that they are generally named after the grape from which they are made, and not, as elsewhere, after their cru* ('growth' or place of origin) – which would seem to support Olivier de Serres' remark that 'Le génie du vin est dans le cépage', i.e. the spirit, or essence, of wine lies in the grape. As exceptions to the general rule Alsace does, nevertheless,

The village of Ammerschwihr, Haut-Rhin, and its vineyards. Phot. Candelier.

have a few crus such as Pfersigberg d'Eguisheim, Kaeferkopf, Kanzlerberg and the Rangen of Thann. This last is the most full-bodied of Alsatian wines. Its ferocity is such that a local curse runs 'Que le Rangen te frappe!' (May Rangen strike you!).

The vine was apparently introduced to Alsace a little later than to most other areas, but vineyards are recorded in 119 different Alsatian villages between AD 650 and 890. The wines of Alsace, as many and varied then as now, enjoyed a great reputation in the Middle Ages, especially in the Nordic countries to which they were exported from the Rhine. Despite the incessant ravages of various wars, Alsatian vignerons have always shown great perseverance in replanting their vineyards. After the occupation of 1870 the planting of noble grape varieties was discouraged in favour of inferior but more prolific vines. However, since 1918 the vineyards have been re-establishing their traditional high standards, and today about three-quarters of the vines are noble varieties.

The Gewurz grape. Phot. M.

13

Nearly all the wines of Alsace are white, and most are dry. Wines produced from common varieties are Knipperlé★, Chasselas★ and Goldriesling. The noble vines produce a unique and marvellously varied range of white wines, from the very dry to the almost sweet and from the fresh and light to the heady. They are Sylvaner★, Riesling★, Traminer★, Gewurztraminer★, Pinot Blanc or Clevner, Pinot Gris★ or Tokay d'Alsace, and Muscat★. There are also some wines made by blending either common or noble wines, e.g. Zwicker★ and Edelzwicker★.

Red wines are rare in Alsace, but are nonetheless excellent. They are in fact made from the Pinot Noir (which the Alsatians, incidentally, call Burgunder) from which the great Burgundies are made – a sufficient guarantee of breeding and distinction.

Rosé or clairet★ wines (Schillerwein) are made from either the Pinot Noir or the Pinot Meunier grape, and are fresh, dry and pleasantly fruity.

Lastly, mention should be made of the magnificent vin de paille★ that used to be made in the Colmar region but which unfortunately no longer exists.

ALSACE, APPELLATION D'ORIGINE CONTRÔLÉE Alsace has only recently (1962) qualified for an appellation contrôlée of its own. The official appellation is Alsace or Vin d'Alsace, accompanied, as is customary, by the name of the grape from which the wine was made. The variety of grape is in some cases followed by the name of the commune which produced the wine: there are ninety-three such communes in the Haut-Rhin and Bas-Rhin departments.

The words Grand Vin or Grand Cru, or similar indications of superior quality, are also used, but are only authorised for wines made from noble grapes whose musts are rich enough in sugar to attain 11° of alcohol by natural fermentation. It is in fact legally permitted for Alsatian wines to be enriched or fortified with up to 2·5° of extra alcohol if the regional committee of experts judges it necessary.

amber A word generally used to describe the golden yellow colour of certain old white wines. This colour should never be accompanied by a taste of maderisation★. The amber tinge is caused by oxidisation of the wine's colouring-matter★ (which, although scarcely visible in young white wines, is nonetheless always present). In a young wine the colour is a fault.

Amboise The vineyards of Vouvray★ and Montlouis★ include several communes grouped around Amboise and its famous château. The white, red and rosé wines made there are all entitled to the appellation Touraine★ followed by Amboise. The white wines produced by the Nazelles and Pocé-sur-Cisse communes are excellent. These communes are on the edge of the official Vouvray area, and their wines were in fact once sold under the name of Vouvray. The other white wines, all grown on the micaceous chalk of Touraine, are also extremely good, possessing elegance and a fine fruity flavour.

The Limeray and Cangey communes produce mostly red and rosé wines. The rosés, made from Cot grapes combined with Gamay and Cabernet, are particularly good. The white wines should have 10·5° of alcohol, the rosés 10° and the reds 9·5°. Amboise wines are produced in fairly small quantities, and are almost all consumed locally.

amer (bitter) The name of a disease (also called amertume) which sometimes affects wines in bottle, particularly red Burgundies. Their taste, though at first negligible, later becomes decidedly bitter, and the colouring-matter★ solidifies and forms a deposit. The disease usually affects wines of low acidity, acting on their glycerine and tartaric acid content. In the early stages of the disease, wine can sometimes be treated by pasteurisation★.

Certain varieties of grape have a definite light bitterness which, far from being offensive, is rated highly. This is the case with the Mauzac grape (Gaillac★, Blanquette de Limoux★) and the Clairette grape (la Clairette★) of Languedoc whose bitter aftertaste makes it a desirable ingredient of quality vermouths.

amoroso A sweetened oloroso sherry made especially for the British market. The full-bodied amoroso called East India gets its name from the days when the

*Aerial view of the château of
Amboise and the Loire valley.*
Phot. Beaujard–Lauros.

sailing ships carried casks of sherry to the
East Indies and back. The sea air and
constant rolling motion were supposed to
improve the sherry. Brown sherry is a very
dark and sweet amoroso.

ample An 'ample' wine has a full, generous taste and its aroma, bouquet and
flavour are rich, well rounded and perfectly balanced.

Ancenis (Coteaux d') This vineyard
covers the hillsides around the town of
Ancenis on the right bank of the Loire. In
addition to the predominant Muscadet★
and Gros-Plant★ vines, the vineyard is
planted with a proportion of the Gamay
grape of Beaujolais and the Cabernet of
Anjou, whose wines are supple, light and
greatly admired. They should be drunk
while young.

*Vineyards of the Loire, Oudon
near Ancenis. Phot. M.*

CABERNET D'ANJOU

APPELLATION CONTRÔLÉE   NICOLAS

The vineyard also produces wines which are made from the Chenin Blanc (or Pineau de la Loire) and the Pinot Gris (or Beurot), locally known as Malvoisie. All these wines are VDQS★ and are supple and fresh, with a pleasant bouquet.

Anjou An old French province whose limits correspond more or less to the present Maine-et-Loire department. Its vineyards continue the viticultural region of Touraine★ to the west along the Loire, covering the hillsides that border the river and its tributaries. They also enjoy a mild climate. The wines of Anjou have always had a great reputation and have been exported to England in great quantities since 1199. Although the white wines are the best known, there is a great variety to choose from, each with a character of its own. There are dry, medium-dry and sweet whites, and pétillant★, sparkling red and rosé wines. For viticultural purposes Anjou is usually divided into four subregions: Saumur★, Coteaux de la Loire★, Coteaux du Layon★ and Coteaux de l'Aubance★.

ANJOU, APPELLATION D'ORIGINE CONTRÔLÉE The red, white and rosé wines which qualify for the Anjou appellation must be produced within the legally-defined limits of the region and made from the following grapes: Pineau de la Loire (or Chenin Blanc) for white wines, Cabernet Franc and Cabernet-Sauvignon for red wines and Cabernet Franc, Cabernet-Sauvignon, Pineau d'Aunis, Gamay, Cot and Groslot for rosés.

ANJOU (MOUSSEUX) Sparkling wines that can be either white or rosé. The official grape variety for the white is Pineau de la Loire, but in practice certain red grapes (Cabernet, Gamay, Cot, Groslot and Pineau d'Aunis) are also allowed, vinified as for white wine, up to a maximum proportion of 60%. The rosé must be made from Cabernet, Cot, Gamay and Groslot grapes. These wines must all have 9·5° of alcohol before their liqueur de tirage★ is added.

ANJOU (ROSÉ D') Anjou produces a great many rosé wines that qualify for the Anjou appellation, all of which have a suppleness, fruitiness and freshness that have deservedly won them great popularity. Only rosé made exclusively from the Cabernet grape is entitled to the Cabernet d'Anjou appellation. Rosés are produced in most parts of Anjou, but particularly around Brissac in the Coteaux de l'Aubance★, around Tigné in the central area of the Coteaux du Layon★, and in the Saumur★ region. The latter produces only Cabernet rosés, which are entitled to the appellation Cabernet de Saumur.

Anjou rosés make good carafe wines, being well balanced, fruity and light, sometimes slightly moelleux★, and best drunk within a year of the vintage. Cabernet d'Anjou has an attractive colour, is fresh and fruity and should have an alcoholic strength of at least 10°. Its liveliness and fruitiness are best appreciated when young. The production of rosés in Anjou has undergone a remarkable expansion, increasing some 80% in the last ten years.

announcement of vendange A proclamation formerly used to notify growers to begin harvesting the grapes. They were forbidden to start the harvest before that moment. This constraint led to the production of quality wines by not allowing the picking of grapes before they were mature. The decision to announce the vendange was based on the appearance and taste of the grapes (modern analytical methods of checking maturation did not

The hillsides of Layon in Anjou. Phot. M.

then exist), and also conformed to local custom.

In Burgundy the vendange began 100 days after the flowering of the vines. Today, the ancient words are proclaimed by the president of the Jurade of Saint-Emilion standing symbolically at the top of the Tower of the King; 'People of Saint-Emilion and the seven communes, the Jurade proclaims the beginning of the vendange. Open the heavy doors of the cuves and begin the picking'.

appellation d'origine Wines labelled *à appellation d'origine* are always designated by a precise geographic term which leaves no doubt where they come from. It may be an entire region (Burgundy), a town (Nuit-Saint-Georges), a château in Bordeaux (Château d'Yquem) or a climat★ in Burgundy (Richebourg).

French legislation obliges producers to comply with stringent requirements for their wines being classed appellation d'origine. These wines are divided into strict official categories drawn up by an organisation called l'Institut National des Appellations d'Origine (INAO★). The categories are: vins à appellation d'origine contrôlée★, vins délimités de qualité supérieure★ (VDQS) and vins à appellation simple. The superior category is represented by the appellation d'origine contrôlée (AOC) under which are classified practically all the great wines of France. Then come the vins délimités de qualité supérieure (VDQS), excellent regional wines which must meet certain standards of quality although not as high as those for AOC wines. Finally, the third category, the wines à appellation simple, includes only a few representatives. The wines of Alsace were classed in this category for a long time, but they have now graduated to the AOC class. The white, red and rosé still wines of Champagne are included in this category.

On wine menus the wines of appellation d'origine must never be mixed with ordinary wines but should always have a special heading.

appellation d'origine contrôlée (AOC) The INAO★ has laid down strict rules for the admission of all the great wines which are included in this prestigious classification. The area of pro-duction must be clearly defined, and all the wine's contributing factors are carefully controlled and specified – variety of grape, minimum amount of sugar in the must and of alcohol in the wine, maximum yield per hectare, methods of pruning, viticulture and vinification. Although these rules are based on long-standing tradition and local practice, they are in no way opposed to scientific innovations provided they bring about an improvement in the quality of the wine. Conformity to the rules is strictly enforced by representatives both of the INAO and the Répression des Fraudes★.

All the famous French crus are AOC wines, and all of them must carry the words 'Appellation Contrôlée' clearly on their label (one exception being Champagne). When being transported, these wines must be accompanied by transit documents and by certificates indicating any particular modifications they have undergone, and the title must also figure on declarations of harvest and stocks, prospectuses, bills of sale and on all containers. France has more than 150 AOC wines.

Arbois Arbois and Château-Chalon are the most famous vineyards in the Jura★ department of France. Several communes share the highly-prized appellation contrôlée of Arbois, the best known being Pupillin, Montigny-les-Arsures, Mesnay and Les Arsures. Although they had been well known for many centuries, Pasteur really made the wines of Arbois famous when he settled there to engage upon his research into the fermentation and diseases of wine, which he afterwards described in his '*Etudes Sur le Vin*'.

The red wines of Arbois are fine and generous, the whites are low in alcohol and dry with a highly individual bouquet. The vineyard also produces sparkling wine (made by the Champagne method), vin de paille★ and vin jaune★ which is almost on a par with Château-Chalon★. The most famous of its quality wines, however, is probably Arbois rosé, an excellent, fruity, dry wine with an attractive light ruby colour that verges on *pelure d'oignon*★. There is a record of it being served at the Royal tables as early as 1298. A local saying about these excellent wines is that '*Plus on en boit, plus on va droit*' (the more one

Following two pages: celebration of the proclamation of the wine-harvest at Saint-Emilion. Phot. Renè-Jacques.

drinks, the straighter one walks) – a saying which it is tempting to put to the test!

Argentina The Argentine vineyards have been expanding rapidly for the last forty years, and their output is now roughly equal to that of Algeria, i.e. 155,000 hl a year. Argentina is the chief producer as well as the chief consumer of wine in South America*. Very little of its wine is exported as practically the entire annual production is consumed locally. The wines, which are all cheap and full-bodied, are harvested in the Mendoza and San Juan districts not far from the Chilean border, at the foot of the Andes due west of Buenos Aires. The red wines are generally better than the whites and the rosés.

Armenia The principal wine-growing centres of this Soviet republic are Etchmiadzin, Ashtarak and Jerevan. The largest vineyard lies around Jerevan and extends as far as Anipemza in the north, and Artachat in the south. The local wine-growers have managed to cultivate various frost-resistant species of grapes on irrigated volcanic soil in the mountainous regions (Lori, Chirak and Zangezour). Although most Armenian wines are dry,

General view of Arbois. Phot. Beaujard-Lauros.

the country is well known for its port-type wine, which is sold in the USSR as 'Portvein'.

aroma Aroma is the distinctive smell which a wine exudes. In French it is also called *fruit, parfum, bouquet primaire* and *bouquet originel*. Aroma is essentially a product of the grape, since it originates from substances that form in the grape skin as it grows. Each species of grape, therefore, has its own particular aroma which is more or less pronounced according to species, soil and vintage. Red and white Burgundies, for example, have technically speaking no aroma, since with one or two exceptions the juice of their grapes has, when freshly picked, only a very slight smell.

The most characteristic aroma is that of Muscat★ grapes, but the Cabernet, Traminer, Syrah and Malvoisie varieties are also quite distinctive. A great deal of aroma is lost during fermentation, and dry★ wines rarely have as much aroma as wines which have retained a certain amount of their natural sugar. Aroma also tends to fade with time. It first combines with the developing bouquet★ and then is superseded by it.

aromatic An aromatic wine is one that gives off a powerful aroma★. Only fruity wines are really aromatic, as aroma depends largely on the grapes from which the wine is made.

artificial wines Various artificial beverages have at one time or another been invented and sold as wine to the public, mostly at the end of the last century during the wine shortage caused by the devastation of French vineyards by oidium★, phylloxera★ and mildew★. Some were made from dried Greek and Turkish raisins, others were simply vins de sucre★ which had nothing to do with grapes at all. Others still were 'improved' vins de sucre. Two, three or even four cuvées★ were made from the same crop by running off the first wine and then pouring sugar, water and other ingredients on to the residue left in the vat to make it ferment again. Also, a 'white wine' was made by adding large quantities of sulphuric acid to extremely coarse, poor quality red wine and thus neutralising its colour.

Vendange at Mendoza in Argentina. Phot. Aarons.

A famous case of falsifying wines occurred recently at Limoges, where the defendant, who had been concocting 'wine' out of purely chemical substances, received a harsh sentence.

assemblage The blending or combining of wines in a vat, e.g. the vin de goutte★ with the vin de presse★ from the same cuvée★, or vat. Wines from different vats are also blended in order to achieve an overall uniformity of the vineyard's production. Assemblage is also used as a technique for the correction★ of wines. Different vintages from the same vineyard are blended to maintain a consistent character and quality from one year to the next. This method is standard practice in Champagne★, but as it requires enormous and costly reserve stocks, as well as a great deal of storage room and much extra labour, it is not really a viable proposition for the average vigneron.

Asti Asti, situated south of Turin, is one of the most important centres of the Italian wine industry. It is best known abroad for its sparkling wine Asti Spumante, which is made from the Canelli Muscat grape (named after a village near Asti) cultivated on the surrounding hills. This grape makes pale, sweet wine with a low alcohol content and a very pronounced aroma★, which is also used in the manufacture of Italian vermouths.

Asti also produces good quality red wines from Barbera and Freisa grapes, and from the excellent Grignolino and Nebbiolo varieties.

Asti Spumante   A very popular sparkling wine (*spumante* literally means 'foaming') made at Asti★. The method of production differs from those generally used in France for sparkling wines in that the basis of the final product is not wine but must, i.e. unfermented grape juice. Another difference is that the carbon dioxide which causes the effervescence is, in the Asti method, produced by the first fermentation, whereas in other methods the sparkle does not develop until secondary fermentation, either in bottle (Champagne method★ and German method★) or in vat (the cuve close★, Charmat process).

At Asti the must of Muscat★ grapes is stored in cellars under refrigeration, which effectively prevents it from fermenting. It is then decanted and transferred to hermetically sealed vats where it is left to ferment and produce the carbon dioxide that forms the wine's effervescence. The great advantage of this method is that it allows the Muscat grapes to retain their characteristic taste and aroma. Great care and delicacy is usually needed to make sparkling wines from Muscat grapes. If they are vinified as for dry wines, i.e. if all their natural sugar is used up in the first fermentation, they will lose their distinctive aroma when extra sugar is added to cause the secondary fermentation.

astringent   Another word used by wine-tasters to describe this trait is tannic, since astringency is generally caused by an excess of tannin★. Astringent wine makes the mouth and face pucker up and can sometimes cause an involuntary grimace. It is thus sometimes said to have 'bite'. Astringent wines are also called harsh★, hard★, angular and thick.

Aubance (Coteaux de l')   An Anjou★ vineyard that stretches from the Loire to the Layon along the Aubance, which is a tributary of the Loire. Although its wines were until the sixteenth century more highly prized than those of the neighbouring Coteaux de Layon★, the latter have since gradually come to be preferred by wine-lovers.

The Aubance shares with the Layon vineyards its schistose soil and its vines, the Pineau de la Loire variety. The white wines entitled to the appellation Coteaux de l'Aubance are usually medium dry, fruity and delicate, with a pleasant earthy taste (*goût de terroir*★). Although they have less strength, vitality and firmness than Layon wines, they nonetheless have a certain character of their own. The best-known domaines, or estates, are at Mûrs, Saint-Melaine, Soulaines and Vauchrétien.

The overall production of Coteaux de l'Aubance is not great, and is consumed locally. The commune of Brissac, which is also in the Coteaux de l'Aubance area, produces a great quantity of rosé and Cabernet rosé under the regional appellation Anjou.

Ausone (Château)   A premier grand cru classé★ of Saint-Emilion. Although it is doubtless only a legend, local tradition has it that Château Ausone occupies the site of the property where the Roman poet Ausonius lived in the fourth century. Château Ausone is a very fine wine that is generous and elegant.

austere   An austere wine does not lack good qualities, but has a high tannin content which tends to obscure its taste and bouquet. It is also a little too rough to please all palates. Immature Médocs, for example, often have this characteristic. It is also said that such a wine is 'severe' and its good qualities are often hidden beneath this severity.

Australia   Vines are not indigenous to Australia. The first ones were planted near Sydney in New South Wales in about 1788. Today the states of Victoria and South Australia both cultivate vines more extensively than New South Wales, and 50% of their production consists of fresh eating-grapes and raisins. As in Europe, the vines were successfully regrafted on to American rootstocks when the vineyards were devastated by phylloxera★.

In the last few years great technical

progress has been made in Australian vinification methods, particularly in the preparation of Australian 'sherry', a fortified wine made in the same way as genuine sherry.

Wines resembling European ones are designated under the appellations claret, Burgundy, Bordeaux, Moselle, etc. But these traditional names are quickly being replaced by labels indicating the grape and viticultural region. The principal vineyards are found in the following regions:

Hunter Valley Produces a Burgundy-type wine which improves with age and can be kept for a long time in bottle.

Central and North-East Victoria Produces dessert wines of the Muscat, Madeira and port types as well as some light, white wines and good full-bodied reds.

Western Victoria Produces light, white wines of the Riesling and Champagne types and also more robust whites and vigorous, flavourful reds.

South and South-East Australia Produces quality red wines.

Adelaide The region around this city is known for its Bordeaux-type flavourful reds as well as delicate whites and sherry-type dessert wines, both vintage and tawny.

Barossa Valley, Eden Valley, Clare One of the largest Australian vineyard areas. Full-bodied reds, light aromatic Rieslings and dessert wines are produced.

Swan Valley There are many small producers, but only four or five large vineyards. The Burgundy-type wines are vigorous and full-bodied and, like those of the Hunter Valley, have a very characteristic aroma.

Murray Valley Sweet wines and Muscats are produced all along the Murray River as are dry, supple, mild whites of the Moselle and Sauternes types, sherry-type wines and also a large quantity of light rosé and red table wines. During the last few years more noble grapes have been planted in many districts, particularly at Cadell, Mildura, Nildottie, Lexton and Langhorne Creek.

Riverina District Forty viticultural enterprises produce red wines, dry and sweet whites and sherry-type dessert wines.

Austria The vineyards of Austria have suffered a great deal from the successive wars fought on her soil, and the remains of the Austro-Hungarian empire were stripped of many good wine-growing regions (such as the Tyrol which is now partly Italian). Today, the total annual production more or less meets national demand and very little Austrian wine is exported.

The best Austrian wines are white. The red ones, made from Spätburgunder (Pinot Noir) grapes, are in no way remarkable, and are all consumed locally. The

Austria: *Wolkersdorf vines, near the Czech border.* Phot. Ségalat.

23

white wines are in quite another class. Made from Riesling, Sylvaner, Gewürztraminer and Müller-Thurgau grapes, together with several local varieties such as Rotgipfler and Veltliner (which is rather like Traminer★ though with less aroma and flavour), they have certain similarities with the wines made in the neighbouring districts of southern Germany and the Italian Tyrol. They are light, dry, fresh, fruity wines which should be drunk young.

Gumpoldskirchener, produced south of Vienna, is probably the best-known Austrian wine today. Loved by generations of Viennese, it is a clear, fragrant, fruity wine and, although it has never been a great one, is always very agreeable. Loibner, Kremser and Dürnsteiner wines are grown and harvested on the steep banks of the Danube

A tavern-keeper savours the new wine of Gumpoldskirche, near Vienna. Phot. Rapho.

to the east of Vienna, and are generally excellent. In addition, the region immediately around Vienna produces good carafe wines that are drunk in the cafés of Vienna and Grinzing. The best of these carafe wines (Nassberger, Wiener and Grinzinger) are sometimes bottled and exported.

Auvergne The wines of Auvergne are classified with those of the Loire★ and are VDQS★. Despite efforts to promote and improve viniculture in the region, the vineyards now cover only one-third of their former area, and wine production has decreased proportionately. Most of the vineyards lie south and south-east of Clermont-Ferrand, though there are also a few in the area between Châtel-Guyon and Issoire. They are divided into three main production areas: the Clermont-Ferrand district, which produces the once-famous crus Chanturgues★ and Corent; the Issoire district, in which the good and fruity wines of Boudes are grown; and the Riom district, with its well-known fruity cru Châteaugay.

Auvergne wines are usually red, sometimes rosé, and are made from Gamay grapes. They are good quality, fresh, pleasant wines with a fine bouquet, and should be drunk young. Local demand for them is great, particularly in the region's many spa towns.

Ayse A Savoie★ cru from the Bonneville region. The sparkling wine of Ayse has great character but also a reputation for 'breaking legs'. To qualify for the appellation Mousseux de Savoie, followed by the name Ayse, the wine must be made from Gringet, Altesse and Roussette d'Ayse (at least 30%) grapes. It is made either by the Champagne method★ of bottling before secondary fermentation, or by the local method of spontaneous fermentation.

Azay-le-Rideau Not far from Tours in the valley of Indre, the flinty soil of Azay-le-Rideau's limestone hills produces a white wine that has been famous for many centuries. Several communes share the appellation (which must always be

The château of Azay-le-Rideau. Phot. Lauros-Geay.

25

Azay-le-Rideau: the first wine festival (1968). Phot. Léah Lourié.

preceded by the word Touraine). Saché, where Balzac wrote *'Le Lys dans la Vallée,'* enjoys the greatest reputation. Production is very low, which is a pity as the wine is dry, fresh and fruity, and is considered one of the best dry white wines of Touraine. Its official minimum alcohol content is 10°.

Azerbaijan Vines have been grown in this Soviet Republic for many hundreds of years. They were even mentioned by the Greek geographer Strabon, who was born in 58 BC. The methods used by Azerbaijani vignerons in the Middle Ages indicate an advanced knowledge of viniculture. The vine-shoots were trained along growing props (young trees) or bunches of reeds tied together in threes, or spread out on the sandy soil. In the colder areas they were covered with earth in winter and carefully loosened again in spring. There is even some evidence of grafting. The entire crop

was made into wine and, given the sophistication of their vinicultural techniques, it was probably extremely good.

With the adoption of Islam as the country's religion, the wine industry declined, and it was only in the nineteenth century that it slowly began to revive.

Today, some forty varieties of grape are cultivated, the best of which are Ag Shany and Gara Shany, both grown on the sandy peninsular of Apsheron. The chief vine-growing areas are, in order of importance: Shamkhor, Shemakha, Kirovabad, Tauz and Agsu (near Shemakha). Wine is also produced all over the Nagorno-Karabakh district from Norashen-Shakhbuz to Paragachai. The most important product of the region is a Soviet port-type wine called 'Portvein'. Azerbaijan's white vins ordinaires are pleasant and light, especially Bayan Shirei. There is also a very velvety red wine called Matrassa.

B

Badacsony A well-known Hungarian vineyard situated on the western shore of Lake Balaton. In ancient times it was the property of the Grey Friars, and was divided into small lots in the seventeenth century. Badacsony is a sarcophagus-shaped hill 400 m high on which the vines grow in terraces giving the area a Mediterranean atmosphere. The peasants say that only the vines 'which are reflected in the mirror of Lake Balaton' give good wine as the undersides of the leaves receive reflected light from the lake.

The wine of Badacsony has been re-

nowned for some years. It is often said that the fire of ancient volcanoes burns in it and that the Romans knew and appreciated its flavour. Altars erected to the Roman God of wine, the 'Liber Pater', have been discovered in the course of excavations. The old wine presses★ are constructed on Roman foundations, and the knife used in the vendange which is passed down from generation to generation resembles the implement used by the Romans. The largest wine cellar in Hungary is found in the community of Badacsonylabdi. It contains more than a million and a half litres.

The best-known wines of Badacsony are the Badacsonyi Kéknyelu, a white wine of the Kéknyelu grape (whose name means blue sleeve), and the Szürkebarat (grey friar). But the region also produces other good white wines from the Rizling (Riesling), Furmint and other grapes, and also remarkable dessert wines.

Baden A wine-growing area of southwest Germany★ bordered by Switzerland on the south and Alsace on the west. The many vineyards planted with different varieties are found at the foot of the Black Forest facing the Rhine Valley. Since the Second World War, considerable effort has been made to regroup and replant the vineyards. The dominant grape varieties are the Müller-Thurgau, the Gutedel (Chasselas) and Pinot Noir, each representing about one-fifth of the total. Pinot Gris, Pinot Blanc, Sylvaner and a little Riesling account for the rest. Almost all of the wine is produced in modern co-operative cellars.

The very varied wines of Baden, which used to be consumed only locally, are now gaining favour on the German market and

18th-century house at Badacsony. This type of building comprised a cellar, cave and press, and was used only in the harvest period. Phot. J.-L. Charmet.

countries – in fact travelling by sea seemed to suit it extremely well and gave it a smooth texture and bouquet that were much admired. It is made from a combination of Mourvèdre, Grenache and Cinsault grapes. As all its most distinctive qualities are contributed by Mourvèdre, the viticultural authorities have decreed a gradual increase in the proportion of this variety (now at least 20%) in an attempt to restore the red wine's former reputation.

To qualify for its appellation the red wine must mature for at least eighteen months before being bottled. At the end of this period it is a fine, generous, robust and well-balanced wine with an attractive dark colour, a distinctive velvety texture and an aroma of violets whose strength varies in proportion to the amount of Mourvèdre grape in the wine's composition. It ages well, acquiring a characteristic bouquet, and is arguably the best red wine of Provence.

The white wine, which is mostly produced around Sanary, is also excellent. It is made from Clairette (50%) and Ugni Blanc grapes and is dry (but not acid), fresh and full-bodied.

The rosé is fruity, supple and fresh and is steadily increasing in popularity. The official maturing period for both white and rosé is at least eight months.

banvin (right of) In feudal days, the time in which the lord could sell his own wine before his vassals had the right to market theirs. The exact number of days was generally determined by custom and varied greatly from one fiefdom to another. The lord owned the oven, the mill and the wine press which his subjects used as a right of their tenure. The lord also sold the wines to other areas and searched for new outlets when the local production was large. In exchange for this last service he was granted the right of banvin, dating from the end of the Carolingian period (AD 987).

The term 'banvin' also means the notice authorising the sale of wine by the subjects on the lord's territory.

Banyuls This Roussillon★ wine is the most famous and perhaps the best French AOC vin doux naturel★. The Banyuls area lies at the extreme south of France on the

are starting to be exported to other countries. Some of the better-known wines of the area are: the Seeweine of Lake Constance; the good cru of Kaiserstuhl, produced on a sort of volcanic island to the west of Freiburg; the Markgräfler grown between Freiburg and Switzerland from the Gutedel; and the Mauerweine produced around Baden-Baden and sold in bocksbeutels like the wines of Franconia.

Bandol The wines of Bandol, which have one of the four appellations contrôlées of Provence★, grow on terraced hillsides (called *restanques*) between La Ciotat and Toulon.

The vineyard's four principal communes are Bandol, La Cadière-d'Azur, Sanary and Le Castellet. The area also includes Le Beausset, Saint-Cyr, Ollioules and Evenos. Wooded hills shelter the vineyard against cold winds from the north, and the proximity of the sea reduces any sudden change of temperature so that the vineyard rarely suffers from extremes of heat or cold. Apart from vines, the arid flint and limestone soil produces nothing but pine trees and scrub.

Bandol's red wine has always been held in high esteem, even in quite distant

Spanish frontier. It is bordered by mountains on every side, those to the east plunging straight into the Mediterranean. This stretch of rocky coast is the most picturesque part of the Côte Vermeille.

The vineyard is divided into four communes, Banyuls, Cerbère, Port-Vendres and Collioure, and is extremely difficult to cultivate as it consists of very steep hillsides that rise to an altitude of 300 m, and extend to the very edge of the cliffs that fall to the sea. The vines have to be grown in terraces in order to withstand the torrential rains and the *tramontane* (a north wind). The vignerons use an interesting system of channelling water called *pied de coq*. The soil itself is hard to work, consisting mainly of shale with a thin covering of arable earth which has to be brought up to the top of the vineyard every year.

Banyuls wine is traditionally made from the Grenache Noir grape. Like all vins doux naturels, alcohol is added to the wine, a process which enables it to retain the full flavour of the grapes. The alcohol is added to bring fermentation to a halt before all the wine's natural grape sugar has been converted into alcohol. If a dry wine is desired, the mutage★ is left until all the sugar has been fermented.

There are two appellations d'origine contrôlée: Banyuls and Banyuls Grand Cru★.

Besides being an apéritif and dessert wine that bears comparison with the most famous wines of its category made in other countries (notably Germany), Banyuls is also a good accompaniment to certain main dishes. It is a warm, racé★ wine with breeding and elegance.

BANYULS GRAND CRU This red wine is subject to much stricter regulations than the Banyuls. Certain features of its preparation are officially specified and rigorously adhered to, such as the species of grape; obligatory égrappage★, or destalking; a minimum five days' maceration of grape juice and skins before mutage★; and, above all, at least thirty months maturing 'in wood'. The wine is first put in small casks to mature in contact with the air, and later transferred to large, hermetically-sealed wooden ones (*foudres*) to complete the process. In addition, the wine is tasted, before being bottled, by a panel of inspectors appointed by the INAO★.

Barbaresco One of the best red wines of the Italian province of Piemonte. It is made from the Nebbiolo grape and produced in limited quantities around the two communes of Barbaresco and Neive. Although the production area is similar to that of the neighbouring Barolo★ and they both come from the same grape, Barbaresco is very different. A lighter wine, it matures more quickly and after two or three years in bottle takes on a *pelure d'oignon*★ tint. It is an excellent and distinctive wine which is classed among the best of Italy. Unlike Barolo, which is generally sold in Burgundy-shape bottles, Barbaresco is often found in the Bordeaux-type.

Barbera A red wine made from the Barbera grape in the Piemonte region of Italy. It is a good table wine with colour, body and plenty of bouquet and flavour.

Vendange near Banyuls on hills overlooking the sea. Phot. Rapho.

29

Barbera is a wine of no great distinction, and is best drunk young and as an accompaniment to Italian food. It sometimes referments in bottle and becomes moustillant★, which, although it may be strange to subtler palates, suits the people of Piemonte very well.

Bardolino   A very good light red wine from the province of Verona in Italy, produced at the eastern end of Lake Garda. Like its neighbour Valpolicella★, it is made from Corvina, Negrara and Molinara grapes. Hardly more coloured than a dark rosé, it is a delicious, fruity wine that rarely has an alcohol content of more than 11°. Bardolino is at its best between one and three years of age.

Barolo   Barolo is possibly the best red wine of Italy and is made from the Nebbiolo grape. Both full-bodied and long-lasting, it is not unlike the wines of the Côtes-du-Rhône★, and sometimes reminiscent of Hermitage★ and Côte-Rôtie★. It is produced in the Piemonte region on eight communes around the village of Barolo, south of Turin. It is usually kept in cask for three years before being bottled (in Burgundy-shaped bottles), and improves even more if left longer. Barolo is strong (from 12–14°) and has an attractive deep red colour. It is always a good wine and often a great one.

barrique   A large barrel, or cask, that varies in size from one region to another (it is often advisable to ascertain its capacity before purchase). A barrique usually holds 228 litres (in the Nantes and Côtre d'Or regions, for example). In Bordeaux it holds 225 litres, an ancient tradition officially established by a law of 1866; and a bordelais tonneau★ holds 900 litres, or four barriques. In Touraine and Anjou it is equal to 232 litres, and in Languedoc, to a third of a muid★. In some regions (e.g. Burgundy) it is also known as a pièce★.

Barsac   This commune, which is part of the Sauternes vineyard, is traditionally and officially entitled to the two appellations Barsac and Sauternes★. Barsac is as outstanding a wine as Sauternes, and is made with the same meticulous care. The differences between the two are, in fact, few and subtle: Barsac is less gras★ and less sweet, but also fruitier and more aromatic when young. The premiers crus of the 1855 classification★ are Châteaux Climens and Coutet, but the seconds crus are also excellent – Châteaux Myrat, Doisy-Daëne, Doisy-Dubroca and Doisy-Védrines. (See Index.)

Baux-de-Provence (Coteaux des)   The wines of this region have recently qualified for the VDQS★ label. The red and rosé wines are made from Grenache, Carignan, Cinsault and Mourvèdre grapes, the white wines from Clairette, Ugni and Muscat varieties, all of which are well suited to a sunny climate. The wines have breeding and elegance.

Baux-de-Provence (Coteaux des)   The wines of this region have recently qualified for the VDQS★ label. The red and rosé wines are made from Grenarche, Carignan, Cinsault and Mourvèdre grapes, the white wines from Clairette, Ugni and Muscat varieties, all of which are well suited to a sunny climate. The wines have breeding and elegance.

Béarn   This former French province covered almost the same area as the present-day department of Basses-Pyrénées. Its vine-growing area, which forms part of the Sud-Ouest★ region, covers picturesque hillsides between the *gaves*, or mountain streams, of Pau and Oloron, sometimes reaching a height of

Baux-de-Provence: aerial view. Phot. Lauros-Geay.

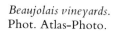

300 m. It has a great many communes, including Jurançon, Gan, Lasseube, Monein, Salies-de-Béarn, Bellocq and Oraas. In the north-east the vineyard extends to the border of the Hautes-Pyrénées department and slopes down to the Adour valley around Lembeye, Crouseilles, Conchez and Portet.

Béarn is mainly known for its appellation contrôlée wines: the great Jurançon★ and its close rival Pacherenc-du-Vic-Bihl★, and the red wine of Madiran★. However, it also produces some VDQS★ sold as vins de Béarn. Most of these wines, which can be either red, white or rosé, are vinified in co-operative cellars. The reds and rosés are good wines that are consumed locally and much praised by visitors. They are made mainly from Tannat grapes, in combination with Bouchy and Pinenc and sometimes Manseng and Courbu Rouge. The dry white wines are made from various grapes such as Baroque, Courbu Blanc, Sémillon and Claverie but output is only about 15% of total red and rosé production. Rousselet du Béarn, which is made near Pau, is probably the most pleasant of these white wines.

Beaujolais The southernmost vineyard of the Burgundy region and also the largest, covering about 15,000 ha. It is situated entirely in the Rhône department, except for the canton of Chapelle-de-Guinchay which is in Saône-et-Loire. The picturesque hillsides of Beaujolais lie on slopes overlooking the Saône valley and rise to heights of 500 and even 600 m.

The predominant variety of grape is the Gamay. Although this grape is also grown in both the Auvergne and Loire regions, it is only in Beaujolais that it develops all its qualities (particularly its fruitiness) to the fullest. This is probably due to the granitic soil of the area since, on clay and limestone soil elsewhere in Burgundy, the same grape makes relatively ordinary wine. A small quantity of white Beaujolais is produced, made like all white Burgundies from Chardonnay grapes.

Beaujolais is the ideal carafe wine, pleasant, smooth and refreshing. It should always be served chilled, which is rare for red wine. For many years Beaujolais was drunk only by the inhabitants of Lyons, but since then the charm of its youth and freshness has won it widespread popularity. Beaujolais' nine crus are, from north to south: Saint-Amour★, Juliénas★, Chénas★, Moulin-à-Vent★, Fleurie★, Chiroubles★, Morgon★, Brouilly★ and Côte-de-Brouilly★. Other Beaujolais appellations are Beaujolais★, Beaujolais supérieur★ and Beaujolais-Villages★.

BEAUJOLAIS and BEAUJOLAIS SUPÉRIEUR These appellations apply to red, rosé and white wines grown all over the Beaujolais area. For Beaujolais, red wines must be at least 9° in alcohol content

and white wines, 9·5°; for Beaujolais supérieur, red wines must be 10° and white wines, 10·5°. Maximum yield per hectare may not exceed 50 hl for Beaujolais and 45 hl for Beaujolais supérieur.

BEAUJOLAIS-VILLAGES Certain wines from the best areas of the vineyard are entitled to the appellation Beaujolais-Villages, or Beaujolais followed by the name of their commune, e.g. Jullié, Emeringes, Leynes and Bellevue. (See Index.) The great charm of these unpretentious, fruity and smooth Beaujolais is their youth. They should therefore be drunk within about a year of the vintage, and always slightly chilled (never at room temperature) to bring out the fruity flavour.

The Hospice de Beaune (view from the courtyard).
Phot. Aarons-L.S.P.

Beaumes-de-Venise A commune that lies a little to the south of Rasteau★ in the Vaucluse department and produces an excellent appellation contrôlée Muscat wine made, like other vins doux naturels★, by mutage★ of the must with alcohol. But whereas Rasteau wine is made almost exclusively from Grenache grapes, Beaumes-de-Venise Muscat can only be made from Muscat-à-petit-grains, a small-graped vine also called Muscat de Frontignan. The vineyard is part of the southern Côtes-du-Rhône region and extends from Beaumes-de-Venise to Aubignan.

Although relatively and undeservedly little known, owing to low production,

Beaumes-de-Venise is one of the best French vins doux naturels. It is golden, sweet (although less so than Frontignan★) and, above all, has exquisite finesse and a marvellous aroma. It ages well, preserving all its finesse and aroma.

Beaune This small, picturesque city is historically, spiritually and commercially one of the great centres of the Burgundian wine industry. It is famous for its magnificent Hôtel-Dieu, an almshouse that was founded in 1443 and has its own vineyards. These produce very fine wines (the *vins des Hospices de Beaune*) which have been famous for centuries and are sold to the public at the wine auctions that take place in the Hôtel-Dieu each November. This annual sale is an important event for wine merchants everywhere, and its proceeds are devoted to the maintenance of the Hôtel-Dieu and its charitable activities.

Some 95% of Beaune's wines are red. However, all its wines, both red and white, are distinguished, graceful and well balanced. The whites have a pronounced bouquet while the reds vary a great deal according to the conditions of their growth (soil, climate, etc.). Some are vigorous and firm, some are velvety and fine, and some again combine finesse with a warm, strong flavour. Erasmus, the humanist philosopher, felt he owed his recovery from ill-health to Beaune, and wrote, 'Fortunate Burgundy! You should be called the Mother of Men since you give them such milk!'

The most famous crus are Grèves, Fèves, Marconnets, les Bressandes, Cras, Clos de la Mousse, Clos du Roi and Clos des Mouches (which produces a remarkably good white wine). (See Index.)

Belgium Vines were introduced to Belgium by the Romans, who planted them principally along the Meuse and Escaut rivers. The most extensive vineyards seem to have been established in the ninth century around Liège and Huy. (It was on the hills overlooking Huy, incidentally, that the last Belgian wine made from grapes grown in the open air was produced, in 1947.) There is mention of vines growing in Namur and Tournai in the tenth century, and in Brussels, Bruges and Malines in the eleventh.

Today, Belgian wine is quite different as

Cultivation of grapes in a glasshouse near Brussels. The wine is made from the 'Royal' grape. Phot. Actualit.

it is made entirely from hothouse-grown grapes vinified by co-operatives. Hothouse cultivation made its first appearance in 1865 near Brussels, in Hoeilaart and Overijssel, where the grapes were sold as fresh fruit. It was not until about 1954, following an unusually large production, that a hothouse owner had the idea of making wine from his crop.

The grapes used are the Frankenthal, Royal and Colman varieties with a small quantity of Chasselas★. Belgian wine is mostly white, sometimes rosé or sparkling. It is made of 95% red grapes and 5% white (the white wine can therefore be called blanc de noirs★). Vintage is totally unimportant as the grapes are always grown in hothouses and are sheltered from changes of climate. Belgian wine should be consumed early and does not keep well.

The hothouse cultivation of Belgian grapes used to be protected by internal taxes which virtually prohibited other European varieties. Since the formation of the EEC, however, these taxes have been abolished and Italian and French grapes are now being sold in increasing quantities on the Belgian market. Today, the government subsidises vine-growers who uproot their vines and plant something else, so viticulture is no longer an economic proposition.

Bellet A tiny vineyard in Provence★ with its own appellation contrôlée. Surrounded by the acres of carnations and other flowers that are grown on the perimeter of the commune of Nice, it lies on hills overlooking the Var valley at a height of 250–300 m. The slopes of these hills are very steep, which means that the vineyard has to be cultivated by hand.

Bellet produces very little wine. Not long ago the vineyard was reconstructed and divided among several owners, one of whom subsequently installed equipment that could vinify the whole crop at once. The wine, which can be red, rosé or white, is excellent, and has a distinctive character. Most of the grapes grown are exclusive to the vineyard: Folle-Noire, Braquet and Cinsault for the red and rosé (there is, however, a large number of supplementary varieties authorised for rosé); Rolle, Roussan, Spagnol or Mayorquin for the white.

The red wine is light, fine and delicate, and has an attractive ruby colour. The rosé is also light and elegant, and has an aroma of iris root. The white wine has a lot of character, having nerve★ and elegance with a fine aroma and freshness remarkable in a southern wine. This is probably due to the cold winds that come from the Alps and to the altitude of the vineyard.

33

bentonite A special kind of clay (silicate of aluminium) which is extracted from deposits in Wyoming and South Dakota in the USA. Used in fining, it causes proteins in solution to flocculate and to form deposits in the bottle. It has very good results when used in large quantities to clarify the wine. Unfortunately, it robs the wine of other substances which contribute to its fullness and sometimes imparts an earthy taste when used indiscriminately.

Bergerac A vineyard that covers most of the Bergerac area of Dordogne. Its wines are classed among those of the Sud-Ouest★ and are entitled to the appellation d'origine contrôlée Bergerac. The vineyard produces red wines which, despite a reputation dating from the Middle Ages, are relatively little known outside their place of origin. Those grown on the right bank of the Dordogne (of which Pécharmant★ is the best known) have more finesse and suppleness, while those grown on the left have more body, colour and tannin.

The wines are made from Cabernet, Merlot and Malbec grapes (all Bordeaux varieties) and contain from 9–12° of alcohol. The white wines are subtle, mellow, rarely dry (except for Panisseau★), and are made from Sémillon, Sauvignon and Muscadelle grapes. Rosette★ is one of the best-known crus. Monbazillac★ should also be mentioned here. It is the region's most famous wine, and has its own appellation contrôlée. Bergerac also produces some rosé wines.

Berry The old French province of Berry, which, with its capital, Bourges, lies at the very heart of France, is today divided into the two departments of Cher and Indre. Its wines have always been highly esteemed: Gregory of Tours mentioned them in 582, and in 1567, Nicolas of Nicolay wrote in his *Description Générale des Pais et Duché de Berry* that, 'The dry, stony region abounds in very good wine that keeps a long time'. Today, four Berry wines have appellations d'origine contrôlée: Sancerre★, Ménetou-Salon★, Quincy★ and Reuilly★. Châteaumeillant★ has a VDQS★ label. The red and rosé wines with these appellations are made from Pinot and Gamay grapes, the white from Sauvignon.

Bikavér One of the most famous red wines of Hungary★, produced on the hills of the village of Eger about 100 km northeast of Budapest. It is made from the excellent Hungarian grape Kadarka, together with a few French varieties such as Cabernet and Gamay. The vineyard was severely damaged by phylloxera★ in 1880, but fortunately not completely destroyed. Bikavér (which means 'bull's blood') is a magnificent, full-bodied, generous wine with an attractive deep red colour and a very distinctive bouquet. It is considered the best red wine of Hungary.

Blagny A hamlet in the Côte de Beaune★ region whose vineyard is divided between Meursault★ and Puligny-Montrachet★, giving rise to an unusual situation: the climats★ in the Puligny area have the appellation Puligny-Montrachet, and those on the Meursault side, Blagny or Meursault-Blagny. The white wine of Blagny is similar to Meursault, though it has an elegance and delicacy more like that of Puligny. The red wine is fine and delicate and not unlike Volnay★.

blanc (vin) White wine. The vinification of white wine differs greatly from that of reds, being more difficult and unpredictable. More precautions must be taken when gathering the grapes and they have to be transported to the vatting sheds without being crushed in the process. There they must be pressed immediately, stalks and all.

The first juice obtained, moût de goutte★, is separated from the skins and put in barrels. Then the rest of the grapes are crushed, a longer process than that for reds because the must has a tendancy to expand. However, it is necessary to press quickly in order to avoid contact with the air which can cause yellowing and maderisation. The moût de presse★ then joins the moût de goutte in the vat and the important sulphur dioxide★ is added. This is left standing for six to twelve hours during which time the must separates from the sediment. Next comes a light racking and transferrence of the juice into new oak barrels (which give the necessary tannin to the wine) for fermentation. This process is always more laborious and delicate than for the red wine as the yeasts need essential elements found in the parts of the grape

34

'The Vendange' by Goya.
Prado Museum, Madrid.
Phot. Scala.

which have been eliminated by cleansing.

The fermentation lasts at least two or three weeks and must be carried out at a temperature of 15–18°C. Occasionally the fermentation stops completely until the spring. Each day the wine must be inspected and analysed and the barrels rolled in order to stir up the dregs and stimulate the yeast. Sweet white wines are even more difficult to make because of their richness and sugar content. When the wine

has finished fermenting, it is placed, like most wines, in barrels.

blanc liquoreux (vin) The fermentation of white wines is always longer and more difficult than that of red wines. The problem is even more complicated when making vin blanc liquoreux or sweet white wines. The must comes from grapes which have been subject to pourriture noble★ and thus contain a large amount of

Vineyards of the Limoux region (Aude). Phot. M.

sugar. All this sugar cannot be transformed into alcohol; when the must attains an average alcoholic content of 14–15° the yeast stops working, the alcoholic fermentation ceases and a significant quantity of natural sugar still remains in the wine. Certain sweet wines contain 14° of acquired alcohol and thus retain nearly 90 g of sugar per litre. In this case a large dose of sulphur dioxide★ must be added to avoid a secondary fermentation.

Before the Second World War there was a great demand for sweet white wine. To make as much as possible despite musts which did not contain enough sugar, certain wine makers stopped the fermentation at 12°, for example, in order to safeguard the remaining sugar. In order to do this they had to use even stronger doses of sulphur dioxide. Besides sugar, sweet white wines also contain gums and a lot of natural glycerine which gives them a special oily, fat consistency. The principal sweet white wines are those of Bordeaux (Sauternes★, Barsac★, Cérons★, Sainte-Croix-du-Mont★ and Loupiac★), Monbazillac★, certain Anjou★ and

Touraine★ wines and the famous rare Trockenbeerenauslese of the German vineyards of the Rhine and Moselle.

Blancs (Côte des) One of the most renowned vineyards of Champagne situated south-east of Epernay. It is called the White Coast because white Chardonnay grapes are almost the only crop grown. The wines show remarkable finesse and delicacy. This vineyard contains the following famous crus: Cramant, Avize, Oger, Mesnil-sur-Oger and Vertus. Cramant and Avize are the best known. They produce Blancs de Blancs★ which are extraordinarily subtle and delicate and have a lot of breeding. Cramant is a rare cru which is sold under its own name from vines harvested solely on its territory without being mixed with those coming from other crus.

Blancs de Blancs An expression that simply means 'white wine made from white grapes', and could, strictly speaking, be applied to any such wine. Its real importance as a qualitative description is in Champagne, where it is used to distinguish wine made exclusively with white Chardonnay grapes from other Champagnes (Blanc de Noirs★) made with Pinot Noir grapes, or with a mixture of the two. Blancs de Blancs are mainly produced in the Côte des Blancs★ region of Epernay, at Cramant, Mesnil and Avize. They are remarkably delicate, fine, light wines of a pale green-gold colour. Recently the expression has begun to be used, incorrectly, in regions other than Champagne.

Blancs de Noirs An expression used in the Champagne region meaning 'white wine made from black grapes'. This is not as contradictory as it sounds, for a grape's colouring-matter is contained in its skin, and the juice of black grapes is almost always quite colourless. (Vines that produce grapes with coloured juices are called *teinturiers*.)

The volume of Pinot (black grapes) grown in Champagne is estimated to be about four times that of Chardonnay (white grapes). Black grapes are grown for various reasons: they are more resistant to spring frosts and also to mold, which in humid years can affect grapes either before or during the harvest. They also have more body, more *sève*★ and a higher alcohol content than Blancs de Blancs★, and keep their whiteness longer.

There are in fact very few absolutely pure Blancs de Noirs. The equivalent of from an eighth to a quarter of their volume in Blancs de Blancs is usually added in order to make them lighter, finer and easier to convert into sparkling wine. There is also some Champagne made from 75–80% white grapes, as well as pure Blancs de Blancs.

Blanquette de Limoux   A well-known sparkling white wine of Languedoc★ which has an appellation contrôlée and is made from the Mauzac grape (sometimes associated with the Clairette), grown in rocky limestone soil around Limoux. Previously, the Mauzac was called 'Blanquette' because of the fine, white down which covered the undersides of the leaves. Thus the origin of the name of the delicious Blanquette de Limoux. Three principal centres produce it, the most important being around Limoux, another near Saint-Hilaire, and a third, more to the south

The Blanquette is obtained by a very moderate pressing – one hl of wine from 150 kg of fresh grapes. The production is therefore very small. In the sixteenth century, the monks of the Abbey of Saint-Hilaire discovered that the wine of Blanquette, when put in small pitchers, became naturally pétillant★ (semi-sparkling) and, by the time of Louis XIII, it was already much in demand. Today, at the cooperative which makes a large amount of the wine, the fermentation of the must is done by the rural method★ of a second fermentation taking place in the bottle. The natural sugar remaining in the wine after the first fermentation provokes the spontaneous formation of the froth. This produces elegant sparkling wine, light and golden, marrowy and fruity, with a particularly pleasant aroma.

Blayais   A vineyard on the right bank of the Gironde estuary opposite the Médoc★ region. Its wines are sold under the following appellations contrôlées: Blaye or Blayais (red and white), Côtes de Blaye (white) and Premières Côtes de Blaye (red and white). The white wines are pleasant and usually dry. Côtes de Blaye is full-bodied, sometimes marrowy, crisp and fine. Premières Côtes de Blaye is rather more marrowy. The red wines have an attractive colour and are moelleux, fruity, supple, and ready for bottling relatively soon after fermentation.

bloom   A fine waxy dust containing yeasts which collects on grapes and other fruits like the plum. It comes off when the grape is rubbed. The yeasts which activate alcoholic fermentation reside permanently in the vineyards and are transported by wind or insects onto the grape and invade the must when the vendange★ is pressed. However, certain of the yeasts can be harmful which is why the must has to be sterilised with sulphur dioxide★.

Bonnezeaux: general view of the Layon vineyard. Phot. M.

Bolivia   Vineyards cover only about 2000 ha of the country and are concentrated around La Paz. The vines, which originated in the Canary Islands, generally produce heavy red and white wines ranging from 13–15° in alcohol. Some fortified wines are also produced. All the Bolivian wines are consumed locally.

Bonnezeaux   One of the grand crus of the Coteaux du Layon★ region, made in the commune of Thouarcé on the right bank of the Layon river. Like Quarts-de-Chaume★, another vineyard in the

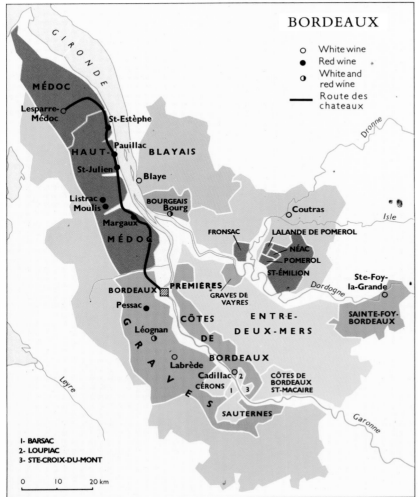

BORDEAUX

○ White wine
● Red wine
◑ White and red wine
— Route des chateaux

GIRONDE

MÉDOC

Lesparre-Médoc

St-Estèphe

HAUT-

Pauillac

BLAYAIS

St-Julien

Blaye

Listrac
Moulis

BOURGEAIS
Bourg

Margaux

MÉDOC

Coutras

FRONSAC

LALANDE DE POMEROL

NÉAC

POMEROL

ST-ÉMILION

BORDEAUX

PREMIÈRES

GRAVES DE
VAYRES

Ste-Foy-la-Grande

Pessac

CÔTES

ENTRE-

DEUX-MERS

SAINTE-FOY-
BORDEAUX

Léognan

DE

G R A V E S

BORDEAUX

Labrède

Cadillac
CÉRONS

CÔTES DE
BORDEAUX
ST-MACAIRE

1   3

SAUTERNES

Garonne

Leyre

Dronne

Isle

Dordogne

1- BARSAC
2- LOUPIAC
3- STE-CROIX-DU-MONT

0   10   20 km

Poster by Hervé Morvan (1957). Bibl. de l'Arsenal. Phot. Lauros-Giraudon.

following the Garonne and Dordogne rivers and their common estuary, the Gironde. The vines grow mainly on rocky, hilly land as the marshy, alluvial soil near the rivers is not suited to quality production.

Bordeaux is divided into several viticultural areas: Médoc★, Graves★ and Sauternes★. on the left side of the Garonne and Gironde, and Blayais★, Bourgeais★, Fronsac★, Pomerol★ and Saint-Emilion★ on the right bank of the Dordogne and the Gironde.

Entre-deux-Mers★ is found between them in the triangle formed by the Garonne and the Dordogne. The wines of Entre-deux-Mers include Premières Côtes de Bordeaux, Côtes de Bordeaux-Saint-Macaire★, Graves de Vayres★ and Sainte-Foy-Bordeaux.

The grapes of Bordeaux are the Cabernet, Malbec and Merlot for the reds, and the Sauvignon, Sémillon and Muscadelle for the whites.

BORDEAUX: APPELLATIONS D'ORIGINE CONTRÔLÉES   There are numerous Bordeaux wines which are AOC: thirty-four reds, twenty-three whites and two rosés. This does not seem an excessive amount when one considers the diversity of fine Bordeaux wine. There are three categories of appellations:

General name: Bordeaux or Bordeaux

same region, it has its own appellation contrôlée. The vineyard, with its schistose soil and steep hills, is barely 3 km by 500 m. The wine of Bonnezeaux has in its way as much distinction as its rival Quarts-de-Chaume. It is as tender★, fragrant, smooth and vigorous as the latter, and is mainly distinguished by its characteristic fruity aroma and flavour. It ages extremely well. The principal domaines are la Montagne and Château de Fesles.

Bordeaux   The wines of Bordeaux have been highly regarded through the ages – the Romans first spread their fame, they were prized by the English in the Middle Ages and, by the eighteenth century, the reputation of Bordeaux wines was known around the world.

The Bordeaux vineyards are located wholly within the Gironde department,

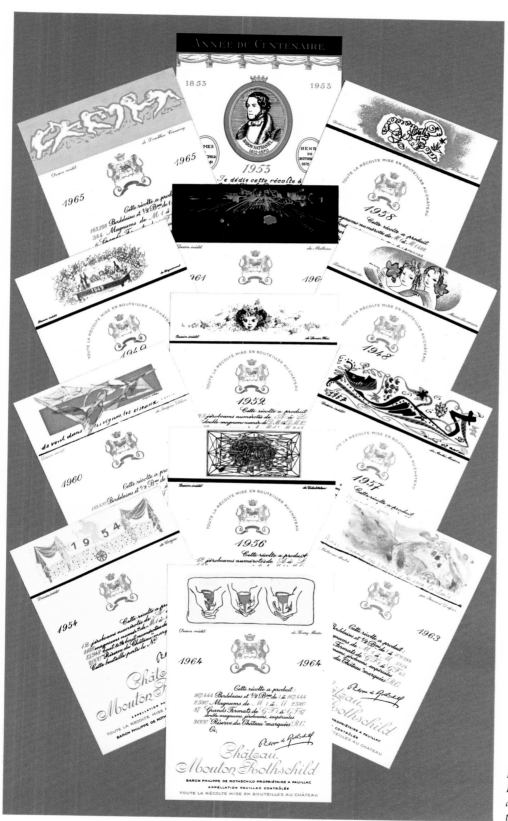

Each year Château Mouton-Rothschild employs a famous artist to provide a design on the theme of wine.

The wine port of Bordeaux.
Phot. Lauros-Geay.

supérieur (red, white, rosé or clairet) some-times followed by the name of the com-mune it comes from.

Regional name: corresponds to the geo-graphical area of the vineyard: Médoc (red), Graves (red and white), Entre-deux-Mers (white), etc.

Communal name: less common, and more reputable: Margaux (red), Pauillac (red), Sauternes (white), etc.

BORDEAUX and BORDEAUX SUPÉRIEUR The white, red and rosé wines falling under this category are of medium quality, sometimes unsteady but make good table wines. The red Bordeaux must have a minimum of 9·5° alcohol and the whites, 10°. The Bordeaux supérieurs, which keep well, must have a minimum of 10·5° for the reds and 11·5° for the whites.

These wines come from areas of Bor-deaux which do not have their own particular appellation, e.g. the districts of Coutras and Guitres. The vineyard owners also use these appellations in a bad year when they think their wine is not of sufficient quality to merit its particular appellation or for the part of their harvest which exceeds the hectarage limit set by law.

BORDEAUX CLAIRET Clairet, a clear, pale red wine, was for a long time the only kind of wine usually available. The relatively recent red and white are made by methods which are much more sophisticated than those which wine-makers used to employ. However, the red wine of Bordeaux is still called claret in Britain.

Today, the Bordelais are trying to re-vive the old clairet, which should not be confused with a rosé wine. It is made from a red wine which undergoes a very short fermentation period, which does not allow all the tannin to dissolve in the must. The result is a supple, round wine with a pleasant bouquet. The clairet, not having much tannin, has very little astringency – a feature which is appreciated by drinkers of young wines. It is also fresh and fruity, and can be drunk in its first year. Clairet does not age well.

BORDEAUX-CÔTES-DE-CASTILLON This appellation covers the wines of Castillon-la-Bataille, Saint-Magne-de-Castillon and Blèves-Castillon, communes that lie on the right bank of the Dordogne. The red wines, which sometimes have the appel-lation Bordeaux supérieur-Côtes de Cast-illon, have a rich colour and are generous and full-bodied. They can be drunk young.

BORDEAUX-HAUT-BÉNAUGE An appel-lation that applies to nine communes in the Entre-deux-Mers★ region. They were once part of the old county of Bénauge, which because of its dark and gloomy forests used to be known as the Black

Bénauge. Today, much of the forest has given way to vineyards which produce an agreeable white wine.

BORDEAUX MOUSSEUX These are white and sometimes rosé wines made by the Champagne method★ of secondary fermentation in bottle. They are entitled to the AOC Bordeaux and are very pleasant and fruity if made from selected grapes and prepared with great care and attention.

bottle (bouteille) The history of the manufacture and use of the bottle is chronicled by James Barrelet in his work '*La Verrerie en France de l'époque gallo-romaine à nos jours*', (Librairie Larousse). He reports that, at first, a leather bottle called a *boutiaux*, which could be attached to the saddle of a horse, was used to carry wine. At the time of the Renaissance, the French imported Italian bottles made of very thin, dull glass and protected by wicker casing. They were used to serve wines at the table.

At the beginning of the seventeenth century, the French began to produce thick glass bottles called 'green glass' or 'black glass' which could be used for serving, transporting and storing the wine. This was an extremely important invention for the future of French wines, and for their prestige.

The shape of the bottle was the same for all wines. At first, the base of the bottle was in the shape of an onion and then, little by little, became cylindrical (like a Benedictine bottle). During the first part of the nineteenth century, the traditional bottle was continually refined (Burgundy type), and at the same time a particular shape was created for certain crus. In 1800 the 'Bordeaux' and 'Champagne' shapes could be distinguished. The first machine-made bottles were used in Cognac in 1894, and standardisation of different types of bottles began. Today, the most widely-used bottles are those of Burgundy, Bordeaux, Champagne and the Rhine, and they appear in clear or tinted glass (green, yellow or yellow-brown).

BOTTLES (CAPACITY OF) This varies a little depending on the region. Burgundy, Bordeaux, and Anjou bottles contain 7·5 dl, Alsatian 7·2 dl and Champagne 8 dl. The Angevine filette (Anjou half bottle) contains 3·5 dl and the Beaujolais 'pot' 4·5 dl.

There is more variation in the contents of Champagne bottles. The split contains 2 dl, the pint 4 dl, the bottle 8 dl, the magnum two normal bottles, the Jeroboam four bottles, the Rehoboam six bottles, Methuselah eight bottles,

Left: the Malbec or Cot grape, a variety much used in making Bordeaux wines.
Phot. M.

The Bordeaux vineyards.
Phot. Atlas-Photo.

From left to right: wine or liqueur bottle often found in the press rooms of Hungarian vignerons. It holds 2 litres. Phot. J.-L. Chamet. Glass oval bottle with hunting scene. Germany around 1600. Musée des Arts Décoratifs. Phot. Lauros-Giraudon. Flat, stoneware bottle decorated with the coat of arms of Liosel. Beauvaisis, second half of the 16th century. Height 25 cm. Musée de Sèvres. Phot. Lauros-Giraudon.

Salmanazar twelve bottles, Balthazar sixteen and Nebuchadnezzar twenty.

bottle sickness A wine should never be drunk immediately after being bottled. It should be left to settle for one to three months depending on the wine, a length of time the specialists call the 'bottle sickness' period. All the operations the wines have gone through (fermentation, etc.) have made the delicate wine somewhat unbalanced. Even the most well-bottled wine is subjected to an unsettling aeration which temporarily hides its bouquet and its other attributes. When the oxidising effect of the air has disappeared the wine regains its delicate equilibrium, then if it is a wine which profits from ageing, the wine begins to take on its new qualities.

bottle washing Despite the care taken in cleaning bottles, a little deposit sometimes remains on the inside. The old remedy of scouring is very good. The cleaning agent should be put in the bottle with a little water, then shaken vigorously to loosen the lees and tartar which stick to the inside. Afterwards, the bottle should be rinsed twice with water, and left to dry in an upside down position.

bouchonné A term used to describe a wine which tastes 'corky'. This taste is so disagreeable and noticeable that it needs no description. A corky tasting wine is not usually the result of a mistake when making the wine, but rather a faulty cork. The taste comes from the cork itself and is due to parasites living in the bark of the cork oaks. The best corks, which come from Spain, especially Catalonia, rarely produce this result. Sometimes, the taste is even worse and comes from mould which has developed in the cells of the cork.

For storage, the bottles must always be laid down to avoid drying out the cork. It is also very bad to keep changing the bottle from an upright to a horizontal position.

If the odour of the cork is faint, it is enough to throw away the first few inches of wine, as the rest of the bottle is usually undamaged. But a wine which is really bouchonné should not be drunk. Restauranteurs and hosts should try to safeguard their guests from this disappointment by always discreetly smelling the cork before serving the wine.

bouquet The fragrant smell of a wine which develops with maturity. The bouquet is one of the great charms of a fine wine and one of the subtlest pleasures for the drinker. Bouquet is the result of a combination of the aroma★ of the grape and a more complex fragrance which develops after the wine has undergone fermentation.

The secondary fragrance, which is affected by the action of the yeasts, is flowery or fruity, or both. Thus, for example, the bouquet which is so pleasant in Beaujolais can be characterised as follows: Saint-Amour, peach, reseda; Juliénas, peach, raspberry; Brouilly, peony, prune, etc.

The bouquet is further developed by oxidation while the wines are maturing in barrels, then to a lesser degree during ageing in bottles. As a result of these changes the wine gives off a smell which is extremely subtle, fragile and complex. To appreciate this bouquet to the fullest, the gourmet adroitly turns the glass in his hand and inhales the aroma time and again.

The fragrances found most often have been classed into a series forming the 'fragrance spectrum'. Plant fragrances, often used to describe young wines, are floral (rose, jasmine, hyacinth, lilac, orange blossom, violet, peony, reseda, pink, lime, etc.) or fruity (peach, apricot, apple, almond, raspberry, banana, blackcurrant and cherry).

Vegetable odours appear in the bouquet of older wines – mushroom, truffle, undergrowth, humus, etc. Old wines which have recently reached their fullness are often described in terms of animals: venison, pheasant and musk deer (like certain admirable old Burgundies). Spices like pepper, sandalwood, clove and vanilla are also mentioned, as are the odours like fine tobacco (certain Châteauneufs-du-Papes), resin, coffee and toasted almond (old white Burgundies).

The wines from northern vineyards which have a temperate climate usually have a higher acid content and also more bouquet than those from warmer southern regions, which have little acidity. In the same way, wines from rocky, chalky soil which receive little sun have more bouquet than those made from more fertile land.

Certain oenophiles can determine the area and grape from which a wine comes and its approximate year merely by smelling the bouquet. When the bouquet expands slowly, taking a long time to reveal itself, it is said that the bouquet has a 'long nose'. On the other hand, if the bouquet is not apparent or fades quickly, it is said to have a 'short nose'.

Bourgeais A vineyard that lies on the right bank of both the Dordogne and the Gironde rivers, facing the Médoc★ district. Its wines are sold under the appellations contrôlées Bourg or Bourgeais and Côtes de Bourg. The white wines are dry, medium dry or sweet. The red wines are full-bodied, well balanced, robust and age well. They are excellent table wines.

bourgeois (crus) The great diversity of Médoc★ wines has led to a natural classification, based on usage of the different crus. They are divided according to merit into crus paysans, crus artisans, crus bourgeois ordinaires, bons bourgeois, bourgeois supérieurs and, lastly, into grands crus. These latter, representing the aristocrats of wine, were classified in 1855 into five categories, called crus classés.

The crus bourgeois were classified in 1858, in a work by M. d'Armailhacq, into thirty-four bourgeois supérieurs, sixty-four bons bourgeois and about 150 bourgeois. Today they are referred to simply as the 'bourgeois supérieurs' and the 'bourgeois'. In 1932, 100 were officially recognised by the courtiers★ of the region. Châteaux Gloria, Phélan-Ségur, Sémeillan and Fourcas-Dupré are among the crus bourgeois supérieurs. Certain crus of some years are called crus exceptionnels. However, this easily misleads the public because, in fact, the crus exceptionnels are officially listed under the five crus classés. These are the Chateaux Angludet, Bel-Air-Marquis-d'Aligre, Chase-Spleen, la Couronne, Moulin-Riche, Poujeaux-Theil and Villegorge.

Bourgogne aligoté This appellation is given to those white wines grown in Burgundy★ which come from the Aligoté grape (with or without Chardonnay). The minimum alcoholic content must be 9·5° and the maximum yield per ha, 45 hl.

Bourgogne ordinaire and **Bourgogne grand ordinaire** These appellations concern the red, rosé and white wines produced in the Burgundy★ area. The red

wines come from the fine Pinot and Gamay grapes (in the Yonne, the César and the Tressot). The whites come from the Chardonnay and Pinot Blanc, the Aligoté and the Melon de Bourgogne (in the Yonne and the Sacy). The minimum alcohol content must be 9·5° and the maximum yield per ha, 45 hl.

Bourgogne passe-tous-grains This appellation is only applied to those red wines made in Burgundy★ from two-thirds Gamay Noir and one-third Pinot grapes. The minimum alcohol content must be 9·5° and the maximum yield per ha, 45 hl.

Bourgueil Formerly, almost all of the Bourgueil country was part of the province of Anjou, and later it was included in the modern viticultural classification with Touraine★.

The vineyards extend in a line for twenty km between Saint-Patrice and Saint-Nicolas-de-Bourgueil, as well as along the Loire (La Chapelle, Chouzé).

The soils have a different composition, going from south to north: alluvium deposited by the Loire, then gravel terraces and thick sands, and finally the coast, where limestone-clay covers micaceous chalk. The wines grown on gravelly soil

are the lightest, with more finesse and bouquet, and can be drunk young. The wines of the coast are more full-bodied, harder when young and must mature before they can be drunk.

Most of the communes produce wines of both the coastal and rocky varieties (the volume of wines from rocky soil is greater). Yet, Ingrandes produces only wine from rocky soil, and Benais, the wines of the coast. The grape, like at Chinon★, is the Cabernet Breton (or Cabernet Franc).

It is difficult to separate Bourgueil from Chinon. Both are located in the 'Kingdom of Grandgousier' and their red wines bear such a resemblance to each other that it is sometimes difficult to tell them apart. Bourgueil takes longer to mature than Chinon, but it has more body while still being fresh and delicate. Its strongest characteristic is a magnificent bouquet of raspberries (Chinon has a violet bouquet), and it is often compared to the bon crus bourgeois of the Médoc★. Bourgueil has, in any case, a singular virtue, if one believes the Prior who said in 1089, 'This wine makes sad hearts happy'. There are two appellations contrôlées: Bourgueil and Saint-Nicolas-de-Bourgueil.

bourru (vin) A vin bourru is one which has not yet deposited its yeasts and impurities at the bottom of the barrel. The wine is therefore full of insoluble matter and still contains unfermented sugar. It has a cloudy appearance.

This sparkling or semi-sparkling grape juice used to be much in demand and was the speciality of certain regions. Unfermented wines are still bought and sold at the time of the vendange. Parisians favour the macadam★, the unfermented wine of Bergerac★, and not so long ago it was esteemed an honour for members of the trade to handle the unfermented wine of Gaillac★. In autumn the unfermented wine of Alsace, the Neuer Susser, comes each day to Paris from the vendange and is quickly consumed.

bouteilles, mise en (put in bottles) Some large houses refuse to deliver their wines in barrels but insist on bottling it on the premises. Bottling is an important job which, if done at the wrong time, can utterly destroy the best wines.

Saint-Nicolas de Bourgueil

APPELLATION CONTRÔLÉE (NICOLAS) CHARENTON.VAL-DE-MARNE

Vendange at Bourgueil. Phot. Phedon-Salou.

Analysis determines the maximum expansion of the wine in the barrel, its clearness and stability. The most favourable time is always chosen to bottle as the bottling period only lasts a maximum of six weeks. March and September are generally the favoured months. The temperature should be constant, the weather dry and barometric pressure stable. Traditional wine-makers wait for a north wind which they believe is a sign of good atmospheric conditions. The bottling must be carried out rapidly with all equipment meticulously clean.

A wooden spigot or a siphon can be used to transfer the wine from cask to bottle. A siphon with a plastic spout is preferable, as the wooden spigot tends to stir up the wine each time the tap is closed. The corking must always be done so as to leave the least possible amount of air between the wine and the bottom of the cork. Then the bottles are left standing for twenty-four hours so that the corks will adhere well to the neck of the bottles. Next the wine is laid down for at least a month (the 'bottle sickness'★ period) before it is delivered for consumption.

The wine-maker who likes to have the adventure of bottling his own wine must wait till he judges the wine is in the right state for bottling. Wine must not travel in hot weather as a refermentation may occur, nor in cold weather as the wine may freeze en route. After transport, white wines should rest from eight to ten days, and red wines from ten to fifteen days, before being drunk.

Bouzy   A village in Champagne★ which has given its name to the Côte de Bouzy, the south-eastern slope of the Montagne de Reims★ that runs into the Marne★ valley. Bouzy is an excellent cru of Champagne and produces an exquisite (though not, of course, sparkling) red wine. This is made in very small quantities, and unfortunately is rather delicate and does not travel well.

In good years Bouzy is a magnificent wine that would seem to justify the famous quarrel between Champagne and Burgundy in the seventeenth century which was begun by Fagon★, the king's doctor. It is a fine, garnet-coloured wine with a distinctive bouquet of peaches (a characteristic of Champagne wines first noted by the Marquis de Saint-Evremond). After

several years in bottle, this powerful, warm and well-balanced wine is sometimes hard to distinguish from an excellent Burgundy.

Brazil   Although vines have been planted since the Portuguese conquest, it was not until the Italian immigration after the First World War that viticulture really started to develop. The chief vineyard area is in the south of the country in the state of Rio Grande do Sul, but the regions of Sao Paulo, Santa Catarina, Rio de Janeiro and Minas Geraes also produce some wine. The American hybrid Isabella is the most widely-planted grape. It produces a vin ordinaire which is often a good, but never a great, wine.

brilliance   A very attractive visual quality, especially in white and rosé wines

Bottling wine in a private cellar at Savigny-lès-Beaune (Burgundy). Phot. M.

BOUZY ROUGE
VIN NATURE DE LA CHAMPAGNE
Paul COLLARD
Propriétaire-Récoltant
BOUZY (Marne)

when they are absolutely limpid. Wines that have clarity and brilliance, however, are not always perfect. The processes (collage★, filtering★ and racking★) necessary to clarify a wine during vinification may impair both the aroma★ and bouquet★ of the wine.

Brouilly One of the most famous Beaujolais★ crus. The appellation applies to wines made in the communes of Odenas, Saint-Lager, Cercié, Quincié and Charentay, which are grouped around the Montagne de Brouilly. Brouilly is a typical Beaujolais, fruity★ and tender★ with a pronounced bouquet. It should be drunk young, as these distinctive qualities fade with age.

Mount Brouilly (Beaujolais). Phot. M.

Brouilly (Côte de) One of the better wines of Beaujolais★, Côte de Brouilly comes from the vineyard which occupies the slopes of the renowned Montagne de Brouilly. The position of the vineyard and its granitic soil produce a particularly fine wine.

It is produced in the communes of Odenas, Saint-Lager, Cercié and Quincié. The wine is a beautiful dark purple colour, high in alcohol and fleshy★, but also fruity★ and fragrant. Although a little firm when young, it can be drunk then or after several years when it becomes truly exquisite. As Côte de Brouilly ages, it loses some of its fruitiness but develops its bouquet.

Bué Although it covers only a small area, this commune of the Cher is well known for its wine, which has the right to the appellation contrôlée Sancerre★. This area produces the well-known crus of Chêne-Marchand, Chemarin and Poussie. The vines of Poussie, the ancient property of the Abbey of Bué, grow both on clay and dry limestone which gives the wines good bouquet, equilibrium and longevity.

Buena Vista A historical vineyard of Sonoma★, California, founded just after the gold rush by the colourful Hungarian Count Agoston Haraszthy, who preferred to renounce his title to become 'the Colonel'. He has been called 'the father of modern Californian viticulture' because of his strong influence on the vineyards of that state. The winery of Buena Vista has suffered a series of misfortunes including the destruction of the caves during the great San Francisco earthquake.

Today, Buena Vista again produces Premium Wines. Most of the time, the wines carrying the Buena Vista label are sold under the name of the grape they come from (Varietal Wines), but there is also some wine that carries two special appellations, Rose Brook and Vine Brook.

Bugey Bugey was the home of the renowned Brillat-Savarin. Its small vineyard, which carries the VDQS★ label, is located in the department of Ain between Beaujolais★ and Savoie★ and has recently been reducing its production. The red and rosé wines come from the Gamay, Pinot Noir and Gris, Poulsard and Mondeuse grapes. These very agreeable wines are generally light and fruity and somewhat similar to a Beaujolais. The white wines are made from the Chardonnay, Altesse, Aligoté, and Mondeuse Blanc. They are light and refreshing, like many of the Savoie wines. The best crus are the Virieu and Montagnieu. Only the white wines from Altesse and Chardonnay grapes can be called Roussette de Bugey.

Bulgaria Viticulture is an important part of the Bulgarian economy and a considerable effort is being made to modernise it. After Italy, Bulgaria is the second largest European exporter of fresh grapes. A large quantity of wine is also exported, especially to the USSR, Czechoslovakia and East Germany.

Vineyards are found as high as 500 m and sixty-three varieties of grape are grown, of which three-quarters are used to produce table wines. The other varieties are used to make dessert wines: Asenovgrad (a sort of Malaga made in the town of the same name), Madara, Slavianka, Tchirpan, Tyrnovo and Melnik.

There are six principal wine-growing areas in Bulgaria:

The Valley of the Roses (Kazanlyk region) with the great centres of Karlova and Troian. It produces the Rozentaler Riesling (Riesling of the Valley of the Roses), and the Karlovski Misket, an amber-coloured muscat.

The South-west (Kjustendil region) The vine, cultivated around Sandanski and Melnik, produces the Melnik, a very sweet and agreeable wine containing up to 35% sugar.

Thracia The most important vineyards are found along the Maritsa between Dimitrovgrad to the east and Thtiman to the west, with the Stara Zagora–Sliven line as the northern boundary. Within this principal zone there are two regions of production around Plovdiv and Tchirpan. The Plovdiv region produces Bolgar, Pamid (red wine), Pirinsko (red wine from the Pirine grape, near Plovdiv) and Trakia (red wine). Tchirpan produces a dessert wine of the same name.

The Banks of the Danube possess rich vineyards whose largest centres are Vidin and Silistra. Vidin produces the Gymza, a well-known red wine.

The Coast of the North Sea The two towns of Varna and Pomerie produce a white wine called Dimiat.

The Tirnovo region in northern Bulgaria gives its name to a well-known dessert wine.

Despite their careful preparation, all the white wines of Bulgaria lack freshness because of the latitude of the country. The red wines, however, have recently become very good table wines which often attain the level of red French VDQS★ and are classed, most of the time, with those of Romania and Hungary, and have a similar astringency.

Bué: the domaine of La Poussie with its natural amphitheatre. Phot. M.

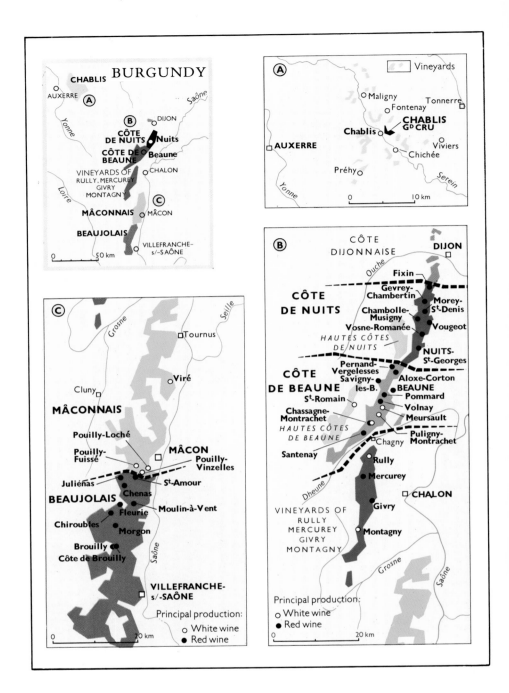

Burgundy Without doubt, the cultivation of the vine began in Burgundy in
the Gallo-Roman period and perhaps even
earlier. However, the Burgundy vineyards
are certainly the work of the monasteries.
From the twelfth century, thanks to the
monks of Cîteaux, the fame of the wine of
Burgundy was widespread. The vineyard
of Lower Burgundy, with Auxerre as its
capital, was known outside the region

before that of Upper Burgundy. In the
fourth century, St Germain had inherited
some vineyards from her parents in Auxerre, and a piece of this ancient vineyard
still exists (Clos de la Chainette★).

It was only towards the thirteenth century that the wines around Beaune began
to be appreciated outside their area.
Beaune established the universal reputation of the wines of Burgundy and,

upon the death of Philip Augustus, the vineyards of Beaune were considered 'the great riches of the duchy of Burgundy'. At the beginning of the eighteenth century the first *maisons* (houses) of wine were founded at Beaune, then at Nuits and Dijon. The *négociants*★ greatly extended the scope of commerce for the wines and were largely responsible for spreading their reputation.

The vineyards of Burgundy today extend into four departments: Yonne, Côte-d'Or, Saône-et-Loire and Rhône. These are divided into five subregions: Chablis★ (Yonne department); Côte d'Or★ (department of the Côte-d'Or) comprising the Côte de Nuits★ and the Côte de Beaune★; Côte Chalonnaise★(department of Saône-et-Loire); Mâconnais★ (department of Saône-et-Loire) and Beaujolais★ (department of Saône-et-Loire and Rhône).

BURGUNDY: APPELLATIONS D'ORIGINE CONTRÔLÉES   Of all the French regions

A village in Burgundy: Rochepot and its 12th-century château. Phot. Aarons-L.S.P.

Burgundy: Château Vougeot. Phot. M.

'The Drinker' by Watteau.
Musée Cognacq-Jay.
Phot. Giraudon.

which produce wine, Burgundy has the largest number of appellations contrôlées. Particularly in the Côte de Nuits and the Côte de Beaune, there are many villages which themselves have numerous crus or climats★, each with its own characteristic and distinctive personality. The legislation then only had to follow the 'usage and tradition' of the area. There are four categories of appellations:

Generic or regional appellations   These are designated wines which are grown in the Burgundy area and which all have the right to the appellation: Bourgogne★ rouge and blanc and Bourgogne rosé or clairet; Bourgogne aligoté★ (white); Bourgogne ordinaire★, or Bourgogne grand ordinaire★ (red and white); Bourgogne passe-tous-grains★ (red).

Sub-regional appellations   This appellation is applied only to wines produced in a particular subregion of Burgundy: Côtes de Beaune-Villages★ (red); Mâcon and Mâcon supérieur★ (red and white); Mâcon Villages★ (white); Beaujolais★ and Beaujolais supérieur★ (red and white); Beaujolais-Villages★ (red).

Communal appellations   Many of the Burgundy villages can legally give their name to the wine grown on their territory: Fleurie★, Beaune★, Volnay★, Nuits-Saint-Georges★, Meursault★, Chablis★, etc.

Appellations of crus   The vineyard of each commune is divided into small vineyards called climats★ in Burgundy. Certain of the best-known vineyards are called by their particular name: e.g. Chambertin, Musigny and Clos de Vougeot. Often the communal appellation is followed by the name of the climat or the expression premier cru, e.g. Chambolle-Musigny-les-Amoureuses.

BURGUNDY: APPELLATION BOURGOGNE   This is applied to red and white wines produced in the Burgundy area. For the rosés, the appellation becomes Bourgogne clairet or Bourgogne rosé. For the red wines, the authorised grapes are the Pinot; in the Yonne, the César and the Tressot; in the Mâconnais and Beaujolais, the Gamay noir à jus blanc. For the white wines, the grapes are the Chardonnay★ and the Pinot Blanc★. The minimum alcohol content for the Burgundies is 10° for the reds and the rosés, and 10·5° for the whites. The maximum yield is 45 hl per ha.

Under certain conditions, the names of Marsannay or Marsannay-la-Côte of the Upper Côtes de Nuits and Upper Côtes de Beaune can be added to the appellation Bourgogne (red, white and rosé).

Buzet (Côtes du)   A small VDQS★ area of the south-west of France, located to the east of Agen on the left bank of the Garonne, and includes the eight communes of the canton of Lavardac. The viticultural co-operative of Buzet-sur-Baïse is well equipped to vinify the production of all the wine-growers in the district.

The region produces good quality red wines which are agreeable and full of bouquet. They come from the Merlot, Cabernet Franc, Cabernet Sauvignon and Malbec grapes. This last variety is being eclipsed more and more by the Merlot, a variety which up till now was used mostly in Bordeaux, and which makes fine wines with a good bouquet. A small amount of white wine is produced from grapes used in Bordeaux: Sémillon, Sauvignon and Muscadelle. The grape-growing area is presently being enlarged.

C

Cabernet Franc This grape has different names depending on the region. It is called Bouchet or Gros-Bouchet in Saint-Emilion and Pomerol, Bouchy in Madiran, and Breton in Touraine and Saumur. It is a hardy variety with small bunches of thin-skinned, bluish-black grapes. It grows well on most soils except chalky ones. The wine from this grape has a lively, sparkling colour like that from the Cabernet-Sauvignon★, but with less bouquet. On the other hand, it takes less time than the Cabernet-Sauvignon to clear after fermentation. The Cabernet Franc is often combined with other varieties in Gironde and the south-west but in the Loire★ it is the sole grape used for Chinon★, Bourgueil★, Saint-Nicolas-de-Bourgueil★, Saumur-Champigny★ and several other reds and rosés.

Cabernet-Sauvignon A typical grape of Bordeaux, principally of Médoc★ and Graves★ where it accounts for 50–70% of the grapes producing good crus. It is also called Petit-Cabernet (Médoc and Graves), and Petit Bouchet (Saint-Emilion★ and Pomerol★). The Cabernet-Sauvignon is often mixed with the Cabernet Franc★, Merlot and Petit-Verdot but very rarely with the Malbec.

The Cabernet-Sauvignon prefers poor, dry soil and it grows in small bunches of little, thick-skinned, bluish-black grapes. This grape produces a dark-coloured wine full of tannin, which is harsh in a young wine but which with time takes on body, suppleness and a very delicate bouquet of violets. Cabernet-Sauvignon has been planted in many other countries by those attempting to imitate the wines of the

Far left: the Cabernet Franc grape, a 'noble' variety found in different regions of France. Phot. M.

Left: the Cabernet-Sauvignon, a characteristic grape of Bordeaux and especially of the Médoc. Phot. M.

Médoc. In California good quality wines have been produced but, elsewhere, the results have not been so successful.

Cabrières One of the appellations of the Coteaux du Languedoc★, classified VDQS★. The red wine, vin vermeil, of Cabrières was known in Montpellier as early as 1357 and was a favourite of Louis XIV. It is an excellent rosé, fruity and full-bodied. It is made mainly from the Carignan and Cinsault grape.

café wines Simple, light, red wines which are easily drunk at the counter or, like table wines, from a carafe. They are very agreeable when served slightly chilled. These wines are made by a short vinification process which gives them a pleasant suppleness. Many of the red wines coming from the Côtes du Rhône and Languedoc are treated in this way. They are also called 'one night wines' because their fermentation time is no longer than a night (from twelve to fourteen hours).

The commune of Saint-Saturnin in the Hérault, and that of Saint-Cécile-les-Vignes in Vaucluse, are well known for their café wines.

Cahors The red wine of Cahors, classified VDQS★, is one of the best wines of south-west France. Well known even at the time of the Romans, it was completely overshadowed by the Bordeaux wines until Louis XVI ended the privilège de Bordeaux★ in 1776. Phylloxera★, then the frost of 1956, almost extinguished the doughty vines, but they soon revived.

Cahors is produced by forty communes on the two banks of the River Lot, both up and down stream from Cahors, in the centres of Cahors, Luzech, Puy-l'Evêque, Catus, Montcuq and Lalbenque. The principal grape (60–80%) is the Malbec, also called the Auxerrois. It is sometimes blended with the Jurançon Rouge, Abouriou, Merlot and others.

Cahors is perhaps the most colourful of French wines. It is a brilliant, dark crimson colour, almost black, which is similar to the deep velvety red of the better wines of Valteline in northern Italy. The Italian wines can be drunk when very young while the Cahors should mature three to five years before being bottled, and is not at its best for another five to ten years thereafter. An aged Cahors is a splendid wine, harmonious and firm without being

The vineyard of Cahors extends around this loop of the river Lot which encircles the town. Phot. Beaujard-Lauros.

hard, and full-bodied with an inimitable bouquet.

The USSR★ gives the name 'Cahors' to something very different – vins de liqueur★ which are dark red, almost black in colour, very sugary and containing about 16° alcohol. The vines which make this wine (also called Karop or Kagor) are descended no doubt from grapes imported a long time ago from Quercy. The addition of alcohol, used to make the Russian version, was probably the idea of a resident of Cahors who used the process with his wine so that it would make the trip to Russia without damage. This expensive wine, which is very much in demand in Russia, has for a long time been that used for the Mass in the Orthodox Church. Even though it is nothing like the French original, the Russians have adopted the name of Cahors for one of their most precious wines.

California California accounts for 90% of the vineyard acreage of the United States. Less than half of its enormous production is actually used for wine; the rest is made into dried raisins or consumed as table grapes. Two-thirds of total wine production (about six million hl) consists of vins de liqueur★ (Muscatel, Angelica, sherry and port).

The vineyards of California are divided into three distinct regions. The first, which produces mainly table grapes, is found around San Francisco along the northern coast of the Pacific. It is divided into several grape-growing areas, the principal ones being, from north to south: Mendocino, Sonoma★, Napa★, Alameda★ (principally in the Livermore Valley), Santa Clara★ and San Benito★.

The second region, in the interior of the State, includes the San Joaquin and Grand valleys and, from north to south, the vineyards are those of Sacramento, San Joaquin, Madero, Fresno and Tulare. This region produces primarily dried raisins, table grapes and lots of cheap sweet wines.

The third region extends further south, eastwards of Los Angeles, to the foot of the San Bernardino mountains, and produces mostly vins ordinaires, comparable to the French wines of the Midi★ region.

The indigenous wild vines were growing to the west of the Rocky Mountains when the first European grape varieties were brought to California by the Spanish Franciscan monks. They planted them to the north of San Francisco (this variety, which has since been named 'Mission', produces only a mediocre wine). But it was a Hungarian immigrant who brought to California the beginnings of modern viticulture. The dynamic Count Agoston Haraszthy (called more familiarly 'the Colonel') is rightly known as 'the father of California wine-making'.

The red wines of California come principally from the following grape varieties: Zinfandel, Carignan, Alicante-Bouschet, Grenache, Mission, Mataro (a common, very productive variety of Spanish origin) and Petite-Syrah (which probably comes from the same family as the French Hermitage). The majority of white wines come from the Sultana or Thompson Seedless (which gives a clear wine without much aroma and a neutral taste, but very inexpensive) and other varieties like the Sauvignon Vert, Burger and Palomino (this last, while excellent for sherry, makes a mediocre table wine).

During the last twenty years, great progress has been made in the production of Californian table wines. The areas planted with good European varieties (Cabernet, Pinot, Riesling, Sémillon) have been extended considerably. The better wineries rival those of Europe from the point of view of technique and equipment. The sometimes arbitrary methods of naming wines are becoming more uniform, so that they can now be classified in three categories: mediocre vins ordinaires, which are simply called reds, whites or rosés; wines which still carry the generic names coined at the beginning of Californian wine-making like 'California Chablis' and 'California Burgundy' (there is no law which regulates the percentage of Chardonnay for the 'Chablis' or of Pinot Noir for the 'Burgundy' contained in these wines, but they are of good quality); and finally, the 'Premium Wines' which represent the aristocracy of Californian wines and are of excellent quality. They are called 'Varietal Wines' because they carry the name of the grape variety from which they are made (for example, Pinot Noir and Cabernet-Sauvignon) and correspond in a way to the French AOC wines. The name of a winery added to that of the grape gives a further guarantee of quality.

Certain producers date their wines, although a vintage year does not have the same importance as in France because the character of Californian wines does not vary very much from one year to another. The stability of the climate gives a consistant quality with no surprises. The vintage year, then, is simply an indication of age, a guarantee of the maturity of the wine.

As well as table wines, California produces a great quantity of sparkling wines which are made for the most part by the Champagne method★. Many of them are mediocre because there is no legal supervision as in France. But some made from the Chardonnay and Pinot Blanc, in well-known wineries (like Almaden, Beaulieu, Korbel and Paul Masson), are of excellent quality. The sparkling wines of California are sold under the name 'California Champagne' and 'Sparkling Burgundy'. The American vins de liqueur★ which are produced in large quantities are generally made from different grapes and by different vinification methods than their European counterparts. However, there are five or six producers, including Almaden and Louis M. Martini, who make sherry and port according to the traditional Spanish or Portuguese methods.

Canada All the Canadian vineyards are found around Niagara between Lake Erie and Lake Ontario (except for a few widely-dispersed vineyards in British Columbia). There are only about 8000 ha planted to vines, which produce some 250,000 hl of wine. The climate of this peninsular formed between the two lakes is very temperate, and conditions are very favourable for the cultivation of the vine.

One of Champlain's companions, Jean de Poutrincount, planted several feet of vines, but the real origins of Canadian viticulture date from 1811 when a German named John Schiller began planting vines and making wine near Toronto. Today, the wines resemble those which are produced in the United States in the nearby state of New York. They are made from some of the same varieties: Concorde, Catawba, Niagara and Delaware. Since the end of the Second World War, some experiments have been tried with hybrids★ of French origin. Most of the production still consists of sweet dessert wines but the demand for table wines is becoming stronger.

Capri One of the most popular dry white wines in southern Italy. Capri is produced not only on the island of Capri but also on the neighbouring island of Ischia and on the nearby mainland. (These other areas, incidentally, often make better wine than Capri itself.) The quality of Capri varies according to individual vineyards. The best wine is probably not exported.

capsule A capsule is the metallic or paper wrapper around the cork and neck of a bottle of wine, and as such has a purely decorative function. When opening a bottle, the capsule should be cut cleanly under the ridge round the top of the bottle. Wine should never come into contact with it when being poured, as this might give it an unpleasant 'capsule taste'.

capucine A wooden receptacle in which the vignerons of Lorraine carry their drinking wine to work every day. A capucine holds two litres and is produced in the shape of a round-bellied bottle with a long neck. It is made of pieces of wood held together by metal rings, like a barrel. The capucine inspired the creation of the *Confrérie des Compagnons de la Capucine*, whose declared mission is to uphold and protect the wines of Lorraine★.

carafe wines Young, cheap, unpretentious wines that are served in carafes and not in bottles. Carafe wines are often excellent, light, fresh wines, providing they are genuine vins de pays★.

carbon dioxide (CO$_2$) This gas is a waste product which is encountered several times during the life of a wine.

It is present during alcoholic fermentation★ when the sugar decomposes into alcohol and carbon dioxide. One hl of must produces about 4·5 hl of carbon dioxide. The gas, being heavier than air, can collect in the cellars and it is necessary to provide good ventilation during the fermentation period.

Carbon dioxide is also formed during malo-lactic fermentation★. It is responsible for the slight effervescence found in certain wines like Crepy★ and Gaillac perle★ which undergo their malo-lactic fermentation in bottle.

It also causes the light sparkle of wines bottled on their lees, and the sparkle in Champagne★ and other sparkling wines made by other methods such as the rural★,

German★, cuve close★ and the Asti★ process. It is also injected into carbonated sparkling wines.

carbonic maceration A method of vinifying red wines used mainly in Beaujolais★. The grapes are put in the cuve without being crushed. The result is an intracellular fermentation by which part of the sugar is converted into alcohol without the aid of yeasts. At the same time, a small amount of grapes at the bottom of the cuve has undergone alcoholic fermentation as the skins have been broken by the weight of grapes above. The ingredients in the skin of these grapes diffuse throughout the pulp creating aromatic substances which would not appear in wine vinified in the normal way.

After several days of maceration the grapes are crushed and normal fermentation takes place. As a result of this method, very fragrant wines having only a small volatile acid content are produced. They mature quickly and conserve well.

Carbonnieux (eau minérale de) Not a mineral water, but an excellent wine made in Graves★. According to an almost certainly apocryphal story, Benedictine monks used to sell the white wine from their domaine★ of Carbonnieux under this name at the court of the Turkish Sultan, where the Moslem laws of abstinence were supposedly in force.

Carthagène Carthagène is a vin de liqueur★, or fortified wine, traditionally made by vignerons in the south of France for their private consumption. It is made in very small casks and in small quantities, as the only alcohol available to the vignerons is the amount officially allowed to distillers. To every five litres of Grenache grape juice (which is very rich in sugar), one litre of 96° proof alcohol is added, and the mixture is then left on the lees for the winter (clarification occurs spontaneously). After one year in cask the wine has acquired a golden colour, is sweet (200–250 g of natural sugar per litre) and has an alcohol content of 16°.

Once, only *eau-de-vie de vin* or wine spirit was used. Nowadays *eau-de-vie de marc* (spirit made from grape pulp) is sometimes used as well, and makes a harsher, much less fine wine.

Similar wines are made in Champagne and Burgundy (Ratafia★ and Riquiqui) as well as in Charentes which produces Pineau des Charentes★, a much less sweet wine than Carthagène, and made with Cognac rather than *eau-de-vie*.

casse brune A disease that commonly affects white wines and is caused by oxidation. As a preventive measure, doses of sulphur dioxide★ are added to the grape juice before fermentation.

casse ferrique A disease that can occur when the iron content of a wine exceeds 10–12 mg per litre. Oxidation causes the ferric salts of the wine to crystallise, which in turn makes either the tannin or the protein content do the same. According to the appearance of the wine, two types of casse are distinguishable, casse bleue and casse blanche. Both of these appear soon after the wine has been exposed to the air (during racking or filtering, for example).

Casse bleue gives red wine a purplish colour, and white wine a leaden tinge and a black precipitate of ferric tannate.

Casse blanche makes the wine look milky and opalescent due to the formation of ferric phosphate, which causes flocculation of the protein compounds.

Ideally, to avoid casse ferrique, no part of any machine used for vinification should be made of iron. In practice, this is virtually impossible since iron is used all over the vineyard, in metal buckets used by the grape-pickers, the crushing apparatus, the chains in the presses, the pipes used for racking and transferring wine from one vat to another and even in the cement from which some vats are made. Iron buckets have now been replaced by plastic ones, and wherever iron is absolutely unavoidable, it is sealed and protected with a layer of varnish. The use of enamelled, plastic-coated, or stainless steel vats is becoming more and more widespread. When the damage has already been done, French law authorises treatment with citric acid, which dissolves the crystallised ferric salts that were the original cause of the casse. The most effective treatment, however, is potassium ferrocyanide, known as blue-fining★.

Cassis An AOC Provence★ vineyard with an exceptional geographical situation. It rises in tiers around the little port of Cassis, surrounded by massive limestone rocks and open to the sun and sea in the south. In winter it is sheltered by the hills from the cold north winds, and in summer the sea air tempers the fierce heat of the sun. The vineyards were considerably developed during the reign of Henri IV (although vines had been grown there many years before) and Cassis has been highly regarded ever since.

The white wine, made from Ugni Blanc, Clairette, Doucillon, Marsanne, Sauvignon and Pascal Blanc grapes, has always been better known than the red. It is very dry though not acid, and has finesse, freshness and character. It is also a perfect accompaniment to *bouillabaisse*, a fish soup which is a speciality of Provence. Particular care must be taken during harvesting and vinification to ensure its clarity★ and brilliance★ and to prevent it from turning yellow.

The red and rosé are made from Grenache, Mourvèdre, Carignan and Cinsault grapes. The red, when successful, is a good wine with a warm and velvety taste. The rosé, although an attractive, supple and fruity wine, has never achieved the reputation of white Cassis.

Castelli Romani A generic name for an immensely varied range of popular Italian table wines that go particularly well with the Roman cuisine. Although lacking great distinction, they are very pleasant, particularly the dry white wines that are served young in carafe. They are produced south-east of Rome around the villages of Frascati, Marino, Rocca di Papa, Velletri, Albano, Genzano, Ariccia and Grottaferrata. The best known is Frascati★.

categories of wine It is easy to get lost in the maze of official French appellations, which are both numerous and definitive, although they were partly devised to protect the customer.

Basically, French law divides wine into three categories: wines with appellations d'origine★, vins de consommation courante★ (which are administered by the Institut des Vins de Consommation Courante), and imported wines.

cave (cellar) The role played by the cave in the preservation and evolution of

wines has always been important. Col-umelle outlined the principal components of the ideal cave: 'facing north, away from the baths, the oven, cooking pit, cistern . . .' In Caton he advised having good caves 'in order to reach the peak of perfection'. However it was Chaptal, the great chem-ist, who gave the definition of the perfect cave in his 1807 work *Art de Faire le Vin*. The cave must face north so as to protect it from great variations in temperature which would occur if it faced south. It must be very low and cool. The best temperature, which should remain con-stant all year round, is from 9–12°C (as is the case in the best caves of Champagne★,

Saumur★ and Vouvray★). If necessary, the ventilators should be closed during ex-treme hot or cold spells, and the floor should be covered with sand which can be moistened in the summer.

The cave should be sufficiently, but not excessively, ventilated. There must also be constant humidity, but not too much; an excess would provoke mould on the casks and corks, and the wine would acquire a bad taste, becoming weak and character-less. Lack of humidity results in dried-out barrels and consequent seepage of the wine through the pores.

The cave should be dim, as bright light dries out the wine. Nearby vibrations are

57

very harmful as they stir up the lees★ and force them into suspension in the wine which can encourage acidity or sourness. Finally, the cave must be clean, free of refuse and any substances which produce an odour (like vegetables, fruits, oil, fuel, etc.) or other matter susceptible to fermentation. Neither vinegar nor green wood should be placed in the cave.

This is the kind of cave still found in some old houses, but it is rare to find these conditions in the cellars of today's oenophiles. It is adviseable, though, to have a 'cellar book' in which to keep track of each wine and to record from whom and for what price it was brought, when it was served and with what dishes. A special column reserved for tasting observations is also worthwhile and often amusing.

If real cellars are not available, special metallic or wooden racks or solid shelves should be used. The bottles must be lying face down so that the wine bathes the cork. Only bottles of Cognac, *eaux-de-vie*, port, apéritifs and liqueurs should be standing.

The beginner can make a good start with a cave of 300 or 400 bottles. Most wine producers sell their wines in cases of six and twelve bottles. All the purchases should have labels with the name, vintage, date and price.

Cérons Bordered by Barsac★ on the south and Graves★ on the north and west, the vineyards of Cérons are situated on the left bank of the Garonne in the area of the great white wines. The appellation Cérons also includes the communes of Podensac

and Illats. The grapes and harvesting are as in Sauternes, with successive and careful picking.

Cérons is a very fine and elegant wine. Less sweet than Sauternes, it is lighter, more vigorous and also fruitier. A part of the harvest is vinified into an excellent fruity dry or semi-dry wine which is classed among the best Graves, while keeping the strong characteristics of the Sauternes-Barsac. The best crus include the Châteaux of Cérons and of Calvimont, Lamouroux, Haut-Mayne and Grand Enclos du Château de Cérons.

Chablis The northernmost vineyard of Burgundy is positioned around the little village of Chablis. The Cistercian monks living in the Abbey of Pontigny in the twelfth century did much to develop its reputation. However, its clear, dry, very fine and fruity white wines have been widely appreciated since the ninth century.

Before the phylloxera★ invasion and the destruction of the vineyards, the region produced one-third of the total production of Burgundy. Replanted in the famous area of the grand crus, the present vineyards suffer from exposure to springtime frost, which in certain years causes considerable damage. In 1957 the vineyards were almost completely destroyed by frost, but the vignerons have obstinately continued production in spite of these trials. First they burned fires among the vines, and more recently organised a network of heaters in the vineyards. Re-

Chablis, the northernmost Burgundy vineyard, has organised an effective system of fighting spring frosts with propane heaters. Phot. M.

search is underway to develop other, more sophisticated devices.

The only grape used for Chablis is the Chardonnay★, the grape of all the great white wines of Burgundy. The soil of the vineyards, which stretch along the hillsides bordering the Serein, is well suited to grape-growing. It is flinty, based on the chalky limestone of the Upper Jurassic period. Chablis, light, dry and vigorous, is an excellent accompaniment to seafood.

CHABLIS: APPELLATIONS D'ORIGINE CONTRÔLÉES The Chablis area has four appellations: Chablis Grand Cru, Chablis Premier Cru, Chablis and Petit Chablis. The appellations Chablis Grand Cru and Chablis Premier Cru should be followed by the climat of origin. The maximum authorised yield per hectare is 40 hl except for Chablis Grand Cru, which is only 35 hl. The minimum alcohol content is 11° for Chablis Grand Cru, 10·5° for Chablis and 9·5° for Petit Chablis.

chabrot or **chabrol** In certain provinces of France, such as the Midi, it was formerly the custom to put a little wine in the main dish or soup before serving it. This custom, termed *chabrot*, now survives

mainly in folklore although it is still practised regularly in Béarn.

chai   A building located above ground where the vinification operations take place. The names *cellier* or, in certain provinces, *cuverie* are also used. The chai must be protected from extremes of temperature. The ceiling should be arched and have lofts above it, and the walls should have small glass windows which are not exposed to the south. The chai must always be kept clean and free from products susceptible to mould or fermentation like green wood or vinegar.

chai (master of the)   A person of considerable importance in all the notable vineyards. The success of a wine depends on his valuation and is subject to his authority alone. The master has absorbed twenty centuries of observation, research and tradition. While the master of the chai makes use of scientific knowledge in handling the wine, he also follows age-old traditions. He understands that the seasons, the cold, the moon, the sap and many other things still have an unpredictable and mysterious influence on the wine.

He alone decides the best moment for racking and bottling, and he alone determines if a new wine shows indications of a promising future. No instrument, no matter how sophisticated, can replace the trained eye, the sense of smell and the infallible taste of the master of the chai, who reigns in the cave wearing a black jacket and leather apron.

Chaînette (Clos de la)   A well-known vineyard situated at the heart of the town of Auxerre in the grounds of the departmental psychiatric hospital. It contains the remains of the vine belonging to St Germain which was bequeathed to her in the fourth century by her parents. The wines of Auxerre were greatly renowned in ancient times and the manuscripts of the Middle Ages commended them. The wines of Clos de la Chaînette were served at the tables of the kings of France and they still are of exceptional quality today.

Chambolle-Musigny   A commune of the Côte de Nuits★ which produces mostly red, and a little white, wine. The Musigny white is excellent, but unfortunately very rare.

Musigny and Bonnes-Mares are the most esteemed vineyards. The appellations such as les Amoureuses and les Charmes, which always precede the name of Chambolle-Musigny, also produce remarkable wines.

More feminine than Chambertin, the red wines of Chambolle-Musigny have an incomparable bouquet and suavity and many oenologists claim that they are the best and most delicate of the Côte de Nuits.

chambrer (to bring to room temperature)   An expression dating from the eighteenth century which means that the wine is brought from the cellar temperature to room temperature. Rooms of that time would seem cold to those

Master of the chai with his traditional apron and the symbols of his trade, pipette and tastevin. Phot. M.

accustomed to central heating and the temperature of the cellar would not be more than 10–12°C.

To chambrer a wine thus originally meant to bring it to a temperature of 14°C (rarely higher), which was the ideal drinking temperature. In time, the expression has gradually changed in meaning and today it is often used in the sense of 'to heat a wine', a practice which will destroy it.

Champagne (the region) It is impossible to really appreciate Champagne without knowing the region from which it comes. Champagne would never have attained its perfection without several conditions unique to the region. Legislation has, among other things, severely limited the area of production of Champagne and certain areas which used to supply their harvest to the Champagne shippers have thus been excluded. The vine was cultivated in Champagne from the beginnings of the Christian era and, by the Middle Ages, the wine was already well known. At that time, the still red and white wines of the area were renowned and became involved in a famous quarrel between advocates of Champagne and Burgundy.

The vineyards of Champagne are situated in three departments, chiefly the Marne, the Aube and Aisne, and several hectares of the Seine-et-Marne. The centre is found in the Marne vineyard which is divided into three large areas: the Montagne de Reims★, Valley of the Marne★ and Côte des Blancs★.

Champagne is the perfect illustration of Olivier de Serres' dictum, 'the air, the soil and the growth are the fundamentals of the vineyard'. In Champagne these three elements unite to produce an incomparable wine. The Champagne area has a very favourable climate despite its location in a latitude which is the most northern for the cultivation of the vine. The rivers and forests assure a constant humidity, the winters are relatively mild, and the summer and autumn often sunny. Thus the vines receive a maximum of warmth and sunlight. The chalky subsoil is counterbalanced by the affect of acids in the soil and ensures perfect drainage. However, this subsoil has also permitted the construction of the caves which are indispensable to the making of Champagne, and there are 200 km of underground galleries.

The noble★ grape varieties which have existed in Champagne from the Middle Ages are vigorous and their wines have a very great finesse. These are chiefly the Pinot Noir and the white Chardonnay. The Pinot Noir produces the great red wines of Burgundy; here it is made into white wines (Blanc de Noirs★). The Chardonnay, also grown in Burgundy, produces in Champagne wines which have finesse, freshness and lots of sparkle (Blanc de Blancs★). The Pinot Meunier produces a less fine wine and is used in the second crus.

In Champagne, crus do not have the same importance as in other areas. Most of

Champagne: The Smiling Angle, 13th century. Rheims Cathedral. Phot. Lauros-Giraudon.

Following two pages: Champagne vineyards. Phot. René-Jacques.

61

CHAMPAGNE

Aisne
SOISSONS

A I S N E

Vesle

Trigny

Ch^au-Thierry

Reuil

REIMS

Mailly-Champagne
Verzenay
Verzy
Villers-Marmery
Trépail
Ambonnay
Bouzy

M^gne DE REIMS

V. OF THE MARNE

4 3
Ay

ÉPERNAY

1
2

Tours-s/-Marne

Moussy

Cramant
Avize
Oger
Le Mesnil-
s/-Oger

CHÂLONS-
s/-MARNE

CÔTE
DES BLANCS

Vertus

Marais de
S^t -Gond

M A R N E

Marne

P^t Morin

SEINE-

G^d Morin

ET-

MARNE

Aube

Vitry-le-
François

Nogent-
s/-Seine

Seine

Marcilly-
le-Hayer

A U B E

Montgueux

TROYES

Brienne-
le-Ch^au

Bar-
s/-Aube

Bar-
s/-Seine

Landreville

Polisot

Les Riceys

1. **Chouilly**
2. **Mareuil-s/-Ay**
3. **Cumières**
4. **Damery**

▨ Vineyard

── Department boundary

0   20 Km

the idea of a cru exists despite everything, because the best houses blend their wines from the vines coming from the three most important areas (the Montagne de Reims, Valley of the Marne and Côte des Blancs).

Champagne (the wine) A wine for feasting, a wine for celebrating, Champagne occupies a cherished place among the wines of France. Present at the *petits soupers* of the Regency period, appreciated by the beautiful Pompadour 'who became more beautiful after drinking it', this pale golden wine is always praised. It is not surprising that the sale of Champagne has more than doubled in ten years and 124 million bottles were sold in 1973.

There is only one Champagne. Other sparkling wines (which can also attain a very high quality) are called vins mousseux★. The Champagne method★, where the second fermentation takes place in bottle, is used for many of the sparkling wines, and some are good enough to have the right to an appellation d'origine contrôlée, e.g. Vouvray mousseux, Saumur mousseux and Saint-Péray mousseux.

But apart from this fermentation method, the wine must undergo a series of special steps before it can be called Champagne. These include the vendange, pressing, first fermentation and blending, all of which must be done with delicate precision.

Only those wines which are produced in the limited area of Champagne and come from the grapes of that area have the right to the appellation Champagne. The grapes are harvested when mature, but not overripe, and are handled with extreme care to avoid colouring the must, especially when using black grapes. Careful hand-picking is the rule here.

Then comes the pressing. The large houses buy the grapes and prefer to use their own premises (called *vendangeoirs*) for pressing. The grapes are never crushed prior to being pressed. This is for obvious reasons, especially with the black grapes, because the end product should be a clear, unblemished juice.

The Champagne presses are unique, being wide and shallow and forcing the juice to leave the skin quickly without dissolving the colouring matter. About 4000 kg are generally pressed at a time,

the wines of Champagne are made traditionally from a mixture of wines coming from different crus. Each house has its favourite proportions and blends and strives to produce a consistent style of wine each year. Nevertheless, there are Champagnes (generally coming from the small producers and not the great houses) which are made from the grapes grown on a single commune, e.g. Cramant, Avize, Le Mesnil, Ay and Mailly. On the other hand,

Two advertising posters (around 1900) by Alphonse Mucha (left) and M. Réalier-Dumas. Bibl. de l'Arsenal. Phot. Lauros-Giraudon.

The 'mountain' of Rheims and the Champagne vineyards. Phot. Lauros.

giving first 20·5 hl of cuvée, then 4 hl of the first taille and 2 hl of the second taille. Only the cuvée is generally used for the best wines, the tailles making quality still wines. The first fermentation usually occurs in the same way as all other white wines.

The wine ferments either in Champagne casks of 205 litres or in large, modern, glass vats. This produces a still wine which is soon clarified by the cold of winter. A racking then separates the deposits.

The period from January to the beginning of March is the crucial time in the constitution of the cuvée as it is then that technique begins to give way to art. There are no crus in Champagne and it is only the way the wine is blended that accounts for differentiation among the various types. Each house has a personal recipe for the cuvée, which brings together the wines that have complementary qualities and which is also designed to produce the type of Champagne appreciated by its clientele. In a normal year the cuvée is composed of about one-quarter of wine from the Ay region (which gives it finesse and racé★), one-quarter of wines from the Marne Valley (body and vigour), one-quarter from the Montagne de Reims (freshness and bouquet) and one-quarter of wines from the Côte de Blancs (grace, elegance and finesse). The proportions vary depending on whether the year is hot or cold.

This idea of marrying the various Champagne wines is attributed to Dom Perignon★. Only Champagne made from white grapes can be called 'Blanc de Blancs'★.

CHAMPAGNE BEATER A barbarous instrument similar to a swizzle stick which suppresses the bubbles in Champagne, removing all the spirit and ruining the distinctive taste.

CHAMPAGNE METHOD (MÉTHODE CHAMPENOISE) A method used to make French sparkling wines which are appellation contrôlée (except for a few made by the rural method★). The principle seems simple enough. It is to encourage a secondary fermentation in a hermetically-sealed bottle by adding sugar to the wine base which has been obtained by the usual process of vinification. In decomposing,

the sugar gives off carbon dioxide which remains dissolved in the wine, and cannot escape. In practice, it is a very delicate operation to produce the sparkle and it took several centuries to perfect the method. At the beginning of the last century, the breakage of bottles was very high at 15–20% and in 1828, 80% of the bottles were broken.

The Champagne method, as it is practised in Champagne, is a collection of strict rules, which is not adhered to in the preparation of Mousseux. From the vendange to the maturing, excluding the composition of the cuvée, there runs a rigid, traditional chain of discipline which allows no flexibility.

The expression *méthode champenoise* on a label of Mousseux simply means that the wine is made by a secondary fermentation in bottle followed by a dégorgement★, or removal of the sediment. The wine must be in bottle for nine months to merit the vins à appellation d'origine title and four months for the wines without appellation (instead of the minimum of twelve months for Champagne).

The Champagne method proceeds as follows. After it has been left standing for a certain period, the still wine is bottled (usually when the sap starts to rise in the spring), and the liqueur de tirage★ is added. The second fermentation slowly takes place after the bottles are laid down. Then the delicate operation of remuage★ begins in order to collect the deposit and lees. Afterwards, the bottles are left for the necessary time, then subjected to the operation of dégorgement to remove the deposit. Next, the 'dosage' takes place in which the liqueur d'expédition★ is added (the dosage depending on the desired taste), filling up the space emptied by the dégorgement. The bottles then receive their final corks by machine and bound solidly by a steel muzzle.

CHAMPAGNE ROSÉ Instead of the classic pale golden wine, Champagne rosé reflects the colour of rubies. It is made according to a traditional and ancient recipe and was much in demand in the Russian and German courts of the nineteenth century. Champagne rosé is not made in the same way as other rosé wines of France. It is a process unique to Champagne.

When the cuvée is made up, a very small

*Champagne labels
and collars.*

quantity of red Champagne wine is added until the desired colour is reached. This operation is very delicate as care must be taken not to alter the initial character of the cuvée. The red wine must be from the Champagne region and a beautiful vintage Bouzy★, colourful and full-bodied, is usually chosen. This small addition of red wine to the cuvée must be made before the racking and in the presence of authorised witnesses. A rosé Champagne is a good quality Champagne that can attain perfection with some brands.

CHAMPAGNE VINTAGES Only the best years are declared vintages in Champagne (those for example, as the old saying goes, 'when the vines have had 100 days of sun'). On the other hand, each house only has the right to declare as vintage a maximum of 80% of its collection and the minimum obligatory maturing period must be at least three years after the vendange. For these three reasons, vintage Champagne is of superior quality to average wines sold under each trademark.

Vintage in Champagne is not as important as in some other wines. The producers of Champagne strive to make a superior

Organised tour of a cave. The miniature train of Mercier Champagne. Phot. Veronese, ©SPADEM.

wine each year. To accomplish this, they blend a mélange of wines coming not only from the different areas of Champagne, but also from different years. All the non-vintage wines are made from a blending of several harvests whose good and bad qualities balance each other. Thus, a very strong wine, for example, will be mixed with a light year, and this is why there is practically no difference among wines of different years produced under the same brand, excluding the vintage years.

Wine-lovers should be warned that they will find resemblances between two different brands of Champagne of the same vintage year, but not between two non-vintage years. The Champagnes of 1870 were the first to have a vintage printed on the label. Then around 1880 it became more common. The most recent vintages have been 1937, 1943, 1945, 1947, 1949, 1952, 1953, 1955, 1959, 1961, 1962, 1964, 1966 and 1969.

Champigny A little hamlet located in the commune of Souzay which produces the AOC Saumur-Champigny, the best red wine of Saumur and all of Anjou. The area of appellation comprises the communes of Chacé, Dampierre, Parnay, Saint-Cyr-en-Bourg, Saumur, Souzay and Varrains. The Saumur-Champigny, renowned as early as the Middle Ages, resembles its cousins of Touraine★, Chinon★ and Bourgueil★, but is more full-bodied. Certain connoisseurs find it has the aroma of a Médoc and is fleshy like a Beaune with a fruitiness all of its own. Ranging from 10–12° alcohol, it has a beautiful dark ruby colour, and is firm and generous with a blooming bouquet of wild raspberries and strawberries. In good years, it is an excellent wine to lay down.

chantepleure A term used in the Vouvray area to describe the wooden tap used for removing wine from the cask. The word is derived from the impression that the tap 'sings' as it is being opened, and that the wine 'cries' as it is being removed. A little before the Second World War, Vouvray created the *Confrérie des Chevaliers de la Chantepleure* whose members are reunited twice a year during the winter and summer solstices in the caves of the Bonne Dame.

Chanturgues A well-known wine of the Auvergne★ which is produced in very small quantities today and seems to turn up only in the coq au vin of Chanturgues. Chanturgues is an agreeable wine of the Gamay grape, is cherry red, light, fruity and delicate and keeps well. In the record years it has a lot of body and richness with a velvety feel and a pleasant, strong, violet bouquet.

chapeau (hat) The name given to the solid elements of the vendange (skins, stones, etc.) which are raised by the release of carbon dioxide and float on the surface of the must during fermentation. They take the form of a floating hat, *chapeau flottant*, or a submerged hat, *chapeau submergé*. As the colouring matter is found in this hat it is necessary, in order to have coloured wine, to put the must in contact with it. The hat can be bathed in the juice by pumping the juice from the base of the vat, or it can be pushed down with a wooden instrument from time to time. It is also possible to keep it in the centre of the must by using a special system.

chaptalisation An operation which is also called sugaring. The process has for some years been the subject of a passionate controversy. The addition of sugared substances to an insufficiently rich must is not new. At first, honey was used and, around 1790, sugar was first introduced at Clos de Vougeot when the wine lacked *vinosité naturelle* or natural vinosity★. But it was Chaptal (1756–1832) who was the real promoter of sugaring the vendange and who gave his name to this operation.

To have the right to an appellation, a minimum degree of alcohol is demanded for the wines, which varies according to region. Certain bad years produce musts that are insufficiently sugared and which will not therefore produce enough alcohol, resulting in poor quality. The sugaring operations are strictly regulated by law. All the controls stipulate that the musts have to reach, before enrichment, a minimum level of natural sugar. Only cane and beetroot sugars are allowed, never glucose, and it is forbidden to use more than 3 kg of sugar per hl of vendange. (1700 kg of sugar in 1 hl of vendange adds 1° of alcohol.)

Chaptalisation is not allowed in the south of France. The addition of an excess of sugar is very harmful to the wine as the finesse and bouquet are altered and the wine becomes disproportioned. Nevertheless, a wine increased in alcohol by 0.5–1° by sugaring, when the must was originally very low in sugar, is certainly improved. Although the added sugar, under the influence of yeast, is transformed into alcohol, it also creates aromatic substances like glycerine★. The wine has more finish and bouquet while, without sugar, it was thin and deceptive.

Chardonnay One of the finest white grape varieties. It has been the most important in Champagne and Burgundy since ancient times and has given its name to a tiny village in the Mâcon area. In Champagne, where it has existed since the height of the Middle Ages, it is called *fromenteau* because of its wheaten colour.

The Chardonnay produces small, shining, golden grapes, full of a delicious, white, sugary juice from which Champagne and all the great white wines of Burgundy are made, e.g. Montrachet, Meursault, Chablis and Pouilly-Fuissé. It thrives on clay and limestone hills facing

The Chardonnay grape.

Chasselas Doré grape.
Phot. Lauros.

Chassagne-Montrachet The great white wines produced by this commune of the Côte de Beaune★ have an obvious relationship with those of the neighbouring village of Puligny★. The king of all these noble wines, the Montrachet★, is grown in about an equal area in these two communes, as is Bâtard-Montrachet.

The elegant and fruity Criots-Bâtard-Montrachet is only produced in the Chassagne area. As in Puligny, these superb wines only carry the name of their vineyard and not that of the commune.

The great white wines of Chassagne and Puligny have in common a light aroma of almonds or hazelnuts, delicacy and finesse and also the ability to mature gracefully. On the whole, Puligny wines are more delicate than the robust Chassagnes.

Chassagne-Montrachet also produces excellent whites and reds carrying the appellation Chassagne-Montrachet followed by the name of the climat★. Certain of the white wines are remarkably like the Chassagne-Montrachet les Ruchottes, Cailleret and Morgeot. The red wines are full-bodied with an excellent bouquet and resemble certain wines of the Côte de Nuits. The best crus include Chassagne-Montrachet, Clos Saint-Jean, Morgeot, la Boudriotte and la Maltroie.

Chasselas There are several varieties of this white grape (sometimes rosé), most of them making a very good table grape (Moissac, for example). The wine made from the Chasselas is not really remarkable, except when it is cultivated in a cold climate. It is commonly grown in Alsace★ where it produces a popular, agreeable wine with little acidity which is best when drunk chilled and young. It is bottled early, at the end of the winter following the harvest, and retains a very pleasant, light sparkle caused by carbon dioxide which dissolves in the new wine.

In France, the Chasselas is the grape of the Pouilly-sur-Loire★ and Crépy★ of Savoie wines. In Switzerland, the Chasselas is widely grown and is made into the Fendant of Valais and the Dorin of the canton of Vaud. It is also grown in the Bade★ area south of Freiburg, where it is called Gutedel.

château A name used traditionally in the Gironde area to designate a vineyard or

east and south-east, where it develops its best qualities and finesse. These conditions exist on the Côte-d'Or and in Champagne, especially on the Côte des Blancs★.

The grape is often called Pinot Chardonnay although it is not related to the Pinot family. It is referred to by this name in California where it produces a good white wine. The Chardonnay should not be confused with the Pinot Blanc, which comes from a mutation of the Pinot Noir; the Pinot Blanc produces wine totally inferior to the Chardonnay (the best is perhaps the Pinot d'Alba in the Piemonte). The Chardonnay itself produces absolutely remarkable wines which are clear, light and fine. Outside Champagne and Burgundy, the Chardonnay is found in several vineyard areas, e.g. Lyon★, Jura★ and Châtillon-en-Dois★.

charpenté A wine which has enough alcohol to give it a good body, and is also rich in other elements, is said to be 'well-built' or *charpenté*. It is always one of a good year made from grapes which have achieved a high degree of maturity.

cru★ having a certain importance, and which has the appropriate buildings for making wine and an impressive dwelling. A judgement of 1938 ruled that the word château in Gironde is synonymous with domaine, clos or cru.

The degree of 30th September, 1949 detailed that the wines sold under the name of château must come from such an estate. This decree abolished the misuse of the word by reserving it for vineyards distinguished as such by custom or charter.

The INAO★ is always watchful to see that this measure is enforced to protect the consumer, because the word château itself exercises a magical attraction, and wines are often preferred when presented under this name.

CHÂTEAU (MISE EN BOUTEILLES AU) 'Bottled at the château' appears on the label as a guarantee of authenticity for the consumer. It was first developed in the Gironde during the last half of the nineteenth century. The wines thus designated are always quality wines, grown solely on the land where they are bottled.

Château-Chalon This extraordinary wine of the Jura★, endowed with a communal appellation, is certainly the quintessence of the celebrated vins jaunes★. The Savagnin or Naturé is the only grape variety used in this vineyard which comprises four communes: Château-Chalon, Minétru, Nevy-sur-Seille and Domblans. It is only in this part of the Jura that the wine is produced in any great quantity. The Savagnin favours the blue, chalky soil covered with limestone scree which is found at Château-Chalon and in the upper hills of Arbois (at Pupillin in particular).

The Savagnin must be protected from cold winds and needs a lot of sun. At Château-Chalon, it nestles in the deep hollows which are natural hothouses. The area of production of Château-Chalon is thus very restricted and one must admire the incomparable quality of this wine which has survived through the centuries despite the problems of the vineyards and the wine-making. Château-Chalon is truly the prince of the vins jaunes because, even if others were to follow the same vinification process, it would still emerge as the most perfect and graceful.

Château-Chalon, in its flask-shaped

Above: the cliffs of Château-Chalon; in the foreground, ancient vines trained on poles. Phot. Cuisset.

Below: Château-Chalon: vineyards of the 'prince of vins jaunes'. Phot. Hétier.

special bottle, the clavelin★, is a rare and fascinating wine the colour of golden amber. Its astonishing bouquet is strong and penetrating. Its characteristic nutty flavour has a lingering aftertaste and conserves well. Certain cellars keep Château-Chalon more than a century and the wine never loses its excellent qualities.

Château-Grillet The production of this exceptional vineyard of the Côtes du Rhône★ is without a doubt the smallest of the appellations contrôlées in France, producing about a dozen barrels (225 litres) from two hectares. As at Condrieu★, the only grape is the Viognier which is planted on stony terrain that makes hard work for the vigneron. It is harvested when very ripe.

The suave and unique Château-Grillet which is the result of this toil is golden and flamboyant, generous and fragrant with an exquisite delicacy and a sensation of being sweet and dry at the same time. It is an unpredictable wine which sometimes keeps well several years, but which often has a tendency to dry out and maderise★.

Châteaumeillant The Berry area produces these good VDQS★ reds and rosés. The vineyard, already extensive in the twelfth century, was very prosperous after the introduction of the Gamay grape around 1830. Sadly, phylloxera★ destroyed all the vines and today's production is still quite small.

Located about sixty km south of Bourges, the vineyard, planted mainly with the Gamay, is found in the communes of Châteaumeillant, Reigny, Saint-Maur and Vesdun in the Cher, and those of Champillet, Feusines, Néret and Urciers in the Indre. In bad years a certain proportion of Pinot Noir and Pinot Gris are sometimes added to reduce the acidity of the Gamay, and also to raise the degree of alcohol.

The red is a quality wine, especially in good years. The rosé (called vin gris) is excellent. Dry, fruity and light, its popularity is now increasing to what it was in the past.

Châteauneuf-du-Pape A prestigious name that is well deserved by this superb wine, the pride of the vineyards of the left bank of the southern Côtes du Rhône★. The majestic château, now in ruins, which was erected by the papacy in the fourteenth century, has given its name to the vineyard. The soil, the old river bed of the Rhône, is covered with sun-scorched pebbles – an environment which would appear to be unsuitable for the cultivation of the vine; in fact, it is said that this hostile soil wears out an iron plough in two hours.

Although only the Syrah grape is used in Hermitage★, thirteen grape varieties are involved in making the marvellous Châteauneuf. These include the Grenache, Clairette, Cinsault, Mourvèdre and Bourboulenc.

The purple-robed Châteauneuf is a

Châteauneuf-du-Pape: the grapes of this famous cru grow on inhospitable soil full of round stones scorched by the sun. Phot. M.

forceful wine, ardent and warm, whose incomparable bouquet combines the smell of burning raspberry and iodine. A little harsh at first, this magnificent wine develops its unique qualities and subtle bouquet with time.

The best vineyards include Château Fortia, Domaine de Mont-Redon, Cabrières-les-Silex, Château des Fines-Roches, Château Rayas and la Solitude. There is also a very rare white Châteauneuf-du-Pape which accounts for only 1% of production.

widespread in the Middle Ages for the abundance and excellence of its wines, and has never diminished. Chavignol has several very good vineyards: la Comtesse, Cul de Beaujeu and la Garde.

Chénas People complain that the vine has replaced the old oak trees (*chênes*) which gave this commune of Beaujolais★ its name, and for some this has been a source of regret. The vineyards, located to the east and south of Chénas, also have the right to the appellation Moulin-à-Vent★.

The village of Chavignol among the vineyards of Sancerre. Phot. M.

Châtillon-en-Diois A small vineyard on the left bank of the Rhône valley in the department of the Drôme which produces red, rosé and white wines having the right to the label VDQS★. The reds and rosés come from the noble★ grape companions: the Syrah (the Hermitage grape), Gamay (the Beaujolais grape) and Pinot Noir (the Burgundy grape).

This is not sparkling wine like that of the nearby Die★, so proud of its Clairette title, and is delicious, fruity, fine and elegant. Sadly, these wines are produced in very small quantities (around 1000 hl).

Chavignol Well known for its *crottin*, a delicious goat cheese, Chavignol is no less famous for its wine, which has the right to the appellation contrôlée Sancerre★. The reputation of Chavignol was already quite

Chénas is an excellent Beaujolais with a fruity and generous bouquet, but is lighter than Moulin-à-Vent.

Cheval-Blanc (Château) A grand cru of Saint-Emilion★ which, although very generous and full-bodied, is also fine and velvety with a delicious bouquet. It has, without a doubt, the strongest bouquet of the wines of Saint-Emilion. Although the wine matures quickly in bottle, it can also be kept for a long time without losing its qualities.

Chianti This famous Italian wine has a well-known, straw-covered bottle, the *fiasco*, which has done much to popularise it around the world. Nevertheless, it is the wines of lesser quality which are presented in these special bottles, so it is true that for

certain of them, 'the habit makes the monk'. The very good Chiantis are sold in classic Bordeaux bottles carrying an authentic vintage and need no special bottle dressing to be appreciated.

In Tuscany, Chianti is the ordinary table wine (nearly always red) that is drunk young, generally in carafe. It is served in all the restaurants of Florence and suits the Italian cuisine admirably.

Chianti is made by a special method of vinification called *governo* which gives it a very particular character. A part of the harvest (about 10%) is not pressed, but laid to dry on straw screens. At the end of November this reserved part, whose juice is concentrated, is crushed and left to ferment, then it is added to the rest of the Chianti which has already undergone normal fermentation. The whole solution is left in a closed vat until spring. The slightly sparkling wine which emerges lightly tickles the tongue and is fresh and agreeable.

The Classic Chianti, grown on barren, dry hills between Florence and Siena, is a very different wine. It is one of the best Italian wines, being firm, steady and full-bodied with a fine bouquet. It improves considerably with age. This Chianti is made from two grape varieties, San Gioveto and Cannaiolo, to which is added a little Trebbiano Blanc and Malvasia Blanc, which were formerly cultivated at a high altitude amidst the olives. The area of appellation covers four communes, Greve, Radda, Castelina and Gaiole, and a part of six others. The Classic Chianti is never bottled outside the zone of production. It carries the seal of the association of producers and often the name of the vineyard, such as Barone Ricasoli (Brolio, Meleto) and Conte Serristori (Machiavelli).

Many Chiantis, however, are produced outside the classic zone in six legally delimited regions: Rufina and Montalbano (the best), Colli Fiorentini and Colli Pisani (quality product, but limited). The two others, Colli Senesi and Colli Arentini, produce mediocre wines which are often mixed with others coming from the rest of Italy to furnish most of the cheap Chiantis. There is also a white Chianti which comes from the Trebbiano (called Ugni Blanc in France). It is a dry, golden, agreeable wine which is rather full-bodied and without great distinction.

Chiaretto or **Rosato del Garda**   A rosé wine produced south of Lake Garda between Milan and Verona which is certainly one of the best rosés of Italy. The best Chiarettos are made around the villages of Padenghe, Manerba and Moniga (in the region of Brescia) from the local red grapes: Gropello, Marzemino and Schiava. The Chiarettos from the east bank of Lake Garda (in the region of Verona) are equally good but of a totally different character. They are made from the Corvina, Negrara and Molinaro grapes which also give the red, light Bardolino★. These last rosés are mostly sold under the name of Chiaretto although the two appellations Chiaretto and Chiarello are almost used indiscriminately.

The Chiaretto is a delicious, pale rosé wine, fresh and light, which generally has 10–11° alcohol. It is now being exported and, if it is young and served chilled, may be very agreeable, but never as good as in its country of origin.

Chile   Although less productive than those of Argentina, the Chilean vineyards yield the best wines of South America★. Chile is the oldest viticultural region of Latin America, and the vine was cultivated there before 1600. Today's vineyards, however, are more recent, dating no earlier than 1850 when the French varieties imported from Europe were planted for the first time. Thus the majority of Chilean wines (at least the best of them) come from grapes of European origin: Cabernet, Sémillon, Riesling, Pinot, Sauvignon, Merlot, Malbec and Folle-Blanche (here called Loca Blanca).

Chilean viticultural and vinification methods are largely inspired by those used in Bordeaux and adapted to a climate similar to the Mediterranean type and to a volcanic soil, which is totally different.

The vineyards are found in the central part of Chile between 30° and 40° latitude, an area tempered by the polar waters of the Humboldt current crossing the Pacific. The best vineyards are located in the centre of this region not far from Santiago. The two best areas are the Aconcagua and Maipo Valleys, which are mainly planted in Cabernet. Chile has two other large viticultural regions, one in the north, the other in the south. The northern region, which extends from the Atacama Dessert

to the Choapa River, is planted in Muscat and gives generous wines high in alcohol. They are often drunk in the same manner as Madeira, port or sherry. The southern region is found between the Maule and Bio-Bio Rivers. It produces red and light white wines which are low in alcohol. The main grape is the Pais, a Spanish grape by origin and one of the oldest planted in Chile.

Chile produces around 70% red wines and 30% white. The good Chilean wines, which really deserve to be exported, come from noble★ grapes and often bear the name of the grape on their label. The others are sold as 'Sauternes', 'Chablis', 'Borgona' (Burgundy) and 'Rhine'. Finally, Chile also produces sparkling wines, some of which are remarkable and others, a little too sweet.

Chilean wines are classified by age into four categories. The first includes those wines less than a year old. The second, the *especiales*, are two years old. The label *reservado* designates four-year-old wines which are generally of good quality. Finally, the best Chilean wines, the 'Gran Vino', are six years old or more, and are excellent.

Chinon The sprawling vineyard of Chinon occupies both the left bank of the Loire★ and the two banks of the Vienne. The soils are comparable to those of Bourgueil: gravelly terraces on the sides of the Vienne and the Loire, limestone and clay slopes and micaceous chalk below. As at Bourgueil, the wine from the gravelly area gives the informed connoisseur a different taste than those from the coast. This red wine, '*pour intellectuels*' as it is called, is produced by Chinon and several communes which have the right to the appellation contrôlée Chinon. These include Beaumont-en-Véron, Cravant, Avoine and Savigny, not forgetting Ligré, the birthplace of François Rabelais, a great lover of 'this good Breton wine'. Chinon, like Bourgueil, comes from the Cabernet Franc★ which is locally called Cabernet Breton.

Chinon is ruby red in colour, fresh, dainty and supple, with a violet bouquet. Lighter and more tender than the Bourgueil, it is drunk earlier but fades more quickly. On the other hand, certain years can be preserved up to forty years in bottle. The wines of Ligré are full-bodied and gain a very beautiful bouquet with

age. The region of Chinon also produces an excellent rosé from the Cabernet which is dry and light and has an agreeable bouquet, making it one of the best of Touraine★.

Chiroubles Situated in the heart of Beaujolais★, this charming hillside village produces an excellent fruity wine which is tender and full of charm with all the characteristics typical of its area. It should be drunk young and chilled.

Chusclan This commune does not benefit from a proper appellation contrôlée but it has the right to add its name to that of the Côtes du Rhône★ printed in identical characters on the label. The vineyard occupies five different areas in the department of Gard, on the right bank of the Rhône north of Tavel and west of Orange.

The wine produced is a remarkable rosé, strong and very fruity with an aroma of prunes and acacia. It resembles Tavel★ and Lirac★, but is more virile. Sadly, the atomic centre of Marcoule is gradually encroaching on the vineyards and soon there will probably be no more of this delicious, aromatic rosé.

The co-operative of Chusclan also produces an excellent red wine which has title only to the appellation Côtes du Rhône.

clairet A very light red wine which is quite different from a rosé.

Clairette A southern variety of grape, white or rosé, mostly cultivated in the south of France in the departments of Hérault, Gard, Var, Vaucluse, Drôme and the Lower Alps, and also to some extent in California. The origin of the name is not known. In the Drôme, the Clairette produces the celebrated Clairette de Die★, a sparkling wine which has long been respected. In Die, the pure Clairette wines are often made by the Champagne method★, while the Clairette wines blended with Muscat★, which are produced in much larger quantities, are made by the old rural method★ perfected by the modern technique of filtration under pressure. Trans, near Draguignan, used to make a sparkling Clairette of the same type.

In the Mediterranean climate, Clairette gives a wine of high alcoholic content (12–14°) as many of the grapes are picked when very ripe. The Clairette is also mixed

La Clape, the appellation of vineyards located between Narbonne and the sea. In the background, a dovecot. Phot. M.

with other varieties in the white wines of Palette★, Cassis★ and Bandol, as well as in the rosé of Tavel and the red wine of Châteauneuf-du-Pape★.

The Clairette wines maderise★ very quickly, which is considered a fault, although in former days when vermouth was in vogue, they were much in demand as an ingredient. The Clairette of Languedoc★, like that of Bellegarde, possesses nearly all the characteristics of a pure Clairette wine.

Clairette de Die The Roman emperors, according to Pliny, were very fond of the Clairette Dea Augusta (the Roman name of Die). On the rocky hills of Saillans at Châtillon-en-Diois, around the little village of Die in the valley of the Drôme, lie vineyards whose golden grapes are related to the southern Côtes du Rhône. The delicious and exhilarating AOC wine Clairette de Die is made from the Clairette grape, which gives it lightness and freshness, and the Muscat which gives it bouquet and its particular character. It is a golden, semi-sparkling wine, marrowy or sweet and very fruity with an extremely delicate aroma of Muscat and rose.

The Clairette de Die is made in two ways, by the Champagne method★ of second fermentation in bottles, or the rural method★ where the bubbles form spontaneously in the bottle as a result of the natural sugar remaining in the wine after fermentation and without the addition of a liqueur de tirage★. The second method, though delicate and troublesome, makes a much superior sparkling wine. The fine bouquet of Muscat is totally preserved and the wines have more sparkle, and are fruitier, than those made by the Champagne method. Today, the vignerons are perfecting the method by eliminating the light cloudiness which sometimes occurs as a result of filtration under pressure before bottling.

Clairette du Languedoc This white wine of the Hérault must be made only from the Clairette grape to qualify for the appellation contrôlée. The Clairette, a classic white grape of southern vineyards, produces a wine in good soil which is very full-bodied and high in alcohol. The Clairette of Languedoc is a pretty, almost golden coloured wine, dry and full-bodied

with a slightly bitter aftertaste peculiar to this grape. It is used as a base for quality Vermouths.

The wine maderises★ very quickly and takes on a 'rancio'★ taste which is very unique. The word rancio must be specified on the label as a notification that the wine has aged naturally for at least three years and contains 14° of alcohol.

The production area includes the following communes: Aspiran, Paulhan, Adissan, Fontès, Cabrières, Péret and Ceyras. The Gard also produces a Clairette of the same type near Nîmes called the Clairette de Bellegarde.

Clape An appellation given to some of the Coteaux du Languedoc★ wines classified VDQS★ having a long-standing reputation. The vineyard lies in the hollow of a massive limestone range between Narbonne and the sea. The wines, reds and rosés, are colourful and the reds age well. Quality white wines are also produced.

clarity Although this is a quality ·demanded by many drinkers, the processes the wine is subjected to in order to attain a

Clarity: racking is one of the operations performed to obtain a clear wine. Caves in Beaune. Production Calvet. Phot. Rapho-Feher.

perfect clarity may rob it of its charm and bouquet. Thus racking, fining and filtering are often not even used for the great wines.

Classification of 1855 A classification of vineyards of the Médoc had been operating since the beginning of the eighteenth century. Several classifications (like those of Jullien in 1816) distinguished four or five categories of crus as well as bourgeois★ and paysans★. But it was not until the Great Paris Exhibition of 1855 that the classification of Bordeaux wines became official. The courtiers★ of Bordeaux (who act in an official capacity) were told to furnish a 'complete and satisfactory display' of the wines of the department. Essentially based on prices which the wines had commanded over the years, the Classification of 1855 grouped wines of different style but of the same quality. Astonishingly enough, after more than a century the classification still has a certain value.

Actually, the methods of cultivation, vinification and breeding of the wines are similar in all the great vineyards. Only the different soil gives each wine its personality and quality. A well-grounded classification like this normally remains constant with only a few exceptions (some crus have subsequently been demoted or promoted; others not classified in 1855 are now sold at the same price as the classified crus).

One can only criticise the classification for concerning itself solely with the wines of the Médoc and Sauternes and only one Graves (Haut-Brion), and for having totally ignored Saint-Emilion, Pomerol and other Bordeaux appellations, and the rest of the Graves. The classification recognised four red grand premier crus, Château Lafite-Rothschild, Château Margaux, Château Latour and Château Haut-Brion, and for the whites, only one grand premier cru, the prestigious Château d'Yquem. All the Médoc crus classified in 1855 in five categories should be considered as old nobility, but the superieur and unclassified bourgeois crus often give the wine-lover as much pleasure.

clavelin The name of a special squat bottle which holds the vin jaune★ of Jura. Its capacity is 6 dl.

climat A term used in Burgundy to distinguish a particular vineyard area. In each village the vineyard is divided into climats. Thus the Côte d'Or, which is only forty km long and four km wide, has sixty appellation contrôlées and each of them comprises from twenty to fifty climats, each so unique in area that those seeking to define them could only follow the traditional usage and classification. Some of the climats have been very famous since ancient times: Chambertin, Montrachet, Clos de Vougeot and others. The climat of Burgundy is the equivalent of the Bordeaux château.

collage (fining) The traditional and ancient practice used since Roman times to clear the wine and give it a desirable clarity★. Before the wine is bottled, several different substances are introduced which combine with the tannin★ to cause precipitation of these undesirable particles in suspension. The principal agents used for this process are de-fibred beef blood, gelatin, casein, isinglass (used mainly for white wines) and fresh egg whites (used for quality red wines). There must, however, be sufficient tannin present to balance the protein content. When there is insufficient tannin, part of the protein content stays in suspension in the wine and forms a kind of white veil. It is over-fined – a disastrous accident which can only be rectified by addition of tannin or bentonite★.

Blue fine is used in certain countries to eliminate iron, which is responsible for casse ferrique★ (iron clouding). Potassium ferrocyanide must be added to the wine as it forms a heavy insoluble compound with the iron. This substance, called *bleu de Prusse* (Prussian blue), is then precipitated with the fining substance.

colouring matter The colouring matter of red grapes is due to pigments of the tannins in the skin. The pulp is colourless except for several varieties of grapes called *teinturiers* (Gamay teinturier for example). Analysis shows that the colouring matter is peculiar to each grape variety. When they are fresh, the cells of the skin retain the pigment and pressing red grapes produces a juice which has very little colouring (vin gris) or no colour at all (Champagne★).

The pigments are insoluble in cold

water but may well dissolve in alcohol. This is why the longer a wine ferments, the more pronounced the colour as the pigment slowly dissolves in the alcohol formed by the fermentation process.

Besides furnishing colour, the pigments also contribute to the formation of the fruitiness of young wines and the bouquet of old wines. Later, the pigment matter becomes insoluble when oxidised, which explains why brownish deposits are found at the bottom of old bottles. Although colouring matter does not seem to appear in white wines, it is nonetheless present and is quite visible in maderised* wines, which take on a yellow tint.

comet (wines of the) Since ancient times, comets have been considered as auspicious occurrences. Among other things, they are supposed to produce wines of exceptional quality in the years they appear. The 'wines of the comet' were always very much in demand and had an enviable place in the hierarchy of grand crus.

The passing of the comet, 1811. Coloured engraving. Bibl. Nat. Phot. B.N.

Whatever the case, the wines of the comet of 1811 have left a reminder which is as celebrated as the beautiful comet which appeared that year. But an exceptional summer and autumn, splendid and warm, should perhaps also account for some of the excellence of the wines of that year.

complete wine A wine which is perfectly constituted. It unites all the qualities – bouquet, elegance, finesse, breeding and harmony. It is the wine of great years.

composition of wine This is very complex as at least sixty elements are known and still others have not been identified. The principal constituents are alcohol, acids, tannins, colouring matter and pectins. There are also salts (phosphates of potassium, calcium and iron, potassium sulphate, etc.), metalloids (chlorine, fluorine, iodine, silicon, zinc, copper) and vitamins (especially B and C). Finally, about 75–85% is water.

Condrieu An appellation of the Côtes du Rhône★ which includes three communes of the right bank of the Rhône: Condrieu, Vérin and Saint-Michel. The area is sometimes called Côte-Chérie. Condrieu is a unique and very rare white wine which only few have enjoyed since it

travels poorly. It is only made in this area, and comes from one grape, the Viognier or Viognier doré, which is harvested late. This grape gives a very rich must whose fermentation is rarely finished before the arrival of frost.

After careful preparation, the wine is bottled in spring and some is left in casks for eighteen months following fermentation. The first process gives a marrowy taste because of the sugar remaining in the wine. The second gives a dry wine which has a remarkable delicacy and suppleness due to the glycerine which is formed during the long fermentation (certain wine-makers obtain this second type of wine in the harvest year). The Condrieu should be drunk when young as it ages poorly, drying out and maderising★.

It is a splendid, full-bodied wine with a penetrating, suave bouquet, unique like the neighbouring, even more exceptional, Château-Grillet★.

consommation courante (vins de) These so-called 'table wines' are regarded as being suitable for everyday consumption. Well chosen, they do not strain the stomach or head and have the best taste next to the appellation contrôlée★ and VDQS★ wines. By law, they must mention their alcoholic content and satisfy requirements such as minimum degree of alcohol, absence of toxic substances, normal content of volatile acid, etc. They are sold in capped bottles or from the barrel and their quality is controlled by the Institut des Vins de Consommation Courante. They are also subject to the Répression des Fraudes Commission. The wines are divided into two categories: vins de pays★ and vins de coupage★.

Constance   A wine produced in the Republic of South Africa by a small vineyard belonging to the State. It is located not far from the village of Cap and was planted around 1700 by the Dutch Governor, Simon Van der Stel. The vineyard was called Great Constantia in honour of the governor's wife whose name was Constance. The French Protestant émigrés contributed to the establishment of the vineyards.

The wine of Constance enjoyed an incredible vogue in the nineteenth century in France and England and the heroes of Balzac often honoured it! Today's production is only a few hundred hectolitres and it is almost impossible to obtain. Good, often very good, the wine is sweet, suave and fine with a light muscadet perfume (due to the Muscadelle of Bordeaux planted by the French Protestants). However, compared with today's wines, it does not seem to measure up totally to its former glory.

co-operative   The wine-making co-operatives had modest beginnings around 1900, after the start of the first dairy co-operatives. Their prime objective was to sell the harvest, and stock in cellars the excess production which would lower the price. Little by little, the vignerons began to make wine together. The co-operative formula offered great practical advantages to the small producers, removing the need for expensive individually-owned wine casks, which demanded costly and delicate upkeep. It also resulted in economy of work, more care in the vinification and storing of wine, and liberated space previously devoted to wine-making.

The co-operative offered its members modern techniques, used modern equipment and assured them of a quality product. The small producers benefited because they often found it impossible to acquire modern equipment or even to maintain the old equipment. This formula was very successful, especially in the Midi, in the Languedoc area and in North Africa.

The method is particularly valuable for making table wines (vins de consommation courante★), wines of genuine appellation and vins de pays★ but, although certain co-operatives made laudable efforts to conserve the individuality of the wines, it is not compatible with the idea of personal art and particular vineyards which characterise the famous crus. Today, there are about 1100 caves including 250,000 members. They make between 25 and 30% of French wine (around 15 million hectolitres of which 12 million is vin de consommation courante). The rest, about 3 million hectolitres, is divided equally among the VDQS★ and the AOC★ wines.

Corbières   This VDQS★ wine, coming from limestone hills south-east of Carcassonne in Languedoc-Roussilon, is very popular.

Red, rosé and white wines are produced but the reds are by far the best known. The grapes are the typical ones of the region: mainly Carignon, but also Grenache, Cinsault and Terret Noir in varying

The vineyard of Corbières stretches to the foot of the walls of Carcassonne. Phot. Hétier.

*Corbières: 11th-century
Roman chapel on the outskirts
of Lézignan (Aude). Phot. M.*

*Stripping cork (Portugal).
Phot. Loirat.*

proportions for the reds and rosés, and Clairette for the white wines. The rosés are full-bodied, nervous★ and fruity. When they are well made, the reds are a beautiful, sombre colour, full-bodied and fleshy, acquiring very quickly a particular bouquet which is refined with age. A well-known saying about this wine is, 'The wine of Corbières has an accent'.

Corbières and Corbières Supérieurs are found in the department of Aude, and the Corbières du Roussillon in the Pyrénées-Orientales. Corbières must have 10° of alcohol and Corbières Supérieurs, 12°. Fitou★, an appellation contrôlée wine, is produced by the best communes of Corbières.

The Corbières du Roussillon are full-bodied, fine-flavoured wines which come from the same grapes as the Corbières, with the addition of the Malvoisie and Macabéo.

Corent   A wine of the Auvergne★ which now exists mainly in legend, like the Chanturgues★. Both are produced in the area of Clermont-Ferrand and made from the Gamay noir à just blanc. Corent has a very pale tint and great charm. It is usually found as vin gris (that is, when it can actually be found).

cork (bouchon)   The cork is the ideal seal for wine. No other natural or manufactured material can match it, and attempts to stopper wines with plastic corks

have failed miserably. A cork should allow the wine to breathe so that it keeps well, but should also continue to expand. The proper supple cork clings remarkably well to the neck of the bottle and, most important, does not rot.

Specialists use different types of cork for individual wines. A supple cork, for example, is used for wines to be drunk young, a stronger cork for wine to be conserved longer and white wines subject to maderisation★.

The idea of the cork stopper is attributed to Dom Perignon★. He is said to have been inspired by the Spanish pilgrims who used large pieces of cork to seal their gourds. Prior to that, either a layer of oil was floated on the wine or hemp impregnated with oil was put over the top.

It is dangerous to economise on the quality of the cork. It should be of top quality and at least 4–4½ cm long. The cork should never be soaked in hot water before use as it will lose its elasticity. It should, instead, be soaked in cool water for about twelve hours.

corkscrew The invention of this instrument apparently dates from the time when all wines, even non-sparkling ones, began to be sealed with cork★ stoppers as opposed to oil-soaked hemp. The first corks, used by Dom Perignon★ for his Champagne, could probably be eased out by hand, aided by the wine's effervescence.

Corkscrews are first recorded around the end of the seventeenth century, but the name of their inventor remains unknown. Nowadays, corkscrews are available in many different shapes and designs, and are usually worked by a screw, lever or gas. Whatever their form, the principal requirement is that they should be functional and, above all, allow the wine to be uncorked slowly, gently and carefully.

Cornas The vineyard of this Côtes du Rhône★ commune is found on the right bank of the Rhône nearly facing Valence. It only produces appellation contrôlée red wines made from the Syrah. Cornas is a little bitter when young, but acquires an agreeable suppleness when mature. Not as noble or aromatic as its neighbour Hermitage, it is nevertheless a wine of great quality, especially when mature. Full-bodied, heady and substantial, it has a characteristic earthy taste. It has been much in demand and appreciated for a long time. Its deep ruby colour prompted Louis XV to call it 'a very good black wine'.

correction of wines Each year the local oenological stations specify corrections which can discreetly improve the imperfections resulting from a harvest in bad weather while preserving the natural composition of the wine. All the changes are limited and controlled by law. Certain wines must establish a normal level of acidity, some by adding acid and others by reducing it. Insufficient sugar may be corrected by chaptalisation★.

Other problems might be an excess or insufficiency of tannin, calling for fining or the addition of tannin respectively. Sometimes the wine lacks colour which is remedied by heating a part of the vendange to release colouring matter★. Finally, the method of assemblage★, as used in Champagne, can also be employed. Two wines coming from the same soil, but of a different year, sometimes complement

each other admirably and give a steady, complete wine.

Corsica Nothing is mediocre on this beautiful island, and the wines that it produces are no exception to the rule. They are all excellent, or at least original. They used to be consumed only on the island, but are now exported.

The principal grape is the Vermentino (Malvoisie), as well as other indigenous varieties: Nielluccio, Rossola, Bianca, Sciaccarello, Barbarosso and Carcajolo. The continental varieties represent about 15% of the acreage and have only been planted since the last century: Alicante, Grenache, Carignan, Cinsault and Muscat. Wine is produced all over the island and, although the Corsican wines are not subject to the French legislation of the Continent, they are regulated under an unique legal statute dating from 1801. The coastal area has most of the good vineyards. The vineyard of Cap Corse, which is as well known outside the island, produces full-bodied white, rosé and red wines. The celebrated sweet Cap Corse wine, made from Muscat and Malvoisie,

Corsica: the vineyard of Patrimonio, in the Bastia region. Phot. Rapho.

is marrowy and delicate and has made it famous. But there are other famous coastal producers: Coteaux de Saint-Florent, which produces without a doubt the best Corsican wines, especially the famous Patrimonio★, and has been AOC★ since 1968; the region of Bastia (with the excellent wines of Vescovato and Cervione); Balagne (Calvi and Calenzana), where the Sciaccarello reigns; Sartène and its strong VDQS★; Ajaccio and its belt of vineyards; Piana which, besides delicious rosés, gives perfumed Muscats; Bonifacia and others.

The interior of the island also produces some interesting, although less esteemed, wines. These are found around Bastelica, Corte and Omessa.

The Corsican wines are well made considering they come from such a poor, flinty soil. Delicious when young, they also age admirably and acquire a delicate

Costières du Gard, on the right bank of the Rhône. Phot. M.

bouquet. The often dry white wines are full of finesse and fragrance and certain of them resemble Hermitage★. The red wines have a remarkable bouquet. Nearly all are heady and strong and possess a particular finesse. Some of them resemble Côtes-du-Rhône★, especially Chateauneuf-du-Pape★. The exquisite rosés are a lovely colour with a fruity, warm taste, blending pepper and smoke.

Since 1968, Patrimonio has been appellation contrôlée and sometimes classified VDQS.

Cortaillod A Swiss wine which comes from the Lake Neuchâtel area around the village of Cortaillod. It is made from the

Pinot Noir of Burgundy which is the only grape allowed in the canton. It is an agreeable pale red wine, fresh and fruity.

Cortese A dry white wine produced from a grape of the same name in the Piemonte region of Italy. It is an extremely pleasant wine, pale, light and fresh, which should be drunk young.

Costières-du-Gard An appellation which groups the red, rosé and white wines classed VDQS★ from this vineyard. The production area is located on the right side of the Rhône Valley south of Nîmes, between Beaucaire and Vauvert.

The vineyard, planted on rolling gravel which reflects the heat of the sun, includes the usual varieties grown in the Midi and the Côtes du Rhône including the Grenache, Syrah and Carignan. The full-bodied reds have a rich aroma resembling the Côtes-du-Rhône.

The white wines, coming from the Clairette, are fine and fruity if the vendange is not too late.

Cot A red grape which is known by a variety of different names – Malbec in Gironde, Auxerrois at Cahors, Cot in Touraine and Quercy, and so on. It is gradually being replaced by the Merlot variety in the best Gironde vineyards, but is still planted in Bergerac★, Côtes de Duras★ and many VDQS★ crus of the Sud-Ouest★ region. It is traditionally the principal variety of grape (70–80%) grown in the Cahors vineyard. In Touraine it is chiefly grown in the Cher valley, at Mesland★ and Amboise★. In Anjou★ it is combined with Groslot, Gamay and Cabernet grapes to make rosé d'Anjou★.

Unlike most other grapes, which grow from offshoots of the previous year's growth, Cot grapes grow from offshoots of old, tough wood which is an advantage in regions where spring frosts occur. It is most productive on clay and limestone soil. The wine it produces has good colour and body, but is slightly lacking in bouquet and flavour. It does, on the other hand, combine well with other, finer, varieties – it contributes colour and moelleux★ to wine and makes it mature more quickly.

Côte Chalonnaise An area in Burgundy that takes its name from the town of Chalon-sur-Saône. It is a natural extension of the Côte de Beaune vineyards, and shares with them the same soil, methods of viticulture and vinification and commercial traditions. The region has four appellation contrôlées (Côte Chalonnaise is not itself an appellation): Rully★, Mercurey★, Givry★ and Montangy★.

The authorised grape varieties for these wines are those grown in the Côte d'Or: Chardonnay★ for white wines and Pinot Noir★ for red. A certain quantity of Aligoté is also grown in the region and, as elsewhere in Burgundy, the wine made from it is entitled to the appellation Bourgogne Aligoté★. Another grape grown here is Gamay which is made into Bourgogne passe-tous-grains★ with Groslot grapes in a ratio of 2 : 1. It also produces the wines of appellation Bourgogne ordinaire and Bourgogne grand ordinaire★.

Côte de Beaune

The Côte de Beaune represents the southern half of the famous Côte d'Or★ vineyards, and stretches from Ladoix in the north to Santenay in the south, covering an area of 2800 ha. Unlike the Côte de Nuits★, whose wines are almost all red, it is chiefly notable for its magnificent white wines, which are the best in Burgundy★. Some of the reds are also excellent, and the area as a whole produces more red wine than white.

Red Côte de Beaune wines have charm and finesse; they are more subtle, less powerful, and more feminine than those of the Côte de Nuits. They are also ready for drinking sooner, but do not keep as long. The white wines have exceptional breeding and distinction. Many find their smoothness and delicate aroma unequalled by any other wine.

Appellations are either names of communes (e.g. Beaune) or of crus (e.g. Montrachet). The most important communes of the Côte de Beaune are Aloxe-Corton★, Pernand-Vergelesses★, Savigny-les-Beaune★, Beaune★, Pommard★, Volnay★, Meursault★ and Blagny★, Chassagne-Montrachet★, Puligny-Montrachet★ and Santenay★.

Other, lesser known communes also produce excellent wines, some of which certainly deserve to be better known by the wine-buying public. They are, from north to south, Ladoix (red and white), Chorey-les-Beaune (red and white), Mon-thelie (red), Saint-Romain (red and white), Auxey-Duresses (red and white), Dezize-les-Maranges, Sampigny-les-Maranges and Cheilly-les-Maranges (red and white). The last three of these communes are in the Saône-et-Loire department.

Ladoix-Serrigny Although this commune has its own appellation, its wines are usually sold under the name Côte-de-Beaune Villages★ and the best under that of the neighbouring Aloxe-Corton, whose characteristics they share. The wines of Ladoix-Serrigny are light and have a charming bouquet.

Chorey-les-Beaune mainly produces red wines which can be sold under their own appellation or that of Côte-de-Beaune-Villages.

Monthelie has several premiers crus whose names can be added to that of the commune: Sur La Velle, Les Vignes Rondes, Le Meix Bataille, Les Riottes, La Taupine, Le Clos-Gauthey, Le Château-Gaillard, Les Champs-Fulliot, Le Cas Rougeot and Duresse.

Vineyard of Monthélie, near Beaune in Burgundy.
Phot. Rapho.

Saint-Romain produces robust reds and fruity whites sold under the AOC Saint-Romain. Some of the production is also sold as Côte-de-Beaune-Villages.

Auxey-Duresses Before the appellation laws the wine was sold as Volnay★ or Pommard★. Some of the climats have the right to the name Côte-de-Beaune accompanied by the name of the commune. At present these include: Les Duresses, Les Bas-des-Duresses, Reugne, Les Grands-Champs, Climat-du-Val (or Clos-du-Val), Les Ecusseaux and Les Bretterins (the climat of La Chapelle is divided between Les Bretterins and Reugne).

Saint-Aubin Positioned on the hills behind Puligny-Montrachet★ and Chassagne-Montrachet★, this commune produces red and white wines having the appellation Saint-Aubin or Saint-Aubin-Côte-de-Beaune or Côte-de-Beaune-Villages. The best climats are allowed to carry the name of their cru in addition to that of the commune: La Chatenière, Les Murgers-des-Dents-de-Chien, En Remilly, Les Frionnes, Sur-le Sentier-du-Clou, Sur Gamay, Les Combes and Champlot.

Dezize-les-Maranges These fruity, light red and white wines are sold under their proper name or under Côte-de-Beaune-Villages.

Cheilly-les-Maranges These red and white wines are often blended with those of other communes and sold under the name Côte-de-Beaune plus the name of the commune. The best crus, Les Maranges and Clos-du-Roi, can label their wines Sampigny-les-Maranges and Sampigny-les-Maranges-Clos-du-Roi.

CÔTE DE BEAUNE: APPELLATION CÔTE-DE-BEAUNE A wine bearing on its label the name Côte-de-Beaune without mention of the commune or village is a wine coming from the Beaune area, and less prized, evidently, than those which only carry the name Beaune on the label. The Côtes-de-Beaune are red or white and must have 10.5° alcohol for the reds and 11° for the whites.

Côte-de-Beaune-Villages This appellation is completely different from Côte-de-Beaune. It is applied exclusively to red wines made from a combination of at least two wines from certain communes in the Côte de Beaune area (but not Beaune itself). They have an alcoholic strength of 10.5°.

Côte de Nuits Occupies about 1200 ha from Dijon to Prémeaux, but the grand crus begin at Fixin. Most of the production is red wine which has great breeding. Some excellent white wines are made at Musigny, Vougeot★, Morey-Saint-Denis★ and Nuits-Saint-Georges★, but they have not attained the excellence of the great red wines.

Like all the Burgundy★ wines, these possess the personality of their climat★, and have in common great breeding, firmness, sumptuous colour, rich bouquet and the ability to mature well. The appellation may be that of the commune (Gevrey-Chambertin★) or the cru (Romanée-Conti). The communes of the Côte de Nuits are: Fixin★, Gevrey-Chambertin, Morey-Saint-Denis, Chambolle-Musigny★, Vougeot, Vosne-Romanée★ and Nuits-Saint-Georges.

Côte d'Or The Côte d'Or forms the most important and the most beautiful area of Burgundy★. Its soil produces the prestigious red and white wines whose names are universally known: Romanée-Conti, Chambertin and Montrachet★. This great viticultural region is divided into two sub-regions: Côte de Nuits★, which produces almost exclusively the great red wines, and the Côte de Beaune★ which produces both great reds and whites.

There are also two parallel regions, the upper Côtes de Nuits and the upper Côtes de Beaune, which produce appellation wines and can, under certain conditions, add their name to the Côte d'Or appellation. From Dijon to Santenay, the Côte de Nuits and the Côte de Beaune forms a nearly continuous line of hills 200–500 m high. These hills, facing east and southeast, are protected from the wind and receive a maximum amount of sun. The best crus are harvested at 250–300 m.

The soil is extremely varied and complex which explains the many crus of Burgundy: white marl, favourable to great white wines like Montrachet; the iron- and limestone-rich soils of the Côte de Beaune; and argillo-siliceous-limestone and iron-bearing soils of the Côte de

Nuits. The only grape varieties approved for the great appellations of the communes and climats are the Pinot Noir for the red wines, and Chardonnay for the whites.

The Aligoté grape, mainly grown in the Upper Côtes, only has the right to the appellation Bourgogne Aligoté★.

Côte-Rôtie On the right bank of the Rhône, bordering the hills south of Lyons, is the celebrated vineyard of the Côte-Rôtie, whose width is no greater than 400 metres. The grapes are grown on the two communes of Tupin-Semons and Ampuis. Two noble★ grapes, the red Syrah and the white Viognier (about 20%) are grown on the acidic soil. The wine of the Côte-Rôtie is a great one, praised as early as the first century. It is a beautiful purple colour, full-bodied and generous, with a unique bouquet combining the fragrance of violet and raspberry.

The Côte-Rôtie is as sumptuous as its rival Châteauneuf-du-Pape★, but has greater distinction.

The best crus of the Côte-Rôtie are the Côte-Brune and the Côte-Blonde, which produce several wines. Those of the Côte-Brune are full-bodied and keep for a long time, whereas the wines of the Côte-Blonde do not age as well, but are lighter and more tender.

Côtes d'Agly A vineyard lying between those of Maury★ and Rivesaltes★ on the hills bordering the Agly, a small, turbulent river in the Roussillon★ area.

The soil is composed chiefly of clay and limestone and is planted with noble★ vines (Grenache, Muscat and Malvoisie) which, scorched by the sun and buffeted by the north wind, produce heady vins doux naturels★. These are either red (when the pulp is left with the grape juice during fermentation) or white (when the pulp is removed before fermentation).

Côtes d'Agly wines are often vinified in very modern co-operative cellars. They have an attractive colour, generosity★, distinction, and an aroma faintly reminiscent of stones warmed in the sun.

Côtes de Bordeaux-Saint-Macaire The area entitled to this appellation is the continuation to the south of the Premières Côtes de Bordeaux★ vineyards. It covers several communes and adjoins the famous

crus of Sainte-Croix-du-Mont★. The appellation only applies to wines made from noble★ grapes grown on clay and gravel soil. These are picked when over-ripe, and there are strict regulations concerning their vinification. The sweet white wines obtained are full-bodied and delicate and have a distinctive fragrance. Their particular character makes them as suitable for serving with desserts as they are for fish dishes, and even some white meats.

Côtes de Canon-Fronsac This appellation is given to wines grown on the best slopes of the Fronsac★ vineyards, particularly on the hill of Canon. These wines have a fine dark colour, plenty of body and a distinctive, slightly spicy flavour. They

Village and vineyard of the Côte de Nuits. Phot. Atlas-Photo.

Côte-Rôtie, on the right bank of the Rhône, south of Vienna. Phot. M.

resemble both Pomerol★ and Burgundy★ wines, and are highly esteemed, especially in northern Europe. They are at their best a few years after bottling. The main crus are Châteaux Canon, Comte and Gaby.

Côtes de Duras The name of this vineyard overlooking the Dropt Valley is one of the appellations contrôlées of the Sud-Ouest★. It lies to the north of the Lot-et-Garonne department between the Bordeaux region and the Bergerac vineyards and comprises about fifteen communes. Although Côtes de Duras is best known for its white wines, it also produces some reds made from the Cabernet, Merlot and Malbec grapes. These are good table wines of an unexceptional character with a minimum official alcohol content of 10°.

The white wines are distinctly superior in quality and have a correspondingly high reputation. They are made from the usual local grape varieties, Sémillon, Sauvignon and Muscadelle, with a proportion of Mauzac and sometimes Ugni Blanc, a grape grown all over the south of France. These wines are slightly sweet and have a distinctive and very pleasant aroma. Their official minimum alcohol content is 10·5°.

Côtes-de-Fronsac This appellation applies to wines grown in the general Fronsac★ area which, although less fine than the wines of Côtes de Canon-Fronsac★, greatly resemble them in other respects, particularly in colouring and body. The principal crus are Châteaux Lavalode, Tasla and la Rivière.

Côtes de Haut-Roussillon Planted on dry, stony soil known as *terre d'Aspres*, this appellation contrôlée vineyard in the Roussillon★ region produces vins doux naturels★ made from Grenache, Muscat and Malvoisie grapes, and comprises about forty communes between the valleys of the Tech and Têt. The region has been renowned for its fortified wines since Pliny the Elder praised them and compared them to Falerno. Overrun and destroyed by the Saracens, the vineyard was gradually reconstructed around the local monasteries and castles – so well that by the eleventh century its wines had regained their former reputation and were being served at the royal tables of France, Aragon, Majorca and Spain.

Côtes-du-Haut-Roussillon are generous wines with a very delicate and original bouquet that develops during a long period of maturation. They can be either red or white.

The Haut-Rousillon region also produces some full-bodied red wines made from Carignan grapes. They have an alcoholic strength of 12° and are used in the preparation of apéritifs.

Côtes-de-Provence The domain of these VDQS★ wines extends from Marseilles to Nice on extremely varied terrain. In this fortunate country, the sun conditions the wine, the soil being only of relative importance. Thus the vine is found on both hills and plains, thrusting its roots into chalky soil mingled with flint.

Three principal regions produce the Côtes-de-Provence : la Côte (from la Ciotat to Saint-Tropez), the northern border of the Massif de Maures and the Argens valley.

The rosés are the most popular, and their vogue is due for the most part to the many tourists who identify the wine with the sun and holidays. They are excellent dry wines, fruity, full-bodied and fragrant, whose clear and pretty colour sometimes hints of gold. They are especially suited to the cuisine of the south.

The red wines, less known, are full-bodied, having a beautiful glowing colour and an enjoyable bouquet. Their character depends on the area of origin. For example, the wines of Taradeau, Pierrefeu and Puget-Ville are particularly heady, while those of Saint-Tropez and Gonfaron are agreeably supple. The reds are made from a variety of grapes: Grenache, Cinsault, Mourvèdre, Carignan, Pécoui-Touar and Oeillade. They age well, but can also be drunk young.

The white wines, which come mainly from the Clairette and the Ugni Blanc, are dry, full-bodied, fruity and pale gold in colour. They maderise★ quickly and should be drunk young.

There is an official classification of crus of Côtes de Provence. The principal ones are the domaines of Moulières, Aumerade, Minuty and la Croix ; the châteaux of Selle and Sainte-Roseline ; Clos Mireille, Cigonne and Bastide-Verte.

Côtes de Toul This narrow vineyard, one of the two appellations of Lorraine★, is

Côtes-de-Provence; vineyards at Croix-Valmer. Phot. M.

perched on the limestone hills overlooking the Moselle around the village of Toul. There are nine communes, of which Lucey, Bruley and Ecrouves produce wines classified VDQS★. The grapes used are the Pinot Noir, Meunier, the Gamay of Toul and of Liverdun, as well as 20% maximum of secondary grapes such as the Aubin Blanc and Aligoté.

The Gamay of Liverdun, a variety adapted from the Gamay of Beaujolais, has become the principal variety today, increasingly replacing the Pinots which were, in the old days, the traditional grape of Lorraine. The region used to provide its harvest for Champagne before the legal limitation of production for that area. Today, most of the wine produced is a vin gris★ of a very pale colour which is quite light. The 8·5° minimum fixed by law is seldom exceeded. It is best drunk young, although it can be kept for several years. This is a very agreeable wine, fresh, aromatic and fruity with a touch of acidity much admired in the area. The red and white wines are much rarer and practically impossible to find.

Côtes du Forez One of the appellations of Lyon which merits the VDQS★ label. The red and some rosé wines come from the Gamay. They are consumed locally.

Côtes-du-Jura This regional appellation contrôlée, applied to the wines which originate in the chalk and gravel of the Jura★ hills, covers twelve cantons: Villers-Farlay, Salins, Arbois, Poligny, Sellières, Voiteur, Bletterans, Conliège, Lons-le-Saunier, Beaufort, Saint-Julien and Saint-Amour (not to be confused with the Saint-Amour cru of Beaujolais).

The appellation applies to white, dry, full-bodied wines having a particular perfume, and generous reds with bouquet and finish. When the Poulsard grape dominates, the red wines have little colouring, but are very fine. The Trousseau gives more colour and body. The rosés are dry and fruity, but have perhaps a little less character than the reds. Under this appellation are also found the vins jaune★, vins de paille★ and vins mousseux★.

Côtes du Luberon This vineyard, located east of Avignon and north of Durance on the slopes of Luberon, is somewhat similar to the nearby Côtes du Ventoux★. The vignerons have made great efforts and met with the same success as their neighbours at Ventoux by gradually replacing the Carignan with the Grenache and the Cinsault.

The Côtes-du-Luberon wines merit the VDQS★ label. The reds and rosés resemble

Vines of Côtes du Luberon.
Phot. Brihat-Rapho.

those of Ventoux and come from the same grape varieties. The rosé is particularly delicious. The whites, made from the Clairette and Bourboulenc, are produced in just as large quantities. These are fruity wines which should be drunk young.

Côtes du Marmandais These VDQS★ wines of the Sud-Ouest★ are produced on the two banks of the Garonne in the cantons of Marmande and Seyches. The region is, in a sense, a prolongation of the Entre-deux-Mers area on the right bank of the Garonne, and of Sauternes on the left bank. The grape varieties planted on these sunny slopes are very varied. Interest has been mainly local in these red and white, good quality wines up till now.

Côtes du Rhône From Vienne to Avignon, the vineyards planted on the slopes of the two banks of the Rhône link those of Burgundy and Provence. No other vineyard offers such diversity as this to the wine drinker. More than 110 communes located in six departments are covered by the general appellation Côtes du Rhône. They produce wines which, for the most part, have only this appellation in common and include dry whites, sweet whites, light reds, robust reds, rosés, sparkling wines, vins doux naturels★ and vins de paille★.

The vineyard is divided into two parts, north and south, separated by a region without vines between Valence and the gorge of Donzère. The northern Côtes du Rhône is found on a narrow band of slopes overlooking the Rhône. The southern part is mostly laid out on both sides of the river as far as the department of Gard on the right and those of Vaucluse and Drôme on the left.

The terrain of the two is very different. The northern vineyards lie on steep slopes, while those of the south are planted on such arid, rocky soil as to defy nature.

A great variety of grapes are used, twenty being authorised including Syrah, Grenache, Mourvèdre, Cinsault, Clairette, Roussanne, Marsanne and Viognier. The following crus are recognised as the best of the northern region. On the right bank, Côte-Rôtie★, Condrieu★, Château-Grillet★, Saint-Joseph★, Cornas★ and Saint-Péray★; on the left bank, Hermitage★ and Crozes-Hermitage★. The southern Côtes-du-Rhône crus include, on the left bank, Châteauneuf-du-Pape★, Gigondas★, Vacqueyras, Cairanne, Vinsobres, Rasteau★, Beaumes-de-Venise★ and Die and its Clairette★ and on the right bank, Tavel★, Lirac★, Chusclan★ and Laudun★. Besides the appellation Côtes-du-Rhône, the same region of the Rhône valley offers a certain number of VDQS wines which are sold under their proper name. On the left bank these are Châtillon-en-Diois★, Haut-Comtat★, Coteaux-du-Tricastin★, Côtes-du-Ventoux★ and Côtes-du-Luberon★, and on the right bank, Côtes-du-Vivarais★ and Costières-du-Gard★.

CÔTES-DU-RHÔNE: APPELLATION The appellation Côtes-du-Rhône is given to a large quantity of wines which are usually generous and heady, and which when made well are good table wines. They particularly complement the food of the Midi region or other highly-seasoned dishes. These whites, reds and rosés come from a mélange of wines in the northern and southern part of the Côtes du Rhône.

Today, nearly all the wine sold under the single appellation Côtes-du-Rhône come from the southern part: Vaucluse, Drôme and Gard. The best wines have the right to their own appellation and certain communes can use their own name, like

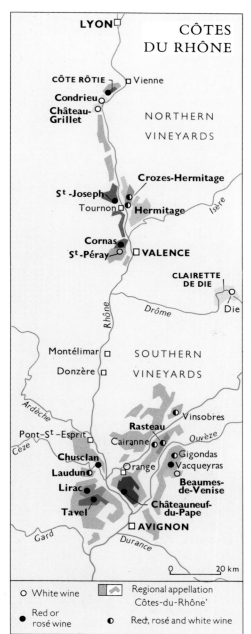

CÔTES DU RHÔNE

LYON

CÔTE RÔTIE □ Vienne

Condrieu
Château-
Grillet

NORTHERN
VINEYARDS

Crozes-Hermitage

St -Joseph
Tournon
Hermitage

Isère

Cornas
St -Péray □ VALENCE

CLAIRETTE
DE DIE

Rhône

Drôme

Die

Montélimar □

SOUTHERN
VINEYARDS

Donzère □

Ardèche

Vinsobres

Rasteau
Pont-St -Esprit
Cairanne

Ouvèze

Cèze

Gigondas
Chusclan
Orange
Vacqueyras
Laudun
Lirac
Beaumes-
de-Venise
Châteauneuf-
du-Pape
Tavel
□ AVIGNON

Gard
Durance

0   20 km

○ White wine   Regional appellation
                     Côtes-du-Rhône'

● Red or   ◐ Red, rosé and white wine
  rosé wine

sun. Thanks to the efforts of the vignerons, who have tried to improve the grape varieties and the methods of vinification, the wine of the Côtes du Ventoux has become one of the best VDQS★ of the Rhône valley.

The reds and rosés come from the Carignan (not more than 50%), the Grenache, Syrah, Mourvèdre and Cinsault grapes. The rosés have a rich bouquet, are fruity and nervous★ with finesse and freshness. The reds are an attractive, clear, ruby red. The whites, made principally from the Clairette and Bourboulenc, are produced in similar quantities.

Côtes du Vivarais   A vineyard of the Ardèche department situated on the right bank of the Rhône around Orgnac, whose chasm is a favourite tourist attraction. It produces red, rosé and white wines from the classic grapes of the region – the Grenache, Syrah, Mourvèdre and Cinsault for the reds and rosés, and Clairette, Bourboulenc and Picpoul for the whites. The fresh and fragrant Côtes-du-Vivarais are classified VDQS★. When the grapes are more vigorous and the wines contain at least 11° of alcohol, the name of the commune can follow the appellation Côtes-du-Vivarais, for example Orgnac, Saint-Montant and Saint-Remèze.

Côtes du Zaccar   Included under this appellation are the Algerian wines produced around Miliana south-west of Algiers which were labelled VDQS★ before Algerian independence. The red, rosé and white wines are grown on limestone-clay soil at an altitude of 400–900 m and share a common, unique bouquet.

The colourful, full-bodied reds were fleshy, sometimes having a raspberry fruitiness. They were counted among the best in Algeria. The whites, made mainly from the Faranah, were generally excellent, fruity and very flavourful.

coulant (vin)   A wine which provides a very smooth sensation, also described as 'glissant' or 'slippery'. It is rich in glycerine★, harmonious and stable and no one element (alcohol, tannin or acid) predominates.

Coulée-de-Serrant   This, along with Roche-aux-Moines★, is the most delicious

Following two pages: 4th-century Roman mosaic depicting boys gathering grapes, transport by cart and treading. Detail. Santa Costanza, Rome.
Phot. Hamlyn Group
Michael Holford.

Châteauneuf-du-Pape and Tavel. By contrast, certain communes can only use their name when it is preceded by Côtes-du-Rhône, for example Gigondas, Cairanne, Chusclan and Laudun.

Côtes du Ventoux   This appellation derives from a vineyard in the Rhône valley of the same name. It is situated on the slopes of a mountain in the department of Vaucluse where the vines are protected from the cold winds and exposed to the

of the Savennières★. The appellation Coulée-de-Serrant must be preceded by Savennières. The domaine, enclosed by walls, only covers three hectares. On this schistose soil of a well-exposed hill, the Pineau de la Loire flourishes, and was always a favourite of Louis XIV and, later, the Empress Josephine. The wine used to be semi-dry or sweet and was harvested late so that the grapes could be conserved by the sun. Today, dry wine is made and no-one complains. It has kept its old delicacy and elegance and has also acquired a certain vigour.

Coulée de Serrant: general view of the vineyards.
Phot. M.

coulure A vine disease. Sometimes, when the weather is bad during the period of the flowering of the vines, the flowers do not fully develop but dry up and fall off. Certain grapes like the Chardonnay are prone to this disease.

coupage (vins de) Offspring of several fathers, these blended wines have an undetermined origin. Their birthplace is in the cellars of wine *négociants*★, for they are made from the careful mixings of various wines. Algeria has always produced blended wines of high alcoholic strength. Vins de coupage always come from the same grapes, though hybrids are also permitted. Their alcoholic content must exceed 9.5°.

Many of the vins de coupage are the vins de marque★.

court en bouche (vin) A wine which may be excellent but which lacks vigour and imparts only a fleeting sensation to the tastebuds.

courtier An indispensable intermediary between the multitude of producers and the wine *négociants*★. The body of courtiers already existed at the beginning of the fifteenth century and the jurors of Bordeaux were officially given office in the sixteenth century. The profession today is controlled by the law of 31st December, 1949. The courtier thus inherits a great tradition and plays an important role, for he tours the vineyards and informs the *négociant* about interesting wines.

The work of the courtier calls for patient observation, great experience and correct judgement. One of the most enchanting tales of the courtier's infallibility is that of a Médoc cask whose certain indescribable taste could not be defined by anyone. The courtier tasted the wine and identified the flavours of iron, string, cardboard and ink. The cask was emptied and on the bottom was found the iron key to the chai which had fallen in. It was tied by string to a cardboard label on which was written in ink, 'Key to the chai'!

courtier gourmet-piqueur de vins The company of Courtiers Gourmet-piqueurs de Vins de Paris is a group of experts (from Paris) attached to the wine storehouses at Bercy. It is one of the oldest of such corporations that still exist. The gourmets, *magistrats de la vigne,* were officially elected jurors, similar to customs officers, whose job was to assure the proper movement of wine from place to place. The sanctions that they had the right to apply against abuses were severe and picturesque (if one can judge from the archives of the communes!).

The role of the gourmet consisted of serving as an intermediary between buyer and seller, then watching the packing and also accompanying the wine on its journey. He had to keep a precise register of the transportation of wine, subject to the control of the municipality and the corporation of vignerons. If the gourmet's function has disappeared, the title is still

carried proudly and legitimately by the modern courtiers.

crémant A Champagne which has less sparkle than usual. Its sparkle forms a 'cream' on the top of the glass (from which comes the name), and disappears very quickly. The crémant is located midway between a mousseux★ and a pétillant★. Its pressure is lower than the average mousseux wines (2.5–3 kg instead of around 5 for mousseux).

A well-made crémant is a good quality wine having the advantage over a normal Champagne of preserving its winey taste and a certain favourable sweetness. A crémant consequently comes principally from the best cuvées. It is a rare wine which is much sought after and very expensive. Unfortunately, very few houses still prepare the traditional crémant.

The word crémant should not be confused with the name of the commune of Cramant, a cru of the Côte de Blancs★, which is south-east of Epernay. This confusion easily arises as Cramant is one of the rare crus of Champagne. Funnily enough, there is actually a crémant of Cramant!

crème de tête An expression which formerly referred to the richest Sauternes carefully made from the earliest grapes. The first harvest, which was small, was composed almost exclusively of *pourris*, or rotten grapes, which were exceptionally rich in sugar (up to 500 g per litre) after attack by pourriture noble★. Subsequent harvests contained less and less of these grapes and the last, the queue, contained few or none at all.

Today, all the grand crus of Sauternes combine the portion of their harvest which they judge worthy to bear the name, and the rest is sold under the name of the château. The expression crème de tête has thus lost most of its importance as the grand crus no longer sell their individual first harvest under this name.

Crépy The wines of this appellation contrôlée of Savoie★ are grown on the banks of Lake Léman. They are the best known of the Savoie wines and the only ones drunk outside the region. The ancient vineyard occupies two limestone hills facing south and south-west on the communes of Loisin, Douvaine and Ballaison.

The Crépy comes from the Chasselas★ roux et vert which produces the celebrated Fendant in Switzerland. The Crépy is a delicious, very dry wine which has a light, natural sparkle found in perlant★ wines. By law it must have a minimum of 9.5° alcohol, but often exceeds this amount. It is clear, pale gold in colour with a hint of green, and the flavour is both elegant and charming, with body and an agreeable acidity. This acidity gives it, among other things, an astonishing vitality.

Crépy improves with age without maderising★, losing its acidity and fresh-

The Crépy of Savoie, like the Swiss Dézaley, is made from the Chasselas, a glorious grape in a cold climate, on the banks of Lake Léman.
Phot. Lauros–Atlas–Photo.

ness, but gaining a subtle perfume and taste of hazelnuts and violets.

Crozes-Hermitage An appellation of the Côtes du Rhône★ which designates the red and white wines produced by a dozen neighbouring communes of the celebrated hill of Hermitage★ on the left bank of the Rhône. The red wines come from Syrah and are close cousins of Hermitage, but with less colour and finesse. Their aroma of wild hawthorn and raspberry gives them undeniable charm. They do not keep as long as the Hermitage and become discoloured with age.

The white wines are made from the Roussanne and Marsanne and are less distinguished by their perfume and body than the whites of Hermitage. Very pale and light, they have an agreeable smell and taste of hazelnuts. Sweet in their youth, they become dry with age.

cru Applied to wine this word, which comes from the verb *croître*, to grow, designates a particular area and the wine produced in that area. In Bordeaux the word cru has a restricted meaning. It designates a château★ with particular standing and personality in the commune. The expression vin de cru therefore implies the notion of renown and superior quality. The château of Bordeaux is similar to the climat★ of Burgundy.

cru (grand) It has taken a long time to define the use of this term, except in Chablis★ where it can be applied to all the AOC wines. The decree of 27th June, 1964 clarified this by ruling that the use of the expression grand cru is forbidden except for Chablis, Saint-Emilion★, Banyuls★ and the wine of Alsace★, and its use must follow the precise conditions fixed by law. The Chablis Grand Cru are always the best of the appellation (Le Clos, Vaudésir, etc.). On the other hand, the Saint-Emilions Grand Cru are the wines which do not come from the classified crus, but which have been awarded this distinction following the recommendation of the tasting commission, and are classified above the wines which have the right to the appellation Saint-Emilion.

cru (premier) A term strictly reserved for those wines of appellation contrôlée which, according to regulation, are in a certain category of premier (first) crus. This is the case for the Burgundy appellations, particularly the communal appellations of the Côte de Nuits and Côte de Beaune, like Chablis, Mercurey, Givry, Rully and Montagny.

In Gironde it is termed premier cru classés, and the first four crus were classified in 1855 (Lafite, Margaux, Latour and Haut-Brion), the premier crus of Sauternes being classified in the same year.

Premier grand cru classé is authorised for certain domaines of Saint-Emilion classified by the decree of 1954, e.g. Ausone and Cheval-Blanc.

cru classé A term reserved for those crus which have been officially designated by the Institut National des Appellations d'Origine★. The crus of Bordeaux which were classified in 1855 have the right to be called cru classé. It is also applied to some AOC Bordeaux wines – Médoc, Sauternes, Graves and Saint-Emilion – and also to classified VDQS of the Côtes de Provence.

cuit (vin) Cooked wine is obtained from a concentration of must which has been heated in a cauldron. The vin cuit of Palette★, a Christmas treat in Provence, is excellent. A cooked taste is also a fault which is found in certain wines which have been warmed in the cuve either to start fermentation or to help those grapes which have been picked too late.

cuvage The area where the cuves are located, also called the *cuverie* or chai★. It can also mean fermentation.

cuvaison or **cuvage** The process of fermenting wine, that is, fermenting the vendange in a cuve★. This operation is most important as it determines the nature and quality of the wine.

The first phase is the delicate operation of pouring the vendange into the cuves. It is tempting to empty the grape-baskets and the carts into the cuves mechanically, and a number of machines have been devised for this purpose, though none are entirely satisfactory.

The choice of cuve and its capacity is also important, as is the vigneron's skill in controlling the alcoholic fermentation.

Several times a day, he tests the cuve with his mustmeter and tastevin. The cuvaison lasts from two days to three weeks according to region, the nature of the wine and its destination. Wines which are drunk young are fermented for less time than those which keep. Usually, however, the period is kept short. At Châteauneuf-du-Pape, for example, the cuvaison used to last until Christmas, just giving the wine sufficient tannin content and time to clear. It kept well but, in order to produce a fuller wine, it needed three years in cask before being bottled, and there was always the risk of the wine drying out. A successful wine therefore depends upon the balance between the time it spends fermenting and the period it remains in cask during the élevage★ process.

cuve The cuves used today are made of wood, cement or stainless steel. However, wood has always been the traditional material and many of the quality vineyards still use it. Wooden cuves have several drawbacks. They are expensive, their repair and detailed preparation before use demands a lot of hard work, and the white wines must be placed in casks or glass cuves after fermentation (thus doubling the necessary equipment). If the cuve is also used to store the wine after fermentation, it must be sealed to protect the wine from the air. Painting and varnishing the exterior to block evaporation also poses certain technical difficulties.

Wood cuves have their advantages, however. The white wine ferments, becoming finer and clearer, more quickly and thus can be sold more rapidly than those made in cement cuves. For the red wines, the wooden cuve is clearly superior as it allows the moderate amount of aeration they need before being bottled.

Cement cuves are less expensive and their upkeep and cleaning are easier. Wine can be kept in them after fermentation without risking oxidation. They do not take up as much space as the wooden cuves but may impart a taste of iron to the wine (casse ferrique★) and sometimes exhibit a certain porosity. The wooden cuve always had a very limited capacity (for fine wines it used to be no more than 100 hl) whereas the cement cuve took on gigantic quantities, from 600–800 hl. Many co-operative caves have thus bought these giant cuves

and the result is not worth waiting for. Such a mass is often attacked by bacteria (*Mycoderma aceti*★ and *Mycoderma vini*★) after fermentation because there is no cooling system.

There are now very expensive modern cuves made of stainless steel which are seen only at the great vineyards. They are extremely easy to maintain and the must in them can be cooled rapidly by interior or exterior cooling methods.

CUVE CLOSE A method of making mousseux wines which is also called the 'Charmat' process. The wines are considerably less expensive than those made by the Champagne method★. A solution of sugar and yeasts is added to the dry wine to obtain a second fermentation. But, unlike the Champagne method, it is not then bottled, and the sparkling level is instead reached in a vast hermetically-sealed vat (called a cuve close). The lining of this cuve is designed to resist the considerable pressure which develops during this second fermentation.

To clarify the wine, it is filtered under pressure and bottled immediately on leaving the filter. Sparkling wines are made in this way in two or three weeks and the delicate and expensive operations of the Champagne method are eliminated. This provides economy of time and manual labour. The mousseux obtained, however, is of inferior quality to those produced by the second fermentation in bottle, slowly and at a low temperature, following the method of Dom Pérignon★.

A cuve of Madeira.
Phot. Léah Lourié.

This method is often used in the Midi to make Muscats★ mousseux, whose base of vin ordinaire is enriched by the Muscat of Hamburg, a process which is not allowed in France for appellation wines.

CUVE FERMÉE A process used nearly everywhere in Gironde for fermenting red wines. The fermentation of grapes coming from Bordeaux varieties is more delicate than that for the Pinot Noir of Burgundy (Burgundy uses the cuve ouverte★ process). The quantity of the vendange is also greater than in Burgundy. The closed cuve allows a layer of carbon dioxide to form over the chapeau★ and protects the must from the risk of acescence★. The must is aerated by plunging the chapeau in and out of the wine at the beginning of fermentation before the yeast is added.

CUVE OUVERTE A process used generally in Burgundy during the fermentation period, which is facilitated by aeration. The floating chapeau★ is pushed down from time to time. Open, wooden cuves are usually used. They are equipped with a drapeau★ which allows heating or cooling of the must.

cuvé (overfermented) A wine cuvé has been left to ferment in the cuve★ too long and has an excess of tannin. It is thus astringent★ and dur★ and needs time to improve.

cuvée The quantity of wine which is made at the same time in a cuve★ or the total amount of wine which has fermented at different times in the same cuve. A cuvée also means the collection of wines from several cuves but which share the same origin. Première cuvée and seconde cuvée are expressions which describe the class and the relative quality of the wine.

cuver To ferment in a cuve★.

Cyprus The wine coming from this island, situated not far from the shores of Turkey and Syria, was celebrated as early as the Crusades. Commandaria, a golden wine produced from the vines planted by the Chevaliers of the Order of Templars around Limassol, was well known throughout the West. After the invasion of the Turks, viticulture languished, though without disappearing entirely, and did not really improve until the English arrived in 1878. By some miracle the vineyards escaped phylloxera★ and today viticulture is an important activity.

Cyprus now produces inexpensive, quality wines. The highly-coloured reds, full-bodied and rich in tannin, go well with spicy foods. The best are the Afames and Othello. The rosé called Kokkinelli is a dark-coloured, fresh, dry wine. The white wines have a unique taste – the best and driest are the Aphrodite and Arsinoé.

The best Cypriot wine is the Commandaria, produced by only twenty authorised villages, including Kalokhorio, Zoopiyi, Yerasa, Arjias and Mancas. This very sweet dessert wine is made from a mélange of red and white grapes and varies from village to village depending on the proportion of red and white grapes, vinification method and maturation time.

Cyprus also produces a great variety of sherry-type dessert wines of which Great Britain is the largest importer.

Grapes from Cyprus, planted in Madeira in the fifteenth century, produce the renowned Madeira wines, and legend has it that the Marsala of Sicily and Tokay of Hungary also originate from Cypriot vines.

Czechoslovakia Czechoslovakia has just over 20,000 ha of vineyards, and produces about 400,000 hl of wine a year. For a long time only dessert grapes were grown, but by the eighteenth century Czech wines had acquired a reputation and popularity that put them on a level with the best wines of Italy and Hungary. Today, wine is produced in the provinces of Bohemia, Moravia and Slovakia and practically all of it is consumed inside the country.

Bohemia's viticultural centre is Melnik, a town in the Elbe valley north of Prague whose red and white wines are considered the best in the region, and which also produces an extremely good sparkling wine. The wines of Moravia are mostly produced around Brno. In Slovakia, viticulture is still the principal livelihood of the peasants of Modra, Pézinok and Sviaty Jůz, and all the sunniest hillsides are traditionally reserved for their vines.

deacidification In a cold, rainy year, the grapes frequently do not ripen normally and the wine made from them is very acidic. Deacidification neutralises part of this excess acidity. It is only permitted under exceptional conditions and administered under the authorisation of the Ministry of Agriculture. Pure calcium carbonate is added to the must. Calcium is a natural product and, when the operation is performed correctly, it does not impair the quality of the wine.

débourbage The operation of separating the must from the sediment before fermentation when making white wine. The first racking after vinification is also called débourbage. This process usually takes place around December when the first lees are very thick and plentiful, and separate easily leaving the clear wine.

decanter A luxurious bottle into which vintage port, which ages in bottle, is transferred before serving. After years in bottle, the port needs to be decanted and aerated in an operation which is necessarily delicate because of the value of the wine. The decanters of olden days were made of glass, often inlaid with gold, and sometimes wore a gold medal around their necks. They were often carried in a container of precious wood. Modern decanters, usually made of glass, are also very elegant.

decanting A very delicate operation designed to transfer the wine, usually an old red one, from its original bottle to a carafe or decanter in order to separate it from its deposits which, if drunk, would impair digestion. The operation of decanting is actually a kind of racking. It is generally done by candlelight, the candle being placed behind the neck of the bottle so that the pourer can see when the wine first appears cloudy.

Despite the progress made in stabilising wines, it is impossible to prevent the deposits of tannin and colouring matter

Decanters of vintage port.
Phot. Casa de Portugal.

99

Dégorgement is one of the last steps in the preparation of Champagne. Caves Pommery. Phot. Lauros.

from collecting as the wine matures in bottle.

Decanting has both champions and opponents. Even if the operation is performed delicately and slowly, the oxidation which takes place may be so chemically violent as to destroy a very old wine whose equilibrium is always a little fragile. Actually, each wine poses a particular problem. The best general method is to stand the bottle up at least two hours before the meal in order to see if it needs decanting. Decanting should be done at the last moment, just before the time for drinking in the case of fragile wines, and a little before the meal for more hardy ones which may benefit from a moderate aeration (such as certain Médocs and Graves).

The adversaries of decanting do not want to risk killing a wine, as they say. They prefer to stand the bottle up two hours before it is drunk and uncork it. Then religiously, with infinite precaution, they pour it into the glasses, and often sacrifice the bottom of the bottle. They feel that if the wine needs aeration to develop all the subtle qualities of its bouquet, it will receive enough while being poured into the glass.

décuvaison The operation of transferring the wine from the cuve, where it has undergone alcoholic fermentation, into barrels. It takes place when most of the sugar has been transformed into alcohol.

definition of wine This was given in the first article of the decree of 3rd September, 1907: 'No drink can be held or transported with sale in mind, be put on sale or sold as wine, unless it is made exclusively from the fermentation of fresh grapes or the juice of fresh grapes'. It goes without saying that this legal French definition excludes drinks prepared with fruits other than grapes, and it also excludes drinks made with dried grapes, which is more important. Wines from other fruits have been made by defrauders, and wines from dried grapes are still produced in Greece and Italy.

dégorgement One of the last steps in the Champagne method★. The Champagne (or sparkling wine), having undergone second fermentation, accumulates deposits on the cork as a result of the turning of the bottle in the course of remuage★. These deposits must be removed. The operation used to be performed haphazardly, and, despite the ability of the workers, there was the risk of loss of gas as well as a certain amount of wine.

Today the process has been facilitated by using the freezing method. The neck of the bottle is frozen to a temperature of -16 to $-18°$C. Within a few minutes the sediment is encased in ice which a specialist removes by pulling out the cork. The wine lost using this process is insignificant. The space left by the removal of the deposit is immediately taken up by the liqueur d'expedition★ which is injected during the dosage★ operation.

dégustation (tasting) A simple, yet extremely complex, operation which is an art and perhaps even a science but, above all, an act of love.

Oenophiles are often as passionate about wine as are music lovers and painters about their respective interests. As art and music are discussed in terms of their own specific vocabulary, so too is wine even though the terms may seem bizarre, pretentious and ridiculous to the unacquainted.

Wine-tasting is not only a source of joy for the oenophile, and a subject of common interest among friends, it is also the most simple and sure test for the vignerons, *négociants*★ and *sommeliers*★. It is by successive tastings that they follow the state of the wine, observe its evolution and are thus certain of the quality of the product to be offered to the consumer.

Tasting affects three senses: sight, smell

and taste. The eye examines the colour (robe★) and the clarity★ of the wine, the nose appreciates the aroma★ and the bouquet★ while the palate distinguishes the diverse sensations from which one can judge the equilibrium of the elements in the wine (sugar, acidity, alcohol, tannin, glycerine, etc.) and the strength of these sensations.

The ability to judge objectively is a vital gift, and demands great concentration combined with the ability to recall and compare.

dentelle (lacy) This refers to a very fine, delicate wine of subtle aroma which is generally a white wine, such as Champagne.

Some old vignerons often say of an old wine '*qu'il tombe en dentelle*', meaning the wine has been killed by age and falls to pieces like an old cloak.

dépouillé The solid deposits contained in the wine after fermentation slowly drop to the bottom of the cask during the winter and form the lees. When the wine has become clear it is said to be dépouillé.

dessert wines Although neglected today, dessert wines were regarded as delicacies by our fathers, who could not conceive of an important repast without ending with such a wine. Sweet wines, fortified wines, Champagnes and the semi-dry sparkling wines can all be served with the dessert. The sweet white wines should be served very chilled, as they have a high

sugar content, and the sparkling wines should also be served chilled but not icy.

Dézaley One of the best dry white wines produced in Switzerland. The Chasselas grapes from which it is made are grown on steep terraces facing Lake Geneva east of Lausanne in the Vaud canton. The wine of Dézaley possesses remarkable finesse, great distinction and generally deserves its high reputation.

discoloured A wine which looks badly tinted and whose colour has faded. This usually happens to very old wines when the colouring matter precipitates with ageing. But discoloured wine can also result from an excess of sulphur dioxide★, or animal charcoal which was used in fining.

diseases (wine) These are caused by bacteria. Aigre★, which sours wine, appears in the presence of air, but a number of bacterial fermentations develop in full, sealed casks and cause profound and often irreversible alterations in the wine. Diseases include tourne★, amertume★, graisse★ and mannite★. Improved hygiene as well as advances in oenological technology have considerably reduced their occurrence.

distinguished A distinguished wine is composed of pure and noble elements which unite in a perfect equilibrium.

Dôle A red Swiss wine produced in the Valais canton in the rocky valley of the Rhône. It is made from the Pinot Noir which is sometimes blended with Gamay and several local varieties. Many consider it the best red wine of Switzerland. It is richly coloured, full-bodied, keeps well and is not unlike the wines of Burgundy and those of the Côte-Rôtie.

dosage Adding a certain amount of sugar in the form of the liqueur d'expedition★ to Champagne★ after dégorgement★. The Champagne is then classified according to the amount of liqueur added: brut – contains from 0 to 0.25% or 0.5% of the liqueur; extra-dry, from 1% to 2%; sec, from 3% to 5%; demi-sec, from 6% to 10%; and doux, 8% to 14%.

Dégustation, Château d'Yquem.
Phot. Rapho-Weiss.

1

5

6

1 Haltica or flea-beetle
2 Yellow spider
3 Red spider
4 Black rot (fungus)
5 Mealy cochineal
6 Vine leaves attacked by a
   fungus
7 Grub of the Cochylis moth
8 Ecaille martre
9 Esca (fungus)
10 Excoriation
11 Meal moth
12 Leaf-roller moth
13 Iron wireworm, click beetle
   larva
14 greyworm, Noctuid larva
   Phot. M.

10

11

In principle, brut does not contain any liqueur, but sometimes a small amount (0·25% to 0·5%) is added when it seems a little hard. Brut Champagne used not to be popular, but today it has many devotees. The French seem to prefer light brut Champagne, the English a full-bodied sec and the Nordic countries, a demi-sec or doux. The Americans used to favour sec but are now switching to brut.

A mediocre Champagne can easily mask its faults by the sweetness of the sugar. The liqueur used to be injected by hand, but the process is now performed quickly and automatically by special machines made of glass and copper.

doux In general the word doux describes an agreeable taste. Applied to wine, the word indicates the presence and taste of sugar in a rather large quantity.

It takes on a different meaning depending on the wine to which it is applied. The sweetness of a wine made from grapes attacked by pourriture noble★, such as a Sauternes or a Beerenauslese, is so marvellous that it is only found in exceptional climatic conditions. But it can also exist in a wine having natural unfermented sugar which is maintained by massive doses of sulphur dioxide.★ This process, which is used for certain white Bordeaux and cheap Liebfraumilch, began because of the demand from consumers for sweet wines. On the other hand, wine such as port, which has natural sugar remaining in the wine when fermentation has been arrested by the addition of alcohol, is legally defined as vin doux naturel★. As well as being sweet because of the sugar, they are also rich in alcohol. Still another sweetness in a wine, such as Marsala, may be caused by the addition of the juice of a very sweet grape.

Therefore, the word doux applied to wine is something very vague and imprecise. It is neither a good nor bad quality and depends on the wine it is applied to. The words demi-sec, moelleux★ and liquoreux describe the taste more precisely.

doux naturels (vins) This expression has an essentially fiscal value in France. It is applied to wines which are naturally rich in sugar, as a result of the addition of alcohol during fermentation, and thus are placed under a certain excise category.

These wines are all products of the Mediterranean sun. In France they are the Banyuls★, Maury★, Côtes-d'Agly★, Côtes-de-Haut-Roussillon★, Grand-Roussillon★, Rivesaltes★, Rasteau★ and the Muscats like Frontignan★ or Beaumes-de-Venise★.

The grapes from which these wines are made are the noble★ Grenache, Muscat, Macabéo and Malvoisie, which undoubtedly came from Spain or the Orient where they grew on arid coasts, burned by the sun on difficult soil. The local inhabitants have devoted themselves to the production of these wines from time immemorial.

The vins doux naturels, whether they be red, rosé or white, are rich in alcohol. The must possesses at least 250 g of sugar per litre. Fermentation is arrested by mutage★, or the addition of alcohol to the must. The wine preserves its fruitiness, a large proportion of its natural sugar and also a high degree of alcohol, often 22 or 23°. This method originated with the Saracens and is not unlike that for making Carthagène★, the liqueur of the Midi whose precise origin is unknown.

In a vin doux naturel the taste of alcohol blends with that of the wine. Sometimes the wine is left to mature in casks which are placed outside in the sun. This produces the exquisite Rancio★. The vins doux naturels are subject to very severe controls which must be observed by the vignerons.

Although they are muted with alcohol, they should not be confused with the vins blancs liquoreux★ produced in Bordeaux, the Loire (Sauternes, Quarts-de-Chaume, Vouvray, etc.) and in Germany (on the banks of the Rhine and the Moselle) which do not have alcohol added to them. They are simply the prized result of the natural fermentation of the juice of grapes which has been attacked by pourriture noble★.

The vins doux naturels belong to the category 'vins de liqueur' but are not included under the same fiscal bracket. They fall for the most part under the fiscal regulations applying to the specific wine.

drapeau Apparatus used to circulate water in the cuves★ during the fermentation period in order to reheat the must in a cold year or cool it in a hot year. Its use has been widespread in Burgundy since the very warm years of 1947 and 1949.

E

Egrappage by hand at Château Palmer in the Médoc. Egrappage results in a less astringent wine which is ready for drinking earlier. Phot. M.

éclaircissage A special vendage method used in Sauternes. When the grapes are mature the pickers skilfully remove half of them from the vines so that the remaining grapes receive more air and sunlight. They then ripen further and regularly attract pourriture noble★. The first grapes picked are made into an excellent dry white wine.

Edelzwicker A white Alsatian wine made from a blending of the noble★ grape varieties including Traminer, Riesling, Sylvaner and Pinot. The Edelzwicker is better than the Zwicker, the German word *edel* meaning 'noble' or superior. It is more full-bodied and fragrant, but is just as light and easy to drink. It makes a good carafe wine and goes especially well with sauerkraut.

égrappage Separating the grapes from the stalks before they are pressed or placed in the fermenting vats.

Egrappage has been practised in the Gironde since the eighteenth century, but has only come into general use in the Côte d'Or in the last thirty or forty years. It is also practised in the Loire (Bourgueil, Chinon, Champigny), the Côtes du Rhône (Hermitage, Cornas, Côte-Rôtie) as well as with grapes to be made into Chianti. On the other hand, it is not carried out in Beaujolais because of the short fermentation period. Egrappage is generally used for wines made from grapes which have a high tannin content (Cabernet, Pinot, Syrah and some Italian varieties) in order to make them less astringent and more drinkable.

In Bordeaux, where the grapes have a high tannin content, it is widely employed although some vignerons use it on only part of the harvest, depending on the maturity of the grapes, the varieties, soil and the year.

The practice of égrappage reduces the

total amount of the vendange, especially the marc. It gives the wine more marrow, finesse and colour and adds about one half degree of alcohol. On the other hand, flabby and flat wines should not have the stalks removed as they need the extra tannin to make them more firm and vinous.

Egrappage is performed mechanically by the *égrappoir* or *fouloir-grappe*, a machine that crushes the grape, then ejects the stalk after separating it from the juice and skin.

Egypt In ancient days the Egyptian wines were renowned, but at the beginning of this century they were practically nonexistent, and the few produced were poor. An Egyptian named Nestor Gianachis undertook the reconstruction of the vineyards. In 1903 he planted the first vines but it was not until 1931, after many attempts, that a decent wine was finally produced. Today, although production is still very limited, Egypt produces some interesting wines and efforts are being made to introduce them on the world market.

elegant All grand cru★ wines are elegant, which is not to say that less *racé*★ ones are not. The elegance of a wine is the result of the blending of different elements into a subtle harmony.

élevage The care lavished on newly-made wine to aid nature in improving its quality and to assure it a long life. It begins with the wine in cask, continues while it is bottled and during the maturing period until the time when the desired perfection is attained.

To begin, the warm new wine is not immediately sent to the cellar. Fermentation must have completely ceased and the temperature dropped below the minimum 20°C necessary for fermentation to occur. Also, before it is bottled, the wine must undergo several processes: ouillages★, débourbages★, soutirages★, collages★ and, finally, filtration★.

The period spent in cask varies according to the nature of the wine and the type of wine desired. Certain wines must mature for about two years before their bouquet is apparent (great Burgundies and Médoc). Others, like Beaujolais and Muscadet, are especially liked for their fruiti-

ness, and several months ageing is enough. On the other hand, the longer the fermentation, the longer the wine must mature in cask in order to remove the excess tannin. Today, however, wines tend to spend less time in cask than they used to. Wines which remain too long in cask dry out and lose part of their bouquet because of oxidation.

élevé (vin) A wine which is ready for bottling.

éleveur A word which has come into use only recently to describe the qualified specialist who cares for the wine from the time it is made until it is shipped from the cellar. The *éleveur* must know, among other things, the character, personality, vintage and origin of each wine.

emaciated A term which is applied to wine in the same sense as it is to humans. An emaciated wine has less substance or body due to repeated separations or racking of the clear wine from the deposits.

enemies of the vine The innumerable diseases which attack the vine pose one of the greatest problems of viticulture. Among the many enemies which impoverish the vine are insects, the innocent butterfly in the caterpillar and larval stages, as well as other larvae (cochylis, eudemis, pyrale, noctuelle), the may bug, red spiders and especially the dreaded phylloxera★ which ravaged the vineyards of Europe.

There are also the cryptogamic diseases caused by fungus, grey rot (pourriture grise★), apoplexy (esca), mildew and oidium★ (powdery mildew).

The vine can also suffer from attacks by physiological diseases: chlorisis (green sickness), leaf reddening (*rougeau*), coulure★, millerandage (shot berries★) and fan-leaf (*court-noué*).

Other enemies include lightning, hail and frosts.

Entre-deux-Mers The vast area occupying the triangle formed by the Garonne and Dordogne from their confluence at the mouth of Ambes to the eastern border of the Gironde department.

Several of the regions included in this territory produce special wines: P r e m i è r e s - C ô t e s - d e - B o r d e a u x ★,

Loupiac★, Sainte-Croix-du-Mont★, Côtes-de-Bordeaux-Sainte-Macaire★, Graves-de-Vayres★ and Sainte-Foy-Bordeaux★.

The name Entre-deux-Mers is applied uniquely to those dry white wines of at least 11·5° alcohol, produced on limestone, clay and gravel soil, from the noble★ grape varieties of Bordeaux. The wines are of excellent quality, particularly the dry whites which are quickly replacing the former sweeter ones due to consumer demand. Entre-deux-Mers is a fresh, fruity wine with its own particular sève★. It goes remarkably well with fish, especially oysters and hors-d'oeuvres.

The area also produces a red wine which is sold under the appellation Bordeaux or Bordeaux supérieur★.

entreillage (sometimes called *mise sur lattes*) After receiving the liqueur de tirage★ the bottles of Champagne are piled in horizontal lots in the cellars. Between each row, laths of wood have been skilfully placed by the cellarmen. In this position the second fermentation slowly takes place under a constant temperature of about 10°C. The slowness is indispensible for obtaining the persistent sparkle which is the trademark of Champagne. The sugar contained in the wine decomposes little by little into alcohol and carbon dioxide. This process takes between two and four months. Afterwards the wine is left to rest a while longer so that the deposits and lees from the dead yeasts will accumulate. The next step is the elimination of these deposits by the processes of remuage★ and dégorgement★.

enveloppé (vin) A wine whose alcohol and glycerine content overshadows the other elements, forming a kind of envelope around them so as to make it difficult to perceive their subtleties. This occurs in wines made from grapes of a high sugar content.

épanoui In full bloom, a term usually applied to the bouquet★ of a wine. The expanding bouquet reveals itself little by little until eventually it reaches its fullness.

épluchage Sorting the grapes by hand, just after picking and before they are crushed or pressed, in order to eliminate the damaged grapes. This is practised during the production of quality wines and is an extremely expensive operation because of the labour involved.

When the harvest is a healthy one and most of the grapes are at about the same stage of maturity, the operation can be performed very quickly. But this is not always the case, particularly in Champagne. In this northern climate the grapes often have difficulty ripening and the unripe grapes, which are acidic and low in sugar, must be discarded so that a sufficiently alcoholic wine can be made. Even more important, the rotten or

Entre-deux-Mers vineyards near Rozan. Phot. M.

Epluchage in a Champagne vineyard. Phot. M.

107

Sicilian vineyards at the foot of Mount Etna. Phot. Aarons-Z.F.A.

mouldy grapes which could impart a disagreeable smell or taste must be eliminated. Thus in Champagne the épluchage is an onerous, but necessary, task. It is performed at the vine itself. The grapes are deposited on wicker trays supported by two narrow wicker crates weighing 80 kg. The sorters cut the grapes with scissors and throw the healthy, ripe grapes in one basket and the green, mouldy, or damaged grapes into the other.

equilibrium   A wine in equilibrium has all its elements in perfect proportion to one another. The alcohol, acid and sugar are in perfect accord, with none dominating the others. Such a wine is also called balanced and harmonious. When a wine has an excess or lacks an element it is obviously termed unbalanced.

Estaing   A small vineyard of the Sud-Ouest★ situated in the Lot Valley on the three communes of Estaing, Coubisou and Sebrazac. The vineyards grow on terraces 300–450 m high which have been carefully constructed by vignerons over the centuries on the slopes of the deep valley. The vines benefit from warm, dry summers, but sometimes experience the rough winters of a continental climate.

The red wines are made mainly from the Fer★, locally called Mansois, and from the Gamay, Merlot, Cabernet, Négrette and Jurançon Noir. They are generally very delicate, excellent wines with a rich bouquet.

The best white wines are made from the Chenin Blanc, Rousselou and Mauzac. They are fine, dry, very pleasant wines which are enjoyed by both locals and

tourists, as are those of the neighbouring Entraygues. Both are classified VDQS★.

Est Est Est   A light, semi-dry, white Italian wine produced around the villages of Montefiascone and Bolsena, north of Rome. It is made from the Moscatello grape (or Moscato di Canelli) which is also used for Asti Spumante★ and the Italian vermouths.

The wine's curious name comes from an often recounted story about a wine-loving German bishop en route to Rome who sent his servant ahead to taste the various wines along the way. He was instructed to write the Latin word Est (is) on the wall of each inn whose wine was particularly good. After trying the wine at Montefiascone, the servant was not content to write Est but scribbled Est! Est!! Est!!! The poor bishop arrived and soon died of intoxication. The story is related on his tomb, which has been piously preserved.

Etna   The wines of Etna are the best table wines of Sicily. The vines grow on the slopes of the volcano and produce good quality red and white wines. The wines from the villages located at high altitudes like Nicolosi, Trecastagni and Zafferana are full-bodied and have a certain *racé*★.

Etoile (L')   This commune of the Jura★ which has a communal appellation contrôlée is the domain of white wine, with no red or rosé produced. The dry white wines have the characteristics of those of the region, but also possess a special delicacy which ranks with the best. The sparkling wines are fine and elegant, and the town also produces a small amount of vin jaune★ and vin de paille★.

évent   The French word meaning flat. A wine exposed to air takes on a different taste, and saying that a wine is flat is far from being a compliment. Such a wine is also described as mealy. A flat taste is acquired at the moment of bottling when the wine is unfortunately exposed to the air. The wine is then said to suffer from bottle-sickness as it appears rough, unbalanced and has a mealy taste which only disappears after a long, quiet rest during which the wine is sealed from the air.

F

Fagon Although he was Louis XIV's doctor it is not for this function that Fagon is renowned, but for his peremptory condemnation of Champagne. He did, however, recommend Burgundy, the wine of kings, to his patients.

Falerne The most famous wine of ancient Rome. Celebrated by Pliny and Horace, it was reputed to be immortal, preserving its splendour for more than a century and not revealing its inimitable, marvellous bouquet until after ten years. Its reputation continued for centuries and the best compliment that could be made to a wine was to compare it to Falerne.

Falerne is produced today on mountainous slopes north of Naples. Its red wine is a solid one and the agreeable white is dry, pale and fruity.

fat A wine containing a lot of glycerine★, an element which contributes to the wine's mellowness and smoothness. Certain wines, especially those made from grapes attacked by pourriture noble★, contain a large amount of glycerine. A fat wine appears oily and smooth and leaves traces (and is said to cry) on the glass.

fatigué (tired) Most wines are not very resilient and need time to recover after each step in the vinification process, e.g. after filtering and bottling, but a robust wine springs back quickly after each of these changes.

Faugères The red wines of this appellation are grouped under the Coteaux-du-Languedoc★ classified VDQS★. They are made north of Béziers not far from Saint-Chinian★. The excellent, full-bodied red wines are made principally from the Carignan, Grenache and Cinsault, while the white wines are made from the Clairette.

feeble A wine which lacks colour and alcohol. These anaemic wines are produced in bad years and, although they are often acceptable, they lack any real distinction.

feminine Feminine wines are full of grace, charm and elegance, such as Musigny. They are the opposite of virile★ wines.

Fendant The Swiss name of the Chasselas★ grape which, except for Pouilly-sur-Loire★, does not produce any remarkable wines. In the canton of Valais, very agreeable, clear, fresh, often fine and delicate wines are made from this grape. The wine is bottled early, before the end of the winter following the harvest, and preserves a light, pleasant sparkle because of the carbon dioxide which has dissolved in the young wine. It resembles Crépy★, which is also made from the Chasselas.

Fer A grape variety grown in the Aquitaine Basin from Landes to the Haut-Garonne. Its name is derived from the hardness of the wood. It is also called Fer Servadou, and Pinenc in the Basses-Pyrénées (where it produces Madiran★ and Tursan★), and blends well with the Tannat and Cabernet Franc. It is the characteristic red of Aveyron, where it is called Mansois, and makes Estaing★, Entraygues and Marcillac★.

If they are well vinified, the wines of this grape are excellent with an agreeable bouquet which hints of the countryside.

ferme A ferme wine is one which is full-bodied and vigorous, has a high tannin content and improves with age.

fermentation (alcoholic) The process by which grape juice becomes wine by the transformation of the sugar content of the must into alcohol and carbon dioxide by yeast. This was explained chemically by Gay-Lussac as $C_6H_{12}O_6 = 2C_2H_5OH + 2CO_2$ (glucose = ethyl alcohol + carbon dioxide).

Other elements are produced during the course of fermentation including glycerine★, volatile acids, succinic acid, esters and bouquet.

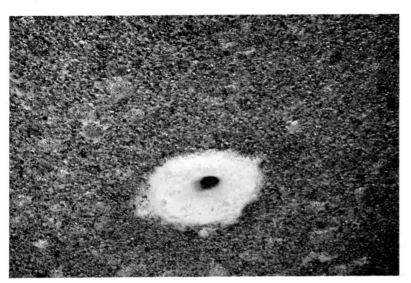

Must fermenting. Phot. M.

In 1857, Pasteur discovered that fermentation was caused by living organisms, the yeasts. Until that time people thought fermentation was a spontaneous action and classified it as a work of God. Since Pasteur's time, modern techniques have evolved and fermentation is not left to chance, but is carefully controlled. Constant surveillance is kept on the temperature of the must and the cellar.

Certain yeasts are selected and sulphur dioxide★ is used for sterilisation purposes. The fermentation of most wines lasts until almost all the sugar in the must has been used up. Fermentation stops when the wine reaches 14 or 15° alcohol. It can be halted by the addition of a foreign alcohol (mutage★) or by sterilisation with sulphur dioxide (used in the production of vins blancs liquoreux★).

fermentation (malo-lactic) This phenomenon sometimes takes place immediately after alcoholic fermentation★ but normally occurs in the spring 'when the sap is rising'. Under the action of certain bacteria the malic acid, which is normally present in the wine, is transformed into lactic acid and carbon dioxide. The wine then becomes slightly effervescent and disturbed. Lactic acid is much less acidic than malic, and the result is a deacidification of the wine as the percentage of malic acid is reduced.

When closely regulated, this process is very useful in the case of green★ and certain Swiss and Alsatian wines which contain too much malic acid.

The wines are best when bottled just after this secondary fermentation has take place, as they conserve a light sparkle due to the carbon dioxide. This is the case with Gaillac perlant★, Crépy★, the wines of Valais and the vinho verde★ of Portugal. Unfortunately this secondary fermentation cannot be regulated as closely as alcoholic fermentation.

When the wine has a normal amount of acidity, the occurrence of secondary fermentation can be a disadvantage. On the other hand, malo-lactic fermentation creates a taste of lactic acid which is slightly perceptible to the palate.

feuillette A measure used at Chablis in the Yonne of 132–136 litres. In Sâone-et-Loire and the Côte-d'Or, it holds 114 litres.

filtration A necessary operation to assure the clarity★ of wine. Unwanted deposits including dead yeast cells are caught in the filters. Filtering purifies the wine and kills certain microbial germs which could cause infection. It is best to carry out filtration at the same time as collage★ as certain protein substances which slip through filtration can show up again in the bottle.

Several kinds of filters are used, including the Chamberland-type candle filter, the hose filter lined with cotton which clears heavily-sedimented wines, and the Seitz filter which works through layers of asbestos.

fine In France the expression fine wine has become a synonym for a wine of appellation d'origine. A fine wine always has an inherent superiority because of its geographical origin, its grape and other factors which have given it remarkable individual characteristics.

Fine is also used in the sense of finesse. Finesse is usually attributed to a wine of class and distinction which has a delicate taste and a subtle aroma. Thus a full-bodied wine which has finesse is a great wine. Without finesse it can only be heavy and common.

Fitou A red AOC★ wine of Languedoc★ produced south of Narbonne by the better communes of Corbières★: Fitou, Caves-de-Treille, Leucate, Paziols, Tuchan, Cascatel and Villeneuve-des-Corbières. Fitou is made from Grenache and Carignan grapes (at least 75%) blended with some of the other classic grapes of the Midi. It is a generous, full-bodied, powerful wine of a beautiful, dark ruby colour which must be left in cask at least eighteen months to two years before bottling. It matures rapidly, casting off its tannic roughness and acquiring its own particular beautiful bouquet. It is really remarkable after five or six years.

Fixin This northernmost village of the Côte de Nuits produces vins fins de la Côte de Nuits★ as well as several great red wines, which are similar to those of Gevrey-Chambertin. The appellation Fixin can be followed by the term Premier Cru or the name of the following climats: les Hervelets, la Perrière, Clos du Chapitre and les Arvelets.

fleshy A fleshy wine has a lot of substance and firmness and imparts a full sensation to the palate. Such a wine always has a marvellous equilibrium between the alcohol, dry extract and glycerine content.

Fleurie The light and fragrant Fleurie evokes thoughts of flowers in spring. It is a very fruity Beaujolais★ which should be drunk chilled and young in order to appreciate its aroma and the taste of fresh grapes. In certain years Fleurie ages beautifully like Morgon★.

flor (vins de) A name applied to a certain group of very good wines whose fineness is due to special yeasts which form a thin veil (or flor) on the surface of the

Filtration: top, alluvial filter; below, plaque filter. Phot. M.

Fixin, a Burgundy vineyard near Gevrey-Chambertin. Phot. Giraudon.

Foulage in the Upper Douro (Portugal). The cuves are made of granite.
Phot. J.-Y. Loirat.

cask. The wine remains for six years or more under the veil without the cask being topped up. During this time it acquires an extremely original suave and powerful bouquet. The process is used in Spain to make sherry, and in France for the vins jaunes★ of the Jura area.

fondu Term for a balanced wine whose elements are all blended into a harmonious whole.

foulage (pressing) One of the first operations performed on the newly-harvested grapes when they arrive in the chai★ or cuvage★. Pressing or treading the grapes was practised even in ancient days by the Greeks, Egyptians, Hebrews, Romans and Gauls. During the pressing, care must be taken not to damage the stones or stalks as they are rich in tannin and oils necessary for the finesse of the wine. For this reason treading by feet is still practised for certain wines like port because it is gentler and more controlled than the mechanical pressers. The mechanical *fouloir-égrappoir* presses the grapes and removes the stalks at the same time.

White wines are always pressed in order to speed up the flow of the juice. It is not performed in Beaujolais where a tender and slightly tannic wine is desired.

foxy A word used to describe the smell and taste of wines made from hybrid vines, especially American ones. American rootstocks were imported into Europe as replacements after the phylloxera★ disaster, and some of these plants have a naturally 'gamey' smell or flavour in the grape, juice or wine. To the great relief of all vinegrowers, however, these characteristics disappeared when European vines were grafted on to them.

The taste can also be imparted to wine by certain diseases. Champagne which is past its prime can also be foxy.

Franconia A German viticultural area located in the Main Valley around Würzburg. The best vineyards, located around the communes of Würzburg, Escherndorf, Iphofen, Randersacker and Rödelsee, belong to the German Government, five or six noble families and charitable organisations. As in the Baden area, several viticultural co-operatives have made great progress.

The wines of Franconia are dry, powerful, full-bodied and sometimes have a *goût de terroir*★ aftertaste. They are made from the Riesling, Sylvaner (which often makes the best wines of the area) and the Müller-Thurgau, a kind of hybrid of the Sylvaner and Riesling which makes common wines.

Würzburg produces, under the name of Steinwein, one of the best wines of the region from the Riesling or Sylvaner grown on steep slopes on the banks of the Main. Good Stein wines are dry, full-bodied, balanced and very agreeable. Franconian wines are traditionally sold in special bottles called Bocksbeutel, on which the name of the grape, the commune and vineyard are indicated.

Frangy The delicious Roussette de Frangy is a white wine of Savoie★ which must by law be made, like all Roussettes, from the Roussette grape (also called Altesse), the Petite-Sainte-Marie and the Mondeuse Blanche, with a maximum of 10% Marsanne. The Roussette grape is mainly grown at Seyssel★, and some at Marestel, Monterminod and Monthoux. Very little real Roussette, certified VDQS★ on the label, is produced in Savoie except at Seyssel. The Roussette de Frangy is a fresh, fragrant, smooth, agreeable wine whose only rival is the neighbouring Seyssel.

frank A frank wine is a pure, plain, well-balanced one which has a perfect aroma and taste. Such a wine is also said to be clean tasting.

Frascati One of the best-known white wines of Castelli Romani★, produced around the little town of Frascati, southeast of Rome. This golden-coloured, dry, full-bodied wine has an alcohol level of about 12° and makes an agreeable table wine which is particularly favoured by the Romans.

Freisa A red Italian wine produced in the mountainous area of Piemonte, east of Turin, from the grape of the same name. Freisa can appear in two guises – it can be a fruity red, often a little acidic and fresh when young, which rapidly takes on a remarkable bouquet and is best at around three years, or a fragrant, fruity, sparkling semi-dry, which is mostly favoured by Italians. As a result it is rarely exported in this form. The Freisa of Chieri is especially renowned.

fresh A fresh wine imparts a lively sensation to the palate. It is generally a young wine or has the attributes of one – fruitiness, vivacity, simplicity and an agreeable acidity. Fresh wines should be served chilled to reveal their best qualities.

Fronsac On the right bank of the Dordogne near Libourne, the vineyard of Fronsac, which includes several neighbouring communes, dominates the hills with its magnificent panorama.

Fronsac is famous throughout northern Europe for Charlemagne's château, as well as for its colourful, robust wines. The Duke of Richelieu, grand nephew of the celebrated minister of Louis XIII, later to be the Duke of Fronsac, was influential in making the wine popular at the French court.

The appellation Fronsac does not legally exist. Two appellation contrôlées belong to two distinct areas: Côtes de Canon-Fronsac★ and Côtes de Fronsac★.

Frontignan A Languedoc★ village well known for its incomparable Muscat★. The rocky hills are planted with the golden, small grape Muscat, also called Muscat doré de Frontignan. The famous Frontignan has been celebrated by Rabelais, Olivier de Serres and Voltaire. Like all vins

Frontignan. Phot. M.

doux naturels, Frontignan is muted with alcohol, a process which is especially good for the Muscat as it preserves its delicate and unique fruitiness.

Frontignan is a very generous wine having at least 15° alcohol. Its beautiful golden topaz colour, its suave aroma, its flavour which blends the taste of grapes and honey, make it a wine of great class and real distinction.

Fronton A VDQS★ wine of the Sud-Ouest★ and named after a small vineyard located north of Toulouse around the town of Fronton. Like its neighbour Villaudric★, Fronton was badly affected by the frost of 1956. The communes producing the wine are found in the departments of Haute-Garonne, (Castelnau-d'Estrefonds, Fronton, Vacquiers and

Saint-Rustice) and Tarn-et-Garonne (Nohic, Argueil and Campsas).

The strongly-coloured red wines are made from Négrette grapes blended with the Gamay, Cabernet, Fer, Syrah and Malbec varieties. The small quantity of white wines are made from Mauzac, Chalosse and Sémillon grapes.

frost (black)   The frost that occurs in the middle of winter. Despite the precaution taken to cover the vines with earth, the frost is sometimes so intense that the buds frost over causing the vines to split. This occurred in Bordeaux in February 1956 and was a terrible disaster in Saint-Emilion and Pomerol. The extreme cold ($-25°C$), arriving unexpectedly after a period of mild days, destroyed thousands of feet of vines.

frost (white)   One of the nightmares of the vigneron as many of the world's good wines are made at the northernmost limit of the vine. Theoretically the danger of frost lasts for around six weeks in France and Germany, from 1st April to 15th May. However, there have been memorable

Warding off the frost: oil heaters. Phot. M.

exceptions. The vineyards of Pouilly-sur-Loire★ were ravaged on 28th May, 1961 and the vines of Chablis★ have been frosted in June. Only 3 or 4 degrees during these critical weeks is sufficient to partially or totally destroy a year's work and endanger future harvests.

The most threatened vineyards have taken precautions. Chablis, the vineyards of the Loire and the Moselle are equipped with oil heaters. The vineyards at the foot of the slopes are more exposed than those on the hills, but also produce less fine wines. The vignerons are slowly abandoning these spots, realising that in the end quality counts most.

fruity   A fruity wine smells and tastes like fresh fruit. The word is also used to describe young wines, whose fruitiness in time will be replaced by bouquet★. Each grape variety has its own particular kind of fruitiness. The best-known fruity wines are Beaujolais, the wines of Alsace, Muscadet, Bourgueil and Chinon and the wines of California made from the Zinfandel grape, and, less pronounced, from the Riesling, Sylvaner and Pinot of California. The word musky★ is used to describe fruity Muscats.

full-bodied   A full-bodied wine is one of good character, rich in alcohol, well coloured and with a pronounced taste. It is also said to have *corps* or body. The term *étoffé* is sometimes used to mean that there is sufficient glycerine★ content.

fumet   The distinctive bouquet peculiar to a wine which has a great deal of personality, such as Châteauneuf-du-Pape★.

furry   A furry wine imparts a unique sensation of velvety smoothness. It is mostly used to describe a fleshy wine with an exceptionally high glycerine content.

G

Gaillac The region of Gaillac, in the Sud-Ouest★ area of France, has been engaged in viticulture since pre-Christian times. In fact it is said that the vine of Gaillac was the likely father of Bordeaux. Gaillac, which is particularly known for its sparkling wine, also produces mildly sparkling wines (perlant★) and still AOC★ wines, some dry and some sweet. They are made from the Mauzac grape (the same variety which gives the Blanquette de Limoux★) and from the grape with the curious name l'En de l'El (far from sight), to which the classic white varieties of the area are added.

The Tarn divides this area, which has a semi-mediterranean climate. The wines from the limestone slopes of the right bank are marrowy and full of bouquet, while those from the granite soil of the left bank are lively, dry and have nerve. This explains the diversity of the white wines of Gaillac, which are all well made.

Gaillac Mousseux is made by the rural method called *gaillacoise*. The sparkle is produced naturally without adding any sugar. Fermentation is slowly halted by successive filtrations. It is then left to mature for two or three years, at which time the wine is marrowy and fruity with a particular, delicate aroma. Wines made by the Champagne method★ have less charm and fruitiness.

The mildly sparkling or perlant wine of Gaillac is made by a completely different method. First, the must is left to ferment at a low temperature until it reaches the state of a dry white wine containing only a small amount of natural sugar. It is then left several months without racking until secondary fermentation begins, at which time it is bottled. The resulting wine is

light, fruity and fresh with a special aroma.

The wines classified as Gaillac and Gaillac Mousseux must have at least 10·5° alcohol, while those called Gaillac-Premières-Côtes must contain a minimum of 11·5°. Attempts have been made for some time to produce quality red and rosé wines at Gaillac, such as those which used to be made at Cunac and Labastide by the process of carbonic maceration★.

Gaillac: the Tarn and the Saint-Michel Abbey, where the monks made the first wine of the cru. Phot. M.

Gamay A white-juiced red grape named after a hamlet near Puligny-Montrachet which is practically the only variety grown in Beaujolais★.

On the granitic slopes of Beaujolais it gives fine, aromatic, young wines which are much in demand today, while on the limestone-clay terrain of the rest of Burgundy it produces only ordinary wines. In 1395 Philip the Bold ordered 'the disloyal plant named Gamay' to be expelled from the kingdom. Happily for us, his subjects did not obey him.

Gamay rouge à jus blanc.
Phot. Larousse.

The Gamay is only planted in very good vineyards in Burgundy, where the Pinot Noir is king. When mixed with one-third Pinot Noir, Gamay produces Bourgogne-passe-tous-grains★. Gamay is also present in the wines of Lyonnais★, Saint-Pourçain★, Auvergne★, Châteaumeillant★ and Giennois★, but none of these wines have the finesse and bouquet of Beaujolais. In California, especially in the Napa★ and San Benito★ counties, it produces very agreeable wines which are sometimes superior to those made from the Pinot

Noir. They are sold under the name Gamay of Beaujolais.

gelée (vin de) Another name for the vin jaune★ of the Jura which, literally translated, means 'wine of the frost'. The Savagnin grapes are left on the vines until the first frost; the grape slowly withers up, concentrating its natural juices (passerillage★).

Gattinara A beautiful, red Italian wine made from the Nebbiolo grape, as are Barolo★ and Barbaresco★. Like these wines it comes from the Piemonte region, but from a different area north of Turin. Gattinara is an excellent wine which can be compared with the best Côtes-du-Rhône. Full-bodied and with a fine bouquet, it has an enveloping taste, and should not be drunk too young as its best qualities develop after some maturing. Unfortunately, production is very limited.

generous A wine such as Chambertin which is rich in alcohol. Such a wine is also said to be warm★ and vigorous and gives a sensation of well-being to the drinker. A generous wine is not, however, a heady one.

In Spain and Portugal, generous wines are usually muted with alcohol.

Georgia The viticultural region of the USSR furnishing the largest number of excellent quality wines and 20% of total production. Georgia has the third largest amount of land devoted to viticulture of the Soviet Republics. At Tchoudari, a vine 0.55 m in diameter with roots running under 2 m of soil covers an area of 80 sq m and each year produces 500 kg of grapes.

Grapes are grown at an altitude of 1000–1340 m which makes up for the unfavourable latitude of the area and accounts for the quality of Georgian wines. Some 400 varieties of grapes are cultivated of which sixteen are eventually made into wine. The vines are trained on horizontal poles, a method called *talavéri*.

Each Georgian province has its traditional viticultural methods. Kakhétie in the oriental part of Georgia is arid and must be irrigated. The vineyards cover about 100 km from Signakhi to Akhméta surrounding the Alazani Valley. Tsinandali and Moukouzani are the most important centres. This region produces notable wines (Kardanakhi, Mtsvane and Teliani), including good white wines (Naparéouli, Gourdjaani no 3, Tsolikaouri no 7 and Rkatsitéli), and excellent reds (Sapéravi, Teliani no 2 and Moukouzani no 4, one of the best of Kakhétie, resembling a Burgundy).

The red and whites of Tsinandali are the most famous Georgian wines. Tsinandali white no 1, for example, is a delicious dry wine.

The Kartélie region of Tbilissi grows the Tchinouri grape from which the white wine Gorouli-Mtsvane is made.

Imérétie (a region of Koutaisi) produces mainly white wines which are named after the grape from which they are made, e.g. Krakhouna, Tsitska and Tsolikaouri. The region also produces the red Khvant-chkara, which was Stalin's favourite.

The western region of Gourie, located near Makharadzé, produces the white Djani and Tchkhavéri wines.

The seaside area of Abkhazie, close to Soukhoumi, mainly grows the Isabelle grape, while in the Valley of Bzyb, the Tsolikaouri of Imérétie is grown as well as the Isabelle.

Georgia also produces a sparkling wine called Soviétskoié.

German method A process of making sparkling wines which is more economical than the traditional Champagne method★ as it eliminates the delicate operations of remuage★ and dégorgement★. However, it differs from the cuve close★ process because the second fermentation takes place in bottle, as in the Champagne method, and not in a hermetically-sealed vat. After the second fermentation has occurred and the sparkle appears, the wine is transferred from bottle and pumped into a cold stainless steel vat where it is stabilised by nitrogen pressure. Then a certain amount of sugar is added (like the dosage of the classic Champagne method) and the wine is then filtered and bottled.

This process is only permitted in France for sparkling wines without controlled place names. The transfer into the vat and the filtering replace the process of dégorgement, but the delicate wine suffers from this treatment. It is far from the skilled and demanding task that the highly-trained *remuers* (men who turn the

bottles in the cellars of Champagne) perform.

Germany Germany's long viticultural tradition dates back to Roman times, when legions visited the Rhine and the Moselle. However, the country as a whole is not really suitable for vine-growing except in the valleys of the Rhine and its tributaries. German vineyards are situated further north than most vine-growing areas, and the vines are planted on hillsides overlooking the rivers so as to have maximum exposure to the sun. Only a few acclimatised varieties of vine are hardy enough to grow at this latitude, mainly Riesling, Sylvaner, Müller-Thurgau and, more rarely, Gewürztraminer, Rülander (Pinot Gris) and a few others. The variety of grape is usually specified on the wine's label. In general, Moselle and Rheingau wines are made from Riesling grapes, while Rheinhessen, Palatinate and Franconian wines are made from the prolific Sylvaner species.

Germany excels in the preparation of white wines, both sweet and dry, and these make up about 80% of her total output, which averages 4 or 5 million hl a year. Although the ordinary wines are unremarkable, the quality wines are outstanding, and have a distinctly original character. Relatively low in alcohol

Vendange in Georgia.
Phot. Lauros-Hétier.

Following two pages: the transport of wine in cask, Chartres Cathedral, north aisle. 16th century.
Phot. Lauros-Giraudon.

(usually between 8° and 11°), they are light, refreshing, fruity and pleasantly tart (though they sometimes show a touch of sweetness). They have great distinction, a delicate aroma, and often a remarkable clarity.

The white wines lend themselves extremely well to the preparation of sparkling wines, and the famous 'Sekt' industry has developed enormously since World War II. It is worth noting that German Sekt is agreeable only if it has been properly made from quality wine and has retained some of its character.

The greatest wines of the Rheingau★

further south on the west bank, near the border of Alsace. Other notable viticultural regions are the area north of the Rheingau between Rüdesheim and Coblenz, the Mittelrhein and the Baden★ vineyards on the outskirts of the Black Forest across the border from Alsace.

Moselle★ wines are produced in the valley of the Moselle River. Although completely different from the wines of the Rhine in character, they equal them in quality.

Distinctive wines are also produced on the banks of other tributaries of the Rhine: the wines of the Nahe★, which joins the

Vineyards growing on terraces along the left bank of the Rhine viewed from Bacharach. Phot. Rapho.

and Rheinhessen★ are made in exceptional years from Riesling grapes grown in favourably positioned vineyards and affected by pourriture noble★. These sweet wines are extremely sought after, and are often sold by auction.

Rhine wines are produced in five regions of the Rhine valley, each having its own individual character. The wines of the Rheingau, on the east bank between Wiesbaden and Rüdesheim, are considered to be the best (one of them is the renowned Johannisberger★). They are helped a good deal by the vineyards' excellent position facing due south towards the Rhine. The Rheinhessen, which lies further south on the west bank, is the original home of Liebfraumilch★. The Palatinate★ lies still

Rhine from the west at Bingen; those of Franconia★, produced in the Main valley; and the wines of the Ahr★, which are red, and thus an exception.

German wines are usually sold in special, long, slim bottles (green for Moselle, yellowish-brown for Rhine wines). Others, such as Würzburger, Franconian Steinwein and Baden Mauerwein, come in squat, flask-shaped bottles with flat sides, called *bocksbeutels*.

The German system of appellations can be quite confusing. For quality wines the system is similar to the French one: they are called by the name of the town or village or origin (e.g. Rüdesheim, Johannisberg). The better wines also add the name of their particular vineyard (e.g.

Johannisberger Klaus, Rüdesheimer Berg Bronnen). There are a few exceptions to this rule, usually very famous wines which are known simply by the name of their vineyard (e.g. Steinberger from the Hattenheim commune, and Schloss Vollrads from the Winkel commune).

German wine labels also contain a certain amount of information which may seem esoteric, but in fact is quite important to the consumer. For example, chaptalisation★ is allowed in Germany, mainly in bad years. (Fine wines, however, are not usually chaptalised.) The words *Natur*, *Rein* and *Naturwein* can only be applied to unchaptalised wines. *Wachstum*, *Creszenz* and *Gewächs* are the equivalents of the French cru★, and are followed by the owner's name. *Cabinet*, or *Kabinett*, can be translated as Special Reserve or Superior Quality, and *Schlossabzug*, *Originalabfüllung* and *Kellerabfüllung* correspond to the

From left to right: multicoloured engraved glass, 16–17th century; engraved glass, Bohemia, 18th century; ceramic flagon, 16th century. Musée des Arts Décoratifs. Phot. Giraudon.

121

French mise en château, i.e. château-bottled or estate-bottled. *Spätlese* means a wine made from 'late-picked' (i.e. over-ripe) grapes, and *Auslese*, one made from grapes affected by pourriture noble. *Spätlese* and *Auslese* wines are excellent sweet wines, and those marked *Beerenauslese* and *Trockenbeerenauslese* are even sweeter and richer. Lastly, the vintage of German wines is very important, as all northern

wonderfully. The climats are: Chambertin, Chambertin-Clos de Bèze, Charmes-Chambertin (or Mazoyères-Chambertin), Chapelle-Chambertin, Griotte-Chambertin, Latricières-Chambertin, Mazis-Chambertin and Ruchotes-Chambertin.

Gewürztraminer Traminer wines which are especially fragrant and heady.

Vineyards on terraces along the Rhine. View taken from the Lorelei rock looking towards Boppard. Phot. Lauros-Candelier.

vineyards are particularly dependent on good weather for the quality of their grape harvest and ultimately, of course, their wine.

Gevrey-Chambertin This Burgundian commune carries the prestigious name of Chambertin which is renowned throughout the world. The wines are an admirable blend of grace and vigour, strength and finesse, with a characteristic liquorice bouquet. The grand crus age

The word *Gewürz* means spicy. These are excellent, original wines, made from the grape of the same name, which also have the same seductive qualities as the Traminer. Their 'nose' and extremely aromatic taste are extraordinarily rich, sometimes even too exuberant. These qualities are even more marked after a late vendange, yet, in Alsace, the Gewürztraminers never attain the elegance of the Rieslings.

Germany and the Tyrol often produce excellent Gewürztraminers as does Cali-

Gustave Lorentz
APPELLATION ALSACE CONTRÔLÉE
Gewurztraminer
RÉSERVE
GUSTAVE LORENTZ, NÉGOCIANT A BERGHEIM (H.-RHIN)

fornia, but the aroma is never as pronounced as in the Alsatian wines.

Giennois (Coteaux du)   Today, the little village of Gien on the Loire★ is more famous for its pottery than its wines, but in former times, right up to the end of the last century, it was an important viticultural commune with more than 800 vignerons. Vines still grow on several hillsides and terraces around Gien, particularly at Bonny-sur-Loire, Beaulieu, Ousson, and Châtillon-sur-Loire.

The reds, rosés and whites, which are all consumed in the area, are VDQS★ but production is limited to 200–300 hl. The light, agreeable white wines made from the Sauvignon are generally the best, while the reds and rosés made from the Gamay are more ordinary.

Gigondas   Although the wine from this charming Provençal village, perched on the north side of Montmirail, does not have its own special appellation contrôlée, the name Gigondas can be added to Côtes du Rhône★ in the same print on the label.

The vineyards are located between Orange and the mountainous region of Ventoux, an area which enjoys a warm, dry climate.

Like all the southern Côtes du Rhône wines, the wines of Gigondas are made from numerous grape varieties. Grenache is the favourite, then Bourboulenc, Clairette, Cinsault, Mourvèdre and Picpoul. The vignerons no longer cultivate the

Carignan, as they wish to achieve a more supple wine.

Gigondas produces red, rosé and white wines. The dry, fruity, original rosé is very agreeable when young, but has a tendency

Gevrey-Chambertin: the vineyard and village.
Phot. Aarons-L.S.P.

123

The fortified village of Gigondas. Phot. M.

From left to right: German coloured glass; French glass; filigreed Dutch glass; Venetian-style glass, Belgium. All 17th century. Musée des Arts Décoratifs, Paris. Phot. Lauros and Lauros-Giraudon.

to maderise★ when it ages. The red is excellent. It is a powerful, full-bodied wine, having finesse, a certain elegance and is a beautiful, purple colour. Although a bit harsh when young, it acquires its true beauty after maturing at least two years.

Givry On the hills of the Côte Chalonnaise★, Givry produces excellent red wines related to Mercureys★. They have the same bouquet and finesse, but are lighter.

Glacier A white Swiss wine produced in the alpine valley of Anniviers in the canton of Valais. The wine receives a rather different treatment, as it is left to age high in the mountains for ten or fifteen years in small larch casks holding 37 litres. Glacier is a very special and, to some, surprising wine which has a certain bitterness when first tasted.

glass The choice of glass is quite important when tasting wine. Every major

viticultural region in France has created its own specially-shaped glass designed to show off its wine to the best advantage, e.g. there are glasses for red and white Burgundy, red and white Bordeaux, Vouvray and Alsatian wine. A glass should be simple and light. Its function is to hold wine rather than to decorate the table, and a lot of carving and ornamentation is merely an obstruction. Its texture should be thin for the same reason. Coloured glass deprives the enthusiast of his first pleasure, which is admiring the wine's colour. However rare and precious such glasses may be, they are never as suitable for a great wine as clear, shining crystal.

A glass should be of such a size that it need not be filled to the top, thus enabling one to release the wine's full bouquet, without fear of spilling, by a gentle circular movement of the hand. The shape is equally important. It should narrow slightly towards the rim in order to concentrate the bouquet, which a wide-topped glass would allow to escape. The traditional Champagne glasses are far from ideal as their width allows all the bubbles to escape, together with the Champagne's fine and subtle aroma, and would make even the greatest wine dull and flat. The most suitable glasses for Champagne are either fluted or tulip-shaped.

The stem of the glass, too, is important. It should be neither too thick nor too thin. Round ones are best to hold and they also make it easier to turn the glass and appreciate the wine's bouquet.

glycerine An element of wine responsible for smoothness and mellowness. Glycerine materialises during alcoholic fermentation★ and normally is present in wine at the level of 6–8 g per litre. Wines which undergo a slow fermentation have a higher level of glycerine.

The vins blancs liquoreux★ contain up to 20 g per litre but, in this case, the glycerine is not caused solely by alcoholic fermentation. *Botrytis cinerea*, the cause of pourriture noble★, has already produced some in the grapes. Must from grapes strongly affected by pourriture noble contains as much glycerine as 12 g per litre before alcoholic fermentation.

gouleyant A term which can be abused in oenophilic circles, probably because it

sounds pleasing to the ear and esoteric to the uneducated. It simply means a fresh, light wine which glides easily and agreeably down the throat.

gourmet In wine parlance this refers to one who knows wines and how to taste them. The derivation of the word is found in the expression courtier gourmet – piqueur de vins★.

goutte When making white wines, moût de goutte is the juice which flows naturally from the grape after crushing and before pressing. In red wines the vin de goutte is the wine which runs from the cuves when fermentation has halted. This first juice accounts for about 85% of the volume. The rest is comprised of marc, which is returned to the press for the extraction of the vin de presse★.

grafting A method of vine propagation which has been used mainly since phylloxera★. It consists of attaching a graft (the shoot depending on the desired variety) on to a stock of American origin (Riparia, Rupestris, Vialla or Berlandieri) which is resistant to phylloxera. The most widely used is the English stock, as the American vines often make a disagreeable foxy★ tasting wine.

When grafting was first tried in France, there were many who feared that the marriage of the vines would weaken the traditional wines. The French oenologists

Grafting. Phot. M.

125

and vignerons have succeeded in classifying and selecting the stocks according to their aptitudes and preferences (precocity, affinity with the scion, exposition, soil, climate, etc.). But before grafting became a science there were many failures and some vineyards did not become revitalised until after forty years.

Certain famous vineyards resisted the practice of grafting for a long time. The prestigious vineyard of Romanée-Conti, for example, injected carbon sulphide into the soil until the Second World War but had to begin grafting during the Occupation when sulphur was not available.

Grafting does not affect the quality of a wine. Its influence is on the vigour of the vine, giving it more or less strength, and retarding or hastening the maturing of the grapes. Grafting has resulted in higher costs and modification of the method of vine cultivation.

grafting (English) A widely practised method in which the graft and stock are sectioned at complimentary angles by a special grafting machine so that they fit perfectly together in a V shape.

graisse A disease which attacks badly constituted or cared for white wines, which are poor in alcohol and tannin. The wine becomes oily and turgid, takes on a strange tint and tastes flat and faded. The treatment consists of trying to kill the bacteria by cleansing the wine with sulphur dioxide★ and to restore its clarity by energetic collage★ with tannisage★.

Grand-Roussillon This appellation contrôlée of Roussillon★ embraces all the vins doux naturels★ contained in the Grand-Roussillon region: Côtes d'Agly, Côtes-de-Haut-Roussillon, Maury and Rivesaltes.

Graves The vineyards of Graves are reputedly the cradle of Bordeaux★ wine. The wines of Graves, which have enjoyed an excellent reputation for hundreds of years, have always been called 'the wines of Bordeaux'.

The Graves region stretches the length of the left bank of the Garonne, between the river to the east and the forest of Landes to the west. It begins in the north at the Jalle de Blanquefort, the Médoc border,

and descends south to Langon, having twined around Sauternes. The average width of the vineyard is only twelve km and the length, sixty km. The name of the region comes from the terrain, called *grave*, which is a mixture of siliceous gravel, sand and a little clay.

Graves differs from other Bordeaux vineyards in that it produces both red and white wines (dry and sweet). The vineyards are customarily divided into two parts: red Graves in the north, and white in the south, but the separation is not really that clear-cut. The northern section also produces excellent quality white wines and the southern part, some reds. It is the nature of the soil that determines the grape grown. The pure *grave* is more favourable for red grapes, and *grave* mixed with other components is preferred for white vines.

Red Graves somewhat resembles the neighbouring Médoc. Both are made from the same grapes: Cabernet Franc, Cabernet-Sauvignon, Merlot and a small amount of Petit Verdot and Malbec. The extremely fragrant red Graves are elegant wines which keep well. They have more body and nerve than the Médocs, but do not possess their sweet fragrance and delicate mellowness. Pessac and Léogran (which also produce excellent white Graves) are the two main centres of production. But, unlike those of the Médoc, the communes of Graves do not have any particular appellation. Château-Haut-Brion, classified Premier Grand Cru in 1855, is the most glorious. Other crus also have a very good reputation, including Châteaux Pape-Clément, La Mission Haute-Brion and Haut-Bailly.

White Graves is grown mostly in the southern area, and is made from the same varieties as the neighbouring Sauternes: Sémillon, Sauvignon and Muscadelle. It is represented by a unique range of wines from dry to sweet (they become sweeter towards the south near Sauternes). The wines have *race*★ and are fine and fragrant, without being acidic like certain dry wines. In good years they age gracefully and, very rarely, maderize. Like the reds, the white Graves do not have a communal appellation. There are many good crus among them, including Château Carbonnieux, Domaine de Chevalier and Château Olivier. (See Index.)

GRAVES, APPELLATION GRAVES This regional appellation is applied to good quality red wines of the Graves area having an alcohol minimum of 10°.

GRAVES SUPÉRIEURS Applies to white wines (never red) which have a minimum alcohol content of 12°. The wines are generally sold with the name of the vineyard and the guarantee of authenticity *mise en bouteilles au château* indicated on the label. The appellation is often absent on the labels of certain well-known crus.

gress has been made since this revival and there are now more than 120 vineyards covering between 500 and 600 acres; the majority are in the south of England, though other areas include Lincolnshire, Norfolk and South Wales. Production is now approaching more than 170,000 bottles a year.

Most British wine is white, an exception being Beaulieu Abbey rosé, grown from Müller-Thurgau and Seyval B, grape varieties which resist disease, ripen early and suit Britain's damp climate. Quality is

Composed of a unique mixture of flinty pebbles, sand and a little clay, the 'graves' soil produces wines of longstanding repute. Phot. M.

GRAVES DE VAYRES An area of Bordeaux which is geographically part of Entre-deux-Mers★ occupying the left bank of the Dordogne, south-west of Libourne. It comprises the gravel-soiled areas of Vayres and Arveyres.

The white wines are fine and mellow with their own personal *sève*★. The supple, agreeable reds resemble the second crus of Pomerol.

Great Britain Viticulture in Britain is not an entirely new industry. There were extensive vineyards, in fact, attached to monasteries in the early Middle Ages and were it not for England's later trade ties with France, this level of wine production may have continued. However, it was not until 1952 that vines were commercially grown again on British soil. Much pro-

improving year by year though the British wine industry is presently handicapped by high excise duty and EEC restrictions covering the planting of new vines, introduced in response to overproduction in other European countries. It may therefore be a number of years before British wines make any impact on the European market.

Greece The ancient Greeks were great wine-lovers, praising it in their literature, religion and art. Ancient Greece is considered the mother of viticulture. The Greeks were the first to prune the vine and to observe that rough soil, which was unsuitable for growing other crops, paradoxically gave the best wines. When establishing a colony the first thing the Greeks planted was the vine.

127

Greece: high vines in Crete.
Phot. Loirat–Rapho.

Greece: vineyards at Corinth.
Phot. J. Bottin.

Little remains of this expertise today. Although vineyards are found in every part of Greece, a good part of the harvest is exported as fresh grapes or dried raisins (the celebrated Corinth grape). Around 5 million hl of wine is produced annually, mainly from the regions of Attica, the Peloponnese, Crete, Thrace, Corfu and the Aegean islands. Vineyards occupy 50% of the surface of the thin strip of land stretching along the Peloponnese coast.

The resin which is added to the famous white or red vin ordinaire Retsina gives the wine an aftertaste of burnt wood and turpentine. To the unaccustomed, it is sometimes considered undrinkable. Most of Greek wine is resinated as it helps to conserve it in the hot climate.

There are non-resinated wines made in the Peloponnese (around Achaia and Messini), Arcadia (around Tegee) and on the islands of Cephalonia, Santorin, Samos, Corfu and Zante. The unfavourable latitude and hot climate produce heavy wines, high in alcohol and full-bodied, which lack finesse, particularly the white wines.

The dessert wines, however, are often remarkable. The best known is the Muscat of Samos, a dry white wine which is very alcoholic (18°). Mavrodaphne, produced in several regions from the grape of the same name, is generally very good, especially that made near Patras.

green Wine made from unripe grapes tends to be over-acid, and is called 'green'. When the acidity is not obtrusive it can be pleasant, especially as it mellows to an agreeable freshness as the wine matures. Very young, immature wines often have a touch of greenness, even when made from sound grapes.

Grignolino An excellent Italian red wine, made from the grape variety of the same name in the Piemonte north of the village of Asti★ in the mountainous region of Monferrato. Produced in only small quantity, the Grignolino has its own very special taste and inimitable bouquet. Although it gives an impression of lightness it usually contains 13 or 14° alcohol.

gris (vin) Although not legally classified, this is a very light rosé made by treating a red harvest like a white one. The process is used in Burgundy and the Loire (rosés of Saumur★ and Cabernet★) and in the east of France (Côtes de Toul★).

Until the eighteenth century, vignerons only made this kind of wine, as they lacked other means. On their arrival in the cuvage★, the grapes are immediately crushed and pressed, but less quickly than the whites.

Gros-Plant du Pays Nantais A very dry white VDQS★ wine which used to be kept for family and local consumption, but which during the past twenty years has been more widely known and drunk. The Gros-Plant (or Folle-Blanche) is made from a grape of the same name which has been in the region perhaps even longer than the Muscadet★.

The grape undoubtedly comes from the Charente where it used to be made into Cognac. However, because it is so susceptible to rot it is seldom grown any more in its area of origin.

In the Atlantic area of the Loire, the grape is grown in certain selected areas principally on siliceous soil around Lake Grandlieu (Saint-Philbert, Bouaye, Legé and Machecoul). It is also found around Loroux-Bottereau, Liré, Champtoceaux and in the Retz area where Muscadet is also cultivated.

The Gros-Plant is a light, fresh, almost colourless wine, usually containing about 9–11° alcohol. It can be kept but is best drunk young. It is always a bit green★ and never has quite the finesse of a Muscadet.

Vines of the Nantes area.
Phot. M.

H

hail One of the natural catastrophes which can harm the vineyard. If a hailstorm does not entirely destroy the vineyard, it still affects the quality of wine which is made from the damaged grapes. In a humid year mildew can more easily enter grapes whose skin has been broken by hail. In a dry year, on the other hand, the grapes become shrivelled and parched and the wine (especially the red) takes on what is called a 'taste of hail', a dry taste which is easily recognised.

Hailstones not only cut grapes and leaves, but often ruin the vines themselves. The vigneron must then prune the vine, a step which may have repercussions on the quality of the following year's wine. At-

tempts are made to fight off this calamity by shooting silver iodide into the air to prevent the formation of hailstones.

hard A term describing a wine which has an excess amount of acid or tannin. When the acid is not balanced by a high enough level of alcohol, which is often the case with young wines, it can be very disagreeable.

harsh A harsh wine is both astringent★ and rough on the tongue, and can even set one's teeth slightly on edge. These characteristics are caused by an excess of tannin, which is due either to a coarse variety of grape being used to make the wine or to bad vinification (cuvé★ wine). This tannin eventually precipitates, and the wine improves a little with age.

Other words used by connoisseurs to describe wines that contain excessive tannin are 'angular' and, when it impairs the delicacy of the wine's texture, 'thick'.

Haut-Brion (Château-) One of the four greatest red wines of Bordeaux and the only Graves officially classified in 1855 with the three greats of Médoc★ (Lafite★, Latour★ and Margaux★). Haut-Brion is a generous, powerful wine, but is also fine and elegant and has a very particular smoky taste. In good years it makes a wine which ages admirably. There is also a small quantity of white Château-Haut-Brion made, which is extremely full-bodied and powerful.

Haut-Comtat A vineyard of the left bank of the Rhône Valley which grows on six communes of the Drôme, around the little town of Nyons known for its olive

Grapes damaged by hail.
Phot. M.

130

trees and lavender. The vines, protected from cold winds by the mountains, grow on arid soil amongst the fragrant plants. The Grenache is the dominant vine (at least 50%) flanked by its habitual companions in the Midi: Carignan, Mourvèdre, Cinsault and Syrah. The VDQS★ reds and rosés are very fruity and agreeable, possessing a special aromatic bouquet.

Haut-Dahra The name given to the formerly VDQS★ wines of Algeria produced in the department of Algiers, west of Algiers between the coast and the Chelif river.

The vines are cultivated on a variety of terrains, the average at an altitude of 600 m. These highly-coloured red wines are powerful, fleshy and marrowy and have an alcohol content of at least 12°.

headache The true oenophile never has a headache from overdrinking, for as Brillat-Savarin aptly said, 'Those who stuff themselves or become inebriated do not know how to eat or drink'.

However, some suffer headaches after drinking certain white wines because of their sulphur dioxide★ content. The excess sulphur combines with the blood to cause this discomfort. About 10% of consumers are especially susceptible to sulphur, experiencing a headache and upset stomach even when the sulphur level is not extraordinary. Others who may experience headaches from rich red or white wines should stick to lighter ones.

heady A heady wine is one with a relatively high alcohol content, which makes it 'go to one's head'. The alcohol is sometimes masked by a high sugar content which may make the wine seem like a vin doux naturel★.

heavy The opposite of a harmonious, balanced wine. It is a wine which lacks finesse and has too much alcohol and tannin. The aroma and bouquet are thus completely hidden. Such a wine (and many of the vins ordinaires fall into this category) weighs heavily on the palate and stomach.

Hermitage or **Ermitage** The name given to the well-known red and white wines of the Côtes du Rhône★ which are

Tain-l'Hermitage and its terraced vineyards.
Phot. Pavlovsky-Rapho.

produced from vineyards growing on terraces in Tain-l'Hermitage. The name comes from a hermitage built in the reign of Blanche of Castille by the chevalier Gaspard de Stérimberg. Red Hermitage, made from the Syrah, is a generous, powerful wine which in its youth has the characteristic bitterness of wines made from this variety.

Rich purple in colour, it has a penetrating bouquet and its warm flavour lingers for a long time in the mouth. Red Hermitage takes several years to attain the height of its power and perfection. White Hermitage, made from Roussane and Marsanne grapes, is a full-bodied, fine wine of a beautiful gold colour which has a very characteristic aroma.

The region also produces a small quantity of the delicious, golden vin de paille★ which contains 15° alcohol and is made from grapes which are dried for at least two months on a bed of straw.

Hippocrates Was the most famous doctor of all time and the acknowledged father of medicine. Oenophiles remember him as the wise doctor who said, 'Wine is the best thing for man, whether he be healthy or sick, if taken in moderation'.

Vendange in Hungary in the Eger region. Phot. Charmet.

Grape-harvest celebrations at Kelebia, Hungary. Phot. Charmet.

honour (wine of) A custom which is without doubt as old as wine itself. Wine offerings were presented by the ancients each time they wanted to honour someone, and the practice is still carried on today though on a less grandiose scale. Dating from the Middle Ages, bishops who owned vineyards would offer their best wines each time they received a distinguished visitor or the king himself. In those days of limited communication, the practice helped to disseminate the wine and spread the reputation of a particular vineyard. It was often after being appreciated as a 'wine of honour' that a cru was regularly served on the royal table.

In humbler homes the best wine was always reserved to honour any important visitor. Today in the country the best wine, colloquially called *derrière les fagots*, is kept for the visitor one wants to cordially welcome.

Hungary This country traditionally had the largest viticultural area in Eastern Europe and produced excellent wines.

Viticulture has flourished in Hungary for a long time, becoming more advanced in the seventeenth century when colonies from Belgium and France were established. Although production has been surpassed by that of the USSR and Romania, the Hungarian vineyards have been in the process of expansion since 1959.

There are a number of viticultural areas. The mountainous region is found in the north, starting at Gyöngyös, north of Budapest, around the villages of Abasár, Visorita, Varkaz, Domoszló and Verpelét. Gyöngyös makes a white wine from the Chasselas grape, which is sweet like honey. At Gyöngyöstarjan there is a cave which was constructed in 1740 by French prisoners of war. Even in wartime, Hungary kept up its vineyards.

North-east of Gyöngyös is the important viticultural zone of Eger, known for its Bikavér★ and Egri Kádárka (two full-bodied reds which keep well) and also for the white wine Egri Leányka, and a Muscat★. This mountainous region ends near the Soviet frontier in the most famous vineyard, Tokaji-Hegyalia (see Tokay).

The vineyards of the great central plain, stretching between the Danube and Tisza, are centred around Kecskemèt which produces a good white wine, the Kecskemèti Leányka. The vines grow on sand-dunes and sandy soil and the region produces some 200,000–300,000 hl of wine, but it is best known for its *eaux-de-vie*.

The hilly area or Badacsony★, west of Lake Balaton, produces remarkable wines which have been famous for centuries.

A fourth area called the region of Szekszárd, located sixty km north-east of Pécs, is known for its Fleuré de Decs (produced in a little village of the same name), its Riesling of Szekszárd and its red wine of Kádárka.

Hungarian wines generally bear the name of the town or region of origin usually ending in 'i', e.g. Badacsonyi, Egri, Szekszárdi and Gyöngyösi. The grape name is sometimes added. For the red wines, these are the Vöros and Kádárka, and for the white (in order of quality) Furmint, Hárslevelü, Rizling (Riesling), Veltelini, Kéknyelü, Muskotály, Ezerjó and Leányka.

hybrid Viticulturally speaking, a hybrid is the result of crossing two varieties of grapes. Botanically speaking, hybridisation is a relatively new phenomenon, having been practised for only about 200 years. By selective breeding, it enables one to combine some qualities and to lose others; it also results in more vigorous and robust offspring. As far as the vine is concerned, hybridisation was first used in France after the phylloxera★ attack as a means of warding off the insect. Laliman of Beaune replanted his vineyards with American vines which are resistant to phylloxera (Noah, Clinton, Elvira, Othello, etc.). However, as the wines were not appreciated, the next step was to cross the American vines with French ones by grafting. Thus a robust hybrid which could withstand phylloxera was created.

In France, hybrids bear the name of their 'inventor' plus a serial number (Seibel 5279, Couderc 4401, etc.). In other countries the hybrids are often called by the name of their parents whose characteristics they claim to possess, or by a name resembling that of a noble★ parent. This creates a regrettable confusion, such as with Emerald Riesling and Ruby Cabernet in the United States, and, in Germany, Goldriesling, Mainriesling and Müller-Thurgau (sometimes presented under the name of 'Riesling und Sylvaner' or 'Reisling-Sylvaner' although it has not been proven that Müller-Thurgau is the result of the crossing of Riesling and Sylvaner).

In France, hybrid production is dying out, as the wines made from them are common and not much liked by wine-drinkers in other EEC countries. Moreover, the use of chromatography soon reveals wines made from hybrids. As a result, the vignerons are replacing more and more of their hybrids with the indigenous vine species.

Hypocras A drink, generally wine-based, which was in great vogue from the Middle Ages up to the time of Louis XIV. Hypocras was a mixture of white or red wine (or beer or cider in the homes of poorer folk), spices (cinnamon, cloves, nutmeg, etc.) and sugar. The famous Taillevent, Charles VII's master chef, left the recipe for posterity.

The nobles always preferred Hypocras

Popular Hungarian vessels: top, Transylvanian wine jugs (mid 19th century); centre, ceramic liqueur gourds (late 19th century); bottom, carved wooden gourd (late 19th century). Various colls. Phot. Charmet.

to wine and liked it enriched with raspberries and costly ingredients like amber. The mixture was clarified in a special filter and kept in air-tight containers.

I

Institut National des Appellations d'Origine (INAO) A unique institution which was created by the law of 30th July, 1935. Although it receives its power from the State, the INAO is a private organisation which brings together government officials (Agriculture, Justice and Repression of Frauds) with specialists in the wine field (*viticulteurs*, *négociants*). Its objective is to improve the quality of French wines and *eaux-de-vie*, and its primary task is to define the requirements which wines must meet to obtain an appellation d'origine contrôlée★ classification. Each step is defined, from the grape variety to the methods of vinification.

The INAO oversees and controls pro-

Irancy, Burgundy.
Phot. Beaujard-Lauros.

duction at every step; it educates, encourages and protects the consumer as well as the producer and subjects vignerons to a very strict discipline. Abroad, the INAO works to protect the French appellations, such as the case of the 'Spanish Champagne' in London where the INAO fought to safeguard the appellation 'Champagne'. After battling for three years it was victorious.

Iran Persia was one of the first countries to cultivate the vine in order to make wine. Even after the Moslem conquest, wine-making still flourished as is attested by Omar Khayyám's praise for the wines of his country.

The Syrah grape, from which Côte-du-Rhône wines are made, was, according to legend, brought to Europe from Persia during the Crusades.

Today the vine is mainly cultivated at the foot of the mountains, in the centre, the south-east and in the north around Alborz. Production is mainly in the form of table grapes which are locally consumed or exported as dried raisins. Only a very small amount of wine is made (around 3600 hl a year).

Irancy A small town south-west of Chablis★ whose vineyard, lying on well-exposed hills, used to be very famous. The wine was exported as early as the twelfth century and today the reds and rosés of Irancy are still excellent, especially the cru Palotte. However, only small sections of the old vineyard remain and production is greatly limited. Even the best restaurants of the region can not get enough to satisfy their clientele.

The wine of Irancy, like the other reds and rosés of Burgundy, is made primarily from the Pinot Noir. In fact the other regional varieties, the César and Tressot, are slowly disappearing.

In good years the red wine is excellent. It is a full-bodied, very fine wine of a beautiful purple colour and its own particular taste. It ages well and gradually unfolds its beautiful bouquet.

Unfortunately, the Pinot does not always mature perfectly in this northern part of Burgundy. Thus it is better in poor years to drink Irancy vinified into rosé, which is fresh and fruity and has an agreeable *goût de terroir*. Irancy has the right

to the regional appellation Burgundy to which it can add the name of the commune.

Irouléguy A VDQS★ wine and typical of the produce of the Basque country. It is produced by a very small vineyard in the Nive Valley located west of Saint-Jean-Pied-de-Port and stretches over seven communes, the principal ones being Saint-Etienne-de-Baigorry and Irouléguy. The vines perch on hills from 100–400 m high not far from the Spanish frontier. The small vineyard, which totals only about 40 ha, does not produce more than 1500 litres

a year of red and rosé wines, which are vinified at the co-operative cave of Irouléguy. The beautifully coloured red is warm and fruity and, like the other reds of Béarn, is made principally from the Tannat, with the addition of some Bouchy and Fer★.

Israel Israeli viticulture has only existed since the State was formed in 1949. From 1955 to 1961, wine production tripled (to 2,700,000 hl). However, the roots of viticulture in the area can be traced back to biblical times. It was revived around 1890

Vendange at Irouléguy.
Phot. Yan-Rapho.

after the Moslem occupation thanks to the efforts of Baron Edmond de Rothschild who began a viticultural experiment at Rishon-le-Zion, south-east of Tel Aviv.

Today, the two principal vineyards are Rishon-le-Zion and Zichron Jacob, south-east of Haifa. Vineyards have recently been planted further south in the regions of Lachish, Ascalon and Beersheba.

The grape varieties are those which adapt to the warm, dry climate of Israel. For the reds these are principally the Alicante, the Grenache, Carignan and Alicante Bouschet, and for the whites, the Clairette, the Muscat of Alexandria and the Frontignan. There is also some Cabernet-Sauvignon, Sémillon, Malbec and Ugni Blanc.

Israel has qualified technicians as well as twenty modern vinicultural installations, mainly co-operatives. The wines are well made and reasonably priced, good but never extraordinary. Most of the production is consumed locally, only about 6% being exported. Great Britain and the United States are the principal importers of Israeli wines.

The co-operative of Carmel Zion has an English branch called the Carmel Wine Company, which was founded in 1897. It also has an American branch, the Carmel Wine Co. Inc., New York.

Italy This has been a wine-producing country from time immemorial, and today accounts for about 20% of world production, rivalling France in actual volume produced. Every region of Italy produces wine, and from the Alps to Sicily there is a remarkable variety of climates, soil and grape varieties and vinicultural traditions. Many of these are ordinary wines without appellation, but are better than certain vins de consommation courante made in the French Midi. If, in recent years, the Italian vines have descended the hills to invade the plains, great progress has been made in vinicultural methods, particularly by the co-operatives. The result is a better balance in quality, and hybrids are now almost non-existent. The taste of the consumer is also changing, as in France, towards lighter, less alcoholic wines favouring rosés or semi-sparkling varieties.

Since the decree of 12th July, 1962 an appellation system inspired by the French classification has been organised for fine wines; the divisions are: *denominazione semplice, denominazione di origine controllata* (DOC), and *denominazione controllata e garantita* (the best wines). These appellations are placed under strict government control and the wines must adhere to stringent regulations regarding area of production, grape variety, production per hectare and alcoholic minimum.

Although the vine is cultivated all over Italy, certain regions are notable. In order of volume of production, they are the

Italy: one of the most famous crus of the 'country of wine', Aleatico is a dessert wine produced on Elba. A view of the island's main town, Portoferraio. Coloured engraving. Bibl. Nat. Phot. B.N.

136

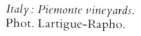

Italy: Piemonte vineyards.
Phot. Lartigue-Rapho.

region of Pouilles, at the heel of the Italian boot, which produces very colourful and alcoholic common wines and some dessert wines, the Piemonte, second in production, but first in quality and famous for its Asti Spumanti★ and Barolo★, Sicily which, besides ordinary wines, produces dessert wines like the Marsala★, Tuscany, the source of Chianti★, Venetia, whose best wines are produced around Verona, and Campanie, producer of the famous Falerne★ and Lacrima Christi★.

Italian wines generally take the name of the town or province of origin or the name of the grape (with some exceptions like Est Est Est★ and Chiaretto★). The principal reds are: Barolo, Gattinara★, Barbaresco★ (made from the excellent Nebbiolo grape), Barbera★, Freisa★ and Grignolino★, all from the Piemonte; the Valtellina★ of Lombardy; Bardolino★ and Valpolicella★ of Verona; Santa Maddalena★, Lago di Caldaro★, Santa Giustina★ of the Italian Tyrol; the Lambrusco of Bologna; Chianti of Tuscany; and Gragnano of Naples.

The white wines are dry or semi-dry. Because of the latitude they are generally heavy except those of the Italian Tyrol in the north. Among the whites are the Cortese★ of Piemonte, the Lugana★ of Lake Garda, the Soave★ of Verona, the Terlano★ and Traminer of the Tyrol, the Orvieto★ and Est Est Est produced north of Rome, the Castelli Romani★, Capri★ and Lacrima Christi around Naples, and the Etna of Sicily.

The rosés are presented by the Chiaretto of Lake Garda and the Lagrein rosato★ of the Tyrol.

Marsala is the most famous dessert wine, but the Aleatico★ of the Isle of Elba is also excellent as is the Vino Santo★, produced mainly in Tuscany, as well as some in Trentin. There are in addition about six good Muscats. Asti Spumante, the king of the sparkling wines, is made by the Champagne method★ from Pinot Blanc or Gris.

The Italians attach little importance to vintage. The differences in quality from one year to the next are less marked than in French wines. Moreover, with the exception of about twelve, Italian wines do not improve after three years. Only wines made from the Nebbiolo (Barolo, Barbaresco, Gattinara, Ghemme, Valtellina) benefit from ageing. It is the same case with good Chiantis.

J K

Japan The vine has been cultivated in Japan since the twelfth century, but viticulture did not assume any importance until the nineteenth century. Grape juice was used solely as an ingredient in medicines until the arrival of the Europeans and Americans. Despite research trips to France and California, the Japanese vineyards are far from achieving any real economic importance.

All the vineyards are located on the island of Hondo, mainly around Yamanashi, Osaka, Yamagata and Nagano. The humid climate is not favourable to the vine and the grapes must mature quickly because of the torrential rains in September. European, American and Asiatic vines (like the Japanese Koshu) are used. Unfortunately, the European varieties are vulnerable to cryptogamic diseases (mildew and oidium) because of the humid climate. The vines are never of great quality, except perhaps for those from the Sadoya vineyard in the Yamanashi region whose very agreeable wines are made from European varieties.

Jasnières A white wine of the Coteaux du Loir★ produced on the communes of Lhomme and Ruillé-sur-Loir. Made from the Pineau de la Loire, it is generally a dry wine which fills out in warm years and when aged. Jasnières is golden yellow in colour and is marrowy and delicate with a very fruity fragrance.

jaune (vin) This wine of the Jura★ and the glory of Château-Chalon★ is made from the Savagnin, a variety peculiar to the region. The vendange occurs late so that the grapes will be completely mature and the juice concentrated. As this is often after the first snows it is also called *vin de gelée*.

The special method of vinifying vin jaune may seem to defy all oenological rules. After the alcoholic fermentation, a year after the harvest, the wine is drawn off into thick oaken casks where it remains for six years without being topped up. During this ageing period, fixed by law, it acquires the inimitable *goût de jaune*. The wine is covered with a thick veil, formed by special yeasts peculiar to the Jura. In other places, a wine left under such conditions would turn to vinegar, but in this region it is transformed into a marvellous wine of a golden yellow colour, which has a curious nut-like bouquet. A similar process is used in southern Spain for sherry, Manzanilla and Montilla.

The vins jaunes are quite rare and

Vin jaune is a speciality of the Jura. A view of an Arbois vineyard. Phot. Cuisset.

consequently expensive. As they must be aged six years before bottling a lot of capital is tied up. Moreover, the wine is sometimes inexplicably invaded by harmful bacteria. Finally, since the contents of the cask are subject to evaporation, the volume is diminished.

Vin jaune should never be served at the beginning of a meal. It is so powerful, full-bodied and penetrating that it would detract from the aroma and taste of any other wine following it.

Johannisberg   A famous German vineyard of the Rheingau★, which is located on one of the hilliest areas overlooking the Rhine. Production is insignificant in proportion to the world fame of Johannisberg, which has been considered for some time as a synonym for racé★ and refined elegance. The wine is all that, and as an assurance the name of the vineyard and the producer are specified on the label beside the word Johannisberg (the word *Dorf* next to Johannisberg signifies nothing more than 'village' in German).

The famous vineyards are Klaus, Vogelsang, Kläuserpfad, Kläuserberg and Hölle. The most famous is Schloss Johannisberg which was, according to legend, planted on orders from Charlemagne. The Austrian Emperor gave the vineyard to Metternich after the Congress of Vienna. The wines of Schloss Johannisberg are sold under two labels: the best known carries the coat of arms of the Metternich family; the other, a coloured picture of the château and vineyard. Different coloured capsules on the bottles distinguish the different wines: a red capsule for dry, less expensive wines; a green capsule for wines made from overripe grapes; a rose capsule for rare and costly wines only produced in certain years from grapes attacked by pourriture noble★. Some experts feel that the wines of Schloss Johannisberg are not living up to their reputation and that certain other Rheingau wines are better.

Juliénas   Documents reveal that Juliénas was making wine before the rest of Beaujolais was even planted. Juliénas is fresh and fruity and has a darker robe and more body than its neighbour Saint-Amour. It should be drunk young like most of the Beaujolais, although certain years profit from ageing.

Jullien   The author of *la Topographie de tous les vignobles connus*, written in 1816 and updated in 1822 and 1832. In this work Jullien gives a complete classification of all the existing crus so that the evolution of the French vineyards can be traced to the present day.

Jullien relied heavily on the topographical position of the vineyards as a basis for classification, e.g. 'dry wines are generally made from vineyards located above 47° of latitude', 'vins de liqueur are ordinarily made from vineyards situated below 39° of latitude and they contain a higher concentration of sugar the closer they are to the equator'.

The vineyard of Johannisberg and its château. Phot. Lauros-Atlas-Photo.

A Beaujolais village. Phot. L.S.P.-Aarons.

Jurançon vineyard. Phot. M.

Jura Within the limits of this department, from Port-Lesney to Saint-Amour, is found the viticultural region of the ancient province of Franche-Comté. The vineyard covers two well-positioned hills bordering the plain of Bresse on a line parallel with the Côte d'Or with the centre at Arbois. Although only eighty km long and six km wide, there is much originality and wine to satisfy every taste: red, white, rosé, sparkling wines, vin jaune★ and vin de paille★. Charles Quint, Francis I, Henry IV and Pasteur were among its admirers.

The vineyard is situated at an average altitude of 300 m on limestone and clay soil, and planted in three noble★ grape varieties peculiar to the Jura region: Trousseau and Poulsard for the red, and Savagnin or Naturé (called Traminer in Alsace) for the white and vin jaune. The Pinot Noir for red wine and Chardonnay for white are also cultivated.

The Jura has four appellations contrôlées: Côtes du Jura★ (whites, reds, rosés, vins de paille, vins mousseux), Arbois★ (whites, reds, rosés, vins jaunes, vins de paille, vins mousseux), L'Etoile (whites, vins jaunes, vins de paille, vins mousseux), and Château-Chalon★ (vins jaunes).

Jurançon Certainly the most illustrious of the appellations contrôlées of the Sud-Ouest★. The king of Navarre is said to have moistened the lips of his son, the future Henry IV, with the wine of Jurançon, and it was in demand throughout all of northern Europe until the French Revolution, thanks to the Dutch traders.

The Jurançon, pearl of Béarn, is produced south and west of Pau. The vineyards are dotted over the hills facing the south and south-east and are difficult to reach. The soil, whether it be sand, gravel, limestone or clay, is planted in grapes peculiar to the area: Petit-Manseng, Gros-Manseng and Courbu.

The vendange is performed late so that the grapes will be passerillaged★, and production is not more than 25 hl per hectare.

Jurançon is an extraordinary wine, without rival. It is a golden coloured, marrowy nectar that has a generous *sève*★, strong aroma and a light, spicy taste of cinnamon and clove. It gives the strange impression of hiding a certain acidity under the softness of its sugar. Jurançon is a wine which conserves and travels well. Sometimes very ripe, but not passerillaged, grapes are harvested and made into dry, nervy, fresh, fruity wines which are generally drunk in the year following the vendange. There is also a small amount of red Jurançon which is locally consumed. It is as old as the white, as is attested by documents reporting a gift made by Jeanne d'Albret in 1564 of 'a vine of Jurançon red and white'.

Knipperlé A small-grape variety grown in Alsace★ which every year is losing ground to the noble★ varieties. It attracts the pourriture easily and produces good quality wines which are fruity and supple.

Knipperlé is also cultivated in Germany and Switzerland under the name of *Räuschling*, but it is consumed locally in all areas of production.

FESTE BACCHIQUE.

'The Feast of Bacchus' after Watteau. Print. Phot. Lauros-Giraudon.

141

L

The vines of Lacrima Christi and Vesuvius. Phot. Gauroy-Atlas-Photo.

The vines of Lacrima Christi and Vesuvius. Phot. Gauroy-Atlas-Photo.

Lacrima Christi A famous white Italian wine produced from vineyards growing on the volcanic slopes of Mount Vesuvius (a little red is also made). Its bouquet and taste as well as its pale golden colour somewhat resemble Graves. This wine, whose name means 'tears of Christ', is extremely rare and today there are hardly any vines on the slopes of Vesuvius. In 1816, Julien stated that very little was produced, and that the wine was reserved for the table of the king of Naples.

Lafite-Rothschild (Château) A premier grand cru classé of the Médoc★ which since the seventeenth century has been extraordinarily famous. Its old proprietor, M. de Ségur, was nicknamed the Prince of Vines. It was bought in 1858 for 5 million francs by Baron James de Rothschild and the nobility of the vines has never slackened. Many wine-lovers think that Château-Lafite is the best of all red wines, or at least the masterpiece of the Haut-Médoc.

It is a perfect wine. Bright, velvety and generous, it has a delicate, suave taste and an exquisite finesse. It can be kept for a long time and still has all its qualities after forty years in bottle, and sometimes even after a century. Only the best cuvées are called Château-Lafite, the rest, although still of quality, are sold under the name Carruades-de-Château-Lafite-Rothschild.

Lago di Caldara An excellent red wine produced from vines growing on hills west and north of the small lake of the same name, which is located not far from Bolzano in the Italian Tyrol. Made from the Schiava Gentile, it is a light, lively, charming wine and is one of the best of the region.

Lagrein rosato A delicious, fresh and vivacious rosé, made around Bolzano in

the Italian Tyrol from the local Lagrein, and which should be drunk young. It was called Lagreiner Kaetzer before the First World War when the region was part of Austria.

Lalande-de-Pomerol A vineyard growing north of Pomerol★ on gravelly and sandy soil which produces wines with the appellation contrôlée Lalande-de-Pomerol. The wines are generous and nervy like Pomerol, but have less finesse. The better crus, which can be compared with the second crus of Pomerol, include Château de Bel-Air (not to be confused with Château Belair, the premier grand cru of St. Emilion), Châteaux Grand-Ormeau, Commanderie, les Cluzelles and Perron.

Languedoc An ancient French province which extends from the Rhône delta to Narbonne and includes the coastal border of the departments of Gard, Hérault and the Aude. The last two departments are, by volume, the most important producers in France – most of the production consisting of vins de consommation courante★, which are often called 'wines of the Midi★'. But, besides these vins ordinaires, the region also produces AOC wines: Fitou★, Blanquette de Limoux★, Clairette du Languedoc★ and the suave Muscats★ of Frontignan★, Lunel★, Mireval★ and Saint-Jean-de-Minervois★. There are also VDQS wines: Corbières★, Corbières supérieurs★, Minervois★, Picpoul-de-Pinet★ and Coteaux-du-Languedoc★. This last appellation includes thirteen others.

Languedoc (Coteaux-du-) Under this VDQS appellation are grouped thirteen red and rosé wines coming from the hills of the Aude and Hérault departments (the whites do not merit the appellation) which are sold under the name Coteaux-du-Languedoc followed by their proper name, or solely by their proper name.

The majority of wines are made from Carignan, Cinsault and Grenache grapes and they must have a minimum alcohol content of 11°. They include the following appellations: Cabrières★, Coteaux-de-Vérargues, Faugères★, Coteaux-de-la-Méjanelle, Montpeyroux★, Pic-Saint-Loup, Saint-Chinian★, Saint-Christol,

Château Lafite-Rothschild. Phot. M.

Languedoc: the vineyards of Aigues-Mortes. Phot. M.

Languedoc: vineyards south of Sète. Phot. Lauros-Beaujard.

Château Latour. Phot. M.

Saint-Drézéry, Saint-Saint-Georges-d'Orques and Saint-Saturnin in the Hérault, and la Clape★ and Quatourze★ in the Aude.

These are excellent quality wines which have been famous since ancient times. Saint-Saturnin is well known for its light and agreeable *'vin d'une nuit'*. Saint-Christol, Saint-Drézéry, the Coteaux de Vérargues and Méjanelle mainly produce rosés. The first three appellations, along with Saint-Georges, were reputedly the best of the region in the last century.

Latour (Château) This premier grand cru classé of Pauillac★ is, with its rivals Château-Lafite-Rothschild★ and Châteaux-Margaux★, one of the three greats of the Médoc★. The dry, pebbly soil of the vineyard, planted in the noble★ varieties of Bordeaux, gives a small production but marvellous quality.

Château-Latour is always a robust, complete wine even in mediocre years, and reveals an exceptional richness in good years. It is a highly-coloured, full-bodied, astringent wine in its youth which, like all great wines, has a subtle taste of resin. On ageing it acquires a splendid bouquet and can be kept for a long time, easily for half a century.

Anyone who has drunk Château-Latour once in his life will not mistake it for another. Although there are a number of crus in France, and especially in Bordeaux, whose name includes 'Tour' or 'La Tour', the label of Château-Latour is unique, being inscribed with the picture of a lion standing atop a tower.

Laudun The vineyard of this village of the Côtes du Rhône★, found on the right bank of the Rhône, north of Tavel★ and Lirac★, produces very good, elegant, fruity reds and rosés, resembling Tavels and Liracs, and whites of excellent quality.

Laudun does not have a proper appellation contrôlée but its name can be added, in the same characters, to Côtes du Rhône on the label.

Lavilledieu A VDQS of the Sud-Ouest★ which scarcely exists any more as the winter of 1956 badly damaged the vineyards. The production area is located between Moissac and Montauban in the triangle formed by the Tarn and Garonne, and comprises the communes of Lavilledieu, Montech and Castelsarrasin.

Layon (Coteaux du) The vineyards of this Anjou★ appellation cover the hills bordering the little river of Layon, which flows into the Loire at Chalonnes. Only the area along the lower course of the Layon from Chavagnes and Thouarcé on the right bank, and from Rablay on the left, produce white wines which can claim the appellation.

Coteaux du Layon is the top producer in both quality and quantity in the Anjou area and is well known outside the region. The Pineau de la Loire matures until October and is often attacked by the pourriture noble★. The wines range from dry to sweet, depending on the year and the grape, but are generally sweet. Tender and smooth, very fine and fragrant, they are usually a beautiful golden colour and are harmonious and full-bodied. They can approach the level of Sauternes, Barsac and the sweet German Rhine wines, while still preserving the fruitiness of the Loire wines.

The best communes are Beaulieu, Faye, Rablay, Rochefort, Saint-Aubin-de-Luigné, Quarts-de-Chaume★ and Bonnezeaux★. The famous crus of the Coteaux du Layon have a distinct appellation of origin.

Most of the production of Layon comprises white wines sold under the appellation Anjou, and also excellent rosés having the appellation Rosé d'Anjou★, as well as Cabernet d'Anjou.

lees Yellowish sediment deposited in the bottom of casks which is separated from the wine during racking. The lees consists of yeast cells and impurities from the wine, and smells like baker's yeast.

Young wines in barrels often have a pronounced taste of lees which disappears after racking. Such a taste is not necessarily a fault, in fact admirers of Muscadet and Swiss wines consider it a virtue.

lees (bottling on) Bottling on lees is a technique used for white wines such as Muscadet which are meant to be drunk young. It is practised to help the wines conserve their freshness and fruitiness. Such wines release a small amount of carbon dioxide which makes the tongue tingle agreeably. Normally, wine is bottled when it is clear, after a series of rackings to separate the wine from its lees or sediments. When the wine is bottled on its lees the yeasts use oxygen from the wine, thus protecting the wine from oxidation and consequent yellowing and ageing.

On the other hand, wine bottled on healthy yeasts is prone to a secondary malo-lactic fermentation★ accompanied by a release of carbon dioxide, part of which dissolves in the wine.

Wine which is bottled early and in cold

weather shows the same qualities; carbon dioxide is very soluble in cold wine and part of it remains in solution. Such wines are like those bottled after malo-lactic fermentation has finished. The Crépy★ of Savoie, Gaillac perlé★ and certain Alsatian wines, as well as the Swiss wines of Valais and Vaud (where the process is called the 'Neuchâtel method'), are made this way.

Bottling on lees is only carried out in good years because the secondary fermentation is always a dubious process, and the wine may be changed, attacked by diseases or developing a bad taste.

lees (wine) A sediment resembling fine sand which is especially visible in white wines and, although displeasing, should not be considered a fault. It is caused by crystals of potassium bitartrate (a compound of tartaric acid, one of the organic acids found in grapes) which precipitates when the wine is cold. The deposit usually appears in casks in winter, but sometimes a part of the potassium bitartrate content does not dissolve. The wine is then saturated with the compound which eventually deposits itself in the bottle; this precipitation improves the wine because it loses some of its acidity due to its tartaric acid content.

Liebfraumilch A German word meaning 'Our Lady's milk' and one of the best-known German wine appellations. It was originally applied to mediocre wine produced by the vineyard of Liebfrauenstift, near the Gothic cathedral in the town of Worms, in the Rhinehessen★. However, the word has now become a synonym for Rhine wine. It is no longer an appellation of origin and is not applied to wines of just one quality. Normally it is the mediocre, cheap wines of the Rhinehessen, sometimes

CHATEAU DU BREUIL

BEAULIEU
1966

APPELLATION CONTRÔLÉE
COTEAUX DU LAYON   NICOLAS CHARENTON VAL-DE-MARNE

with those of the Palatinate★, which are sold under this name.

However, there are some quality wines sold as Liebfraumilch, but the name of the seller is the only way of distinguishing these.

Leichtenstein Two-thirds of the small amount of wine produced by this tiny, independent principality, situated between Switzerland and Austria, is called Vaduzer (after the capital, Vaduz). Vaduzer is a light red wine which is so clear that it almost appears to be a rosé. It is made exclusively from the Blauburgunder grape. The best cru is Abtwingert, a vineyard of the Rote Haus. The principality also produces other wines, including Schaaner, Triesner and Balzner.

light When applied to wine, this term is the opposite of full-bodied and heavy and is therefore a compliment. A light wine usually contains little alcohol, which makes it easy to drink.

liqueur (vin de) Wine which has kept a large amount of its natural sugar thanks to mutage★ by alcohol. Port is one of the best-known wines in this category, but certain Madeiras★ made from the Malvoisie grape are also vins de liqueur.

In France, the title has a very precise meaning. It is only applied to those wines muted with alcohol and whose alcoholic content is not greater than 23°. All the vins doux naturels★ fall into this category: Banyuls, Côtes-d'Agly and Frontignan, for example. However, for tax purposes, vins de liqueur are classified as spirits, while vins doux naturels are not.

The mutage is performed before or during fermentation, the proportion of added alcohol depending on the appellation. The degree of alcohol must be mentioned on the label, although this is not the case with vins doux naturels.

liqueur d'expédition A mixture of old wine and cane sugar which is added to Champagne★ immediately after dégorgement★. The liqueur fills the empty space left by the expulsion of sediment which had amassed next to the cork. The amount of liqueur d'expédition injected depends upon the desired taste: brut, extra dry, sec, demi-sec or doux. Some-times, certain brands of Champagne use Cognac.

This dosage is called liqueur d'expédition because it is one of the last steps performed before Champagne leaves the premises (actually, the bottles remain for a few weeks before being shipped).

liqueur de tirage Provokes the sparkle in Champagne★, and vins mousseux★ made by the Champagne method★. First, the amount of natural sugar in the still wine is measured; then a certain amount of cane sugar dissolved in old wine, the liqueur de tirage, is added. A good sparkle is expected when the wine contains around 25 g of sugar per litre. If the wine does not contain enough sugar there will not be enough bubbles; if it contains too much, the pressure will burst the bottle.

Formerly, the exact quantity of the liqueur to be added was not known and in some years there was a great loss due to broken bottles. An ordinary bottle will not support an internal pressure five to six times atmospheric pressure, which is that of sparkling wines. Thus, special bottles of a certain thickness are necessary. These are carefully filled with the wine mixed with the liqueur de tirage. They are then corked with a provisional cork and wire, and laid down to rest for some time.

Lirac The vineyard of this village of the Côtes du Rhône★ occupies dry, flinty hills north of its neighbour Tavel★. The appellation Lirac is applied to excellent, vigorous, fragrant rosés, which are not quite as good as the Tavel wines. Lirac is made from the same varieties as Tavel, as well as the Syrah, Mourvèdre and Ugni Blanc, and is vinified with the same care, whether it be at Château de Segries, Château de Clary or a co-operative.

Lirac also produces powerful and generous red wines having a pronounced bouquet from the same varieties as the rosés, and fine, fragrant white wines from the Clairette.

Listrac A commune of the Haut-Médoc★ producing red wines which, without being highly classified, are nevertheless very good wines of a pretty ruby colour, full of body and nerve and possessing a certain finesse and agreeable bouquet.

Listrac has several good crus bourgeois supérieurs (Châteaux Fonréaud, Fourcas-Dupré, Lestage, Sémeillan, Clarke) and several good crus bourgeois. The co-operative cave at Listrac vinifies a wine comparble to the crus bourgeois supér-ieurs.

lively A lively wine proclaims its viv-acity and bursts with health. Young and clear, it stimulates the palate because of its agreeable, but never overbearing, acidity.

Loir (Coteaux du) This vineyard oc-cupies well-exposed hills bordering the Loir north of Tours in the departments of Sarthe and Indre-et-Loire. Although lo-cated on the boundary between Touraine, Anjou and Maine, it is actually a Touraine★ vineyard with which it shares the same soil, climate and grapes.

The vineyard used to be more famous than it is today. Ronsard and Rabelais sang of the vineyard of La Chartre and Henri IV praised the wines of the area.

The white wines made from the Pineau de la Loire are the best known. They are a beautiful golden colour, fine and fruity, often lightly sparkling and keep well – somewhat resembling the Vouvrays. They

have an alcohol content around 10°, and are mainly produced by the communes of Château-du-Loir, Saint-Paterne, Chah-aignes, Bueil and Vouvray-sur-Loir. The red wines are colourful, generous and fragrant. Saint-Aubin, Chenu, Nogent and Saint-Pierre-de-Chevillé all produce good reds.

The region also produces rosé wines and some twenty communes produce wines of the famous cru Jasnières★.

Loire The longest river in France can boast many well-known châteaux as well as magnificent wines. The wines of the Loire are produced from more than 200,000 ha of vineyards. Vineyards flourish on both banks from its source to the Atlantic, growing on various soils, experiencing different weather and planted in many grape varieties.

The appellations d'origine contrôlées★ include those of Nivernais and Berry★, Sauvignon★, Pouilly-sur-Loire★, Sancerre★, Menetou-Salon★, Quincy★ and Reuilly★; those of Touraine★: Vouvray★, Montlouis★, Chinon★ and Bourgueil★; those of Anjou: Saumur★, Coteaux-de-la-Loire★, Coteaux-du-Layon★ and Coteaux-de-l'Aubance★; and, finally, in

Following two pages: Velasquez, 'Wine Drinkers or the Triumph of Bacchus', detail. Prado Museum, Madrid. Phot. Giraudon.

Luynes, Indre-et-Loire. The château in autumn. Phot. Phédon-Salou.

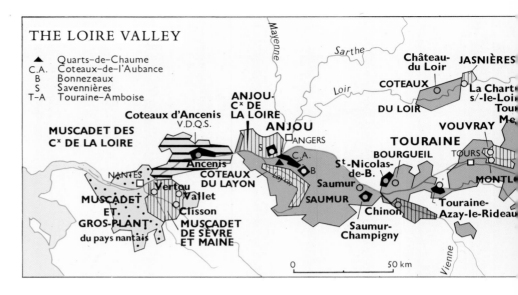

THE LOIRE VALLEY

▲ Quarts-de-Chaume
C.A. Coteaux-de-l'Aubance
B Bonnezeaux
S Savennières
T-A Touraine-Amboise

the area of Nantes, the mischievous Muscadet★.

There are numerous VDQS★ wines from the Auvergne to Nantes: vins d'Auvergne★, Saint-Pourçain★, Château-meillant★, Coteaux-du-Giennois★, vins de l'Orléanais★, Montprés-Chambord-Cour-Cheverny, Coteaux-d'Ancenis★ and Gros Plant du pays nantais★.

Loire (Coteaux de la) The appellation contrôlée Anjou-Coteaux de la Loire is reserved for those communes located on the banks of the Loire★ around Angers:

Saint-Barthélemy, Brain-sur-l'Authion, Bourchemaine, Savennières★, La Possonnière, Saint-Georges, Champtocé and Ingrandes on the right bank; Montjean, La Pommeraye and a part of Chalonnes on the left bank. The vines grow on rocky hills next to the river and get plenty of exposure.

The white wines, made from the Pineau de la Loire, are not as sweet as those of Layon★. Fine and nervy, they are dry or semi-sweet and are always elegant wines with a fruity bouquet. The minimum alcohol content is 12°.

Ars-sur-Moselle. 'Vins de Moselle' is one of the two appellations reserved for the wines of Lorraine. Phot. M.

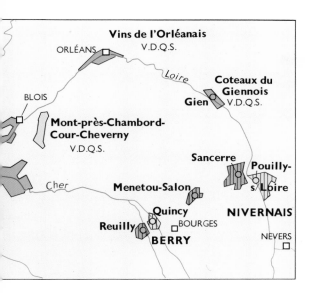

The village of Savennières has its own particular appellation contrôlée. The region also produces reds and rosés from the Cabernet which carry the appellation Anjou★.

The expression Coteaux de la Loire is also part of one of the three appellations contrôlées of the Nantes area, Muscadet des Coteaux de la Loire★.

Lorraine The wines of Lorraine, like those of Alsace, were at one time in great vogue. From the sixth to eighth centuries, the wines were in great demand and several of the large religious orders of Belgium and Luxembourg owned vineyards in the area. Later, the grapes were sold for making Champagne.

Today the vineyards possess only a shadow of their former glory. Wars, phylloxera★, disinterest by the youth in viticulture, and the replacement between 1904 and 1911 of most of the vineyards by orchards, have all taken their toll.

Although the vineyards only occupy about one-tenth of their area a century ago, some very good VDQS★ wines are produced. Two appellations designate the wines of Lorraine: Vins de la Moselle★ (Moselle) and Côtes-de-Toul★ (Meurthe-et-Moselle).

louche A louche wine is dull and feeble. This disorder may be caused by an incomplete alcoholic or malo-lactic fermentation or the onset of a microbial disease such as casse.

Loupiac This commune is situated on the right bank of the Garonne facing Barsac★. Although it is geographically part of the Premières Côtes de Bordeaux★, it forms a distinct region which has its own appellation.

Loupiac is a Sauternes-type wine made in the same way. Its qualities are similar to the neighbouring Sainte-Croix-du-Mont★. Full-bodied, fragrant and fine, Loupiac is an excellent, sweet white wine. The principal crus are those of the Châteaux of Ricaud, Gros, Loupiac-Gaudiet and Rondillon.

A tastevin is used to verify whether or not a wine is louche. Phot. M.

loyal A loyal wine is honest, sincere, and is also said to be frank. From a commercial point of view the expression designates a wine which can be delivered for sale without worrying about it undergoing any change. The complete expression is 'vin loyal et marchand' (a loyal and saleable wine).

Lunel A village between Nîmes and Montpellier in the Languedoc★ which produces an excellent AOC Muscat★. The production area includes the flinty terrains of Lunel, Lunel-Viel and Vérargues.

Like Frontignan★, the wine is made from the Muscat Doré and is a vin doux naturel of high quality, which is delicate and elegant. Although not as sweet as Frontignan, it has the same musky smell and taste of the grape.

Lussac-Saint-Emilion This vineyard of the Lussac commune, which can add Saint-Emilion to its proper name, is found almost entirely on well-exposed hills. The wine is highly coloured and full-bodied and the good crus also have finesse. The principal Châteaux are those of Lyonnat, Bellevue, Vieux-Chênes and Lion-Perruchon.

Lussac also produces white wine sold under the name Bordeaux or Bordeaux supérieur★.

Lugana A very pleasant dry white wine produced on the south bank of Lake Garda in northern Italy around the little village of Lugana. It is normally the best white in the region of the lake and is made from the Trebbiano, known in France as the Ugni Blanc (which is made into the white wine of Cassis). In Italy, the Trebbiano is also one of the two principal varieties from which Soave★ is made, and it also produces the white Chiantis★.

Lugana is a beautiful, pale golden coloured wine which is full-bodied and harmonious.

Luxembourg After leaving France and giving its name to certain wines of Lorraine★, the Moselle penetrates the Grand Duchy of Luxembourg before going on to Germany.

The wines of Luxembourg should not be ignored. Formerly part of the German Confederation, Luxembourg became independent in 1866 when Grand Duke Adolph of Nassau ascended the throne. Since then, Luxembourg has made great efforts to improve the quality of her wines. Viticulture is flourishing and production is

152

growing. Some 70% of the wine is consumed locally and the rest is bought by the Belgians.

Since 1935, the State has upheld a national standard, with every step in the vinicultural process subject to rigid standards and surveillance. The small neck label, the emblem of quality, is only awarded after severe controls.

As in Alsace, the wines of Luxembourg, which are nearly all white, are designated by the name of the grape from which they are made. They are light, clear wines which are low in alcohol and should be drunk chilled. Among them are Elbling, a popular, dry, refreshing vin de consommation courante; the light Riesling-Sylvaner which is mellower than Elbling and has a special fragrance; the supple, tender Auxerrois whose taste varies greatly from one year to the next, but unfortunately does not have any aroma; the slightly acidic, very fresh and fruity Pinot Blanc; the fragrant Ruländer (Pinot Gris) which is especially full-bodied in sunny years; the full-bodied, fragrant Traminer which has a touch of sweetness; and finally the fresh, distinguished Riesling which keeps well and has a discreet bouquet similar to that of German Moselle.

The most famous communes are Wormeldingen, Remich, Wintringen, Ehnen, Grevenmacher and Wasserbillig.

Lyons The third largest French city and a gastronomic capital which opens onto Beaujolais★ and the Côtes du Rhône★. From its founding as the Roman city Lugdunum in 43 BC until the advent of the railway, the town was known for its wine. It is often said that Lyons is watered not by two rivers, but by three: the Rhône, the Saône and the Beaujolais.

Lyonnais The Lyonnais region produces wines not unlike those of the neighbouring Beaujolais★. They share a similar geographical area, climate and grape variety – the white-juiced Gamay Noir.

There are three appellations among these VDQS★ wines: Vins du Lyonnais in

the Rhône department, Vins de Renaison-Côte Roannaise★ and Côtes-du-Forez★ in the department of the Loire.

The red wines under the appellation Vins du Lyonnais are fresh, fruity and light, but do not quite equal those of Beaujolais. The rosés are agreeable. The appellation also includes those whites made from the Chardonnay and Aligoté.

'*The Vendage'. Apocalypse of Lorvão (1189), Torre do Tombo, Lisbon.* Phot. Y. Loirat.

M

The château of Conches in the Mâconnais. Phot. René-Jacques.

Macadam The name under which the sweet white wines of Bergerac★ used to be sold. A good deal of the wine was sold in Paris and other large cities as vin bourru★.

Mâcon and Mâcon supérieur An appellation designating red, rosé and white wines. The white wines, made from the Chardonnay and Pinot Blanc, are dry, fruity and agreeable. They somewhat resemble the Pouillys, although with less finesse and body.

The reds and rosés are made from the white-juiced Gamay Noir, Pinot Gris or Pinot Noir. Nevertheless a 15% maximum of Gamay with coloured juice, or 15% of white vines (Gamay Blanc, Aligoté, Pinot-Chardonnay) is tolerated. These make very good carafe wines which are fruity, like Beaujolais, but have more body.

Mâcon-Villages An appellation which is only applied to white wines, never reds. The wines having this appellation can sometimes add the name of the commune (e.g. Mâcon-Viré).

Mâconnais A vineyard around the city of Mâcon which had a very good reputation until the seventeenth century. The area stretches from a point near

Tournus through the Saône-et-Loire department to the limit of Beaujolais. Although production is mainly white wine, there are some excellent red and rosé table wines which are full-bodied and fruity. They are best when drunk young although they can be kept for a long time.

The famous Pouilly-Fuissé★, made from the Chardonnay grape, is the pride of Mâconnais. The two neighbouring appellations, Pouilly-Vinzelles★ and Pouilly-Loché★, although very similar in character and quality, do not attain the standard of Pouilly-Fuissé. The other appellations of Mâconnais are Mâcon and Mâcon supérieur★ for the reds, whites and rosés, Mâcon-Villages★ solely for whites and, since 1971, Saint-Véran.

Madeira A wine made on the Portuguese island of the same name. Some 25% of the cultivated area of Madeira is devoted to viticulture, the grapes being grown between 350 and 600 metres altitude.

Madeira, which has been famous for over 400 years, was a great favourite of Americans in the Colonial period. Ships called at the island on their way from Europe to America and took on board casks of Madeira for Charleston, Philadelphia, New York and Boston. The sea voyage seemed to improve the wine. British officers returning home after the American War of Independence brought with them a liking for the wine they had drunk in the Colonies.

Today, America and the Scandinavian

Vendange in the Mâconnais. Phot. René-Jacques.

countries are the principal importers of Madeira, with France also a good client.

Madeira is muted with alcohol like the vins doux naturels. The characteristic bouquet is obtained by a maturation period in heated cellars called *estufas*. There are various kinds of Madeira, ranging from very dry to very sweet and from a pale straw colour (Rainwater) to a sombre gold (Malmsey). Sercial, the dryest, often has a very special bouquet. It is excellent served chilled as an apéritif.

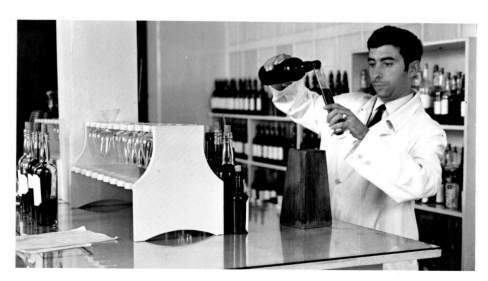

Oenological laboratory in Madeira. Phot. F. Roiter, Casa de Portugal.

Madeira: 19th-century mosaic 'azulejos', which depicts wine being transported by sled.
Phot. F. Roiter, Casa de Portugal.

du-Vic-Bihl★. The red wine, which used to be so popular, lost favour for quite some time and is only just coming back into vogue, the vineyards having been re-planted some twenty years ago.

The Tannat grape gives the wine its dark colour and generosity, while the Bouchy or Cabernet Franc adds finesse. Although, from the beginning of the nineteenth century, the Tannat was nearly the only grape cultivated, the growers are now returning to the traditional varieties. The appellation contrôlée is given to wines made from the Tannat (30% to 50%), the Bouchy (50%) and the Pinenc (or Fer★) which contain 11° alcohol.

Wine from the Tannat is better in its youth, but conserves well. The wine used to be matured in cask for thirty-two months, but the period has been shortened to twenty months. The vigorous Madiran is sometimes compared to the Burgundies.

magnum A bottle whose capacity is double that of a normal bottle. It is often used for red wines and Champagne. Red wine is supposed to mature more slowly in larger bottles and can be kept longer. Thus reds of great years are often bottled in magnum. However, this bottling does not add any qualities to Champagne; on the contrary, the wine may wear out more quickly than in a normal-size bottle.

Malaga A famous Spanish fortified wine produced around the town of Malaga in Andalusia, southern Spain. It is a sweet, fragrant, generous, dark brown wine made from Pedro Ximénez and Muscat grapes. The best, called P.X., is sweetened by the addition of wine from Pedro Ximénez grapes which have been sun-dried.

The cheaper Malagas are sweetened with *arrope*, the juice of a grape which has been concentrated by boiling, and which yields only one-fifth of its original volume, imparting a brown tint and caramel taste to the wine. Malaga, like sherry, is matured by the Solera system.

Malta Most of the vineyards are found on the south coast of this island, with the majority of production consumed as table grapes. The Maltese wines, whether they be red or white, are very ordinary and often astringent and rough, totally lacking

Others include Verdelho which is less brilliant than Sercial, the sweeter and more golden Boal and the suave, fragrant dessert wine Malvasia (Malvoisie).

Madeira of Périgord The Dutch term for Monbazillac, which was an important trade item from the fourteenth century. The repeal of the Edict of Nantes sent 40,000 protestants from the region as immigrants to Holland. Relatives and, later, traders supplied them with their favourite wine which may have received its name from its physical resemblance to Madeira.

maderise To oxidise a wine. As one oenologist put it, 'a maderised wine is like rancid butter'. The term is usually applied to white and rosé wines. Maderised wine is quite apparent to the eye: white wine takes on a characteristic amber tint and rosé, a brickish colour. The taste is also altered. The wine acquires a Madeira-like flavour from which the term is derived.

Madiran A powerful red wine of the Sud-Ouest★ produced north-east of Pau and north-west of Tarbes in the Pyrenees, on the same communes as the Pacherenc-

softness. The torrid summer and torrential rains are not conducive to the production of good quality wines.

However, the island does produce a sweet, full-bodied dessert wine from the Muscat grape which is exported to the United Kingdom.

Malvoisie The wine originally bearing this name was made in Monemvasia, Greece, from the Malvoisie grape. As the grape was transported around the Mediterranean, its name was often changed, e.g., it was called Malvoisie in France, Malvagia in Spain and Malvasia in Italy. Malvoisie is not an appellation of origin but designates a wine made from the Malvoisie grape, whether it comes from Crete, Madeira or elsewhere. In Britain, such a wine is called Malmsey, and is a variety of Madeira.

mannite Although rarely encountered in northern viticultural areas, this wine disease used to be quite common in the hot regions of the Midi and Algeria, where it caused a great deal of damage. The bacteria occurs in cuves which are warmer than normal and supplants the yeasts, imparting a strange, sickly sweet, sour taste to the wine.

Manzanilla Although it legally has the right to the name sherry, Manzanilla is totally different, even though it is made from the same grapes and by the same methods. Some say the Atlantic sea breeze which blows through the vineyards and *bodegas* is the reason for this diversity.

Manzanilla is produced west of Jerez around the little town of Sanlucar de Barramedo. The word Manzanilla is the diminutive of Manzana, and is a combination of the Spanish for camomille and apple. However, Manzanilla has no connection with cider and even less with the herb camomille. When prepared for local consumption and not export, Manzanilla is a very clear wine of about 15–17° alcohol. It is an extremely dry wine with a very pronounced bouquet and a slightly bitter taste which some consider salty. Like sherry, Manzanilla becomes darker and its alcohol content rises when aged in casks. Some brown, full-bodied sherrys reach an alcohol level of 21°.

Manzanillas are classified into five

types: Manzanilla Pasada, Manzanilla Olorosa, Manzanilla Fina, Manzanilla and Amanzanillado.

Marcillac The wines from this Sud-Ouest★ vineyard north of Rodez have recently been classified VDQS★. The vineyards flank the hillsides in eleven communes including Marcillac-Vallon, Balsac, Clairvaux and Saint-Christophe-Vallon.

The excellent red wine, which ages well, is smooth and colourful with a raspberry bouquet. It is made from the Fer★, locally called 'Mansois', blended

with Gamay, Jurançon Noir, Merlot and Cabernet. The rosés and whites have less *race*★, the latter being made from Sémillon, Mauzac, Clairette and Muscat grapes.

Marcobrunn A famous German vineyard which is one of the best of the Rheingau★. It takes its name from the *Marcobrunnen*, a charming little fountain which marks the boundary between the villages of Erbach and Hattenheim. Marcobrunner is a fruity, full-bodied wine with *race*★ and an astonishing bouquet.

Malaga: maturation caves.
Phot. Pedro Domecq.

157

The wines from Erbach are generally sold as Erbacher Marcobrunn, and those of Hattenheim as simply Marcobrunner.

Margaux This famous communal appellation of the Médoc★ is applied to the commune of that name as well as the neighbouring ones of Cantenac, Soussans, Arsac and Labarde. Margaux wines have a suave bouquet and are exceptionally delicate. Velvety and elegant, they are generous without being too full-bodied. The premier cru is Château Margaux★, followed by Châteaux Rauzan-Ségla, Rauzan-Gassies and Durfort-Vivens. (See Index.)

Damery and Hautvilliers, in whose abbey Dom Pérignon★ perfected the Champagne method★.

marque (vin de) Brand name wines without appellation of origin which are produced by blending, and are sometimes of good quality. Wines from different regions are selected by the *négociant*★ who blends them according to the amounts particular to each trademark. In order to avoid confusion with appellations of origin, certain words are prohibited on the label of these wines: *clos, château, tour, domaine, cru, mont, moulin, côte* and *camp* (but the word *monopole* is tolerated). The

Margaux, famous communal appellation of the Médoc. Phot. M.

Margaux (Château-) The premier cru of the commune of Margaux★ and one of the greatest red wines of Bordeaux. Château-Margaux is a delicate, velvety, suave, well-balanced wine with an incomparable bouquet. The vineyard also produces a small amount of white wine sold under the name 'Pavillon-Blanc-de-Château-Margaux'.

Marne (Valley of the) An important Champagne★ vineyard found between Epernay and Dormans★ on both banks of the river and continuing into the Aisne department.

The 'wines of the river' are light and tender and have been important commercially since the ninth century. Ay is the most famous cru, and others include Mareuil-sur-Ay, Avenay, Cumières,

alcohol degree must be stated on the label, although the name and address of the *négociant* does not.

Marsala The most famous of the Italian vins de liqueur★, obtained by mutage of the must with alcohol. The wine is produced around the village of Marsala in western Sicily. In the second half of the eighteenth century, several English families living on the island desired a wine similar to sherry and created Marsala.

The wine is a beautiful amber colour, sometimes dry, but often sweet. It is produced by a strictly delimited region from Grillo, Catarratto and Inzolia grapes.

The original Marsala, called Marsala Vergini or Solera, is a dry wine containing 17 or 18° alcohol which has been blended and aged in casks. A sweeter wine is obtained by adding *sifone*, a concentrated, sugary grape juice of a syrupy consistency.

The official names of the different types of Marsala are, besides Marsala Vergini, Italia, the lightest and cheapest of the Marsalas, containing about 5% *sifone* and 17° alcohol, and Marsala Fini or Italia Particolare (or I.P.). Many Marsalas are exported as Marsalas superiori. They have an alcohol content of 18° and can be dry or sweet depending on the amount of *sifone* added.

Many of the Italian apéritifs have a Marsala base, e.g. Marsala Chinato (with added quinine) and Marsala all'uovo (with eggs).

Marsannay-la-Côte A Côte-d'Or village famous for its rosé, made from the Pinot Noir, and which is one of the lightest, freshest and most delicious French rosés.

The formal appellation contrôlée is Bourgogne-Marsannay-la-Côte.

Mascara An appellation applied to Algerian★ wines produced south-east of Oran, which were classified VDQS★ before independence. The reds and rosés are generous and full-bodied but lack finesse, and the whites are rather ordinary. Mascara wines were made from grapes growing on limestone hills about 200 metres high, while those having the appellation Coteaux-de-Mascara were cultivated at between 600–800 metres. These colourful reds are full-bodied, heady and velvety, having a violet fragrance, while the rosés and whites are both fragrant and fruity.

maturation (control of) Thanks to the work of the INAO★ and the Institut Technique du Vin, French viticulturists know the best moment at which to begin the vendange. A team of professionals regularly test the grapes on different parts of the vine, beginning some three weeks before the supposed date of the vendange. The specimens are analysed in the laboratory and the results sent to the mayor and published in the local papers.

Two curves represent the evolution of maturity: the decreasing curve is that representing acidity, and the increasing one, the sugar level. The level of maturity is the balance between sugar and acidity, which differs depending on the year and grape variety. During the final days of maturation, the grape juice often shows a daily increase of 10–20 g of sugar per litre.

Maury Perched on a hill in an arid valley bordered by the ridges of Corbières

The Marne valley from Epernay. In the foreground, the vineyards of Moët et Chandon. Phot. Lauros.

and Albèze is the little town of Maury, which lends its name to the famous vin doux naturel★ of Roussillon★. The vines grow on schistose, rocky hills scorched by the sun.

Maury is a great wine which is usually red. A vin doux naturel, it is velvety, sweet and powerful and is made from the Grenache Noir.

measures Officially, the litre, along with its multiples, is the only measure of volume recognised by law. But old mea-sures better adapted to the wines of different regions are still used.

The basis of each unit of measure is the container used by the labourers in the vineyards, and the measures therefore vary from region to region. As a result, we have the terms barrique★, muid★, pièce★, tonneau★, feuillette★ and tierçon.

méchage (fumigation) An operation which consists of releasing sulphur dioxide★ by burning a wick of sulphur. Fumigation of amphoras was practised by

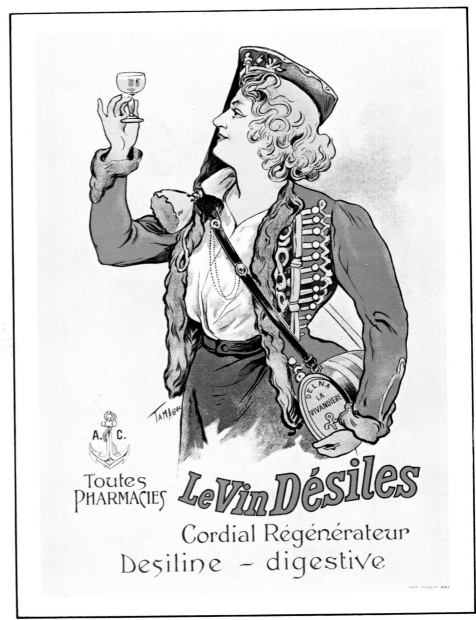

Poster advertisement for a medicinal wine. Coloured engraving by Tamagno (1900). Phot. Lauros.

160

the Romans, and for a long time it was the only source of sulphur dioxide at the disposal of the vigneron. The method is still used to sterilise casks. Before wine is transferred into a cask it is cleansed with about 3 g of sulphur per hl of capacity.

Médéa (Coteaux-de-) Algerian wines produced south of Algiers which were classified VDQS★ before 1958. The vineyard, located on sandy or chalky hills 600–1200 metres high, gives full-bodied reds having finesse and an agreeable bouquet. Although pleasant, the whites do not come up to the standard of the reds.

médecin (vin) A wine added to blends to improve feeble wines. Such a wine is usually very colourful, rich in alcohol, and has a high proportion of dry extracts.

Before it was appreciated as a wine in its own right, Corbières du Roussillon was greatly sought after for this purpose. Other wines in this category include Algerian wines, wines made from the Raboso grape and the red wines of Cahors★, called 'black wines' because of their sombre colour.

medicinal wines Along with vins de liqueur★ and highly spiced wines, these have been a speciality of Languedoc since as early as 1251, as an order from the King of England for clove and nutmeg wines from Montpellier attests. Montpellier's fame for producing medicinal wines is due, no doubt, to its school of medicine which was famous in the Middle Ages and inspired Arabian medicine. Medicinal wines are still used today, the proportion of wine being fixed by law at 80% of total volume. The best known are wines utilising coca, quinine, cola, gentian and the wines of Trousseau and Charité.

Médoc The Médoc occupies a triangular peninsula bordered by the Atlantic on the west, the Gironde estuary on the east and a line connecting Arcachon and Bordeaux on the south. Vineyards only occupy the eastern part of the Médoc, covering an area about eighty km long and ten km wide.

The Médoc is divided into two regions: the Haut-Médoc, from Blanquefort to Saint-Seurin-de-Cadourne, and the Bas-Médoc which stretches from the northern

limit of the Haut-Médoc to the estuary, and has its centre at Lesparre.

The subsoil of the Médoc, consisting of clay, flint and hard limestone, is covered by a pebbly layer called *grave* which, although not very fertile, is especially suited to the vine. The best wine is made from vines growing on this gravelly crust facing the river. (The wines from the recently deposited alluvial soil are not entitled to the appellation Médoc, and are sold as Bordeaux★ or Bordeaux supérieur★.) The principal grapes are the Cabernet Franc, Cabernet-Sauvignon, Merlot and Malbec.

The Médoc only produces red wines and these have a great reputation. A bit astringent in youth because of their high tannin content, they have vigour, bouquet and finesse and keep very well. All the elements are balanced, and they possess certain dietetic qualities which have earned them the respect of many doctors.

There is no Bas-Médoc appellation, the wines of this region being called Médoc. The wines of the Haut-Médoc, which are usually superior to the Médocs, have the appellation Haut-Médoc.

Montpellier: the school of medicine for which medieval Languedoc was famous because of its medicinal wines. Phot. Bottin.

161

Médoc: view of Château Palmer. In the foreground, a worker prunes the vines.
Phot. M.

The best regions of the Haut-Médoc, where the illustrious crus are found, also have a communal appellation. The most famous are Margaux★, Saint-Julien★, Pauillac★, Saint-Estèphe★, Listrac★ and Moulis★. (See Index.)

Menetou-Salon An AOC applied to wines from this commune south of Sancerre★, as well as several neighbouring communes including Morogues, Parassy, Aubinges and Soulangis. The Sauvignon grows very well on the limestone hills of this Loire vineyard and produces wines similar to Sancerre, although with less finesse. The appellation is also used for reds and rosés made from the Pinot, but production is insignificant.

mer (vins pour la) A title which was formerly applied to the better Loire wines, produced between Blois and the coast, which were to be exported. In 1789 the Customs Department at Ingrandes imposed a heavy tax on wines shipped to Nantes and from there abroad. The vignerons of Touraine, Anjou and Orléans could not afford to pay this high duty on their excellent wines. As a result, Dutch and Belgian traders came up the Loire in barges as far as Rochefort and Ponts-de-Cé, and set off for the sea with their precious cargo of wines. As the better wines of the area, the *vins pour la mer* were

exported and the inferior wines, *vins de terre*, were sent to Paris, often to be blended. France for a long time neglected the wines of Saumur and Anjou for this reason. However, she has now made up for lost time.

Mercurey This appellation is applied almost exclusively to red wines produced on the communes of Mercurey, Saint-Martin-sous-Montaigu and Bourgneuf-Val-d'Or, on the Côte Chalonnaise★. The wines have a beautiful red robe, are warm and vivacious while remaining light, and have a bouquet similar to Cassis. Their finesse and distinction are similar to that of certain wines of the Côte de Beaune★. The appellation Mercurey can be followed, in some circumstances, by the expression premier cru or the name of the climat of origin. (See Index.)

The white wine is practically never sold commercially and is often very delicate.

Mesland The Mesland vineyard of Loir-et-Cher is geographically the final point of the Touraine vineyards. It extends over Mesland, Monteaux, Onzain and Chouzy and produces a large volume of white, red and rosé wines having the appellation Touraine, followed by the name of Mesland. The fine, light white wines made from the Pineau are delicious when young, but production is limited.

The region is particularly devoted to rosés made from the Gamay, which owe their delicacy to the granitic soil. The rosés of Touraine-Mesland are clear, light and fruity, especially in their youth. The best are dry, as the sweeter ones tend to lose their character. The whites and rosés must contain 10·5° alcohol, and the reds, 10°.

Meursault   The great white vineyards of Burgundy begin at Meursault. Although the Côte de Nuits★ and the communes of the Côte de Beaune★, north of Meursault, produce good quality white wines, the Pinot-Chardonnay★ begins its reign at Meursault.

The white wines of Meursault, classed among the best whites of France, are both dry and marrowy. A rich, golden colour, limpid and brilliant, full-bodied and developing a rich bouquet, they are famous for their suavity. The best climats are les Perrières, les Genévrières, les Charmes and Goutte-d'Or. (See Index.)

Meursault also produces great reds which are fine, rich in bouquet and very powerful. They are little known, being eclipsed by the whites. The reds have the appellation Volnay-Sante-Nots and are made from the Meursault.

Mexico   Although vineyards occupy about 10,000 ha, the country produces only about 40,000 hl of wine per year, three-quarters of production being sold as table grapes. The national drink of Mexico has an alcohol base fermented from cane sugar. As the tropical climate is not really conducive to the vine, the vineyards are mainly found on the peninsula of Lower California and in the Sierra Madre around Durango and Chihuahua, where the altitude helps to balance some of the defects imposed by climate.

The majority of Mexican wines are of mediocre quality, with the exception of those produced at Ensenada, on the US border around the old Spanish mission of Santo Tomás, but even these are no better than heavy vins ordinaires.

The principal producers of Mexican wines include the following firms: Compania Vinicola de Saltilla, Bodegas del Marques de Aguayo, Bodegas de Delicias and the best known, Bodegas de Santo Tomás in Lower California.

Midi (vin du)   A Midi wine is usually a red ordinaire from the large production area of Languedoc★-Roussillon★ which includes the departments of the Aude,

Meursault and its vineyards.
Phot. Aarons-L.S.P.

The effect of mildew.
Phot. M.

Hérault, Pyrénées-Orientales and Gard. The area accounts for more than half of France's total wine production.

Vineyards have flourished in this region from the eighteenth century, but it was not until the railway penetrated the area that they became known in other parts of the country. The expression vin du Midi is not necessarily slighting. When well vinified and honestly prepared, the wines are a healthy, family drink. The most common grapes, the Aramon, Carignan, Oeillade and Petit-Bouschet, seem to have somewhat replaced the old noble★ varieties: the Muscat, Grenache, Macabéo and Malvoisie.

mildew A destructive mould seen for the first time in France in 1878 and believed to have been imported from America. It attacks the leaves (causing them to dry up and fall) and the grapes (making them turn brown and also drop). The survivors produce an acidic wine containing little alcohol. The treatment, which consists of spraying with copper sulphate, was discovered accidentally by a vigneron who habitually sprayed his vines blue with copper sulphate before the harvest to ward off plunderers. Only these grapes seemed to resist the mildew.

Copper was unobtainable during the Occupation, and other synthetic products such as Captane and Dithane were developed.

General view of Minerve.
Phot. M.

millerandage (shot berries) An ailment caused by incomplete fertilisation of the flowers of the vine, which results in very small grapes lacking pips.

mince (thin) An adjective describing a wine which is light in alcohol and has insufficient bouquet and flavour. A wine which is exceptionally thin is termed *maigre* or *grêle* (skinny).

Minervois This VDQS★ wine of Languedoc★ takes its name from the historic capital Minerve. Minervois occupies an immense circular area north of Corbières★ and west and north-west of Narbonne. The climate is warm and dry and the vineyards enjoy well-exposed positions on the hillsides and in the valleys. Roman soldiers, who colonised the Narbonne area, introduced viticulture and the wines rapidly became famous, being praised by Pliny the Younger and Cicero.

Although some whites and dry, fruity rosés are produced, the red wines are superior and, along with Corbières, are the best in the region. The reds are made from the traditional Languedoc grapes, Grenache, Cinsault and Carignan, and age well. They have a lively, red robe and are fine, fruity, delicate and well balanced with a characteristic bouquet and flavour.

mise en bouteilles à la propriété This phrase on a wine label attests that the wine was bottled by the producer in the same place it was vinified. Thus it is a guarantee of quality and authenticity; for example, it would not appear if a proprietor's wine was sent to a bottler.

Other terms have a similar meaning: *mise en bouteille au domaine* (or *mise du domaine*), *mise d'origine*, estate bottled and *mise en bouteilles au château*★ (used in the Gironde). In Burgundy, where there are few châteaux, the name of the wine *négociant*★ is referred to and this name becomes the guarantee of quality and authenticity.

On the other hand, the term *mise en bouteille par le propriétaire* or *mise en bouteille dans nos chais* is no guarantee that the wine has been bottled at the original château or domaine, nor is the mere mention of the name of a château or domaine.

mistelle The name given to the must of grapes to which alcohol has been added in a proportion of 5–10% to arrest fermentation. The operation is rigidly controlled, as is the use of mistelles. Before 1958, Algeria was a large producer of mistelles as the climate produced grapes having a high sugar content whose musts were powerful and rich in alcohol. The first mistelles were produced at Mostaganem in 1880 and, by 1910, Algeria was the largest producer of mistelles used in producing French apéritifs, and false Madeiras and Malagas as well. From 1940 Algeria continued to send mistelles to the French producers, but no longer made the vin de liqueur herself.

moelleux A white wine termed moelleux or marrowy is one whose sweetness is

vineyards, they are gradually being replaced by European varieties. The best white wine produced in Moldavia is the Aligoté, while Kaberné, which has a violet fragrance, and Bordeaux wines are the best reds.

The château of Monbazillac.
Phot. M.

between that of a vin blanc liquoreux★ and a vin sec★. There is no precise rule for applying this term, but some consider that a wine containing 6–15 g of natural unfermented sugar should be considered moelleux.

Moldavia The second largest viticultural area of Russia and producer of one-third of all USSR wines.

The vine is cultivated in the valleys, particularly in the Dniestr valley around the towns of Kichinev, Oungheni, Rezina, Tiraspol and Bendery.

Although hybrids★ still dominate the

Monbazillac This famous, sweet white wine (vin blanc liquoreux★) of Dordogne is an appellation contrôlée of the Sud-Ouest★, which is sometimes wrongly classified as a Bordeaux. The vineyards flank the hills on the left bank of the Dordogne south of Bergerac★ in the communes of Monbazillac, Pomport, Colombier, Rouffignac and a section of Saint-Laurent-des-Vignes. The grapes are the same as those of Sauternes★: Sémillon, which gives flavour and moelleux★, Sauvignon, which assures finesse and body and Muscadelle, which gives a Muscat aroma.

CHÂTEAU
MONBAZILLAC
APPELLATION MONBAZILLAC CONTROLÉE

MISE EN BOUTEILLES DU CHÂTEAU

As at Sauternes, the harvest is performed in successive stages when the pourriture noble★ has withered the grapes. Fermentation is slow, sometimes taking several months, during which time an important quantity of glycerine is produced which gives the wine its marvellous smoothness. Monbazillac contains a minimum of 12·5° alcohol and its sugar level varies from 30–100 g per litre. In good years Monbazillac is the richest of the French vin blancs liquoreux, containing 15–16° alcohol and 80–100 g of sugar per litre.

Monbazillac has been exported to northern Europe since the fourteenth century. The French émigrés of the region who fled to Holland after the revocation of the Edict of Nantes spread its fame and, in the eighteenth century, all the wine of Monbazillac was sent to Holland. In its youth Montbazillac has a lovely straw-coloured robe which becomes more or less amber with time, and the wine itself improves with age. This fine wine smells of honey and is particularly suave.

Although it bears some relationship to Sauternes, the two should not really be compared as each has very individual characteristics.

Mondeuse An excellent red and white grape which grows mainly in Savoie★ and the neighbouring region of Bugey★. The red Mondeuse produces a very good, fruity, light table wine whose bouquet, smelling of violet, raspberry and sometimes of truffle, develops with age. The delicious rosé of Montagnieu, a wine of Bugey, is made principally from the Mondeuse.

Montagne-Saint-Emilion The commune of Montagne has the privilege of adding Saint-Emilion★ to its name. Two distinct areas of the vineyard produce very different wines. The wine made from grapes grown on limestone soil found at higher altitudes are full-bodied, colourful and robust; the lower, flinty-clay soil gives a lighter, more supple wine resembling those of Pomerol★ and St Emilion. Some crus mix the two kinds of wine.

The best châteaux are Montaiguillon, Tours, Négrit, Roudier and Corbin.

Montagny An appellation of the Côte Chalonnaise★ applied to fresh, light, fragrant white wines made from the Chardonnay grape.

Montesquieu Venerated by the Bordelais, not only for his writings which include 'Esprit des Lois' and 'Lettres Persanes', but also for his love of the grape – as the vigneron of La Brède. He wrote, 'I do not want to make my fortune in the Court, I dream of making it from the value of my land.

Montesquieu, the gentleman vigneron of La Brède. 18th-century French School, Musée du Château de Versailles. Phot. Giraudon.

Montilla An excellent Spanish wine made from vines growing on arid limestone hills around the villages of Montilla and Los Moriles, south of Cordoue. Until recently most of the production was sold to Jerez as sherry (the word Amontillado originally was applied to the type of sherry made from the wine of Montilla) but Montilla has recently been given its own particular appellation.

Montilla is made from the Pedro Ximénez grape which, according to legend, is really the Riesling of the Rhine Valley, having been introduced in Spain by a German soldier named Peter Siemens. The wine produced from this grape is more alcoholic than that from the Palomino from which sherry is made.

Unlike sherry, Montilla is unfortified, as its own alcohol content is sufficiently high. Like sherry it is a flor★ wine, vinified in *bodegas* and aged by the Solera system. However, it is not aged in wooden casks in

its youth as sherry, but in enormous man-sized jars called *tinajas,* which are similar to Roman amphoras.

Montilla can be a Fino- or Oloroso-type sherry, the latter being rare. It is generally a clear, dry wine, which is perhaps easier to drink and more agreeable than Manzanilla and Fino sherry, because it has less body and bouquet. It is delicious as an apéritif and with sea food, and is served chilled as are all the dry, sherry-type wines.

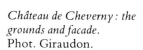

Montlouis Opposite Vouvray★ be-tween Tours and Ambiose, the charming village of Montlouis snuggles in a bend of the left bank of the Loire★. The white wines, made from the Pineau de la Loire, are similar to Vouvray, and were sold under that name until 1938. However, after a long lawsuit, Montlouis was for-bidden to use the appellation Vouvray on her wines. The soil, grape and methods of viticulture and vinification are identical at Vouvray and Montlouis, but the Loire separates the two.

The wines of Montlouis offer the same range as those of Vouvray : secs, demi-secs, liquoreux, tranquilles, pétillants and mousseux. They have less body and more *sève*★ with an expanding aroma. They can be drunk as young and keep just as well because of their lightness and great finesse.

Montpeyroux VDQS★ reds and rosés of Languedoc★ produced on the hills north of Béziers. These are very good wines, especially the reds, being full-bodied and beautifully coloured.

Mont-près-Chambord-Cour-Cheverny This vineyard, whose name recalls two famous châteaux of the Loire, stretches twelve km south-west of Blois to the boundary of Sologne. Its wines have been classified VDQS★ since 1951. Four communes share the appellation: Mont-près-Chambord, Cour-Cheverny, Chev-erny and Huisseau-sur-Cosson. The char-acteristic grape, the Romorantin, grows well in the flinty soil, but a mixture of the Sauvignon and Pineau de la Loire is also authorised. These white wines, nearly all of which are vinified at the co-operative of Mont, are light, rarely surpassing 11° alcohol. Sec, sometimes demi-sec, agree-able, fresh and fruity, they are mainly

Château de Cheverny: the grounds and facade. Phot. Giraudon.

consumed locally, although a few make their way to Paris.

Montrachet The greatest white wine of Burgundy, a title no-one disputes. This dry, sumptuous, powerful, velvety wine is absolutely perfect. Everything is admirable, from its pale golden robe tinged with green to its suave bouquet and rich flavour. Montrachet is certainly the best vin blanc sec, as Château-d'Yquem is the best vin blanc liquoreux.

Montravel An appellation contrôlée of the Sud-Ouest★ applied to white wines produced on the right bank of the Dordogne in the canton of Vélines. Although it occupies an area of Bordeaux, Montravel is not a Bordeaux appellation.

The region of Montravel has been called the cellar of Montaigne. Montaigne was born at Saint-Michel and seems to have been an admirer of the wines, of which he said, 'drinking little and moderately is too much of a restraint on the gifts of this God'.

Made from the Sémillon, Sauvignon and Muscadelle, the white wines of Montravel are divided into three appellations contrôlées: Montravel, the wine of the plain containing 10·5° alcohol, Côtes-de-Montravel and Haut-Montravel, both containing at least 11° and often more. These are moelleux or liquoreux wines of undeniable charm, which are fine and well balanced with a particular sève★ or vigour and fragrance.

An excellent red wine is also produced around Vélines under the appellation contrôlée Bergerac★.

Monts-du-Tessala An appellation applied to a group of Algerian★ wines produced south of Oran, which were classified VDQS★ before independence (Oued Imbert Lauriers Roses, M'Silah, Crêtes des Berkêches and Parmentier). These wines, made from grapes harvested on various soils at about 600 m altitude, were among the finest of Oran. A beautiful red colour, with a subtle raspberry fragrance, the wines of Tessala are full-bodied like all the Algerian wines, but they are also fine, delicate, fruity, velvety and smooth.

Morey-Saint-Denis The great red wines produced by this commune have distinction and a rich strawberry, violet or sometimes truffle bouquet.

The famous climats are Bonnes-Mares, Clos Saint-Denis, Clos de la Roche and Clos de Tart. The cru Bonnes-Mares is applied to the communes of Morey-Saint-Denis and Chambolle-Musigny.

Morgon The wine of Morgon is completely different from the other crus of Beaujolais. Some say it has too much Burgundy and not enough Beaujolais. With its deep garnet colour, currant and kirsch bouquet, generous and robust constitution, full, firm body and its ability to age well, it is evidently in a class apart from the other Beaujolais. Morgon is not as fruity as other Beaujolais but lasts a lot longer. In describing a wine similar to Morgon, the term *morgonne* is used. Le Py, a hill overflowing with vines, is the pride of Morgon.

Morocco This country was producing wine even in the days of ancient Rome.

Montaigne, son of Montravel.
Musée Condé, Chantilly.
Phot. Giraudon.

Morocco: certain vineyards around Fes produce some of the best Moroccan wines.
Phot. Phédon-Salou.

The principal viticultural areas are found in the eastern part of the country around Berkane and Oujda, Taza, Fèz, Meknès, Rabat and Casablanca. Others are located in the south between Safi and Mogador, along the Tensift wadi and in the mountainous region of Bon Assida.

Morocco has no grand crus, and reds and rosés make up the majority of production as the whites have a tendency to maderise in the hot climate. The country also produces sparkling wines, dessert wines and vins gris (vin gris de Demnate). The fragrant, heady reds are made from the Cinsault, Carignan, Grenache and Alicanti-Bouschet.

The north-east region produces the Muscat of Beikani and excellent rosés similar to those of Algeria. In the centre, Taza makes a wine which is used for blending. The reds produced in Meknès have the best reputation of Moroccan wines – they are full-bodied, colourful and have a characteristic fragrance. East of Rabat, the colourful Dar Bel Hamri is made around Sidi Slimane.

Although the red wines made around Casablanca are drunk very young, they can improve with age. Dry and fruity vins gris, considered a speciality of the country, are produced at Boulaouane and El Jadida.

Although some appellations of origin are printed on Moroccan wine labels, the system has nothing to do with the French classifications. The Moroccan Ministry of Agriculture has inaugurated quality control for wines and vines. Only healthy wines which meet the specified standards, which include an alcohol level of at least $11°$, are eligible for export.

Moselle Before joining the Rhine at Koblenz, the Moselle flows past miles of different vineyards. In France, it passes the VDQS★ wines of Lorraine which have the appellation Vins de la Moselle★; further on, it passes the wines of Luxembourg★; and finally it reaches Germany, where it gives its name to world-famous vineyards.

The German vineyards, planted almost exclusively in Riesling, occupy steep slopes alongside the river starting at Trèves. The most favoured wines come from that part of the valley (Middle Moselle) which extends from Trittenheim to Traben-Trarbach. The best communes are Piesport, Bernkastel, Graach, Wehlen, Zeltingen and Brauneberg.

Moselle vineyards are also found in the valleys of its two small tributaries, the Sarre and Ruhr, in the communes of Wiltingen, Kanzem, Oberemmel, Ockfen, and Ayl (Sarre), and Maximin Grunhaus and Eitelsbach (Ruhr). The official name of the region is Mosel-Saar-Ruhr.

170

In poor years the wines are thin, deceptive and often very acidic, but in good years they are, without doubt, the most fragrant, delicate and *racé*★ of all the German wines. Clear and limpid, with their characteristic bouquet which is both flowery and spicy, they have an incomparable distinction.

The label of Moselle wines bears the usual terms of German wines: the name of the commune, the name of the vineyard of origin and an indication of selected picking (Spätlese, Auslese, etc.).

Moselle (vins de la) This appellation is applied to VDQS★ wines of Lorraine★ produced in three different areas of the Moselle department: Sierck in the north near the Luxembourg border, Metz and Vic-sur-Seille, near Château Salins.

The red, rosé and white wines are made from the Gamay of Liverdun, Auxerrois Blanc and Gris, Pinot Noir and Pinot Blanc, Sylvaner and Riesling. The wines differ depending on the area of production: Sierck, for example, produces mainly white wines, Metz, light rosés (clairet of the Moselle), and Vic-sur-Seille, vins gris. The whites and rosés are very light and fruity and sometimes have a disconcerting acidity; the reds are light, but have less charm (Vic, Ancy, Jussy).

Mostaganem and **Mostaganem-Keneda** An appellation applied before independence to VDQS Algerian★ wines made east of Oran near the coast around Mostaganem, Mazagran, Rivoli, Cassaigne and the Dahra (a zone between the sea and the Chélif River). The best wines came from limestone or limestone-clay soil at about 500 m altitude. These extremely full-bodied wines which had an alcohol level of 13° were supple, fruity and delicate.

The wines from the flinty plateau situated between 100–200 m altitude were also supple, but had less finesse. In his book on the wines of Algeria, Paul Reboux wrote of the wine of Saoura (in the Dahra) that it was distinguished by 'its finesse, delicacy and vigour', and added, 'From this Bordeaux-shaped bottle flows a velvety liquid which Burgundy would not disown'.

mou (feeble, weak) When applied to wine this adjective has the same meaning as

The confluence of the Moselle and the Meurthe. Phot. A. Perceval.

Moulin-à-Vent, Beaujolais.
Phot. M.

when applied to man. A mou wine is one which has no character. Lacking a normal level of acidity★ and tannin★, it is flat and insipid.·

mouldy   Some wines smell and taste of mould. This serious fault, which cannot be rectified, is caused by a badly cleaned cask or one in which water has been left and which has been attacked by mould. Wine placed in the cask contracts the offensive smell and taste.

Wine not so badly affected is said to have a stagnant taste or to smell of the cask. A mouldy taste can also come from grapes attacked by pourriture grise★.

Moulin-à-Vent   This Beaujolais wine takes its name from an old windmill overlooking the vineyard. The appellation Moulin-à-Vent is applied to wine produced by the communes of Romanèche-Thorins and Chenas★. Moulin-à-Vent is always a full-bodied wine with a dark ruby robe and is generally considered one of the best Beaujolais. In certain years the wines are splendid, with a bouquet, body and

distinction resembling the wines of the Côte d'Or★.

Moulis   An appellation applied to red wines produced by this commune of the Haut Médoc★ and parts of six other communes, particularly Listrac★. The wines of Moulis have a very particular character due to the presence of a larger amount of limestone in the soil than is found in the rest of the Médoc. The Moulis are colourful, full-bodied and robust. They have a strong bouquet and accentuated flavour which does not exclude finesse.

In the classification of 1855, Moulis was not among the crus classés, but rather the crus bourgeois supérieurs, the excellent Château Chasse-Spleen being classified 'Cru exceptionnel'.

mousse (foam)   This is the heart of Champagne★. It must be light, firm and abundant and quickly disappear in the glass, yet remain in the bottle so as to renew the pleasure each time the glass is filled. A quality Champagne, chilled just the right amount, will not explode noisily

when the bottle is opened and its cork will not leap from the bottle and hit the ceiling. A large, explosive foam is evidence of a poorly conducted champagnisation.

When the froth has died away in the glass, the effervescence of the wine is revealed as an incessant gushing of little, light bubbles. A large, heavy bubble is slurringly called 'toad's eye'.

Mousseux Grouped under this general term are different kinds of sparkling wine, some being of inferior quality which can give a bad name to the others. Champagne★, although a sparkling wine, should never be described as mousseux – it is Champagne.

Different processes are employed to make vins mousseux. The oldest is the rural method★, which was formerly used in several regions including Champagne, and is still practised at Gaillac★, Die★ and Limoux. The Champagne method★ is, by definition, that used today in Champagne and is employed for all the AOC French vins mousseux: Anjou★, Arbois★, Blanquette de Limoux★, Bordeaux★, Burgundy★, L'Etoile★, Montlouis★, Saint-Péray★, Saumur★, Seyssel★, Touraine★ and Vouvray★.

There is also a German method★ in which the operations of remuage★ and dégorgement★ are eliminated, and which may only be used for sparkling wines not having an appellation.

The cuvé close★ method (Charmat process) allows the fabrication of a cheap Mousseux, but its use is prohibited for French AOC sparkling wines. The method used at Asti★ is different, because the sparkle is obtained during the first fermentation, since the must – not still wine – is treated.

Finally, there are several sparkling vins mousseux made by the injection of carbon dioxide. These wines have large bubbles and none of the creaminess of Champagne which they pretend to imitate.

MOUSSEUX ROSÉ Some regions produce sparkling rosés which can be of very good quality. The sparkling rosés of Touraine are made exclusively from the black grapes of the Cabernet, as are those of Bordeaux. Burgundy also produces sparkling rosés which for some time enjoyed great popularity in England and the United States, but never had quite the same success in France.

moustillant, moustiller Terms used to describe a wine which releases a small amount of gas. This shortcoming is often found in young wines which prick the tongue slightly when tasted. This pricking or tingling is quite acceptable to many people when it is not exaggerated, as in a *vin nouveau* like Beaujolais.

A moustillant wine is the result of a refermentation caused by yeasts or malolactic ferments. As a result there is some carbon dioxide in solution. This light release of gas is often deliberately induced, especially in the case of vins perlants★.

muid A measure used for the sale of large volumes of wine. The quantity varies from one region to another: it is 685 litres in the Hérault, 608 litres at Montpellier and 260 litres in the Aisne.

Murfatlar The best wine of Romania★, cultivated and produced at Basarabi in the Dobroudja from Pinot Gris, Riesling and Chardonnay grapes. Between 1957 and 1962, Murfatlar was awarded forty-five different medals for excellence. Before 1914, the wine rarely had an alcohol level higher than 15°. However, since 1945, the methods have changed, and the wines are now sweeter and have a higher alcohol level, from 16–18°. Murfatlar has a complex, modern vinicultural plant which is remarkably well organised and mechanised.

Muscadet Since 1930 this light, supple, fruity white wine, which originates in the Nantes area, has been a favourite of wine drinkers in Paris, the rest of France and other countries. Muscadet is made from the Melon de Bourgogne grape, which derives its name from its round leaves, and which is hardly grown any more in Burgundy. The grape was brought into Brittany in the seventeenth century and planted in large quantities after the terrible winter of 1709, which destroyed the vineyard. And then the miracle occurred. This grape, which had produced only mediocre wines in other areas, found on the banks of the Loire its perfect soil and climate.

The grape is probably called 'Muscadet' in Brittany because of its slightly musky

173

Muscadet: the vineyard of Saint-Fiacre. Phot. M.

taste, but it has absolutely no relationship with the Muscadelle of Bordeaux.

The Muscadet is harvested early, before the grapes are overripe. Fermentation is conducted slowly and the wine is kept for a long time on its lees★. This method of vinification accounts for the bouquet, suppleness, fruitiness and the very pale, almost colourless, tint of the wine. Muscadet is never acid because, in a cold year (like 1963), the vignerons reduce the excess acidity by malo-lactic★ fermentation. Dry without being tart, Muscadet has a great deal of finesse, an indefinable yet personal fragrance, and charms with its youthful brightness and clarity.

MUSCADET: APPELLATIONS D'ORIGINE CONTRÔLÉES Legislation distinguishes three appellations contrôlées: Muscadet, Muscadet de Sèvre et Maine★ and Muscadet des Coteaux de la Loire★. The appellation Muscadet is applied to wines with an alcohol level of 9·5°, yielding 40 hl per hectare and produced in the delimited area.

Between them, the two other appellations produce 90% of Muscadet. Bottling on lees★ is the special process by which the wine is made. It is not racked after fermentation, but is left on its sediment from which it gains its fruitiness and youthful character which are so appreciated. The wine preserves a small amount of dissolved carbon dioxide which makes the tongue tingle.

Muscadet des Coteaux de la Loire The limited area of production is situated around Ancenis on the rocky hills bordering each bank of the Loire. The communes producing the wine on the right bank are found in Loire-Atlantique (Ancenis, Thouarcé, Mauves and Le Cellier). Those on the left bank are in Loire-Atlantique (Saint-Sébastien-sur-Loire and Barbechat) and Maine-et-Loire (La Varenne, Liré and Champtoceaux). The Muscadet des Coteaux de la Loire is generally more full-bodied, drier and fruitier than the Muscadet de Sèvre et Maine★. Sometimes it seems a bit acid, but it retains its youthful character for a long time.

Muscadet de Sèvre et Maine This region located south-west of Nantes produces 75% of the total amount of Muscadet. Here the vine is king, stretching fifty miles over pebbly, flinty, clay soil. The region is divided into four principal cantons, Vertou, Vallet, Clisson and Loroux-Bottereau. The best and most famous Muscadet is produced in this area. It is very fine and light, delicate and supple.

Muscat There are numerous varieties of this grape, whose colours range from a pale yellow to bluish-black. But all possess, to a varying degree, the fragrance and inimitable musky taste so liked by its admirers.

The Muscat is found in the warm soils of Italy, southern France, Spain, Portugal,

Greece, Tunisia and the islands of the Aegean and Mediterranean (Elba, Sardinia, Sicily and Cyprus), as well as the more inclement areas of Alsace, the Tyrol and Hungary. Although the Muscat of Alexandria is the most productive, the best is the Muscat doré of Frontignan. There is also a Muscat of Hambourg which makes a good table grape, but only a mediocre wine; the red Aleatico of the island of Elba; the Muscadelle of Sauternes; the Muscat Ottonel of Alsace; and the Moscatello of Italy from which Asti Spumante★ and Est Est Est★ are made.

The Muscats must be vinified delicately as the essence of their charm and suave, fruity fragrance is capricious and ephemeral. For example, vins mousseux having a Muscat base (Clairette de Die★) should not be vinified à sec, but should finish their first fermentation before being bottled. For this reason, the rural method★ is superior to the Champagne method★, because it preserves the aroma and taste of the grape. At Asti★ the sparkling wines are obtained from the first fermentation. The fragrance of the exquisite French Muscats liquoreux is preserved by mutage★ with alcohol which interrupts fermentation.

Muscat (France) Fragrant vins doux naturels★ from the Muscat grape are produced in the south of France in the Languedoc★ and Roussillon★ areas. The most famous is the Muscat de Frontignan★, with its robe of golden silk. But there are also rivals, including the Muscats de Lunel★, Mireval, Saint-Jean-de-Minervois★ and Rivesaltes★. There is also the suave and fragrant Muscat of Beaumes-de-Venise★, produced on the left bank of the Rhône in the Vaucluse department from the Muscat doré, as is the Frontignan.

The fine and fresh Muscat d'Alsace is the only dry French Muscat. It has the characteristic aroma and musky taste of the Muscat, as well as great delicacy and distinction.

Muscat (Italy) Italy produces much appreciated Muscats from several varieties. The Aleatico grape makes a red, generally sweet wine. The best, Portoferraio, is produced on the island of Elba.

The Muscat of Canelli is the base for Asti Spumante★, the Italian vermouths

Muscat Blanc.
Phot. Larousse.

Around Taormin in Sicily the Muscat predominates in the vineyards. Phot. Hétier.

Muscat vines in Tarragona, Spain. Phot. Aarons.

and the Est Est Est★ of Montefiascone. The Giallo Muscat of Trenton and the region north of Adige produces a vin blanc liquoreux of the Sauternes type which contains 12–15° alcohol. There are also true vins de liqueur, very sweet and full-bodied (from 15–17°), which are made from local Muscats in Sardinia (Muscat de Cagliari), the island of Pantelleria, and Sicily (Muscat of Syracuse).

musky A wine having the special aroma of Muscat grapes is said to be musky. This pleasant aroma vanishes almost completely when the must is entirely fermented, e.g. when all its sugar has been converted into alcohol. For this reason, fermentation of wines with a Muscat base are either arrested before completion by the addition of alcohol (Muscat de Frontignan★, Rivesaltes★) or by using the rural method★ to produce a sparkling wine.

must The juice of unfermented grapes.

must meter An instrument which determines the sugar level of must or grapes by measuring the density. A table gives the corresponding sugar concentration. The must meter is used at harvest time as it can record the increase in the sugar level and thus the appropriate time the grapes should be picked. This simple method is not strictly precise. The control of maturation★ tests carried out at oenological stations in the different wine areas are much more reliable, as they examine the development of the principal constituents

of the must, including the sugar and acid content.

mutage A special operation used in making vins doux naturels★ which consists of arresting fermentation by adding alcohol. In its original state the must has a natural sugar level of at least 250 g per litre (the equivalent of 14° alcohol), a characteristic of very sweet grapes which have often undergone passerillage★.

In order to arrest fermentation, pure alcohol of 90° is added to the must in a proportion of about 6–10% of the must's volume. There remains in the wine a quantity of natural grape sugar (40–150 g per litre) which is not converted into alcohol. The wines are then more or less sweet and always generous and rich in alcohol, some of them containing as much as 23°. Wines preserve the fruitiness of the fresh grape when fermentation is stopped early. This is particularly the case with the Muscats★, which lose more of their fragrance and fruity taste the longer fermentation is allowed to continue.

Thus mutage is performed on vins doux naturels by the addition of alcohol. For other purposes, fermentation can be arrested by treatment with sulphur dioxide★.

Mycoderma aceti The 'mother of vinegar' bacteria described by Pasteur★. It forms a greyish veil on the surface of wine in the presence of air (because the bacteria is aerobic). When the veil thickens, it wrinkles, becoming reddish. The bacteria develops rapidly and little by little transforms the alcohol of the wine into acetic acid and water. *Mycoderma aceti* is the bacteria responsible for creating wine vinegar★, but it turns wine sour.

Mycoderma vini A whitish veil of *Mycoderma vini* often develops on the surface of wines with a low alcohol content. It is easy to get rid of as it can only exist if air is present in the casks; regular ouillage★ is therefore an essential precaution. If this is not done, the alcohol is changed into carbon dioxide and water, and the fixed acidity slowly diminishes as a result of oxidation of the malic, lactic and succinic acids. The wine becomes faded, flat and feeble. *Mycoderma vini* is often accompanied by *Mycoderma aceti*★ which is more formidable, making the wine sour.

N

Nahe An important German viticultural area located around Bad Kreuznach on red sandstone slopes overlooking the Nahe, a tributary of the Rhine.

The white wines of Nahe, made from the Riesling and Sylvaner, are rich, full-bodied and often excellent. They can be compared to the better wines of the Rhinehessen★, like Niersteiner and Nackenheimer, with the added vivacity which characterises the wines of the Nahe. The most famous vineyard of the region is that of Schloss Böckelheim, south-west of Kreuznach, owned by the German government. Other excellent wines are produced around Bad Kreuznach, Niederhäuser, Norheim, Roxheim, Münster, Bretzenheim and Winzerheim.

Nantais The fatherland of Muscadet★ and the two famous VDQS★ wines Gros-Plant★ and Côteaux d'Ancenis★. These are the last vineyards the Loire passes before it flows into the Atlantic.

Napa A valley north-east of San Francisco, California★ which is famous for its vineyards. St Helena mountain, often still covered with snow in March, towers over the northern end of the valley, while the southern end is bordered by San Francisco Bay. The vineyards are cultivated on the gravelly soil of the valley and at the feet of the neighbouring hills.

Napa produces almost exclusively table wines, including a number of the best Californian wines. Excellent Cabernet-Sauvignons, good Pinot Noirs and Pinot Chardonnays, agreeable Chenin Blancs and other good wines are made in the valley. The wines of generic appellation 'Burgundy', 'Claret' and 'Chablis' are usually superior to those produced by the other Californian regions. Many famous 'wineries' are located in the Napa Valley, including Beaulieu, Inglenook, Charles Krug, Louis M. Martini and Beringer Bros, all old establishment, some dating from as early as 1860.

Some sparkling wine and 'sherry' is also vinified by certain producers.

nature (vins nature de la Champagne) Still (non-sparkling) wines from the delimited Champagne★ area and made from the authorised grapes. The expression Champagne nature, often used to designate these wines, is incorrect, as the appellation Champagne is legally reserved for the sparkling wines. Today the largest part of the vendange is vinified into Champagne. However, prior to the heyday of sparkling wine, the still wines of Champagne, the Clairets, whites and, especially, reds, had a very strong reputation.

The majority of vins blanc nature of

Nantais vineyards. Phot. M.

*Vendange, Château Matras
near Saint-Emilion.*
Phot. Peter Titmuss.

Champagne now come from the Côte des Blancs★ and are made from white grapes, although occasionally a still Blanc de Noirs★ is found. These are dry, refreshing, charming wines, especially in good years, which should be drunk young.

Those made from the Mesnil grape are delicious, fruity and fine, while those of the Cramant have more body. Some houses prepare a vin blanc nature by blending several crus. However, the quality is often irregular as the true still white wines are made only with the must of the first and second pressings. Moreover, vins nature are often capricious and unstable and do not travel well.

The red wines of Champagne were very famous in the Middle Ages. In 1816, Julien classed them among the best fine wines of the kingdom and found them to have great finesse. Their bouquet and flavour could be compared with the best wines of Burgundy, which is not surprising as they are made from the same grape, the Pinot Noir. Certain vignerons still produce good reds at Cumières, Ambonnay and especially Bouzy★. They should generally be drunk young, although the good years age admirably. They are tender, smooth and fragrant.

Another still wine of Champagne is the extraordinary rosé of Riceys★ produced in the Aube department. It should not be confused with Champagne rosé★.

Néac   The wine of this appellation contrôlée comes from a vineyard found north of Pomerol★, between Lalande-de-Pomerol★ and Montagne-Saint-Emilion★.

These good quality wines are colourful, generous and fragrant, having both the *sève*★ of the Pomerols and the richness of Saint-Emilion. The premier crus (Châteaux Tournefeuille, Moncets, Siaurac, Belles-Graves and Teysson) are equal to the second crus of Pomerol.

négociant   The *négociant* is not a simple wine merchant. He plays a multiple role. He must first know how to choose wines, and judiciously select his purchases in the cellars with the aid of the courtiers. There is considerable risk attached to this profession, as it is almost impossible to predict how every wine will evolve.

The *négociant* must raise the wine. In this role he is called the *éleveur*★. This calls for the expenditure of a large amount of capital in order to purchase the young wine, as well as a great deal of talent and knowledge in order to raise it properly. He must also despatch the wine and make sure that it arrives at the point of sale in a drinkable state, and must also prospect for clients and arrange for sales.

Although many vignerons have all the facilities needed to raise, bottle and despatch the wine, there are many thousands who do not have the space or equipment. The *négociant*, in fulfilling these roles for them, assures that many marvellous wines, which otherwise would have been unknown, are brought to the attention of consumers.

nervosité (nerve)   This quality of a wine is based on its acidity. When the acidity is not excessive and is within the normal limits, the different sensations which can come from a wine are revealed more strongly. A nervous wine always has character.

New York   The vineyards of this state are neither numerous nor widespread. In terms of production it ranks second to California★, but there is a considerable difference in volume between them. Vineyards are found around Buffalo, Lake Erie and the Hudson Valley, but their main production effort is table grapes, as opposed to wine. A viticultural region of some importance is situated south-east of Rochester around two of the four Finger Lakes, Keuka and Canandaigua.

Most of the wines come from indigenous varieties planted around 1829 (Delaware, Catawba, Elvira, Concorde, Niagara and Isabelle) but, since the end of prohibition, hybrids★ of French origin (Baco, Coudero and Seibel) have been grown and attempts are now being made to cultivate European grape varieties in this area.

This region produces most of the sparkling wines made in the USA, as well as sweet and table wines. European appellations such as Burgundy, Sauternes, Port and Sherry, followed by their appellation, New York State, are used on the labels.

New Zealand Two Australian pioneers, James Busby and the Reverend Samuel Marsden, planted the first vines in New Zealand in 1830 at the Bay of Islands. Then, around 1835, the Marist Fathers introduced the vine at Hawke's Bay. Production remained small until the Second World War when imports of wines were reduced. Viticulture did not progress significantly until the 1950s, when the Australian companies MacWilliams and Seppelts invested heavily. Today, the most important viticultural areas are found on the North Island at Auckland and Henderson in the north and Hawkes Bay in the south.

Both white and red wines are produced, the whites being the better of the two. The whites are made from the Müller-Thurgau, Chardonnay and Chasselas and have an agreeable acidity which assures a certain vigour, a characteristic of New Zealand wines. The reds made from the Cabernet, and two hybrids, the Pinotage and Seibel 5437, have a tendency to be overacid. Chaptalisation★ is allowed because of the low level of sugar in the grapes.

Production was formerly geared to fortified wines and 'Sherry', but today's trend is towards light, white table wines.

Nuits-Saint-Georges This commune has given its name to the 'Côte de Nuits'. Certain plots of vineyards in the neighbouring village of Prémeaux are legally included in the commune of Nuits. A small quantity of excellent white wine is produced but Nuits is most famous for its reds, which are generous and well balanced, falling between the Gevrey-Chambertins and Chambolle-Musignys. They are less firm and vigorous than the Gevreys, but have more body and colour than the Chambolle-Musignys. Although they are vinified earlier than the Gevreys they keep just as well.

There are a number of climats on the two communes of Nuits and Prémeaux, including Saint-Georges, Vaucrains, les Cailles, les Pruliers, les Porrets, Clos de la Maréchale and Clos des Argillières.

The vineyard of Nuits-Saint-Georges. Phot. Aarons-L.S.P.

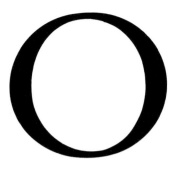

O

oeil-de-perdrix (partridge eye) A very light, indecisive colour attributed to lightly coloured vins gris★.

oenologist (from the Greek *oinos*, wine, and *logos*, science) A technician whose knowledge of wine is certified by a national diploma. The title of oenologist was officially recognised by the law of 19th March, 1955.

The oenologist can take total responsibility for vinifying and raising wines and is able to perform the most delicate analyses on the grape.

oenophile A person who loves wine and devotes much time and attention to it. The oenophile treats the study and selection of wine as a hobby, sometimes becoming involved to the point of making his own wine, or at any rate building up quite a respectable cellar.

As early as 210 BC, the Greek historian Polybe described the love of the Celts for wine and, in the first century AD, Diodore of Sicily wrote that the Greek wines had a good market in what is now France. The Phoenician colony of Massalia (Marseilles) supplied wine to the Gauls in the sixth century AD, and the beautiful wine vessel in the famous 'treasures of Vix' of Châtillon-sur-Seine dates from the same time, proving the interest its owner had in wine.

Office International de la Vigne et du Vin (OIV) An organisation which was created in 1924 and now has a membership of twenty-four countries, which accounts for about 90% of the world's vineyards. It has a considerable influence on governments and oenological organisations, which is not surprising in view of the calibre of its absolutely impartial experts.

The OIV first of all provides an information service to supply governments with official documentation. It is also a technical forum whose members exchange information on their researches and international experiments. Finally, it is an economic organisation which tries to align the legislation and rules of the different viticultural countries in order to arrive at a rational world viticultural policy.

Ohio The first vineyards of this viticultural state of the USA were planted by German immigrants east and west of Cincinnati along the Ohio River, whose steep banks resemble those of the Rhine. One of these planters, Nicholas Longworth, was particularly successful with his

Oenological·laboratory at Saint-André-de-Cubzac, Gironde. Phot. M.

vines and did so much to further viniculture that, by the Civil War, Ohio was by far the largest wine producer in the United States, making highly respected wines, including sparkling wines, from the Catawba grape.

Today there is little evidence of these once-successful vineyards along the Ohio. The vines are now found on some islands and on the south shore of Lake Erie, particularly around Sandusky, an area which provides a mellowing influence on the climate, protecting the grapes from early frosts. Although it produces a large quantity of wine, Ohio has lost its former importance.

oidium A disease of American origin, provoked by a microscopic mould which attacks the leaves, flowers and grapes, covering them with a whitish, flour-like dust. The grapes are then prey to pourriture grise★. In 1846 oidium attacked the French vineyards and did enormous damage over the next few years. Production fell from 45 million hl in 1850 to 10 million in 1854.

A remedy, consisting of regular sprayings with sulphur dioxide★, was soon discovered, but not before several vignerons were ruined.

oily An oily wine has the appearance and consistency of oil and is caused by graisse★. It should not be confused with a fleshy wine, which owes its oily quality to a high level of glycerine★.

old When used in connection with wine, the term 'old' does not carry any derogatory implication – in fact, an old wine takes precedence over all others in the cellar, and however casually gourmets may treat young★ wines, they always respect an old one.

It is pointless to compare the merits of old and young wines, since they are essentially quite different. Generally speaking, wines are called old when they are between five and fifteen years of age. The great red and white Burgundies, the sweet wines of Bordeaux and the Loire, Monbazillacs, the great red wines of the Gironde, white and red Côtes-du-Rhône and vins jaunes★ should all be drunk within this period. Among these, some veterans can happily age fifteen or twenty years, or

Grapes attacked by oidium.
Phot. M.

Casks in a maturing cave in the Côtes-du-Rhône. Phot. M.

183

even longer. This is always true of vins jaunes but, of others, only in good years.

If the qualities of youth are fruitiness and freshness, age gives a wine inimitable bouquet and flavour as well as subtlety. When a wine has lost some of its qualities with age, the French no longer call it simply *vieux*, but say *il vieillarde* (i.e. 'it is ageing'). This is half-way to the final stage of *sénilité*, by which time its beauty and quality have definitely gone, and various changes have taken place; it has oxidised, has deposited its colouring matter and tartrates, and lost its bouquet.

Orléans The reputation of this vineyard dates back to the seventh century, when the wine of Orléans conquered Paris. A large vineyard in the area, created by Saint Mesmin, received a gift from Clovis in tribute to its well-known wine. Orléans quickly became the great wine market of the region, and the Orléanais wines at the time of Louis XIII were compared to those of Bordeaux for their richness and reputation.

The red was the most famous at this time, although Villon praised the white wine of Mauves (Meung-sur-Loire). Although its importance lasted up to the end of the last century, vineyards are now only found in about fifteen communes, mainly on the right bank of the river below Orléans (Baul, Messas, Meung-sur-Loire and Beaugency).

The VDQS★ wines are white, red and rosé. The Pinot Meunier, here called 'Gris-Meunier', is by far the most cultivated variety. The Pinot Noir is also encountered, its name here being 'Auvernat', but it has been supplanted by the Gris-Meunier. A small amount of Chardonnay, Pinot Gris and Cabernet Franc are also cultivated. The clear reds are fresh and light and may be drunk in the year following the vendange. However, for some thirty years, the Pinot-Meunier has been vinified into rosé; this is the famous, fragrant Gris-Meunier made by pressing★ after a short maceration of the vendange.

Finally, Orléans uses its wine in making its celebrated vinegar.

Orvieto A very popular Italian white wine produced around the town of Orvieto in Umbria. The vineyards of Orvieto are quite unique, as most of the grapes are cultivated in a fashion the Italians call *coltura promiscua* – the vines are mixed among the apple trees and cabbage plots. The wine is often good, despite this fantastic method of culture. Always light, it is generally *abboccato* (demi-sec), more rarely *secco* (sec). It is sold in a squat, straw-covered bottle called a *pulcianelle*.

ouillage or **remplissage (topping up)** An operation which consists of keeping the casks constantly full of wine while they are in the cave. The first topping up is done when the wine has stopped fermenting. At first, wine of the same quality is added to the cask twice a week, then every fifteen days. An air pocket forms at the top of the cask for several reasons – cold makes the wine shrink in volume and some wine is lost in evaporation through the pores in the cask. Altogether, about 1% of the wine's volume is lost each month. If the casks were not topped up to replace the lost wine, harmful ferments would begin to alter the wine. At first this would be revealed as flor★, then by an increase in acidity (*piqûre*).

Vineyard at Orvieto.
Phot. M.

PQ

Pacherenc-du-Vic-Bihl This is the white relative of Madiran★, with which it shares the same terrain in the Pyrenees. It is made from Ruffiac, Manseng, Courbu, Sémillon and Sauvignon grapes, which grow at a high altitude like those of Jurançon.

The Pacherenc-du-Vic-Bihl is an AOC★ wine which must have a minimum of 12° alcohol. Lively and marrowy, it slightly resembles its rival, the Jurançon, which is generally sweeter. The wines that come from the area around Portet are the finest.

paille (vin de) Today this rare dessert★ wine is made almost exclusively in the Jura★ region. The Hermitage★ vineyards have almost stopped production, and it is no longer made in Alsace. The grapes from which it is made (the Jura's noble★ varieties: Savagnin, Trousseau, Chardonnay and Poulsard) are carefully picked and then laid on beds of straw (*paille*) for at least two months – sometimes until Christmas – during which time a slow concentration of their natural sugar takes place. The must from these grapes has an exceptionally high sugar content and, after a long and often difficult fermentation, results in a liquoreux★ wine with an alcoholic strength of 14 or 15°. Vin de paille is extremely rare, and few people have the good fortune to taste it on the spot. It is smooth and aromatic, and has a pronounced bouquet.

VIN DE PAILLE
19___

VICHOT-GIROD
PROPRIÉTAIRE A NEVY-SUR-SEILLE (JURA)

CÔTES DE JURA Appellation Contrôlée

Grapes hung to mature in the production of vin de paille.
Phot. Cuisset.

In the days when transporting wine was a hazardous undertaking, the parish priests in the north of France used to make their communion wine by the same process which, particularly in wet or cold years, enabled them to produce wines that were less acid than if the grapes had been pressed straight after the harvest.

generally considered the best, closely followed by those of Bad Dürkheim, Kallstadt, Leistadt and Königsbach. Most of the region's production consists of red and white vin ordinaire, with a predominance of white. A great deal of the wine it exports comes from the area between Neustadt and Bad Dürkheim, known as

Palatinate: a view of the vineyards from the Rhine.
Phot. Candelier-Lauros.

Palatinate One of the four great vine-growing regions in Germany★, and in good years often the chief producer. Its viticultural tradition dates back many hundreds of years; the province was for a long time known as 'the cellar of the Holy Roman Empire'. Its name is derived from the Palatine Hill in Rome, where the Roman Emperors had their official residence.

Today, the Palatinate is bordered by the states of North Rhine-Westphalia to the north, the Rhine to the east and by Alsace-Lorraine to the south and west. The vineyards lie around the foot of a small chain of hills called the Haardt (a northern continuation of the Vosges mountains in eastern France) and also cover a large part of the fertile plain which borders the Rhine. The vineyards of Wachenheim, Forst, Deidesheim and Ruppertsberg are

Mittelhaardt, which produces a few red vins ordinaires and a great many white ones. The most noteworthy are made chiefly from Riesling grapes, and some others from Sylvaner.

The Rieslings from the best vineyards are extremely good, and are almost on a par with the excellent Rheingau★ wines. They are full-bodied, heady and aromatic, and have finesse, breeding and a marvellous bouquet. As in all German vineyards, the 'Beerenauslesen' are outstanding, and command high prices.

Palette A Provence appellation contrôlée which belongs to a small vineyard located on a part of the communes of Meyreuil, Tholonet and Aix-en-Provence. The vines are grown on soil derived from the Langesse limestone geological formation.

186

The red and rosé wines come for the most part (about 50%) from Grenache, Cinsault and Mourvèdre (not less than 10%) grapes. About 55% of the white wines are made from different varieties of Clairettes.

Palette wines are, for the most part, fine and elegant with a very pleasant freshness and lightness. The reds are warm, the rosés full of bouquet and the whites have great distinction. The best cru is Château-Simone. The vineyard also produces a sweet vin cuit★ which is greatly liked in the region and is traditionally drunk at Christmas. It is produced by heating the must in cauldrons before it is left to ferment.

palus This word, which is derived from the French for swamp, is used in Bordeaux to describe the recently deposited alluvial soil which lies along the river banks.

There are not many vines planted on this soil and the *palus* is rarely found in appellation contrôlée zones. The vines which grow on the *palus* are usually very productive but never give quality wines.

panier verseur The use of this wine basket for pouring wine is highly recommended for an old wine containing a little deposit. The deposit, which is mainly composed of tannins, colouring matter, potassium bitartrate and gums, sometimes adheres to the sides of the bottle, though more usually falls to the bottom. It is then mobile, and with each change of position is put in suspension in the wine.

A useful precaution when one is preparing an old bottle is to place it cautiously in the cellar in a wine basket, keeping it in the same horizontal position that it had in the cave. Thanks to the basket, each glass can be subsequently served with the necessary delicacy needed to avoid mixing the deposits with the wine. Some very refined baskets have a small handle which regulates the level of the bottle, thereby enabling the wine to be drunk to the last drop, leaving only the deposit. If the bottle is stored in an upright position and then placed into the wine basket immediately before serving, the deposits may be disturbed. In this case it is better to leave the bottle standing on the table and decant it.

It is not necessary to serve a young wine, which does not have a deposit, in a wine basket, however elegant this may look.

Panisseau A dry white wine produced around Sigoulès which merits the appellation contrôlée Bergerac★. It is one of the rare dry wines of the area. Unlike the marrowy wines of the Sud-Ouest★, it is picked early. It is an aromatic, nervy★, very agreeable wine.

Parsac-Saint-Emilion The commune of Parsac has the right to add Saint-Emilion to its proper name. Its rocky hills produce very colourful, full-bodied wines which have considerable bouquet. The principle châteaux are Langlade, Binet and Piron.

passerillage A very late vendange which can only take place in exceptional weather conditions and with certain thick-skinned grape varieties. It is necessary to leave the grapes on the vine past the normal maturation state. The grape shrinks up and looks withered, the contents, especially sugar, becoming concentrated. The quality of the must which is produced from this is remarkable. This overmaturing is done to obtain the strongly concentrated Muscats★ which are used for vins doux naturels★.

The vins de paille★ are also made from passerillage of the grapes, not on the ground but in closed, warm areas. The grapes are hung in barns or laid on clay or on beds of straw. In certain years, overripening is also used in Sauternes★, Anjou★ and Touraine★, but the wines have neither the character nor the quality of those obtained from grapes which have been affected by pourriture noble★.

Pasteur, Louis (1822–1895) He is justly considered to be the father of modern oenology. This illustrious scientist began his studies on wine at the request of Napoleon III, who wanted an investigation into the numerous changes which could alter a wine. The first step was to determine the exact nature of alcoholic fermentation by which wine is made. He also investigated diseases of wine and their treatment. The sum of this considerable work was reported to the Emperor at Compiègne in 1865 in his famous 'Studies on wine, its diseases and the causes which

Louis Pasteur in his laboratory. Painting by Edelfeld (1887). Phot. Musée Pasteur, Paris.

pasteurisation A method of stabilising wine which was named after Pasteur who, along with Appert and Gayon, pioneered the process. The wine is heated for a minute to a temperature of around 60°C (55°C for wines high in alcohol and acidity, 65°C for light wines). This process destroys the bacteria in the wine and acts as a cure for diseases caused by acetic and lactic bacteria. It has often been used not only to stabilise wine but also to age it artificially or treat casse★.

The only real pasteurisation is that done by putting bottles in a bain-marie. It destroys the development of bacteria but also, at the same time, any chance of improving the wine. This process is occasionally used for ordinary table wines. It

is a delicate operation, since the wine's qualities may be altered by heating it.

Patrimonio One of the best-known Corsican★ wines, produced around Saint-Florent between Ile-Rousse and Bastia. There is some good red wine, and the white is interesting, dry, fragrant and full-bodied. The most famous, however, is the rosé, which is of exceptional quality and generally considered the best in Corsica. It is full-bodied, quite powerful and has a delicious fragrance. Since 1968 Patrimonio has been entitled to an AOC★, subject to certain conditions. Principal varieties of grape are Nielluccio for red and rosé, and Vermentino, Ugni Blanc and Rossola for white.

Pauillac The small town of Pauillac, unchallenged viticultural capital of the Médoc★, lies between Saint-Estèphe★ and Saint-Julien★. The appellation Pauillac comprises parts of Saint-Estèphe, Saint-Julien and Clissac. Pauillac's magnificent red wines fully justify their prestigious reputation. In good years they have all the essential characteristics of true Bordeaux. They are full-bodied, moelleux★ and *séveux*★, have a fine, fragrant bouquet and age extremely well.

Of all the Bordeaux communes, Pauillac is outstanding for having had eighteen châteaux listed in the 1855 classification★. Two of them were premier crus, the prestigious Château Lafite-Rothschild★ and Château-Latour★, and the others included equally distinguished names, such as Mouton-Rothschild (now a premier cru), Pichon-Longueville, Pichon-Longueville-Lalande, Pontet-Canet and Batailley. (See Index.)

paulée Originally a *paulée* was a communal meal held every year in the Côte d'Or at the end of the grape harvest. Proprietors and vignerons were united around one table, and in each village people brought out their best bottles to drink with the substantial regional dishes. The tradition gradually fell into disuse, and then, after a long lapse, was revived by the city of Meursault in 1923. A *paulée* was instituted in Paris in 1932. It takes place every year in a big restaurant, and is attended by both wine-lovers and vineyard-proprietors.

pays (vin de) A regional wine, usually made by blending, which is not subject to the appellation of origin controls. These wines, having an alcohol content of at least 8·5°, are hardly known outside their particular region as they are only consumed locally.

Vins de pays should not be confused with vins à appellation d'origine★. They are titled 'vins de pays du canton de . . .' unless the name of the canton is an appellation d'origine, in which case the name of the commune is substituted. If the commune is also an appellation d'origine the name of the locality is used, followed by the name of the department.

acquire with age. Certain light red and rosé wines possess this colour naturally.

Pérignon (Dom) A monk who was given the job of cellarer in the Abbey of Hautvillers in 1668, and occupied this post until his death in 1715. Popular tradition attributes him with the 'invention' of Champagne. The white wines of Champagne did, in fact, have a natural tendency to effervesce, a tendency which caused the local vignerons considerable annoyance and which remained largely unaffected by their various attempts to restrain it. Moreover, since the fashion at the time was for red wine, no-one bothered much about

The vines of Patrimonio.
Phot. Botin.

Pécharmant The appellation of some red wines of Bergerac★ produced on the hills near the town of Pécharmant, between the Dordogne and the main Bergerac-Périgueux road. The name (sometimes also written Pech-Charmant, meaning 'charming peak') applies to certain *parcelles*, or divisions, of the Saint-Sauveur, Creysse, Lembras and Bergerac communes, whose flinty, clay soil produces well-coloured, full-bodied warm wines with a characteristic *sève*★ and an alcoholic strength of at least 11°.

pelure d'oignon 'Onion-skin' is the name given to the slightly orange, reddish-brown or tawny tinge that some red wines

white, which was kept mainly for local consumption.

The fashion subsequently changed and people started to ask for white wine. (In those days it was called *clairet* or *fauvelet*, and was actually a pinkish or greyish colour, rather than white.) Dom Pérignon managed to create a really white wine a few years after taking up his cellarership. He studied the behaviour of its once-maligned effervescence, determined to transform the defect into a positive quality and to discover a method by which he could induce effervescence regularly and be certain of success every time.

His 'secret' was basically the addition of a certain, precise quantity of sugar to the

Above: the Abbey of Hautvillers; right: relief of Dom Pérignon in the gallery inaugurated in 1932 in honour of the inventor of Champagne. Phot. Lauros-Giraudon.

still wine. The many hopeful imitators who tried to reproduce the wine after his death had a high percentage of burst bottles for their pains, and it was not until a century later that his methods and expertise were rediscovered by a French chemist and wine-lover named François de Châlons, who has undeservedly been forgotten.

Dom Pérignon's real and indisputable merit was to have invented, or at any rate perfected, the blending and 'dosing' of different crus in order to balance and combine their various qualities to the best advantage. He was gifted with an extraordinarily sensitive palate which could distinguish not only one wine from another, but also the species of grape from which each one was made, and he used this skill to produce blended and unblended wines of incomparable quality.

Among other ideas ascribed to him is that of using the famous *crayères* (underground cellars cut out of the chalk during the Roman occupation of Gaul), where the low temperature allowed wine to mature more slowly, and a fining method by which wine could be cleared of sediment without being decanted. (The formula, whose basic ingredients were crystallised sugar, wine and *eau-de-vie*, served in any case as liqueur de tirage★ and to ensure secondary fermentation.) Some people even attribute to him the invention of the long, thin glasses that some purists consider to be the only proper ones for Champagne, and he is also alleged, albeit

without proof, to have been the first to substitute cork for the stoppers made of oil-soaked hemp which had, until then, always been used for wine bottles.

perlant   A word which describes a wine with a very slight effervescence, somewhere between a still wine and a vin pétillant★. The best-known perlant wines are Fendant du Valais, Crépy★ and Gaillac perlé★. The wine is bottled immediately after malo-lactic fermentation★, which transforms the malic acid contained in young wines into lactic acid and carbon dioxide. The carbon dioxide is trapped in the wine and produces the attractive light effervescence. The process is helped by leaving the lees in suspension and bottling the wine early in cold weather after filtration.

Pernand-Vergelesses   A small village in the Côte de Beaune on the borders of

the Aloxe-Corton★ commune. Certain divisions of the Pernand-Vergelesses vineyards produce excellent red or white wines, and these are entitled to the appellation Corton and Corton-Charlemagne.

The reds have warmth, firmness, longevity and a bouquet that has a distinct flavour of raspberries. When produced from a good rootstock, the red wines from the Ile des Vergelesses climat★ can, in good years, be compared with the best Cortons. The white wines have finesse and are excellent.

persistence The quality of a wine whose taste lingers pleasantly on the palate for some time after swallowing. Basically, a wine's bouquet is produced by its volatile elements, and its taste derives from the non-volatile ones (sugar, tannin, acids and their salts).

A *vin long* is one whose flavour persists on the palate, and is always a good wine; a *vin court* is merely average. Gauging the duration of their taste is a useful way of distinguishing different crus. The method is quite simple: after swallowing a mouthful of wine, count the seconds until the taste has completely disappeared from the palate. (A taste of tannin, which occasionally persists by itself, should be ignored.) The taste of red wine never lasts as long as that of white; even a very great red rarely lasts longer than eleven seconds. The following scale is a rough guide to the quality of wine: vin ordinaire: 1–3 seconds; good wine, 4–5 seconds; great wine, 6–8 seconds; very great wine, 8–11 seconds and more (the same as for dry white wines); vin blanc liquoreux★: 18 seconds; and the best Sauternes. Vouvray and Château-Chalon, 20–25 seconds.

pétillant (vin demi-mousseux) Semi-sparkling wine with more effervescence than vin perlant★ but less than vin mousseux★. Pétillant wine has a carbon dioxide pressure of not more than 2 or 2·5 kg at 20°C whereas the pressure of vin mousseux, like that of Champagne★, must be at least 4 and often 5 kg.

There are strict regulations governing the use of the word when applied to the AOC★ Loire wines (Vouvray, Montlouis, Touraine, Saumur, Anjou) made by the Champagne method★ of secondary fermentation in bottle. Wines from other vineyards, however, are unaffected by these rules, which is why some wines customarily called pétillant have no pressure at all, merely containing a small amount of dissolved carbon dioxide (for example, wines bottled on lees★, and immediately after malo-lactic fermentation★).

Pétrus (Château) Although there is no official classification of the wines of Pomerol★, the best of them is indisputably Château-Pétrus, an excellent wine that ranks with the premiers grands crus★ of Médoc★ and Saint-Emilion★.

Château-Pétrus is a 'complete' wine, velvety and admirably well balanced, with plenty of body and bouquet. Its quality is remarkably consistent and even a mediocre year produces good wine, although this should not be kept too long.

Vine leaves attacked by phylloxera. Phot. M.

phylloxera This tiny aphid, *Phylloxera vastatrix*, is the most destructive of all vine pests. The species originated in the USA and was accidentally introduced into Europe in the course of some viticultural experiments in about 1864. From the Gard

'The Vendange' by F. Van Valchenborch. Detail of a spinet cover, late 16th century. Phot. Scola.

expense that was borne entirely by the industry. The traditional structure of the European vineyards was completely altered as a result of this reconstruction. For some, like the Ile-de-France, the catastrophe was fatal and they disappeared forever. The reconstituted vineyards did, on the other hand, benefit from the regenerative effects of technology.

Picpoul-de-Pinet A white VDQS★ wine from Languedoc★ made mainly (about 70%) from the Picpoul grape, which gives it its name, with a proportion of the white Terret and Clairette varieties. This wine, produced by the Pinet commune and four or five others nearby, is generous, dry but not acid, and the ideal accompaniment to Bouzigues oysters.

pièce A hogshead. A measure used in the Burgundy region, roughly the equivalent of a barrique★ (i.e. 228 litres). Its capacity does, however, vary from region to region. In Mâcon it is 216 litres and in Beaujolais, 214. The unit of measure used in Chablis is the feuillette★.

pied de cuve Thanks to the contrôle de maturation★, the vigneron knows beforehand when the vendage will take place and has time to prepare carefully the base of his cuve. With this in mind, he chooses from the best parts of the vines several hundred beautiful, healthy, ripe grapes. After destalking and pressing★, the grapes are placed in a very clean container. If necessary, the vigneron heats the must to between 22 and 25°C. Alcoholic fermentation begins within twelve hours, during which time the vigneron takes care to aerate the must. The resultant leaven, the pied de cuve, contains such a high level of active yeast that 1 hl can activate 40 hl of the vendange.

Pierrevert (Coteaux de) The VDQS★ red and rosé wines from this Provence★ vineyard are made from the traditional grapes of the region, combined with the Syrah variety. The white wines, made from Clairette, Marsanne and Roussane grapes, are reminiscent of Côtes-du-Rhône★. The appellation Clairet de Pierrevert applies to white and rosé wines grown at Pierrevert, Manosque and

department of France, where it was first noticed, it proceeded to ravage virtually every vineyard in Europe, and some never fully recovered. Vignerons tried various countermeasures such as submerging★ the vines, planting them in sand and injecting the soil with carbon bisulphide, but despite all their efforts these methods proved useless. Finally, they tried grafting European vines on to American root-stocks, which are immune to the insect, which was finally successful. It was feared at first that the imported strains would have a detrimental effect on the taste of the wines (see foxy★), but these fears were unfounded and grafting has been standard practice ever since.

The restoration of the vineyards of France alone cost 1800 million francs, an

Sainte-Tulle. These are sometimes sparkling, and have a musky flavour.

pinard A French slang word (sanctioned by the Académie Française since 1943) for vins ordinaires rich in colour and tannin. The word received official recognition during the First World War, when Marshall Joffre called the wine drunk by the common soldiers 'le Général Pinard', and he was well qualified to assess its virtues since his father was a cooper in Rivesaltes, a famous vineyard near the Pyrenees.

As to the origin of the word, various theories have been suggested: some think it comes from *pino*, classical Greek for 'to drink'; others recall that, in the sixteenth century, a Burgundian named Jean Pinard was renowned as the best vigneron of his time, a fact noted in a book printed at Auxerre in 1607 and reprinted in Paris in 1851.

pinçant A pinçant wine has an excessive fixed acidity★ which makes it seem to 'pinch' the tongue. *Pointu*, or 'sharp', is used in the same sense.

Pineau d'Aunis A red grape grown mostly in the Vendôme and Loir-et-Cher departments of France, and sometimes known as Chenin Noir. Like Chenin Blanc, otherwise called Pineau de la Loire★, it is in no way related to the Pinot★ varieties. Its name comes from a small village in the commune of Dampierre not far from Saumur.

Pineau d'Aunis is probably descended from indigenous wild vines, and is generally acknowledged to be the ancestor of the famous Pineau de la Loire, which is itself the result of years of carefully selective cultivation by the vignerons of the Loire valley. It is one of the varieties grown for the red and rosé wines of Anjou★ and Saumur★.

Pineau de la Loire The only grape used for the great white wines of Touraine★ and Anjou★. It is also known as Chenin Blanc, which is what Rabelais called it. It is sometimes, mistakenly, written as Pinot de la Loire, although it has no connection with the Pinot family. The Pineau de la Loire is ideally suited to the Loire valley, being perfectly adapted to its climate and able to grow on any kind of soil. Elsewhere, however, the wines it produces are not outstanding.

Pineau de la Loire is responsible for the great wines of Vouvray★, Montlouis★, Saumur★, Savennières★ and Coteaux-du-Layon★. The grape, during good years, is frequently attacked by pourriture noble★. It is harvested very late, sometimes during November, producing well-coloured wines with a wonderfully delicate bouquet. It also lends itself very well to the preparation of sparkling wines, e.g. the vins mousseux of Vouvray, Montlouis and Saumur.

Pineau des Charentes An AOC★ liqueur★ wine, Pineau des Charentes is made by muting with alcohol, in this case Cognac, and the must or grape juice is harvested in the Charentes vineyards. The method of preparation seems to have originated in the sixteenth century. Like Ratafia de Champagne★, Pineau des Charentes was for a long time made only for private consumption, and it was not until just before the Second World War that it was sold commercially. It can be drunk as both an apéritif and a dessert wine, and is extremely pleasant chilled. It can be either red or white, and has an alcoholic strength

Pineau de la Loire. In good years this famous grape may be attacked by pourriture noble, as is shown here. Phot. M.

A farm and its vineyards at Pineau, Charentes. Phot. Lauros–Atlas–Photo.

of at least 16·5° (sometimes as much as 22°), masked by a deceptive smoothness.

Pinot Gris   An Alsatian grape, a member of the great Pinot family. It is also incorrectly known as 'Tokay', which can cause confusion with the famous Hungarian wine. It is difficult to cultivate, and generally has a poor yield. The white wine it makes is full-bodied, heady, solid and powerful, but somewhat lacking in delicacy, and is most appreciated in its native region. In good years, however, it has more grace and an agreeable smoothness. The grape is also grown in Baden, Germany, where it is called Ruländer, and in northern Italy where it is one of the varieties used to make Terlano, one of the best white wines of the Tyrol.

Pinot Noir   One of the most important red grapes, Pinot Noir has been the mainstay of the great red Burgundies since the Burgundian vineyards were first planted, producing the excellent wines of Romanée-Conti, la Tâche, Musigny, Chambertin, Clos-de-Vougeot and Pommard.

With Chardonnay★ it is one of the two principal varieties of grape grown in both Burgundy and Champagne. In the latter region, where it has been cultivated since the Middle Ages, it was given the name *morillon* (probably in reference to its colour, which is black 'as a Moor'), and used to make excellent red wines that rivalled

Pinot Noir, the great variety of Burgundy and Champagne. Phot. M.

194

those of Beaune★. Of these, only Bouzy★ and Cumières have survived to the present day. Nowadays, the production of Pinot Noir, which is grown mainly on the Montagne de Reims★, is roughly four times as great as that of Chardonnay, whereas in the Middle Ages the proportions were the other way round.

Pinot grapes are small, tight and blue-black, with a sweet and colourless juice. In Burgundy the skins are left with the juice while it ferments, the pigments contained in them dissolve as the temperature rises and give the wines their magnificent colour. In Champagne, Pinot grapes are never crushed; they are picked and then immediately placed in special presses whose large surface area enables them to be pressed very quickly. This is to prevent the juice from being discoloured by contact with the skins.

A proportion of Pinot is used in the preparation of the wines of Saint-Pourçain★, the Orléannais★, Châtillon-en-Diois★ and the Jura★, as well as the excellent red wines of Alsace★ and the exceptional rosés of Marsannay-la-Côte★, les Riceys★ and Sancerre★.

piquette   When the vin de presse★ has been removed from the press, marc still

remains in the cuve. Water is added and, after about fifteen days, a thin, rather strong wine called piquette is produced which is usually consumed by the vigneron and his family. If the operation is repeated a second time, more acidic piquette is produced.

Piquette is also used in a derogatory way to describe wines which are low in alcohol but high in acidity

plein   Full, a word used to describe a wine rich in alcohol, agreeably full-bodied and well balanced.

Pomerol   The little vineyard of Pomerol, bordered to the east by the gravelly region of Saint-Emilion★, lies just outside Libourne on the right bank of the Dordogne. Vines have been cultivated in the Pomerol region since the Gallo-Roman era, but it was the Hospitalers of St John who really developed the vineyards when they established a Commandery there in the twelfth century. The vines were for a long time confused with those of Saint-Emilion, and it was not until the nineteenth century that their great reputation was finally established.

The soil of Pomerol is particularly suitable for the cultivation of vines, being composed of flint and gravel, clay and gravel, or sand, with an iron-bearing subsoil that gives the wine its particular *sève*★ or strength. The wines, all red, are made from the noble★ grapes, Cabernet Franc, Cabernet-Sauvignon (or Bouchet), Merlot and Malbec (or Pressac).

Pomerol is a generous, full-bodied, very attractive wine with a brilliant, dark ruby colour, a distinctive flavour and a marvellous velvety taste which fulfills the promise of its bouquet. It has been called 'a mesh of savours and aromas'. It has a curious similarity to Burgundy, but is more notable for combining the best qualities of the Médoc★ and Saint-Emilion. It has the finesse of the former and the *sève* and vigour of the latter.

The appellation Pomerol comprises the Pomerol commune and a small part of Libourne. Although there is no official classification of Pomerol crus, Château-Pétrus★ is generally acknowledged to be the best, followed by the Châteaux Certan, Vieux-Certan, la Conseillante, Petit-Village, Trotanoy, l'Evangile, Lafleur,

Pinot Meunier or 'Gris-Meunier' grape. The most popular variety around Orléans. Phot. M.

Above and right: Pomerol vineyards near Libourne. Phot. M. and René-Jacques.

POMMARD-RUGIENS
TÊTE DE CUVÉE
APPELLATION POMMARD 1ᵉʳ CRU CONTRÔLÉE
ANNÉE 1966
RÉCOLTE PAR
FÉLIX CLERGET
PROPRIÉTAIRE A POMMARD, CÔTE-D'OR

Joseph Drouhin

POMMARD-ÉPENOTS
APPELLATION CONTRÔLÉE
MIS EN BOUTEILLE PAR
JOSEPH DROUHIN
Maison fondée en 1880
NÉGOCIANT A BEAUNE, CÔTE-D'OR
AUX CELLIERS DES ROIS DE FRANCE ET DES DUCS DE BOURGOGNE

Gaxin and La Fleur–Pétrus. (See Index.)

The Pomerol vineyards also extend into two neighbouring communes which produce wines that have more or less the same characteristics: Lalande-de-Pomerol★ and Néac★.

Pommard Pommard, which is always red, is perhaps the best known of all red Burgundies, at any rate outside its native country. The commune from which it comes in the Côte de Beaune★ has, in fact, cultivated the vine for many hundreds of years, and in the days when vinification and conservation techniques were far from perfect, Pommard had two important qualities: it kept well and travelled without spoiling. It was therefore known far beyond the borders of Burgundy at a very early stage.

Besides possessing these qualities, all Pommards are full-bodied, vinous, well coloured and powerful, and acquire in ageing a flavour of truffles. Their taste has bite and fullness. These characteristics are more or less pronounced according to the climat: Argillières is lighter, Rugiens is very full-bodied and firm, and Epenots has finesse and breeding. Also worth mentioning are Clos-Blanc, les Arvelets, les Croix-Noires and la Platière. (See Index.)

Port The most famous, as well as the most widely known, of all liqueur★ wines, port comes from a strictly delimited region in Portugal, the Upper Douro and its tributaries, including the Cima Corgo and the Baixo Corgo above and below the Rio Corgo. The vine-growing region of the Upper Douro covers barely 2500 square km and is particularly harsh and inhospitable. The ravines, enclosed by schistose mountains and mercilessly scorched by the sun, produce about 250–280,000 hl of port a year, which is strictly controlled by Portuguese wine laws. Due to the special character of the region, the variety of

grapes planted is of only secondary importance. There are about sixteen red varieties, including Avarelhào and Touriga, and six white ones, amongst which are Malvasia Fina, Moscatel, Rabigato and Codega. However, it is the soil and the climate which with skilful human assistance make port wine really what it is.

At the beginning of the eighteenth century, a commercial agreement was made between Portugal and Britain concerning the exchange of English wool and Portuguese wines, which had always been popular in England. Thus it was in response to the preferences of the British palate that the preparation of port was gradually established. Some Englishmen were such enthusiasts that, not content with having installed themselves as wine merchants in Oporto, they became vine-growers in the Upper Douro. One of the

Pommard, near Beaune.
Phot. Lauros-Beaujard.

Barge designed for the transport of casks from the Upper Douro to the town of Oporto. Phot. Casa de Portugal.

best known of these was the celebrated Joseph James Forrester who was born in Hull in 1809, came to Oporto in 1831 and was drowned in the Douro in 1861. His thirty years in Portugal were so full of achievement that the Portuguese made him a baron. One of his original ideas was to transport the wine casks from the vineyards to Oporto in flat-bottomed boats called *barcos rabelos*, which were able to negotiate the fierce torrents and rapids of the Douro. More important, he was the first to explore thoroughly the valley of the Douro, making a map of the vineyard area and conducting a geological survey.

Although grapes were traditionally trodden by foot in the Upper Douro, mechanical pressing is now gradually becoming the rule. Port is made by mutage★, like the vins doux naturels of France. Fermentation, which converts the must's natural sugar into alcohol, is stopped at a certain point by adding more alcohol, the timing depending on whether a sweet or dry wine is desired. Since 1907, the percentage of alcohol added to the wine has been legally fixed at a minimum of 16·5%, and must be in the form of a natural *eau-de-vie* made in the Douro vineyards.

After its arrival in Oporto, or rather in Vila Nova de Gaia, the capital's twin-city on the other side of the river, the wine is left in cask for three years, during which time it is constantly checked and examined by experts who decide which kind of port it is most suitable for – Tawny★, Vintage★, etc.

England has 95% of the vintage port market and used to be the chief importer of other types of port, but has recently been overtaken by France. The French usually drink port as an apéritif, an increasingly popular habit which accounts for the trebling of French imports over the last ten years. As an apéritif it should be white, dry and chilled. In England and Portugal it is more often served at the end of the meal, where its warm, smooth and generous nature has made it the traditional and perfect accompaniment and stimulant to after-dinner conversation.

The ideal age for port is generally considered to be between twenty and thirty years. Its qualities usually start to decline after forty years, although there are some marvellous exceptions. Once opened, a bottle should be consumed within a few days as if left longer, it tends to go flat and sour and loses its aroma.

There are a great many ornate and extremely expensive 'port glasses' on the market, but they should be avoided. Whatever kind of port is being served, the glasses should be clear, to show off its colour, and preferably tulip-shaped, i.e. closing a little towards the rim. They should never be filled more than two-thirds full, so that enough room is left to trap the bouquet.

Portugal Together with cork, wine is the country's chief export. Port★ and Madeira★ have long been known and admired the world over, and vinho verde★, long unknown outside its native country except by tourists, has recently started to appear in the rest of Europe. But as well as these famous wines, Portugal produces a considerable quantity of red, rosé and white vins ordinaires which are generally quite full-bodied and often pleasant.

The country's total annual production is about 15 million hl, of which three-quarters is red. Vinho verde accounts for 3 million hl, port for barely 280,000 hl, and Madeira, only 80,000 hl.

Portugal has fifteen viticultural regions including Madeira, which is an island off the west coast of Morocco. All Portuguese wines are subject to strict wine laws, and

Portugal: vineyards of the Upper Douro near Pinhão.
Phot. Y. Loirat.

port, Madeira and vinho verde are very rigidly controlled. The regions of Dão, Colares, Carcavelos, Setubal and Bucelas produce characteristic wines whose production area is legally delimited and which have an official appellation of origin.

The Dão wines, considered the best of Portugal, are made from grapes growing along the banks of the Mondego. Most of the wines are red and are made from the Tourigo grape, which gives a sweet, slightly astringent wine. The less numerous white wines are made from the Dona Branca and Arinto grape and are light, fresh and fragrant with a beautiful blond colour. The Colares vineyards are situated

on the seacoast close to Lisbon, growing in sandy soil which is difficult to cultivate. The Ramisco grape makes the wines of Colares full-bodied and velvety. They are kept in cask for two years and do not fully mature for at least five years. Unfortunately, the vineyards are slowly disappearing as a result of expanding tourist facilities. The Setubal region south of Lisbon produces the well-known Muscatel of Setubal whose pronounced aroma, colour and fruity taste are attributed to the special method of vinification, in which the stalks are left in the must and the wine is matured in cask for five or six years. The Muscatel of Setubal is a vin de liqueur

which is a perfect apéritif, dessert wine or accompaniment to cheese. The dry, astringent, pale yellow wines of Bucelas, north of Lisbon, are made from the Arinto grape.

Eight other regions of Portugal are in the process of being officially limited and classified AOC★. Pinhel produces light, agreeable clarets, and Lafões, red wines somewhat similar to the vinho verdes★. Bairrada, not far from Dão, makes the pétillant★ white or red Anadia and the Ruby of Bairrada. Other viticultural regions include Bucaco, Sangalhos, Alcobaca, Ribatejo and Torres Vedras.

Portugal also produces sparkling wines like Lamego, and rosés such as Mateus and Faisca (sold under the name Lancers).

Pouilly-Fuissé This excellent dry white wine from the Mâconnais★ vineyards is, like all the great white Burgundies, made from Chardonnay★ grapes. It is produced by four communes: Fuissé, Solutré-Pouilly, Vergisson and Chaintré.

It is a very attractive wine with a fine, greeny-gold colour and an exquisite, delicately shaded bouquet. It is vigorous and dry, though moelleux, and has a pronounced character of its own. Some people find it a little heavy and difficult to digest. It ages extremely well and may well improve after even twenty years in bottle.

Vineyards on the banks of the Loire near Pouilly. Phot. A. A. Petit-Atlas-Photo.

Pouilly Fumé An appellation contrôlée that applies only to Pouilly-sur-Loire★ wines made from Sauvignon★ (also known as Blanc Fumé) grapes. The appellation is sometimes Blanc Fumé de Pouilly. Nobody knows why Sauvignon should be called Blanc Fumé at Pouilly, though it may be because of its colour and smoky flavour. Whatever the reason, it makes excellent wines and has been responsible for Pouilly-sur-Loire's longstanding and well-merited reputation. Unfortunately, its success is not as widespread as it deserves to be, since annual production is not only low but is also sometimes drastically reduced by spring frosts.

It is an attractive, clear, green-tinted wine that has a minimum alcoholic content of 11° and a distinct character of its own. It has a pronounced, slightly spicy and musky fragrance and, although dry, is always pleasingly supple. It is ready to drink quite soon after bottling and loses none of its qualities with age. The best crus are les Loges, les Bas-Coins, Château du Nozet and les Bernadats.

Pouilly-Loché An appellation which applies to wines produced by the Loché commune, next to Pouilly★ in the Mâconnais★. It is a dry, fruity wine with the same characteristics as Pouilly-Fuissé★.

Pouilly-sur-Loire Celebrated for its wines since the Middle Ages, the vineyard of Pouilly-sur-Loire surrounds the village of the same name on the right bank of the Loire in the Nièvre department of France. The communes of Pouilly-sur-Loire, Saint-Andelain, Tracy, Garchy, Saint-Laurent, Saint-Martin and Mesves all produce wine entitled to this AOC★, but the first three are the most important. There is a great variety of soils, with marl and Kimmeridge clay predominating, as at Chablis★.

The appellation Pouilly-sur-Loire applies to wines made from Chasselas★ grapes, whereas the appellation Pouilly Fumé★ is restricted to wines made entirely from Sauvignon★ (or Blanc Fumé). Chasselas usually grows best in siliceous clay (on the hill of Saint-Andelain, for instance), a type of soil not altogether suitable for Sauvignon, which has largely taken over the best, or at any rate the most calcareous, slopes. Chasselas here produces

wines which are totally different from the ones it makes in Switzerland and Savoie (Crépy★). The region suits it perfectly and an expert has declared that, 'the soil of Pouilly is to Chasselas what Beaujolais is to Gamay'.

Pouilly-sur-Loire is a clear, light, fruity wine, very pleasant in its youth but lacking the character and distinction of Pouilly Fumé. It is fine and delicate and has a low acid content, a minimum alcoholic strength of 9° and occasionally a nutty flavour.

Pouilly-sur-Loire bailiffs at Saint-Emilion. Phot. René-Jacques.

Pouilly-Vinzelles Like those of Loché, the limestone-clay hills of the Vinzelles commune in the Mâconnais★ produce a dry white wine which has a well-deserved reputation and various similarities to Pouilly-Fuissé★. Like the latter, Pouilly-Vinzelles keeps for a long time without losing any of its bouquet or flavour.

pourriture grise (grey rot) *Botrytis cinerea*, responsible for the famous pourriture noble★ which attacks ripe grapes, also produces the disastrous pourriture grise (grey rot) which affects green grapes. It invades the immature grapes after a long

Above: pourriture grise;
below: pourriture noble. Phot.
M. and Weiss-Rapho.

period of humidity when many have split – some may have burst as a result of the flow of strong saps, others by insects. As the fungus moves in and rapidly propagates, the grapes darken, become covered with a grey dust and fall.

The damage can be considerable. The wine made from such an infected vendange will be of poor quality, having a mouldy, 'oxide' taste and will reach old age precociously.

Several methods can be used to treat that part of the vendange which has been infected by grey rot. If the must is heated to 80°C the oxidising fungus will be destroyed and the resulting wine is a bit better than if the operation had not been performed. However, bouquet is still changed and the wine still ages rapidly.

Alternatively, the wine can be made a rosé, in which case the musty taste acquired from the stalk and pulp during a one- or two-day fermentation would not be noticeable.

pourriture noble 'Noble rot' is the literal translation of this French name for the mould, *Botrytis cinerea,* which attacks ripe grapes when the temperature and humidity are favourable. Unlike pourriture grise★ or 'grey rot', it is heartily welcomed by the vignerons, as it produces exquisite and much sought after wine. At first, small, brown marks appear on the grape skin and these gradually grow to cover the whole fruit until it is the colour the Loire vine-growers call '*patte-de-lièvre*' (hare's foot). The grape then turns a dark purplish-brown, a stage known as '*pourri plein*', and finally withers, wrinkles and looks shrivelled, or '*rôti*'. The grapes do not all reach this final stage at the same time, so the pickers have to go through the vineyard very carefully at intervals and only take those that are ready. The grapes are picked individually with special scissors, and the whole meticulous process can last from September until the beginning of November.

Pourriture noble causes the composition of the grape to change considerably; the grape juice is condensed, causing a greater concentration of the natural sugar, an overall diminution of acids and the formation of gums and of citric and glutinic acids. Mere overripening, or passerillage★, of the grapes does not

produce the same results. Ideally, *Botrytis* should attack really ripe grapes; if it comes too soon, it is less effective.

The fermentation of the grapes is extremely slow, as the activity of the yeasts is inhibited by the high sugar content of the must, and may take from several weeks to several months. This long period in vat produces a considerable quantity of glycerine★, which gives the wine exceptional smoothness. The wine has to be racked★ and topped up (ouillage★) frequently, and is usually bottled about three years after the vintage. All this complicated and painstaking preparation results in the great vins blancs liquoreux de pourriture noble – rare, delicious, and absolutely natural sweet white wines that are prized and admired the world over.

Although the wines made by pourriture noble in Sauternes★ are generally considered the best, the neighbouring vineyards of Loupiac★, Cérons★ and Sainte-Croix-du-Mont★ also produce their own, as do Monbazillac★ in Touraine★, the regions of Anjou★ and Alsace★, and the Rhine and Moselle valleys in Germany.

Premières Côtes de Bordeaux A region which stretches roughly sixty kl along the right bank of the Garonne from Saint-Maixant to Bordeaux, and consists of about thirty communes entitled to use the appellation. Loupiac★ and Sainte-Croix-du-Mont★, although geographically part of the region, qualify for their own appellation contrôlée.

Both red and white wines are produced, the red mainly in the south, and the white in the north of the district, with the Cambes commune on the dividing line. The white wines are made from Sémillon, Sauvignon and Muscadelle grapes, harvested as at Sauternes★. They are full-bodied, fine and fragrant, often moelleux★, sometimes liquoreux. Some people prefer them dry, and a small quantity is made to cater for this taste. The Langoiran and Cadillac communes produce what are probably the best white wines of the region. The red wines are warm and generous with a good colour. They are a little hard in their youth, but acquire suppleness and softness with age.

press There are various types of winepress in use. Ideally they should combine speed and economy of labour with efficiency. A bad press, for instance, could crush the grape stalks, which would make the wine taste very unpleasant. In ancient times, grapes were pressed by hand in linen

Winepress owned by Hattstatt (1687). Musée d'Unterlinden, Colmar. Phot. Lauros.

Automatic presses in a co-operative cave on the island of Oléron. Phot. M.

wine. The vin de presse has a higher tannin★ content and a higher volatile acidity★ than the vin de goutte, but a lower fixed acidity★. The percentage of vin de presse added to the vin de goutte varies according to the type of wine desired, and whatever is left over is sold without an appellation. To prevent white grapes being overpressed, a precise ruling obliges vine-growers to distil the remainder and sell it as alcohol to the State.

pressing   An operation which consists of extracting the juice from grapes or the wine from marc by means of a press★. For white wines and vins gris★, the grapes are crushed and pressed as soon as they are picked. For red wines, the skins and stalks are left in the juice during fermentation to add colour and tannin★. They also form the marc, which is afterwards pressed to extract the vin de presse★, which varies in amount from about 10–20% of the vin de goutte★. In certain vineyards the marc is never pressed more than once, in order to avoid crushing the stalks which would give the wine an excessive tannin content and result in an unpleasant astringency known as *goût de rafle*.

privilège de Bordeaux   A statute introduced by Henry III in 1224 gave the people of Bordeaux the right to protect their wine trade, i.e. the sale of the wine produced in Bordeaux and its immediate environs. The citizens interpreted this as

bags; later, in presses worked by levers and capstans; and by AD 23, screw-presses were in use. Grapes were always pressed before fermentation, and wine was generally rather pale. Today there are hydraulic presses, mechanical presses, horizontal and vertical presses and screw-presses. There is even a pneumatic press, in which the grapes are crushed against the sides of a cylinder by an expanding bag filled with compressed air.

presse (moût de, vin de)   In the vinification of white wines, the moût de presse is the juice obtained from the grapes put in the press after the moût de goutte★ has been run off. In Champagne★, the juice from the last pressing of the must (about 7·5 litres per hl of must) is called rebêche★ and is not allowed to be sold commercially.

In the vinification of red wines, the vin de presse is that obtained by pressing the marc which is left after running the vin de goutte★ off from the vats of fermented

Automatic pressing. Phot. René-Jacques.

authorising them to forbid any wine from the inland areas of Aquitaine access to the port of Bordeaux before a certain date. This became known as the privilège de Bordeaux and, although it had no real legal basis, it nonetheless had the force of law for six centuries. The date they fixed was originally 11th November, then 30th November, and finally Christmas, by which time the foreign ships moored in the Gironde had long since made provision for their journeys – including, of course, stocks of Bordeaux wine.

This measure meant that there was, in seilles in about 600 BC. The Provençal viticultural tradition, therefore, goes back 2500 years, longer than any other French vineyard.

As in all southern vineyards, a great many varieties of grape are used: Grenache, Cinsault, Mourvèdre, Tibouren and Carignan for red wines, Clairette, Ugni Blanc and Bourboulenc for white. The INAO★ has divided them into two categories, authorised varieties and supplementary varieties. The proportion of the latter in any wine is strictly limited by law.

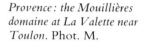

Provence: the Mouillières domaine at La Valette near Toulon. Phot. M.

effect, no foreign outlet at all for the wines of Cahors★, Gaillac★, Moissac and even the Médoc★. The only vineyard to get round this harsh law was Bergerac★, which could ship its wines to the sea on the Dordogne without having to go through Bordeaux. The privilege was abolished, after an enquiry which disclosed its origins, by an edict of Louis XVI in 1776.

This boycott by Bordeaux had a significant effect on rival vineyards. Moissac and Agen turned to producing fruit (prunes and table grapes), and Cahors dug up all its vines.

Provence The present vine-growing region of Provence is much smaller than was the former province of the same name, consisting nowadays of only the Bouches-du-Rhône, Var and Alpes-Maritimes departments. Vines were first planted there by Greeks from Phocea, who founded a colony on the site of present-day Mar-

The Ugni Blanc grape is widely used in Provence, particularly around Cassis. Phot. M.

Provence has four appellations contrôlées, Palette★, Cassis★, Bandol★ and Bellet★, and also four pleasant VDQS★, Côtes-de-Provence★, Coteaux-d'Aix-en-Provence★, Coteaux-des-Baux★ and Coteaux-de-Pierrevert★.

provignage Layering, a method once employed to propagate vines. A shoot of the growing vine is led down into the ground, where it eventually takes root. It is then cut from the main stem and replanted as a new rooted plant.

Puisseguin-Saint-Emilion The pebbly slopes of the Puisseguin commune, which is entitled to add the name Saint-Emilion★ to its own, produce firm, full-bodied wines that have a strong colour and keep well. The good crus also have a certain finesse. The best known are Châteaux des Laurets, du Roc-de-Boissac and Teyssier.

Puligny-Montrachet This village of the Côte de Beaune, together with the neighbouring one of Chassagne-Montrachet★, produces superlative dry white wines which are considered among the best in the world. The most famous of them, the great Montrachet★, is grown in both communes as is Bâtard-Montrachet, whereas Chevalier-Montrachet and Bienvenues-Bâtard-Montrachet are grown only in Puligny. Chevalier-Montrachet scarcely falls short of Montrachet's exceptional quality, equalling it in delicacy if not in body. Bienvenues-Bâtard-Montrachet is lighter than both of these, but has a certain elegance and a more fruity taste which have won it an enthusiastic following. These outstanding wines are sold under the name of their cru and not of their commune. Other wines, with equal breeding though less prestige, bear the name Puligny-Montrachet followed by the name of their particular climat★ (e.g. Puligny-Montrachet les Combettes, le Cailleret, les Folatières, les Pucelles and les Chalumeaux). (See Index.)

The red wines are produced in limited quantities (le Cailleret, for example) and have body, finesse and a smooth bouquet that develops with age.

Q

Quarts-de-Chaume One of the great white crus of Anjou★, made on the hillsides bordering the Layon★ and possessing its own appellation contrôlée. Its superior quality can be largely attributed to its quite exceptional location. It forms a part of the Rochefort-sur-Loire commune, and slopes down from the village of Chaumes to the banks of the river Layon, sheltered by hills from the north, east and west winds. Thus protected, the grapes ripen quicker and pourriture noble★ develops better than in the neighbouring vineyards. Even very ordinary years produce remarkably good wines, and good years are outstanding – the 1921 vintage, for example, will long be remembered.

Quarts-de-Chaume is a rich, powerful, velvety, sweet wine with exceptional qualities of both bouquet and taste. Some

people claim to detect in it the flavours of amber, lime and apricots, and it has a slight, distinctive touch of bitterness which brings out its fragrance further. It is at its best several years after bottling, indeed it ages magnificently and is well worth waiting for. The principal domaines are l'Echarderie, Bellerive and Suronde. Annual production is extremely low, which is unfortunate as it is generally considered to be the greatest of all Anjou wines.

Quatourze The wines of this appellation are made in the Coteaux du Languedoc★ area and are classified VDQS★. They are either red or rosé, as the small quantity of white wine does not qualify for the appellation. The vineyard is situated on a pebbly plateau not far from the town of Narbonne in the Aude department. The red wines, which are undoubtedly the best, are full, warm and powerful, have a certain finesse and age well.

queue (vin de) The vin de queue is made from the last batch of grapes gathered in the Sauternes★ vineyards. The grapes are picked in successive stages, only the ones with pourriture noble★ being taken each time. In the end the only grapes left are those which have not been, and now never will be, affected by the mould and it is these which make the vin de queue.

A queue is also a measure of capacity equal to two pièces★, i.e. 2 × 228 litres. Lastly, *taille à queue*, or 'tail pruning', is a method of pruning vines.

Quincy A small vineyard of about 200 ha which lies in the commune of Quincy and part of Brinay on the banks of the Cher, to the west of Bourges in the Loire valley. The wine's distinctive character is largely due to the type of soil in the vineyard. Quincy is situated on a limestone plateau which, in prehistoric times, formed the riverbed of the Cher, and the soil is composed of the gravel and siliceous sand deposited by the river over a layer of clay of varying depth. This soil, which is

otherwise barely suitable for cultivation, suits the Sauvignon★ grape extremely well. Sauvignon is the only variety planted in the Quincy vineyard and the wines made from it are AOC★. It is grafted on to an excellent vine-stock called Riparia which ripens quickly, giving Quincy an advantage over the nearby vineyards of Sancerre★ and Pouilly-sur-Loire★ in years of high humidity and late harvests.

Although Quincy keeps well, it is as good as it is rare when young, so that it is perhaps best to drink it as soon as it is found. It is a very dry wine with a good bouquet, a finesse imparted to it by the gravel of the soil and, besides the usual characteristics of wines made from Sauvignon, a particular and very agreeable flavour of its own. It has a minimum alcoholic strength of 10·5° and sometimes exceeds 11 or 12°, although in these cases the finesse of its fragrance is impaired.

Quarts-de-Chaume: view of the vineyards. Phot. M.

R

racé A French word used to describe a wine that has all the characteristics of its 'race' or origins (variety of grape, soil, etc.). It implies more elegance and 'personality' than *type*, which is used for more ordinary wines. The equivalent phrase in English would be 'a wine of breeding'.

racking (soutirage) An operation which separates the clear wine from its deposits (or lees). It is a long and delicate process. First the wine is drawn off from the fermenting-vats into casks fumigated with sulphur dioxide★ and then, when the winter is well over, in about March or April, it is racked a second time, the lees now being mainly composed of tartric crystals. For wines which are going to remain in cask to mature, the third racking generally takes place around September. When wine is left in cask for more than a year, it is ouillaged★ as well as racked, i.e. more wine is added to replace that lost through evaporation and absorption by the wood.

rancio A name given to certain wines which acquire a particular bouquet and flavour in the course of a long and slow maturation in casks exposed to the sun. The process is a kind of beneficial maderisation★ which heightens and refines the qualities of the wine. Madeira, some Marsalas and the older French vins doux naturels★ are all included in this category. There is no precise legal definition of the term rancio. It is simply applied to all wines that have this particular colour and taste.

Rasteau This commune, which is situated in the south of the Côtes du Rhône★

region in the Vaucluse department, produces appellation contrôlée vins doux naturels★. Its vineyard covers the sunny hillsides between the Aygues and Ouvèze rivers, and consists of Rasteau and some parts of Sablet and Cairanne. It is mainly (90%) planted with Grenache vines.

Like all vins doux naturels, Rasteau is made by muting★ must with alcohol during fermentation. The must is then left to ferment with or without the grape skins and stalks, depending on whether a red or golden-coloured wine is desired. Rasteau is an excellent dessert wine, generous and sweet with a pronounced bouquet.

The commune also produces red, rosé and white wines sold under the regional appellation Côtes-du-Rhône.

Ratafia de Champagne A liqueur made by adding alcohol to the must of grapes from the Champagne★ region. The

Racking by pump. Phot. M.

208

Vines around Rasteau.
Phot. Lauros.

alcohol is either *eau-de-vie* from Champagne or from another source. Although the fruity tasting Ratafia is very agreeable, it is not often sold commercially, being highly taxed. Some prefer the appellation contrôlée Pineau des Charentes★, whose must is dosed with Cognac. Carthagène★ and Riquiqui are liqueurs of the same type made in certain areas for the personal consumption of the vine-growers. (In several European countries, particularly Spain, the designation Ratafia is used for those liqueurs made by the addition of alcohol to must.)

rebêche The juice from the last pressing of Champagne grapes. Only the first few pressings are allowed to be made into Champagne★ and officially qualify for the name. According to present laws, every 4000 kg of grapes yields 26.66 hl of juice allowed to be used for Champagne, of which 20 hl are cuvée and 666 litres, the first and second tailles. The rebêche is the juice left in the marc gras, or pulp, after these pressings. It is extracted and made into a vin de consommation courante★ for the vine-growers and their employees. The remaining dry marc is made into *eau-de-vie de marc*, or grape brandy.

refermentation The relatively high proportion of natural sugar remaining in vins blancs liquoreux★ after fermentation makes them liable to referment in bottle. This can result in clouded wine, a taste of lees, and corks which either leak or explode under the pressure of the carbon dioxide produced by fermentation. The tendency can be corrected by treatment with sulphur dioxide★, which is the only stabilising agent authorised by French law. Sulphur dioxide is only antiseptic, and thus effective, when pure, and it has to be added in fairly large quantities since a certain proportion always combines with the wine's sugar. The amount necessary varies from one wine to another, depending on the sugar content.

Nowadays, laboratories have equipment that can calculate the right dosage with complete precision, and thus avoid the unpleasant effects of excessive sulphur dioxide which gives wine a disagreeable and obtrusive taste and sometimes causes headaches. Overdosing was largely responsible for the decline in popularity of vins blancs liquoreux and other sweet white wines before this scientific accuracy was possible.

refrigeration, or cooling Vignerons have long known that the coolness of cellars is beneficial to wine after fermentation: it helps the wine to clear, the lees to settle and excess tartric acid to precipitate. In really cold weather at Beanne, they used to take the barrels outside and roll them

Following two pages: detail of a fresco depicting a wine-harvest (c. 1400) from the Tower of the Eagle, Château Bon-Conseil, Trente, Italy.
Phot. Giraudon.

209

around on the ground; the wine would freeze around the sides of the barrel, trapping the deposits and leaving the clear, unfrozen wine to be racked off. Modern science has now largely superseded these methods, and refrigerated *cuveries* are both more reliable and more efficient.

Subjecting a wine to a temperature of around 0°C causes its deposits to settle, so that after being filtered it becomes clear and stable. Refrigerated *cuveries* are indispensable for vinification in hot countries like Algeria and in the south of France, since to obtain a healthy and good quality wine the temperature should never really exceed 32°C. If the must from a crop which has been overexposed to the sun is not cooled down, the weakened alcohol yeasts★ will be supplanted by bacteria present in the fruit, which will seriously impair the wine and give it a high volatile acidity★ and an unpleasant bitter-sweet taste.

reginglard   A local wine which is often a bit sour.

reheating of the must   The best temperature for alcoholic fermentation is between 22 and 30°C. If the must is warmer than 30–32°C, the yeasts' action is impaired and the wine may suffer; below 22°C, yeasts act too slowly and sometimes not at all. In the first case the must has to be refrigerated★, and in the second, reheated to keep the yeasts active until fermentation is complete. Reheating is often necessary in cold countries where winter sets in relatively early. It can be carried out in two ways, either by taking a small quantity of must from the vat, heating it separately and then putting it back with the rest, or else by circulating warm water through pipes called drapeaux★ immersed in the must.

Remuage in a Champagne cave. Phot. J. Bottin.

remuage   Remuage (from the verb *remuer*, to move, shift or stir) is an essential stage in the preparation of Champagne★. During secondary fermentation★, a deposit composed of dead yeasts and mineral salts settles on the side of each horizontally-placed bottle. In order to remove this deposit it must be worked down to the cork end of the bottle. This is an extremely delicate operation that requires specially-skilled workers called remueurs.

The bottles are stacked in wooden racks called *pupitres* which allow the angle of inclination to be adjusted. Every day the remueur takes hold of the base of each bottle and gives it a twist of a quarter-turn accompanied by a slight shake and a fractional change of angle (neck downwards) towards the perpendicular. A good remueur sometimes handles 30,000 bottles in one day.

This gradual progression from horizontal to vertical lasts about two or three months, at the end of which time the bottles are standing on their heads and the deposit has all collected on the corks, leaving the wine quite clear. The bottles are left like this for as long as the wine needs to develop and mature, which is sometimes several years.

The next stage is the removal of the deposit by dégorgement★.

Renaison-Côte Roannaise A VDQS★ wine produced in the Lyonnais★ vineyards. It is made from Gamay grapes and produced around the town of Roanne in about thirty communes on either side of the Loire in the Loire and Saône-et-Loire departments. It is a very pleasant red vin de pays★, and is fresh, light and best drunk young.

repression of frauds The *Service de la Repression des Fraudes et du Contrôle de la Qualité*, a sort of 'wine fraud squad', is a department of the French Ministry of Agriculture authorised by law in 1905. It is concerned with controlling the quality of all French wines, not only AOC★ and VDQS★, but also the vins de consommation courante★ which account for a large proportion of the country's total wine production. It is responsible for the application of various recent decrees which have laid down a higher minimum alcohol content for vins de pays★, it has prescribed the varieties of grape allowed in the composition of each wine, and set a lower limit for proportions of volatile acidity★ and sulphur dioxide★. A *casier vinicole* – a kind of 'vinicultural register' – has been set up for each department to help the administration deal with all the viti- and vinicultural information it collects, to give the necessary instructions at harvest-time and to forecast future developments for the benefit of both producer and consumer.

The Service was set up by decree in 1919, and consists of laboratory and administrative staff divided between a central office, travelling inspectors and teams of specialists. Its job is to clamp down on fraudulent marketing of goods and misleading advertising, and also to decide what 'additional substances' are permitted.

Reuilly An AOC★ wine of central France made in a vineyard on the banks of the Arnon, a tributary of the river Cher. The soil varies from marl and limestone, like that of Sancerre★, to gravelly sand like that of Quincy★, which is a commune ten km away on the banks of the Cher. The wine is produced by four communes: Reuilly and Diou in the Indre department, and Chéry and Lazenay in the Cher department. A long succession of mediocre vintages has unfortunately rather disheartened the vignerons, who now produce only a very small quantity of wine each year – which is a pity, as Reuilly possesses the same characteristics as other wines made from the Sauvignon★ grape, although it is perhaps less distinguished. It is fruity, full-bodied and dry, and reminiscent of both Sancerre and Quincy. A medium-dry Reuilly is sometimes made to suit local taste. The appellation also applies to rosé wines made from the Pinot grape.

Rheims The historic cathedral city of Rheims is, with Epernay, one of the two great commercial centres of Champagne★. The Montagne de Reims, which lies southwest of the city, is one of the principal vine-growing areas in the Marne department. It forms the southern side of the Vesle valley and faces north and east. According to tradition, it is the place where St Remi harvested the wine he presented to Clovis in order to establish good relations between them, and thus pave the way to the latter's eventual conversion.

The Montagne de Reims comprises the mountain proper (with the communes of Beaumont-sur-Vesle, Verzenay, Mailly and Sillery), the Petite Montagne de Reims (with Hermonville and Saint-Thierry), and the Côte de Bouzy★, which runs into the Marne★ valley (with Bouzy, Ambonnay, Louvois and Tours-sur-Marne). The 'wines of Montagne' are full-bodied and have a pronounced bouquet and flavour.

Rheingau An important viticultural region in Germany which produces very high-quality white wines. The vineyards are perfectly situated at the foot of the Taunus range overlooking the Rhine – which at this point makes a curve of almost 180° – facing full south and catching the sunlight reflected from the river. The appellation officially includes the vineyards of Hochheim overlooking the Main (although these are, properly speaking, east of the Rheingau district) and the wines of Assmannshausen and Lorch, which are grown further north on the steep slopes of the Rhine gorges. Between Hochheim in the east and Rüdesheim in the west, there are fourteen villages which make Rheingau wine, and ten or eleven of these have great reputations: Erbach, Hattenheim, Winkel, Johannisberg★,

Rüdesheim, to name but a few. The success and renown of Rheingau, which some connoisseurs class among the best wine in the world, can largely be attributed to the Riesling grape, with which 70% of the region is planted.

The cheaper wines are usually chaptalised★ in order to attain the official alcoholic strength, and are entitled only to the name of the village which produces them (e.g. Rüdesheimer and Johannisberger). Certain world famous crus are sufficiently well known to have just one appellation, e.g. Steinberg★ (from Hattenheim), Schloss Vollrads (from Winkel), Marcobrunn★ and Schloss Johannisberg.

The best Rheingau wines, the rare and renowned Auslesen, Beerenauslesen and Trockenbeerenauslesen, are admirable dessert wines (especially those from the Steinberg, Johannisberg and Rüdesheim vineyards) on a par with the best Sauternes★, although less rich in alcohol. The other Rheingau wines are dry (but not excessively so), extremely fruity, and have a characteristic and inimitable bouquet.

A small quantity of good quality red wine is made at Assmannshausen, but it is very much an exception in this region of white wines.

Rheinhessen An important viticultural area of Germany whose capital is Mayence. The region is bordered on the east and north by the Rhine, on the south by the Palatinate★ and on the west by the Nahe★ valley. About 155 villages make their living by the vine, but only ten of them produce wine of really remarkable quality: Nierstein, Nackenheim, Oppenheim, Bingen, Dienheim, Bodenheim, Laubenheim, Guntersblum, Alsheim and Worms. The lesser quality wines are sold as carafe wines or a Liebfraumilch★ or Domtal (famous vineyards which have become generic names). Although Sylvaner is the dominant grape, the better wines are made from Riesling.

The communal wines produced in the Rheinhessen are often mediocre, being almost sickly sweet and smelling of sulphur dioxide★. But the fine wines made by the better communes are generally excellent, having a great deal of class and distinction. They are fruity and fragrant, distinguished and expansive and can be compared with the best wines of the Rheingau★. The best carry the name of the vineyard from which they come. The wines called Beerenauslesen are, like those of the Rheingau, splendid dessert wines comparable to Sauternes.

Riceys, Rosé des An excellent AOC★ wine made in the commune of les Riceys in the Aube department of France. Although the commune lies within the boundaries of the Champagne★ district,

Vineyards in Riceys, Champagne. Phot. M.

Rosé des Riceys is not a Champagne Rosé★ or pink champagne (although les Riceys produces this too), but a real rosé – and one that is particularly delicious. Vines have been grown in the commune since the beginning of the eighth century, and Rosé des Riceys has always been the most famous of all its wines.

The vineyard is situated on the steep sides of the Laignes valley, facing south and east. Some of these slopes are locally famous in their own right for the rosés they produce: la Velue, la Forêt and Violette, for instance. As at Chablis, the soil is pebbly clay and limestone, and many of the vineyards are equipped with heaters to combat the winter frosts.

The basic grape variety is the Pinot Noir of Champagne and Burgundy, together with a small proportion of Svégníe rose (a pink variety of the Jura Savagnin and the Traminer of Alsace) which gives the wine firmness, crispness and bouquet. The vinification of the wine is extremely delicate. The cuvaison, or vatting, is stopped the moment the wine has acquired a 'taste of rosé'; this may take anything from under two to four days. Only the vigneron's judgement can decide the right moment, and this requires great precision, as a few hours too long in vat can mean failure, producing a wine that is neither a rosé nor yet a red wine. The wine is bottled after eighteen months to two years in cask – and here again great precision is necessary, since if it stays too long in cask it turns the colour of *pelure d'oignon*★ and loses its characteristic and lovely deep rose colour.

Rosé des Riceys' only fault is its rarity. Justly rated among the best French rosés, it is a wine of breeding, originality, delicacy and great finesse, with a full bouquet and an exquisite, slightly nutty taste which persists for a pleasingly long time on the palate.

Riesling   Riesling is without a doubt the most distinguished of all the noble★ grape varieties of Alsace★. It is a small-graped, unprolific vine that is not at all easy to cultivate, needing plenty of sunshine and exactly the right kind of soil. Given these, it produces excellent wine; without them, its wine can be acid and hard. The areas where it grows best are Eguisheim, Riquewihr, Ribeauvillé and Guebwiller.

Riesling wine is the best and most popular Alsatian wine. In great years it attains perfection, and shows outstanding breeding and distinction. It has few faults. It is a crisp, dry white wine with a delicate and subtle fragrance, and a smooth taste in which the flavours of lime, acacia and orange blossom are perceptible, with occasionally a touch of cinnamon. It is easy to drink, but without ill effects. It leaves both head and mouth fresh and clear.

Riesling is grown all over the world and, given the right conditions, always produces high quality wine. Besides being

Riesling, the most 'noble' of Alsatian grape varieties. Phot. M.

grown in Germany (in the Moselle★, Hesse★ and Palatinate★ vineyards) and in the Italian Tyrol, where it also makes good wines, it is cultivated extensively in most parts of central Europe. Riesling grapes also produce a fairly good wine in Chile, and in California produce a wine of distinction and bouquet called 'Johannisberg-Riesling'.

Rioja   A viticultural region of Spain, near Pamplona, not far from the French border in the western Pyrenees. It takes its name from a tributary of the Ebro, the Rio Oja. The region produces more – and better – table wines than any other area in Spain. It is mountainous and has a harsh climate. The mountains at the northern

and southern ends of the valley are often still covered with snow at the end of April. The officially defined area of production includes Elciego, Fuenmayor, Cenicero and Ollauri, as well as Haro and Logroño, the two principal centres of the Rioja wine industry.

Rioja wines, particularly the red ones, have a curious similarity to those of Bordeaux. This is due to the emigration of several Bordeaux vine-growing families to the Ebro valley after the ruin of their own vineyards by phylloxera★ in the nineteenth century. They settled around Haro and Logroño, bringing with them their traditional methods of viti- and viniculture. Even now, the wines are made just as they were in Bordeaux more than eighty years ago.

The principal white grape varieties are Viura, Maturana, Calgrano and Turrantés, which make dry white wines of no great character or distinction. The red varieties – Garnacha (Grenache), Graciano, Mazuela and Tempranillo – are not quite what are usually called 'noble' grapes, but the wines they make are excellent, particularly in view of their price, which is always very reasonable. They are fine and light but quite full-bodied. None of them has a legally defined appellation of its own, which unfortunately means that one has to rely on the producer's name or the brand-name on the label. The best known are Marqués de Riscal, Marqués de Murrieta, Federico Paternina, Bodegas Bilbainas, Bodegas Franco-Españolas and La Rioja Alta, all of which usually appear under the initials CVNE (*Compañia Vinicola del Norte de España*).

Very little importance is attached to vintage, which is practically never specified. Quite a lot of producers do, however, call their young, light and inexpensive wines 'Clarete', while the descriptions 'Gran Reserva' and 'Imperial' are reserved for older wines, which are usually of excellent quality.

Ripaille A white cru of Savoie★ made from the Chasselas grape near the town of Thonon-les-Bains. Like most white wines of Savoie, it is a fresh, tart, dry wine and is rarely found outside its native area.

Rivesaltes A famous Roussillon★ vineyard, north of Perpignan, whose deep red earth produces excellent vins doux naturels★. It comprises about a dozen communes of which Salses, situated more or less in the centre of the area, has always been particularly renowned for its wine. Writing to the governor of the fort there, Voltaire said that it always gave him great pleasure to drink Salses, even though his feeble frame was not worthy of it. Rivesaltes makes two kinds of vin doux naturel, Rivesaltes and Muscat de Rivesaltes.

Rivesaltes is made from Grenache, Muscat, Malvoisie and Macabéo grapes, and can be either red or white (the latter vinified by fermenting the must without the pulp). It is a fine wine, and gets even better with age.

Muscat de Rivesaltes is made entirely from Muscat Doré (or Muscat de Frontignan) and Muscat d'Alexandrie grapes. It was in the Rivesaltes area that Muscat, probably of Spanish origin, made its first appearance when it was served at Pope Benedict XIII's table in 1394. It is an outstanding wine with finesse, a fruity taste and a marvellously fragrant bouquet – qualities which are earning it a steadily growing reputation among connoisseurs.

robe Robe is the word professional wine-tasters and connoisseurs use when referring to the colour of a wine. The colouring matter★ contained in the grape skins dissolves in the juice during fermentation and gives the wine its colour. This process can produce an enormous variety of colours, from dark to light. Red wines range from a deep cherry-red through bright red, ruby, garnet and purple to *rouge tuilé*★, or brick-red, and *pelure d'oignon*★. White wines vary from white to ochre, with intermediary shades of greenish-white, light yellow, lime, golden-yellow, straw and amber★. Rosé wines are gris★, bright pink, saffron-pink or brick-pink.

In red wines, a bluish tinge denotes a young wine (or one made from *teinturier* grapes), and a yellow tinge (tawny, rancio★ and *feuille-morte*, or autumn-leaf) an old one. In white wines, green denotes youth and a rusty colour is evidence of maderisation★.

robust A description applied to powerful, full-bodied wines which seem to assert

216

themselves on the palate with energy and authority. The words 'vigorous' and 'solid' describe more or less the same qualities.

Roche-aux-Moines A cru of the Savennières★ vineyard entitled, like Coulée-de-Serrant★, to add its own name to the appellation Savennières. It was given its name by monks from the abbey of Saint-Nicolas of Angers, who came and planted their vines on the hillsides there in the twelfth century, and now covers about 25 ha. Although it has much in common with the nearby Coulée-de-Serrant, it differs primarily in always being a dry wine. It is also less full-bodied and not as powerful, and should in general be drunk sooner. It does, however, share Coulée-de-Serrant's elegance and delicacy.

Romania The wines of the old Roman province of Dacia (present-day Romania) were famous even in very ancient times, as documents written in the third century attest. In the Middle Ages, the Romanian provinces sold wine to Russia, Poland and the Republic of Venice. Nowadays Romania has about 200,000 ha of vineyards, and her six wine-growing districts produce 4·5 million hl of wine a year.

Dobrudja or Dobrogea is the largest region, and the one which produces the most famous Romanian wine, Murfatlar★, which is grown near Basarabi and Nazarcea. Other well-known wines of the region are those produced at Ostrov in the south, and at Sarica and Niculitel in the Danube delta.

The Moldavian vineyards in the northeast are a continuation of the vineyards of Soviet Moldavia, and chiefly produce white wines. The best of these are Cotnari, Odobesti, Nicoresti, Panciu, Husi and Dealul-Mare ('Great Hill'), the last of which is rather like a French wine.

Munthenia, the region around the cities of Bucharest and Ploesti, produces the wines of Valea Călugărească, Urlati and Ceptura, while Oltenia, in the Olt valley, is known for its white wine, Drăgăsani, and Segarcea. Banat, in north-west Romania, produces only one wine worth mentioning, a red one called Minis, which is again not unlike a French wine.

Transylvania, in the west, has several wine-growing centres, amongst which are Alba Iulia, Aiud, Bistrita Năsăud and Tîrnaveni, the last of which produces a very pleasant white wine.

A southerly latitude is normally unfavourable to the production of white wines, but this is counterbalanced in Romania by the height at which the vines are grown, and the country produces more white wine than red. In recent years all Romanian wines have shown a definite improvement in quality. The most popular drink, incidentally, is a mixture of white wine and soda water, which is served very cold and called *sprit* (pronounced 'schpritz'). The reds are good table wines, despite a certain astringency.

Methods of vinification are the same as those used in Hungary★ and Bulgaria★. The wines tend to have a relatively high tannin content and are at their best with Romanian food, which is fairly strong and spicy.

rosé A rosé is never just a mixture of red and white wines, which is statutorily prohibited by French law. However, what is permitted is to mix red and white grapes, or their juice. Although rosé is mostly made only from red grapes, certain rosés are traditionally made by adding a small proportion of white grapes to the red. Until the eighteenth century, rosé was the only type of wine that could be made with complete success, but it suffered an eclipse when the vinification techniques for red wines became widespread in the nineteenth century. Recently, however, it has become more popular than ever.

Various methods are used to make rosé. The first consists of treating the red grapes as if they were white, i.e. pressing★ them as soon as they are picked, and separating the must from the skins and stalks before leaving it to ferment. The vins gris★ of Burgundy are made in this way, and so are the very pale rosés of Saumur and the Loire valley. To obtain 'real' rosé, with a firmer, more pronounced colour, the crushed grapes are put in a vat and left to start fermenting. As the temperature of the juice rises and its alcohol content increases, the colouring matter★ in the skins dissolves and is absorbed by the liquid. The vigneron takes a sample of the juice every hour, and when he judges it to have reached the right depth of colour, he runs it off into another vat to complete its fermentation. The marc left behind is then pressed and its juice, which is now too dark for rosé, is used for red wine.

Another method is to 'bleed' the vats. After at least two hours of fermentation the vigneron turns the tap at the base of the vat and runs the juice out at intervals until it starts to get too dark. In both these cases it is often extremely difficult to judge the colour with accuracy. The period in vat (cuvaison) can vary from five or six hours to as many as forty-eight (as is the case in the Jura★, for example). The rosés of Tavel★, Provence★, Jura★ and les Riceys★ are all made by these methods. They have a good colour, are full-bodied and seem to retain the characteristics of the grapes they were made from. Rosés made from Pinot, for example, are always excellent, whether they come from the Côte-d'Or, Alsace or les Riceys.

Although some rosés have a long tradition behind them (les Riceys and Marsannay-la-Côte, for instance), a great number have appeared comparatively recently, in response to public demand. Vignerons also make rosé out of crops badly affected by pourriture grise★ to avoid the taste of mould the wine would acquire if vinified by the usual methods, i.e. left to ferment in contact with the grape skins.

Successful rosé vinification requires extremely accurate judgement and balancing of the various processes involved. In achieving a good, firm colour the wine may also acquire excessive tannin and become too heavy, but on the other hand the procedures employed when a pale, delicate colour is desired may well leave it lacking in bouquet. Despite their current popularity, rosés are not always up to standard. They sometimes have an unpleasant salmon-pink colour which is due to the grapes being picked too late or to the oxidisation of the colouring matter. In the

*'Young Bacchus' by
Caravaggio. Uffizi Gallery,
Florence.* Phot. Giraudon.

Midi, the proportion of white grapes sometimes rises above 20%, or the grapes are left to macerate too long before fermentation, and in both cases the wine is disappointing. Rosés have the further disadvantage of ageing badly. They must be bottled very early (in the February or March following the vintage) and drunk quite soon, generally within two years.

Rosette   A white wine grown on hills just north of Bergerac★. The three classic vines of the Sud-Ouest★ region, Sémillon, Sauvignon and Muscadelle, grow on clay and siliceous-clay – types of soil which suit them particularly well. The appellation applies to wines produced by certain *parcelles*, or divisions, of the communes of Bergerac, Lembras, Creysse, Maurens, Prigourieux and Ginestet. It is a medium-dry, fruity wine with finesse, body (a minimum 12°) and character.

rouge (vin)   Red wine is made in several steps. After the vendange the grapes are pressed★ and eventually separated from their stalks. The pressed grapes are put into a cuve★ where they undergo alcoholic fermentation★ caused by the action of certain yeasts, some naturally existing in the bloom on the grapes, and others added. This fermentation can take place in open or closed cuves. The vigneron must be sure that the must is aerated and that the temperature is between 25 and 28°C; if not, the yeast stops acting and it is sometimes necessary to reheat or refrigerate★ the must. The must has to be aerated in order to stimulate fermentation, and to help diffuse the colouring matter★ by putting the juice in contact with the chapeau★.

Finally, the vigneron must sterilise the grapes by adding sulphur dioxide★ and sometimes, acting on the advice of the oenological stations, he must make other additions to correct the must.

The length of the fermentation period varies from two or three days to three weeks depending on the region and type of wine desired. After fermentation has ended the wine must be drawn off from the marc; this is the vin de goutte★. The marc is then pressed and yields the vin de presse. After blending in a cask, the young wine is sent to the cellars to mature in cask for a certain period before bottling.

roundness An agreeable quality of wines with a good alcohol★ and glycerine★ content and not too much acidity★, resulting in a generally 'well-rounded' sensation on the palate.

Roussillon This old French province, with Perpignan as its centre, consists of the department of Pyrénées-Orientales and a part of the Aude. As a wine-growing area, it presents several similarities to the neighbouring Languedoc★. It produces large quantities of vin ordinaire and several good VDQS★ table wines, amongst which are Corbières du Roussillon★ and Roussillon-Dels-Aspres★. Its main claim to fame, however, is that it produces three-quarters of all French vins doux naturels★, all with appellations contrôlées: Banyuls★, Rivesaltes★ and Muscat de Rivesaltes★, Côtes-d'Agly★, Maury★, Côtes-du-Haut-Roussillon★ and Grand-Roussillon★.

Roussillon-Dels-Aspres These wines greatly resemble the neighbouring Corbières★ and Corbières du Roussillon, and like them are VDQS★. The red wines have body, colour and warmth, and although they are made from the same grapes as Corbières du Roussillon, they have a particular flavour of their own, derived from the soil on which the vines are grown. The reds, rosés and whites must contain a minimum alcohol content of 11°.

Rully A very distinctive, dry, fruity, golden-yellow AOC★ wine made from Chardonnay grapes by the commune of Rully in the Côte Chalonnaise★. This wine, which lends itself remarkably well to effervescence, was the first sparkling wine to be made in Burgundy. Nowadays,

Typical vineyard area of Roussillon. Phot. Phédon-Salou.

sparkling Burgundies are widely known, though less appreciated in France than in other countries. The appellation Rully may in certain cases be followed by the words Premier Cru or by the name of a particular climat★. Rully also produces a little red wine of average quality.

rural method A very ancient method of preparing sparkling wines, employed before the Champagne method★ had been perfected, and nowadays scarcely in use at all except in Gaillac★, Die★ and Limoux★. With this method, the carbon dioxide★ is formed entirely by the natural grape sugar left in the wine, without the addition of any liqueur de tirage★. The procedure consists of slowing down, without actually stopping, primary fermentation (which converts grape juice into still wine) by repeated filtration and racking, and then bottling the wine when its remaining sugar content is judged sufficient to ensure a good *prise de mousse*, or secondary fermentation. Once the wine is bottled and firmly corked, fermentation slowly starts again, producing carbon dioxide which is trapped in the wine and remains in suspension as its 'sparkle'.

This method is in some respects similar to the one used at Asti★, where sparkling wines are also made by primary fermentation (although at Asti this takes place in vat), as opposed to the Champagne method, in which still wine is made to ferment twice. The wines it produces are excellent and marrowy with a very fine bouquet. The rural method is also the best way of preserving the characteristic aroma of Muscat★-based wines, such as Clairette-de-Die. It is, however, an extremely delicate operation which can go wrong in many ways. Fermentation may be either too fierce and make the bottles explode, or too weak, even non-existent. Refermentation★ sometimes occurs and quality may vary from one bottle to another. In addition, the wine is always slightly hazy. This is not due to solid deposits of lees and yeasts that can be collected on the cork and removed by dégorgement★ as in the Champagne method, but is a side-effect of the rural method itself, and can be eliminated by isobarometric filtration. At Die this filtration is carried out individually on each bottle.

Russian Soviet Federal Socialist Republic (RSFSR) Vineyards have flourished for a long time in the European part of this republic. They are planted on the banks of the Don and Kouban at Astrakan, Stavropol, and in the south at Saratov. European grape varieties were imported by Peter the Great. Today, the important viticultural centres are Tsimliansk, Derbent (Daghestan), the Kouban Valley (up to Maikop), Rostov-on-Don (which makes Tsimliansky, a sparkling wine) and the coastal areas of Novorossiisk, Touapsé and Sotchi, from which comes the good red wine Abraou-Diourso.

S

sables (vin de)   One of the by-products of the desperate struggle against phylloxera★. When a vigneron of Vaucluse discovered that this destructive aphid was not able to survive in sand, people hurried to plant vines wherever they could find enough fine sand, e.g. around Saint-Laurent-de-la-Salanque in the Roussillon district, on the edges of the Thau d'Agde basin at Sète and on the dunes around Aigues-Mortes in the Gard department. The product, a vin de sables, was also made until quite recently near Soustons in the Landes region of south-western France.

The sandy islands of Oléron and Ré off the west coast of France, however, were producing this type of wine long before phylloxera had even been heard of – in fact, their wine was famous as early as the thirteenth century. Nowadays, the two islands make as much wine as ever, producing dry white wines which are greatly appreciated by visitors and tourists. The Ile de Ré also makes a curious-tasting red wine.

Sables–Saint-Emilion   These wines are made in a vineyard just east of Libourne between Pomerol and Saint-Emilion. The soil is sandy and produces a wine which has the generosity of a Saint-Emilion and the suppleness and bouquet of a Pomerol. It is a pleasant wine that does not require a long vinification. The principal crus are Châteaux Cruzeau, Martinet, Doumaine and Gaillard.

sack   One of the first names used in England for sherry★. It is also used for sweet wines resembling sherry, like Malaga sack and Canary sack.

Saint-Amour   A popular red wine and one of the most pleasant Beaujolais★, produced in the region's northernmost commune. It has an attractive ruby colour and a delicate, fairly light bouquet.

Saint-Chinian   The excellent red wine made in this village is one of the VDQS★ of the Coteaux-du-Languedoc★. The vineyard covers several pebbly hillsides in the north-west of the Hérault department, and produces an attractive ruby-coloured wine that is fairly full-bodied, but has a delicate bouquet which acquires depth with age.

Vin de sable. Vendange at Oléron. Phot. Léah Lourié.

222

Saint-Emilion The vineyard of Saint-Emilion is situated on the right bank of the Dordogne several kilometres from Libourne. It is one of the oldest in France and the chief producer of fine wines in the Bordeaux★ region. Louis XIV called Saint-Emilion 'the nectar of the gods'.

The appellation Saint-Emilion extends to all the communes formerly administered from Saint-Emilion: Saint-Laurent-des-Combes, Saint-Christophe-des-Bardes, Saint-Hippolyte, Saint-Etienne-de-Lisse, Saint-Sulpice-de-Faleyrens, Vignonet and Saint-Pey-d'Armens.

All Saint-Emilion wines have generosity, body and warmth, as well as an attractive, dark garnet colour and a fragrance reminiscent of truffles. More powerful than Mèdocs, they are sometimes called 'the Burgundies of Bordeaux'. An average tannin★ content ensures them a long life (sometimes thirty to forty years) without giving them the unpleasant astringency of wines that contain too much tannin.

Enthusiasts recognise two distinct kinds of Saint-Emilion: the wine grown on the hillsides, and the wine from the flat, gravelly parts of the vineyards. The *vin de côtes*, or hillside wine, is generous, full-bodied and firm (e.g. Château-Ausone★); the *vin de graves*, or gravel wine, has finesse, suppleness and a distinctive bouquet, and resembles Pomerol★ wines (e.g. Château-Cheval-Blanc★).

As in all the best Bordeaux vineyards, wines grown on the alluvial flats are excluded from the appellation. Only noble★ vines are grown: Cabernet Franc, Cabernet-Sauvignon (or Bouchet), Merlot and Malbec (or Pressac). It is interesting that the species of white grape called Saint-Emilion (or Ugni Blanc) is, despite its name, rarely found in the region.

The premiers grands crus classés are Château-Ausone and Château-Cheval-Blanc, followed by the Châteaux Beauséjour, Bélair, Canon, Figeac, la Gaffelière, Magdelaine, Clos Fourtet, Pavie and Trottevieille. (See Index.) In addition, six communes on the periphery of the Saint-Emilion area are officially permitted to add the name of Saint-Emilion to their own on their labels (although their name must always precede Saint-Emilion, and be printed in characters of the same size). These are Saint-Georges★, Montagne★, Lussac★, Puissegin★ and Parsac★, all of

Saint-Emilion: above, the Great Walls; below, the Jurates at the proclamation of the wine-harvest. Phot. René-Jacques.

223

Maturation cave, Saint-Emilion. Phot. M.

which are north of Saint-Emilion, and Sables-Saint-Emilion★, which lies west of Libourne.

Saint-Estèphe   Very distinguished red wines made in the Médoc★. The grands crus (Châteaux Cos-d'Estournel, Montrose and Calon-Ségut) have great finesse. They are lighter in body than the neighbouring Pauillacs, but more fruity and supple. The appellation Saint-Estèphe also applies to a large number of secondary crus (classified in France as *crus bourgeois, crus artisans* or *crus paysans*) which make very good wines, especially those at the upper end of the scale (although they lack both the finesse and distinction of the classed growths).

Saint-Georges d'Orques   One of the Coteaux-du-Languedoc★ VDQS★ wines. The area of production comprises the village of Saint-Georges and some parts of the neighbouring communes just outside Montpellier. The red wines, made mostly from Cinsault and Carignan grapes, have good texture and finesse and are very popular locally. They improve greatly with age.

Saint-Georges-Saint-Emilion   The commune of Saint-Georges is officially entitled to add the name of Saint-Emilion to its own name on its labels. Its wines do in fact have all the characteristics of the

'*vins des côtes*' of Saint-Emilion: they are an attractive purplish-red colour, and are full-bodied and powerful without being coarse. Robust and well rounded, they age extremely well and retain a remarkable bouquet reminiscent of truffles. The best crus are Châteaux Saint-Georges-Macquin, Saint-Georges, Saint-André-Corbin, Samion and Tourteau.

Saint-Jean-de-Minervois   Although still relatively unknown, this AOC★ Muscat wine from the Languedoc region is a vin doux naturel★ of excellent quality. It is both delicate and elegant, and dryer than other Muscats.

Saint-Joseph   Wines made in the north of the Côtes du Rhône★ region, on the right bank of the Rhône facing the Hermitage★ vineyards. The vineyard's output is mainly red, made from Syrah grapes. These reds are very full-bodied, strongly coloured wines with a slightly bitter taste when young. Age refines their bouquet and often makes them excellent wines. The appellation also provides a small quantity of rosé and white wines made from Marsanne and Roussanne grapes. The crisp, fragrant white wines can show remarkable qualities in good years.

Saint-Julien   A small commune in the heart of the upper Médoc★ region. (The appellation Saint-Julien also includes a few divisions of the Pauillac, Cussac and Saint-Laurent communes.) Saint-Julien is an excellent red wine, being supple and fine with a pronounced bouquet. In character it tends to be midway between Margaux★ and Pauillac★ wines. It is more full-bodied but has the same finesse as Margaux, and less full-bodied than Pauillac though its bouquet develops more quickly. It also keeps for a long time in bottle. The best-known châteaux are those of Ducru-Beaucaillou, Gruaud-Larose, Léoville-Las Cases, Léoville-Poyferré, Beychevelle and Talbot. (See Index.)

ling wine (by the Champagne method★) at the beginning of the nineteenth century. Saint-Péray-Mousseux has been extremely popular ever since, and is more widely known than the original, still Saint-Péray. It is one of the best French sparkling wines and some class it next to Champagne★. It has a deeper colour and more body than the latter, yet always preserves its characteristic aroma of violets.

Saint-Pourçain-sur-Sioule The Saint-Pourçain vineyards stretch for about thirty km, at a height of around 300 m, along hillsides bordering the Sioule, Allier

General view of Saint-Péray. Phot. M.

Saint-Nicolas-de-Bourgueil A commune in Touraine★ situated very near Bourgueil★. Although its wines are similar to the latter's, it has its own appellation contrôlée. The soil here is particularly favourable to the Cabernet Breton grape and brings out its best qualities. Saint-Nicolas-de-Bourgueil is usually rated higher than Bourgueil, which has less tannin and does not age as well.

Saint-Péray Situated on the right bank of the Rhône, opposite Valence, this Côtes du Rhône★ commune produces excellent dry white wine made from Roussanne and Marsanne grapes. Saint-Péray is a fine, crisp wine with an aroma of violets.

Saint-Péray was first made into spark-

and Boule rivers in central France. About twenty communes produce Saint-Pourçain, which is considered a Loire wine and has a VDQS★ label. The chief of these are Saint-Pourçain, Besson, Bramsat, Contigny, Chemilly and Bresnay. Although once served at the tables of the kings of France, its present reputation has for a long time been purely local.

The white wine is made from the Tresallier grape often found in the region (and known as Sacy in the Yonne department), of which the proportion is officially fixed at a minimum of 50%. To this are added the supplementary varieties Aligoté, Sauvignon, Chardonnay and Saint-Pierre-Doré (an unimportant species limited to a proportion of 10%). This

Saint Pourçain-sur-Sioule: the vineyard on a level with Châtel-de-Neuvre on the bank of the Allier. Phot. M.

delicious, clear white wine has an attractive greenish-white colour. It is dry, light, fragrant and fine, with a fruity flavour that is curiously reminiscent of apples. Germany buys considerable quantities of it for use in the preparation of sparkling wines.

The red and rosé wines are made from Gamay and Pinot Noir. The red is very smooth and pleasant, a little reminiscent of Beaujolais, but with an agreeable *goût de terroir*★. The rosé is excellent, fresh and fruity, with an attractive, sometimes very pale colour (vins gris★). It is very popular with those who come to take cures at the nearby spas in the summer. The white, red and rosé should all be drunk young.

Saint-Véran This new Mâconnais cru received its title as an appellation contrôlée area on 6th January, 1971. The little village, formerly known as Saint Véran des Vignes, borders on Pouilly-Fuissé★, and the area of appellation includes seven communes: Chanes, Chasselas, Davaye, Prisse, Leynes, Saint-Amour and Saint Véran. The wine has the same subtle bouquet and taste of hazelnuts as its neighbour Pouilly-Fuissé.

Sainte-Croix-du-Mont The steep slopes of this commune overlook the right bank of the Garonne facing the Sauternes★ region. The regulations governing its

vinification procedure are the same – and as exacting – as those applied in Sauternes, and this has given its wine particular prestige among the other famous white wines of the right bank. Sainte-Croix-du-Mont is a lovely, clear, golden colour, is liquoreux and smooth, fine and fruity, and fully deserves its reputation.

Sainte-Foy-Bordeaux A region which occupies the north-east corner of the Gironde department on the left bank of the Dordogne. Although geographically a part of the Entre-deux-Mers area, its wines are quite different and have their own appellation. The white wines are moelleux★ or semi-liquoreux★, with a pleasant fragrance which has led to their being called 'the poor man's Sauternes'. Sometimes they are made dry or medium dry, and in these cases are similar to Anjou★ and Saumur★ wines. The red wines have good body and colour, and mature rapidly.

saints de glace These 'ice saints' are called *Eis Heilgen* in Germany, where they are the patron saints of the four days in May when the vignerons think their vines most susceptible to the spring frosts, particularly in the Moselle and Saar regions. From the 12th to the 15th May, Saint Pancras, Saint Servais, Saint Boniface and the cold Saint Sophie (*die kalte Sophie*) hold

the fate of the vineyards in their hands. It seems that the vines are in fact very rarely attacked by frosts after these dates.

San Benito A vine-growing county in California★ located east of Monterey Bay and south of San Francisco. The vineyards, which cover steep hillsides and the slopes of high valleys, have spread considerably in recent years as a result of the replanting around Paicine of the Almaden vineyard, which was forced out of Santa Clara★ by a housing development. Almaden is currently California's most important producer of 'premium wines' (i.e. quality wines), sparkling wines and sherry, which is made by the traditional Spanish methods. More than half of San Benito's vines are ungrafted French or German varieties (Chardonnay, Pinot Noir, Cabernet and Gewürztraminer), and the vineyard's future seems to be a promising one.

Sancerre Perched on a hilltop on the left bank of the Loire★, the tiny, picturesque town of Sancerre huddles round the remains of its feudal castle, overlooking the river and practically opposite Pouilly-sur-Loire★. The vineyards cover the neighbouring hills, which are composed of two kinds of soil: marly Kimmeridge clay, locally known as *terres blanches*, and dry limestone called *caillotes*. The appellation includes several villages around Sancerre, of which Amigny, Bué★, Champtin, Chavignol★, Reigny and Verdigny make the best-known wines. The superiority of these wines compared with others in the Sancerre region, although always discernible, is most evident in poor years.

Sancerre and its vineyards.
Phot. Lauros-Beaujard.

227

Sancerre owes its reputation to its dry white wine, which is made from Sauvignon grapes. Wines from the *terres blanches* take time to acquire their character and bouquet, but preserve them for a long time. They are fruity, supple and full-bodied. Those from the *caillotes* have great finesse and bouquet from the start, but lose their qualities more quickly. All the wines, however, justify the traditional oath taken by honorary vignerons of Bué: 'I swear I will drink the first glass of wine neat, the second without water, and the third just as it comes out of the barrel'.

Sancerre also produces red and rosé wines, which must be made from Pinot Noir grapes to qualify for the appellation. These wines were famous in the late Middle Ages, but nowadays Pinot is grown only on the slopes unsuitable for Sauvignon. The rosé is excellent, being pale, fruity and full-bodied, and it is considered one of the best Pinot rosés in France. The small output of red wine, made only in good years, is mostly consumed locally.

Santenay, at the border of the Côte-d'Or. Phot. Aarons-L.S.P.

sangria This is a refreshing drink made throughout Spain from oranges, lemons and wine; it is drunk with ice at the table or between meals. Additional sugar is often added to this fresh and pleasant drink, which is often deceptively strong at first.

Santa Clara A valley and county south of San Francisco Bay and Alameda★ in California★, named after an old Spanish mission established near San José. Santa Clara wines have long been known for their quality, but unfortunately there will soon be none of them left, as the vineyards are being encroached upon by the area's rapidly increasing population. Urban growth is gradually forcing the walnut trees from the valleys and the vines from the surrounding hillsides and replacing them with buildings. Many vineyards have succumbed completely or, like Almaden, have had to be replanted further south in a less populated area.

Nowadays, all that is left of the fine Santa Clara vineyards is a scrap of the old Almaden, a few insignificant patches of vines and the Novitiate of Los Gatos, a vineyard owned by Jesuits. Their production is primarily Communion wine, with a small quantity of good table wine and some dessert wines (e.g. Muscat Frontignan and Black Muscat).

Santa Maddalena An excellent red wine made in the Italian Tyrol as popular in Switzerland and Austria as it is in Italy. It is grown north-east of the town of Bolzano, and the vines are principally three varieties of Schiava (Schiava Gentile, Meranese and Grigia). The wine, which is a very pale cherry-red, is fresh, tender, light and fruity, and yet quite full-bodied.

Santenay The old and picturesque city of Santenay is on the boundary of the Côte d'Or★ and produces white and excellent red wines. The reds, which account for the bulk of wine production, resemble Chassagne-Montrachet and are ferme★, full-bodied, and moelleux★ with an original bouquet which improves with age. The best cru is Gravières. (See Index.)

The white wines are produced in small quantities and are fine and dry. They do not, however, enjoy the same reputation as the reds and are best drunk young.

Saumur Although the Saumur vineyards are officially in the Anjou★ district, they are more like an extension of Touraine★, having similar topography, identical methods of cultivation and vinification and, above all, the same type of soil (subsoil of Tufa chalk, out of which great underground cellars are cut, as at Vouvray★, and covered with pebbly, siliceous sand). The vines cover two lines of hills which meet at Saumur, where the best-known crus are to be found. One of the lines starts at Montsoreau and follows the course of the Loire, and the other stretches from Saix to Saumur along the banks of the Thouet and Dive rivers. Other areas of production are from Ranton to Pouançay on the right bank of the Dive, between Montreuil-Bellay and Saint-Hilaire-Saint-Florent on the left bank of the Thouet, and on a chalky hill further to the west (Puy-Notre-Dame and Vaudelnay). Altogether, thirty-seven communes produce AOC★ Saumur wine, the most famous being Montsoreau, Turquant, Parnay, Souzay, Dampierre, Saumur, Varrains, Chacé, Saint-Cyr-en-Bourg, Brézé, Epieds (part of the Bizay commune) and Saix. The wine of Saumur has been renowned since the twelfth century when it was exported in large quantities to the Netherlands.

The white wines, made from Pineau de la Loire grapes, are always dry or medium dry (to qualify for the appellation they must contain no more than 10 g of sugar per litre), and have a minimum alcoholic strength of 10°. They are remarkably light, fine, vigorous wines which keep extremely well – the best vintages always used to be buried in sand where they kept their youthful qualities for a particularly long time. Fruity and fresh, they have a smooth fragrance that deepens with age and a very original taste known as the *goût de tuf*, which derives from the subsoil and distinguishes them markedly from other Anjou wines. In rich years, the most sumptuous and fragrant sweet white wines are made from grapes which the sun has dried on the vine, or, even better, which have been attacked by pourriture noble★.

Apart from its still white wines, Saumur has since 1830 made fine and distinguished sparkling wines, which are produced in greater quantities than any other sparkling wine in France. The natural lightness of

The château of Saumur.
Phot. Hétier.

Saumur's wine makes it particularly suitable for this treatment, and the deep cellars cut out of the chalk under the vineyards are a further advantage in their vinification. The wines are made by the Champagne method★ of secondary fermentation in bottle. The same method is used to make pétillant★ wines, which have much less effervescence than the mousseux. Pétillant Saumurs are sold in the same bottles as the still wines, with a clamp over the cork.

A very small quantity of red Saumur is made (at Turquant, Montsoreau and Montreuil-Bellay), from Cabernet Franc and Cabernet-Sauvignon grapes. These are only harvested if the conditions are right for production from these varieties. The best known is made at Champigny★ and has the AOC Saumur-Champigny.

Finally, Cabernet de Saumur has become more and more popular during the last fifty years, benefiting from the current vogue for rosés. It is a fine, fruity, bright and refreshing wine made

from Cabernet Franc and Cabernet-Sauvignon. It is also extremely pale, as the grapes are not crushed but pressed as soon as they are brought in from the vineyards. With the eyes closed, it is sometimes very difficult to tell from the taste whether it is a white or a rosé wine.

Sauternes The small region of Sauternes, which produces world-famous vins blancs liquoreux★, lies a few kilometres from Langon on the left bank of the Garonne. The appellation contrôlée Sauternes includes, besides Sauternes itself, the communes of Bommes, Preignac, Fargues and Barsac★. The area is extremely fortunate in its soil which seems to produce only wines of exceptional quality. It is a mixture of pebbles and sand which give the wines finesse, limestone which gives strength and vigour, and clay which makes them smooth. The noble★ vines have a naturally low yield which is further reduced by severe pruning. The main variety, Sémillon, produces smoothness, Sauvignon adds body and a distinctive aroma, and the small proportion of Muscadelle contributes a subtle bouquet to the whole. The unique feature of the vineyard, however, is the way the grapes are harvested. They are cut from the vine individually, and only when absolutely ripe,

in a series of 'pickings' over a period of one or two months in late autumn. The warmth and humidity of the season favour the growth of *Botrytis cinerea*, the fungus that causes pourriture noble★.

The grapes affected by this mould over-ripen in a particular way, and provide a must which is rich in sugar, glycerine, pectins and other substances, resulting in an inimitable bouquet and flavour. The wine is liquoreux★ and rich in alcohol (officially at least 13°, but usually quite a bit more). It is also entirely natural. No extra sugar or alcohol is added to it, as the slightest 'enriching' of the must, even by legally permitted methods, would automatically mean the loss of the appellation. Sauternes is a smooth, sweet, golden wine that combines a rare strength with great elegance and finesse, and has a rich and delicate aroma of honey, lime and acacia. Sauternes crus were classified in 1855 with the eminent and universally-renowned Château d'Yquem★ in first place, followed by the Châteaux la Tour-Blanche, Lafaurie-Peyraguey, Clos-Haut-Peyraguey, Rayne-Vigneau and Suduiraut. (See Index.)

Sauvignon This white grape gives wines a special spicy taste. It is best grown in the Nivernais and Berry where it produces the celebrated 'wines of Sauvignon': Pouilly-Fumé and the white wines of Sancerre★, Menetou-Salon★, Quincy★ and Reuilly★.

In Bordeaux it is united with the Sémillon and Muscadelle to make Graves and the sweet wines of Sauternes. It is also found at Bergerac, Vic-Bihl and Cassis, where it adds distinction and aroma. In California it produces a full-bodied wine which has the same aroma and delicate taste as the French wines made from this grape.

Savennières A small village in the Coteaux de la Loire★ district on the right bank of the Loire which qualifies for its own appellation contrôlée. The vineyard is ideally situated on slopes of the river bank between the towns of la Pointe and la Possonnière. Its fine, golden wines·are elegant, crisp, full-bodied and delicate, and have won a well-deserved and longstanding reputation. Their aroma suggests lime and quince. Usually dry, with occasional touches of softness, they are ready for drinking quite early but also keep well. Savennières has two outstanding crus, Coulée-de-Serrant★ and Roche-aux-Moines★. After these two, the best known are Bécherelle, Goutte-d'Or, Clos du Papillon and the Châteaux d'Epiré, de Camboureau, de Savennières and de la Bizolière.

Savigny-lès-Beaune This commune, located north-west of Beaune★, produces mainly light, fragrant red wines which should be drunk young. The best crus are Aux Vergelesses, les Marconnets, la Dominade and les Jarrons.

Savoie It is only recently, with the increase in the popularity of winter sports, that the vineyards of Savoie in southeastern France have really begun to make a name for themselves. They are, however, of very ancient origin. The excellent Altesse vine species is said to have been brought back from Cyprus by a crusader, who introduced it very successfully all over the province.

Savigny-lès-Beaune.
Phot. Lauros Beaujard.

The Sauvignon, the white grape which is popular in the vineyards of central France. Phot. M.

231

Savoie: the vineyard of Saint-Jean-de-la-Porte. Phot. Serraillier-Rapho.

It seems incredible that grapes should manage to ripen so rapidly at the very foot of snow-covered mountains, but the vines grown here are tough and have adapted themselves over the years to the harsh climate. The varieties grown are, for white wines, Altesse and Jacquère (a species only found in Savoie), Chasselas★ (also grown in Switzerland and at Pouilly-sur-Loire★), Petite-Sainte-Marie (Chardonnay), Mondeuse Blanche, Aligoté and Gringet; and for red wines, Mondeuse, Persan, Gamay-noir-à-jus-blanc and Pinot. The vine-growing region covers the Savoie and Haute-Savoie departments, and in general produces light-bodied, dry, fruity white wines with a pleasing touch of acidity. (In bad years this acidity is sometimes too pronounced.) There are also some good red and rosé wines made mainly around Chambéry and in the Chautagne area.

SAVOIE: APPELLATIONS CONTRÔLÉES Savoie has only two AOC wines – Crépy★ and Seyssel★. Most of its other delicious wines are VDQS★ and have the appellations Vin de Savoie, Roussette de Savoie, Vin de Savoie Roussette, Vin de Savoie Mousseux or Mousseux de Savoie. The appellation Roussette de Savoie can only apply to wines made from Altesse, Petite-Sainte-Marie and Mondeuse Blanche grapes, with a maximum proportion of 10% Marsanne. Roussette de Frangy enjoys a well-deserved reputation.

The name of the grape can also be added to the appellation when the wine is made entirely from that variety (e.g. Mondeuse★). Some individual crus can also add their names – Ayse★, for example. There are many of these fresh and delicious Savoie crus: Marestel, Monthoux and Chautagne on the left bank of the Rhône, Monterminod, Chignin and Charpignat on the picturesque banks of the Bourget and in the Chambéry valley, and Abymes, Apremont, Montmélian, Arbin, Cruet and Saint-Jean-de-la-Porte on the right bank of the Isère and south-east of Chambéry.

scorching When grapes which have not attained their full maturity are exposed to intense periods of sunlight, they dry up, blacken and fall off the vine, and are said to be scorched.

sec (dry) A term applied to wines, usually white, which contain, or at least give the impression of containing, no sugar. Most people only notice the presence of sugar in a wine when the level is higher than 5 g per litre, and even the dryest wines contain 1–2 g per litre. Entre-deux-Mers★, for instance, which has to be dry to qualify for its appellation, has an official maximum sugar content of 3 g per litre.

Acidity is another important factor as the higher a wine's acid content, the dryer it will taste. Similarly, a wine rich in glycerine★ will seem almost sweet even if it contains no sugar, as is the case with wines which have been harvested late and fermented very slowly.

As very dry white wines contain practically no residual sugar, there is no danger of their refermenting in the bottle. This means that they do not need the large doses of sulphur dioxide★ given to other wines to prevent refermentation★, and are consequently always pleasant and easy to drink.

When applied to Champagne, dry (sec) is a precise qualitative description: Champagne sec (which the French call *goût americain*) contains a proportion of 3–5% liqueur d'expédition★ (authorised sweetener), and is thus not as dry as extra-dry or brut. The next in the scale, demi-sec, contains 6–10% liqueur d'expédition. (See Champagne★.)

séché Dried out, a term applied to a wine which has stayed too long in the barrel and lost its freshness and fruitiness, becoming dull and unattractive. Sometimes it even has a slightly bitter aftertaste. The word can also apply to very old wines spoiled by too many years in bottle. Their colouring matter★ solidifies and they lose both bouquet and flavour. A *séché* wine produces an uncomfortable dry sensation on the palate, and can be positively unpleasant.

sève, séveux *Sève* literally means sap. A *séveux* wine has pronounced fragrance as well as vitality and a certain alcoholic strength. *Sève* tends to fade after a certain number of years in bottle, so a *séveux* wine is always in its prime.

Seyssel White AOC★ Savoie★ wines grown in the Rhône Valley communes of Seyssel (in the Haute-Savoie department) and Seyssel-Corbonod (in the Ain). The long-established vineyards face south and south-west at a height of 200–400 m. The pronounced aroma of violets so characteristic of Seyssel wines is attributed to the soil, which is siliceous limestone and siliceous clay. This theory is borne out by the fact that the perfume-makers of Grasse for a long time extracted their essence of violets from irises growing on the right bank of the Rhône in the same area of the valley.

The only authorised vine is the Roussette and at Crépy★ the grapes are harvested late, at the peak of their ripeness. No more than 25 hl of wine is produced per hectare, and its minimum alcoholic strength is 10°. Seyssel is a delicious, pale golden wine, delicate and supple, with a distinctive aroma of violets.

SEYSSEL MOUSSEUX For this appellation the Molette and Bon Blanc (or Chasselas) grape varieties are authorised, although the wine must still contain a minimum proportion of 10% Roussette. Minimum alcoholic strength is 8·5° and maximum yield per hectare is 40 hl.

Seyssel mousseux, made by the Champagne method★, is an excellent, fine wine that has an enthusiastic following.

sharp Sharp is an adjective used when a wine's acidity★ is not balanced by its alcohol content. The acid completely dominates the taste, making it very strong and sour. Sharpness is generally a characteristic of wine made in years when cold weather has hindered the ripening of the grapes.

Sherry A pale gold or amber apéritif or dessert wine produced in southern Spain between Cadiz and Seville around the little town of Jerez de la Frontera. The controlled vineyard zone includes the communes of Jerez de la Frontera, Puerto de Santa Maria, Sanlucar de Barrameda, Chiclana, Puerto Real, Chipiona, Rota and

Sherry casks.
Phot. Pedro Domecq.

Trebujena. The Superior Sherry area is formed by a triangle linking Jerez de la Frontera, Sanlucar de Barrameda and Puerto de Santa Maria and includes the neighbouring communes of Rota and Chipiona. Manzanilla★ is produced on the Atlantic coast near Sanlucar de Barrameda.

The soil, more than anything else, determines the nature of the wine, the best being the *albarza*, an arid, white, chalky soil like that of Champagne which produces wines possessing great finesse and a splendid bouquet. The dominant grape is the famous Palomina which gives the best Finos and Amontillados. There are some six secondary varieties, including the Pedro Ximenez whose grapes are dried for two weeks in the sun after the vendange, giving a very strong, sweet wine used in varying proportions in blends called P.X. The vendange takes place in early September and the grapes are pressed after twelve or fourteen hours of exposure to the sun. The must is then brought into the *bodegas* where it is made into wine. The wine ferments until December when the experts decide on its destiny. Light, clear wine having a fine bouquet becomes Fino and

Amontillado after adding *eau-de-vie de vin* until an alcohol content of 15·5° is obtained. The more full-bodied wine with less bouquet is fortified up to 17 or 18° and is called Oloroso or Cream Sherry.

The different wines are stocked in separate *criaderas* or nurseries for one or two years, or more. There, in three-quarters filled oak casks, the wines undergo an evolution caused by the indigenous yeast particles called the *flor*. Afterwards they are blended and aged in the *Solera* system. In time the sherry tends to darken slightly and the wine takes on its inimitable bouquet. It also becomes drier and, unlike other wines, richer in alcohol. Thus the Finos and Manzanillas, which began at 15·5°, can easily reach 21° after five years or more in cask.

Soave One of the best dry white wines of Italy, produced east of Verona from the Garganega (90%), Trebbiano and Riesling vines, which are trained high above the ground on pergolas. Soave is made by two communes, the picturesque little town of Soave and the neighbouring village of Monforte. Virtually the entire harvest is vinified by the local co-operative (*cantina sociale*), which is one of the best equipped in Italy.

Soave is sold in tall green bottles similar to those used in Alsace, and is a pretty, green-tinted, straw colour. Light and fresh, dry but not acid, it is a delicious wine that has a faint almond-flavour, and should be drunk within three years.

sommelier A wine-waiter. In certain restaurants the *sommelier* is the man in charge of all matters relating to the cellar and drinks generally. His jobs include ordering and receiving supplies, organising and constantly checking the cellars, advising customers and serving at table. Since the Belle Epoque it has become the custom in France for *sommeliers* to wear long aprons and short black jackets with a symbolic bunch of grapes embossed in gold on the lapel. The *sommelier*'s responsibilities are as great as the chef's; the *maître d'hôtel* can advise the customer on his choice of food, but only the *sommelier* has the knowledge and skill to suggest the most suitable wines.

The profession goes back an exceedingly long time – some might say even as

The head sommelier of a large Paris restaurant examining a Bordeaux in the cellar.
Phot. Réalitiés.

far as Ganymede, who served ambrosia and nectar to the gods on Mount Olympus. Whatever its precise origin, the Merovingian and Carolingian kings (fifth to tenth centuries) were quick to adopt the idea from the courts of Rome and Byzantium and establish similar appointments at their own.

The derivation of the word is still disputed. Some people think a *sommelier*'s job was originally to receive the wine which was brought by *sommiers*, or *bêtes de somme* (pack-animals or beasts of burden; the origin of the obsolete English word 'sumpter'). Others assert that the word *somme* in Old French meant 'duty' or 'office', and that in great households the *sommelier* was the servant in charge of provisions: there was a *sommelier de panneterie* (bread-store) and a *sommelier d'échansonnerie* (wine-room). Although there does not seem to be a very clearly-defined distinction between the duties of the wine-room and those of the cellar, it seems that none of the great old households of ancient France ever dispensed with the services of this important functionary. Nowadays, when restaurants have no resident *sommelier*, the *patron* or manager should perform the services himself.

Sonoma   One of the most important vine-growing counties in northern California★, Sonoma is situated north of San Francisco and borders San Francisco Bay in the south. Although the mission of Spanish Franciscan monks, from whom it takes its name, introduced vines there in the eighteenth century, viticulture did not really start to develop in the area until the arrival of Colonel Haraszthy, the 'father of Californian viticulture', who established the famous Buena Vista★ vineyard in the vicinity.

Both the climate and the soil of Sonoma vary a good deal, and vines are only grown in certain areas. The Pacific coast is too cold and rainy for them, but the northern part of the country, from Healdsburg to Asti in the Russian River Valley, has a climate similar to that of central Italy and its pebbly hills produce a great number of good quality red vins ordinaires (made from Zinfandel, Carignan, Petite-Syrah, Grenache and Mataro grapes) and several mediocre white ones. The best region

stretches across the middle of the county from San Francisco Bay to Guerneville, and includes Sonoma and Santa Rosa. Its climate is comparable to that of Burgundy in France, and is perfect for viticulture.

The biggest, 'wineries' are those of Buena Vista and Korbel, founded in 1881 by émigré Czechs of that name. The latter is concerned almost exclusively with the production of excellent sparkling wines which are made by the Champagne method★ and conform to the rigorous standards of quality that the Korbel brothers learned at the School of Viticulture at Melnik, near Prague.

sour   A sour wine gives a very disagreeable sensation to the palate. It is acid, astringent and biting like an unripe apple.

South Africa   Vines were first planted in this country when the Dutch colonised it in the seventeenth century. Its climate is favourable to viticulture, being similar to that of the Mediterranean area. The best-known vineyard, Groot-Constantia, which produces the once-famous Constantia★ wine, was planted in 1684.

Vendange near Cap (South Africa). Phot. Rapho.

The vineyards are clustered in the province of Cap and are divided into two distinct sections. The first, the coastal section, comprises the regions of Stellenbosch, Paarl and Wellington, the area from Malmesbury to Tulbagh, and finally the peninsula of Cap. The second is a high altitude area called Little Karoo. It extends from Ladysmith to Oudtshoorn between Drakenstein and Swartberg and includes Worcester, Robertson, Bonnievale and Swellendam. This second region produces mainly port- and sherry-type dessert wines, while the coastal region also produces dry red and white wines.

The vineyard of Paarl Valley, located just east of Cap, produces what are considered the best wines. But the wines of Cap have never recovered the popularity they enjoyed in the nineteenth century, particularly in France. They are mainly consumed locally.

South America Since the vine needs a temperate climate, it is mainly grown in the one-third of this vast continent which lies south of the tropic of Capricorn. Argentina★ is by far the largest producer and Chile★, which produces the best wines in South America, is the second largest. Vineyards are also found in Uruguay, where they are rapidly expanding, and in Brazil★, mainly in the southern region of Rio Grande do Sol. Although Peru lies north of the tropic of Capricorn, it also has some vineyards. The high altitude of the country compensates for its unfavourable latitude.

Spain Although vines are cultivated in almost every region of Spain, and the vineyards occupy an extensive area, the volume produced is much less than that of France or Italy. The arid soil and inhospitable climate limits production to around 25 million hl, about one-third of French production and half of the Italian.

Sherry is the only Spanish wine known to many, but it only represents 2% of the country's wine production. There is also a

Spain: a vineyard in Aragon.
Phot. J. Bottin.

wide range of reds, rosés, whites, sparkling wines, vins de liqueur and mistelles.

Vinification methods are still rather primitive in many areas and most of the wines fall into the table wine category and are drunk locally, as they are not bottled. These very inexpensive wines often surprise the visitor with their originality. The regions of Valencia and Aragon produce full-bodied, highly-coloured wines which are for the most part exported. They are used in Switzerland to give colour and alcohol to more anaemic wine. The best Spanish wines (particularly the reds) come from the Rioja★ region not far from the French border in the valley of the Ebro. The best of these wines resemble good Bordeaux.

The Atlantic region stretching from Galice to the Basque area produces well-known Spanish wines. Next is the important production area of Valdepenas★ south of Madrid in Nouvelle-Castille, followed by the Alicante region near Valence which produces a large quantity of red wine made from the Grenache grape, and also good rosés at Yecla. Several good quality reds and whites are produced around Barcelona (Panades, Perelada and Alella) and good reds, rosés and whites in Galice, which is located near the Portuguese border.

Catalonia produces a sparkling wine often labelled Xampan (pronounced Champagne). But Spain is most renowned for its fortified wines, especially sherry★, Manzanilla★ and Montilla★. Tarragona, south of Barcelona on the Mediterranean coast, produces a full-bodied, fortified red wine called Priorato in Spain and Tarragona when exported. Tarragona, like Malaga, has lost its once commercial importance, but is still a very agreeable wine.

stabilisation Being organic, wine is never really stable. The vigneron therefore has to use his skill to eliminate the ferments (or leavens) after fermentation, and to prevent their growth without impairing any of the wine's qualities or inhibiting its development. Cold weather has always helped vignerons to stabilise wines, though nowadays they also have modern refrigeration★ methods at their disposal. Heat, as used in pasteurisation★ and infrared treatment, is also helpful, but must be used with great caution as it can easily

harm the wine. Another important process is racking, which separates the wine from the ferment-laden lees. But the vigneron's most important stabilising agent is sulphur dioxide★, which has been used since Roman times and is still indispensable.

Stabilisation also presents the vigneron with the extremely complex problem of achieving a lasting and perfect balance of the wine's elements (its present and future acidity, its sugar content and its colour) and also of eliminating all suspended matter (*voltigeurs★*) and preventing cloudiness. Each barrel, each year and each cru presents its particular problems, and has to be treated with great care, as each may react in a totally unforseen way.

Steinberg A well-known German vineyard located in the heart of the Rheingau★, which was created in the twelfth century by the Cistercian Saint

Saint Bernard, founder of the Abbey of Clairvaux and creator of two great vineyards, Steinberg and Clos de Vougeot. Miniature by Fouquet (c. 1445). Musée Condé, Chantilly. Phot. Giraudon.

Left: Schloss Ehrenfels.
Right: Schloss Vollrads and
vineyard in the Rheingau.
Below: Workers on their way
to the vineyards at Hochheim.
Phots. Colin Mahler.

Bernard of Clairvaux, who also established Clos de Vougeot. The wines of Steinberg are sold under different names as the wines, as well as the years, may vary considerably (e.g. Steinberger, Steinberger Kabinett, Auslese and Trockenbeerenauslese). But they all share the family traits of being full-bodied and powerful and having a delicate, expanding bouquet.

still A still wine is neither sparkling nor pétillant★. The term is generally used to describe the basic wine which is to be converted into sparkling wine to distinguish it from the finished product.

suave A word employed by connoisseurs to describe wines of refinement that have a delicate fragrance, perfect balance and great smoothness. It is often used in connection with the great vins blancs liquoreux★ of France.

submersion of vines In the course of the desperate fight against phylloxera★, it was noticed that the insect hibernated on the root of the vines. One of the remedies suggested was therefore to submerge the vines in water (in places where this was possible) and thus drown it. Many vignerons hastened to adopt this measure, which was not, however, as successful as they had hoped. The areas most favourable were, naturally, the low-lying plains of the Hérault, Aude, Gard and Bouches-du-Rhône departments. There are still a few hectares of these submerged vines near the Mediterranean coast.

Submersion in water, a technique used against phylloxera. Phot. M.

Sud-Ouest The Sud-Ouest (southwestern) region of France produces an enormously varied range of wines that includes those of the former provinces of Aquitaine (except Bordeaux), Béarn, the Basque country and Languedoc. Its wines are officially divided into two categories, AOC★ and VDQS★.

The AOC wines are those of the Dordogne (Monbazillac★, Bergerac★ and Montravel★), Côtes-de-Duras★, Gaillac★ and the Basses-Pyrénées (Jurançon★, Madiran★ and Pacherenc-du-Vic-Bihl★).

There are a great many VDQS: Côtes-du-Buzet★, Côtes-du-Marmandais★, the wines of Tursan★, Cahors★, Béarn★, Irouléguy★, Fronton★, Villaudric★ and Lavilledieu★ and those of the Aveyron region (Entraygues, Fel, Estaing★ and Marcillac★).

sugar Grape juice contains two basic sugars, glucose and fructose, which are converted into alcohol by the action of yeasts★. A certain quantity of unfermented sugar is always left in the wine – even dry wines contain from 1–3 g of sugar per litre. In vins blancs liquoreux★, whose musts have a high sugar content, the amount of unfermented sugar left is very great as yeasts cannot work when the alcohol content of the must exceeds about 15°. Fermentation, therefore, comes to a halt of its own accord. In vins doux naturels★ the vigneron stops the yeasts' activity by adding alcohol to the wine himself in order to keep some of the natural sugar unfermented.

Another element always present in a wine which can make it taste sweet is glycerine★. Strictly speaking, it makes the wine moelleux★, but also gives an impression of sweetness.

sulphur dioxide (SO$_2$) Sulphur dioxide is an indispensible aid to vignerons at all stages of vinification, from vatting to bottling. Its use as an antiseptic dates back to Roman times, and it is still the only sterilising agent permitted by law. The work of Pasteur and other modern scientific developments have led to its widespread use by vignerons all over the world, and so far nothing better has been found for the purpose.

It has several functions. It kills bacteria and the germs of wine diseases without affecting the yeast cells that cause fermentation, and can therefore even be employed to sterilise must in the fermenting-vat. It is equally useful in the treatment of grapes that are not too badly damaged by pourriture grise★, as it eliminates the mould that causes casse brune★. It has also been found to improve the quality of must, making it richer in alcohol, fixed acidity★, extract content, flavour and colour.

Sulphur dioxide is particularly valuable in the preparation of vins blancs liquoreux★, sweet white wines whose high residual sugar content always makes them liable to a second fermentation in bottle, and its use for this purpose has become standard practice. Sulphur, as it is commonly called, is used in various forms, sometimes as a pressurised gas or as a powdered tablet, or, more commonly, as a solution of sulphur and water. A certain proportion of sulphur always combines with the wine's sugar (and in fact contributes to the bouquet), but it is only effective as an antiseptic when pure – which is unfortunately also when its flavour and smell becomes noticeable in the wine. It is usually at the bottling stage that vigernons tend to be heavy-handed out of a commendable desire to prevent oxidation or refermentation. Excess 'free' (uncombined) sulphur gives the wine an unpleasant smell and taste, can cause headaches and, in bad cases, sometimes causes the disagreeable smells of rotten eggs or garlic. In France the maximum dosage authorised by law is 450 mg per litre, and the proportion of free sulphur must not exceed 100 mg per litre – although some experts can often detect as little as 40 mg.

supple A supple wine produces a pleasant sensation of smoothness and softness on the palate. Its alcohol★ and acidity★ are perfectly balanced, it has no excess tannin★, and contains a certain proportion of natural glycerine★. Suppleness is now an increasingly sought-after quality.

Switzerland Switzerland is justifiably proud of its wines. The climate restricts vine-growing to sheltered areas in the hollows of its steep slopes and along the shores of its lakes, and the wines are chiefly the result of the great tenacity and unremitting labour of the vignerons.

About two-thirds of the country's total wine output is white and consumed locally. The rest, which is not a great deal, is exported to Germany and the United States, and very rarely to France or Britain where Swiss wine is virtually unknown. Total production never exceeds one million hl a year, and one-quarter is supplied by the Valais canton. On the other hand, Switzerland – despite its size – imports twice as much wine as Britain.

There are about 230 Swiss crus, but the legislation which governs their classification is different from that of France. Vines are grown in a dozen cantons, though only five of them are at all important: Valais, Neuchâtel, Vaud, Ticino and Geneva.

Valais, sometimes called 'the California of Switzerland', produces the best red wines and many of the best white ones. The vineyards are situated in the upper Rhône valley, stretching from Martigny at the foot of Mont Blanc to the northern end of the Simplon tunnel. Altogether it has seventeen crus, of which the best known are Dôle★, Hermitage, Johannisberg, Malvoisie, Arvine, Martigny, Glacier★ and a number of white wines called Fendant made from Chasselas★ grapes.

There are about 1000 ha of vineyards in the canton of Geneva located along the two banks of the Rhône, with the bulk on the right bank. The wines are grouped into large categories depending on the grapes and characterised by their origin, soil and aspect. Most of the vignerons belong to co-operatives (Cave de Lully, Cave de la Souche and Cave de Mandiment de Satigny). Among the wines produced are: Bouquet Royal, Coteaux de Lully and Perle de Mandiment, which are perlant★ wines from the Chasselas grape; Gout du Prieur, Clavendier and dry whites; Rosé Reine, Rosé de Pinot and rosés; and Clefs d'Or, Camerier and generous reds.

The canton of Neuchâtel, in the northwest of Switzerland, primarily produces white wines made from Chasselas grapes grown along the northern shore of Lake Neuchâtel. Often pétillant★, they are bright, fresh, pleasant wines, but are sometimes criticised for being 'sharp and green' in years of insufficient sunshine. Neuchâtel's red wine, which is made from Pinot Noir★ (its only authorised grape variety), is excellent. Many people find it

not unlike the French wine of Chiroubles★. The canton has about eighteen appellations, amongst which are Auvernier, Cormondrèche, Hauterive and Cortaillod★.

The wines of the Vaud canton are nearly all white and are made almost exclusively from Chasselas grapes. The most important vineyards are on the northern shores of Lake Geneva between Nyon and Lausanne (in a region known as La Côte), and then from Lausanne to beyond Vexey (the Lavaux region, which has the good cru Dézaley★). The region known as Chablais, with the well-known white crus Yvorne and Aigle, is also in this canton, as is the Côtes de l'Orbe near Neuchâtel.

Ticino is the Italian-speaking region around Locarno and Lugano. Its wines are mostly red vins ordinaires, and the best are made from Merlot grapes (one of the Bordeaux varieties).

Sylvaner Sylvaner is one of the principal vine varieties of Alsace, and produces good, average wine that has a certain charm. This pale, green-tinged wine is lively, light and refreshing – especially when it retains the light sparkle of its early youth – although it somewhat lacks bouquet and flavour. The best wine is made in Barr and around Rouffach, where it sometimes achieves a distinction that puts it on a par with Riesling★. The Sylvaner vine goes under different names in different parts of the world. It is very common in Germany, the Italian Tyrol and Austria, where its wines have more or less the same characteristics as those it makes in Alsace, and it is also grown in California and Chile.

Syria, Libya, Jordan As the Bible attests, the vine has been cultivated in these areas since ancient times, the wines of Helbon and Chalybon having been carried long distances by the caravans. Since the three countries embrace the Moslem religion, most of the production is consumed as table grapes or dried raisins, although some table wine and a little sparkling wine is made by Christian vigernons.

T

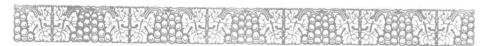

tannin An organic material found in the stones, skin and stalks of grapes. Normally the tannin contained in wine comes mainly from the skin and stones.

The quantity of tannin varies depending on the grape variety (the Cabernet, for example, is rich in tannin) and also on the vinification method. Egrappage★ (destalking), a short fermentation period, a moderate pressing, all lessen the strength of tannin in the wine. White wine has little tannin while red wine contains much more, especially when it has undergone a long fermentation.

Tannin forms deposits which are normally found in old red wines. A mature wine always contains less dissolved tannin than a young one. A normal amount of tannin is an indispensible element in wine as it contributes to the wine's steadiness and clarity. Too much tannin can be eliminated by the fining process. When the wine lacks tannin the process of tannisage★ is used to raise it to a normal level. The strength of tannin in a wine determines the use of certain expressions and terms such as astringent★, thick, thin★ and sour★.

tannisage A treatment sometimes necessary when a wine has a tannin deficiency, which may, for example, be due to unripe grapes. Tannin, a natural product derived from gallic acid, is added in order to prevent the wine from being thin★, and to facilitate the essential process of fining. Sometimes the wood of new oak casks itself imparts enough tannin to the wine to remedy the deficiency and can contribute considerably to its bouquet.

Tavel Tavel, in the Côtes du Rhône★ region, produces the most famous rosé in France. It was the favourite wine of François I and was praised by the poet Ronsard. The vineyard is situated in the Gard department on the right bank of the Rhône, not far from Avignon. A number of different vines are planted, the predominant variety being Grenache followed by Cinsault, Clairette Blanche and Clairette Rouge, Picpoul, Bourboulenc and a little Carignan. Only rosé wine qualifies for the appellation. Its colour – pale ruby with shades of topaz – deepens with age. Heady, dry and fruity, it is an elegant, fresh wine with a slightly pungent flavour and is quite different from other Côtes-du-Rhône wines. It is at its best when drunk slightly chilled. Although some people say it is the only rosé that keeps well, the vignerons themselves drink their Tavel within two years, and regard a bottle more than five years old as a curiosity.

Tavel. Phot. M.

A small quantity of red wine is also made in Tavel from the traditional grape varieties of the area, but is entitled only to the appellation Côtes-du-Rhône.

Tawny This kind of port★ is a blend of carefully selected wines from a legally defined area, and is always matured in cask. The name refers to the colour which all port acquires with age (whether originally red or white), and has come to mean a wine that has matured in cask, as opposed to vintage★ which matures in bottle. The object of the blending is to achieve a sustained and consistent quality from one year to the next. Vintage port, on the other hand, is always the product of one outstandingly good year, and is never blended.

The casks in which this eminent wine matures are usually made of Baltic oak or, failing that, of Portuguese or Italian chestnut. Their shape and volume (usually 550 litres) has been established by practical experience. The wine slowly oxidises as a consequence of the air which penetrates the wood, the colouring matter★ collects around the sides of the casks and the wine throws its deposit and gets lighter and lighter in colour. As it evaporates, the casks are continually filled up with younger wines which enrich the rest. The wine is bottled after a minimum of eight years in cask.

Chai of tawny port, Vila Nova de Gaia, Portugal. Phot. Y. Loriat.

These vinicultural techniques are continually being improved at the instigation of the Portuguese Wine Institute which exercises a strict control over this most important of Portugal's products. The method not only ensures a remarkably consistent quality, but also offers enthusiasts an ever-increasing range of bouquets, flavours and shades, from ruby to light tawny. Tawny port does not have to be served in a decanter★ as it has matured and thrown its deposit in cask. Its original bottle, with the seal of a reputable firm on it, does it ample justice. Port is traditionally passed clockwise around the table.

temperature of wine Temperature is a very important factor when serving wine. There is one golden rule: whether the wine is being chilled or brought to room temperature, it should be done slowly and gently. A young wine can more or less survive a sudden change of temperature, but an old and venerable bottle may be irreparably harmed. The barbaric practices of standing red wine on a corner of the stove or over a radiator, or immersing the bottle in hot water, are as reprehensible as they are harmful. Likewise, that of extra quick chilling by putting the bottle in the refrigerator or, worse still, in the freezer. Conditions were more satisfactory in the old days when the temperature of cellars was never higher than 12°C (which is by no means always the case today), and when living rooms were not overheated, as they nearly always are now. Two mistakes to be avoided at all costs are lukewarm red wine and frozen white wine. To be on the safe side, it is best simply to serve the wine at cellar temperature.

The temperature a wine should be served at depends primarily on the wine itself, on its age, the personal preferences of the guests and the temperature of the dining-room. However, some general rules always apply: young wines should be served at a lower temperature than old ones, and it is always better to serve a wine at slightly less than the ideal temperature, as it will get warmer during the meal. It should also be remembered that the warmer the room, the cooler the wine will appear to be, and vice versa.

Red wine, with one or two exceptions, should always be brought to room temperature. If the wine comes from an ideal cellar★ with a temperature not exceeding 12°C, two hours in the dining-room away from all sources of heat should be enough. This also leaves the guest the pleasure of releasing the bouquet and flavour of the wine himself by the warmth of his hand as he holds the glass.

Generally speaking, and according to the *code du sommelier*, red Bordeaux and Touraine wines are best at about 15–16°C, Burgundies and Côtes-du-Rhone at about 13–14°C, and Beaujolais and light regional wines a little cooler, at cellar temperature. Red vins doux naturels should also be served cool, owing to their alcohol and sugar content.

White wines should be drunk chilled, never frozen: from 6–11°C for dry wines and about 5°C for sweet wines. Château-Chalon and vins jaunes are exceptions and should be drunk at the same temperature as reds. Full-bodied white Burgundies (Corton Charlemagne, Montrachet and Meursault) also require a relatively high temperature, about 10–13°C, to bring out all their excellent qualities. Champagne is drunk chilled, at about 4°C, other sparkling wines even cooler at about 2°. Rosés, too, should be chilled even though the low temperature can often disguise their potency and lead the unwary to underestimate their alcohol content. To chill wine, the old system of an ice-bucket is always preferable to putting the bottle in the refrigerator.

tender A term applied to a wine that has little acidity but is delicate, fresh and light. Its character is not particularly pronounced and it is usually in the prime of its life. A tender wine pleases by reason of its softness and gentleness, and never imposes itself on the palate.

tenue 'Steadiness' is a rough translation of this word, which for the professional denotes a wine's resistance to cloudiness and casse★. For the wine-lover it means a good balance between the wine's various elements.

Terlano One of the best and most famous white wines of the Italian Tyrol. It is grown around the village of Terlano in the deep and picturesque gorges of the Adige, between Bolzano and Merano. Sold in tall, green bottles like the wines of

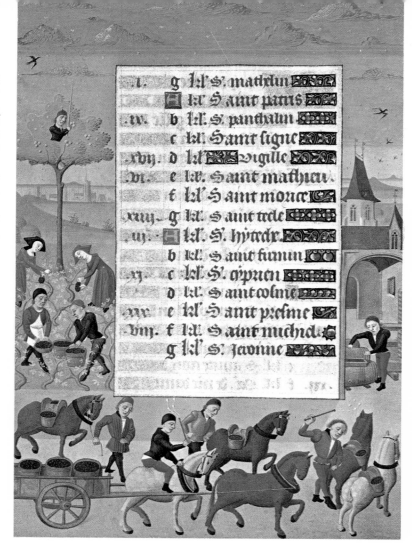

September, the month of the grape and nut harvest. 15th-century miniature. Musée Condé, Chantilly. Phot. Giraudon.

Alsace, Terlano is usually a dry white wine with a pale, greenish-gold colour. It is delicate and extremely pleasant, but has no great bouquet nor a particularly distinctive taste.

It is made from various grapes: Riesling, Pinot Blanc, Pinot Gris and Terlano (a local variety). Its quality and character depend on the relative proportions of these in its composition, something which can only be determined empirically.

terroir This word either means 'soil' or 'patch of ground', i.e. a particular plot of land that makes one cru different from another. There is also the expression *goût de terroir*, which means the characteristic though often indefinable flavour that a wine acquires from a particular type of soil.

thin A thin wine is like a thin person – it has less body★ and less substance than normal. This is usually due to excess racking★ rather than any disease in the wine.

tierçon   A measure of capacity that varies from region to region. In Languedoc it is a third of a muid★, i.e. 228 litres. It is mainly used for Muscat★ wines.

tisane à Richelieu   This is a nickname given many years ago to Bordeaux. Louis XV sent Duke Armand de Richelieu, Marshall of France, to govern the province of Aquitaine as a rest from his exhausting life of pleasure at the court. Predictably, the Duke greatly appreciated the wines of Bordeaux, with whose help he soon resumed the life to which he was accustomed.

Tlemcen (Coteaux-de-)   An Algerian★ wine made south-east of Oran near the Moroccan border, which was VDQS★ when Algeria was under French administration. Coteaux-de-Tlemcen is a mountain wine, grown on limestone at a height of 800 m. It is generous, full-bodied and firm, and has an attractive ruby colour (it is usually red, sometimes rosé). It also improves with age, acquiring moelleux★, finesse and a very pleasant velvety taste.

Tokay   A world-famous Hungarian wine. Real Tokay, which is very rare, is one of the best white wines. It is produced by the small viticultural region of Tokaj – Hegyalja, located in north-east Hungary on the banks of the Bodrog, thirty km north-west of Nyiregyhaza. The wine is made mainly from the Furmint grape whose name came from the old French *forment* (the wine from the Furmint takes on a yellow tint like that of wheat).

The soil is composed of volcanic debris mixed with feldspar and the area is favoured by dry, sunny autumns which are conducive to the supermaturation of the grapes.

The special method of harvesting was discovered in the seventeenth century at Tokay as a result of the beneficial effect of the harvest being delayed one year because of war. The most common and least expensive Tokay is called Szamorodni. Its name, originally Polish, means 'as it grows'. To make it, the overripe grapes are added to the other grapes in the presses.

The quality depends on the year and it is always high in alcohol.

Another variety is the Tokay called Aszú, marvellously sweet and very rare and expensive. It contains a certain fixed proportion of carefully chosen grapes which have been attacked by pourriture noble★. The harvested grapes are laid on large tables and the dried, wrinkled grapes are separated from the others. From the pressing is obtained what is called the 'heart' of the wine which is kneaded into a sort of dough. This dough is added in variable quantities to the must of ordinary grapes which have already been pressed.

The quantity is specified on the label in terms of *puttonyos*. The *puttonyos* are 25-litre baskets used in the region. Depending on the number of *puttonyos* of chosen grapes added to a *fut* (136 litres), you get different labels – 'Aszu 2 puttonyos', 'Aszu 3 puttonyos' – up to six *puttonyos*. It follows that the more *puttonyos*, the better and more expensive the wine.

Tokay ferments in small casks which can be stored in very low cellars. (This has given the vignerons the opportunity to hide their wine in the course of many invasions.) Low cellars apparently make the best wine. Tokay is exported by the government in long-necked bottles of 5·0 dl. Its bouquet and unforgettable taste justify its reputation of being one of the best wines in the world. The best Tokay is grown on the commune of Tallya. Voltaire praised Tokay, saying 'Tokay, the golden liquid which fires the brain and inspires the most brilliant talk. Tokay leaps and sparkles on the brim of the glass'.

tonneau   Before the invention of the *tonneau* or barrel (attributed to the Gauls), wine was kept in earthenware amphoras and carried in leather bottles. Amphoras had to be lined with pitch to make them watertight, which must have given the wine a very strong flavour. The resinous wines of Greece are probably the nearest we can get to the taste today.

Barrels have always been their present functional shape. The wood allows the wine to breathe, and also allows the evaporation necessary for its development. The rounded shape makes the barrels easy to move and, more important, facilitates the racking★ process as the lees remain in the bulge while the clear wine is drawn off.

Barrels are usually made of oak, which contributes considerably to the bouquet★, and white wines are often left to ferment in new oak casks to supplement their low tannin content. The small-scale vignerons of Bordeaux buy barrels second-hand from the great châteaux in the hope that some of the wine will have impregnated the staves and eventually improve the quality of their own. The barrels used for shipping wines are called *fûts perdus*, or lost casks, and are made of chestnut, not of oak.

The tonneau is also a trading unit in Bordeaux, although there is no actual barrel this size. It takes four barriques★ of 225 litres to make a tonneau of 900 litres.

Touraine This peaceful and attractive province, with its marvellous châteaux, is often called 'the garden of France'. Its vineyards date back to the sixth century, and its wines have been praised by a long line of French poets and writers, including Rabelais, Ronsard, Vigny, Balzac and Alexandre Dumas. The vineyards are mostly in the Indre-et-Loire department and produce a great variety of wines. The climate is particularly favourable to viticulture, as are the various types of soil found in the area. These range from granitic and pebbly sand over 'Touraine tufa' (the yellow chalk out of which the cellars at Vouvray are dug), to *aubuis*, the mixture of siliceous sand, clay and limestone at the foot of the hills which brings out all the best qualities of the Pineau de la Loire grape. This delightful region is justly renowned for the great white wines of Vouvray★ and Montlouis★ and the smooth red wines of Chinon★, Bourgueil★ and Saint-Nicolas-de-Bourgueil★.

The Coteaux du Loir★ vineyard, situated at the meeting point of the Touraine, Anjoy and Maine provinces, is also included in the Touraine viticultural region.

TOURAINE: APPELLATION D'ORIGINE CONTRÔLÉE To qualify for this appellation the delicate, fruity red wines of Touraine must be made from Cabernet Franc★ (locally known as Cabernet Breton) and certain other authorised, supplementary varieties: Cot, Malbec, Noble, Gris-Meunier, Pinot Gris and Gamay. The region's light, fruity rosés are made from Cabernet Breton, Cot, Gamay and Groslot. Both dry and sweet (sometimes sparkling) white wines are made from Chenin (or Pineau da la Loire) or, more rarely, Sauvignon. The minimum alcohol content is 9° for reds and rosés, and 9·5° for whites.

The alcohol content of Touraine pétillant★ (red, white or rosé) must be 9·5° before their secondary fermentation in bottle. The white is made from Pineau de la Loire, a white grape, whereas the red and rosé are made only from the red Cabernet variety.

Some Touraine wines are permitted to carry the name of their commune as well as the appellation Touraine (Azay-le-Rideau★, Amboise★ and Mesland★).

tourne A malady liable to affect badly made wines which are deficient in alcohol★ and acidity★ (having a pH greater than 3·5) and still contain a certain amount of

Cooper at work.
Phot. René-Jacques.

A Touraine vineyard between Azay-le-Rideau and Chinon after the vendange.
Phot. Lauros.

unfermented sugar, or wines made from damaged grapes. Wine affected in this way tastes extremely unpleasant, and is both sour and flat; it looks murky and has little, shiny threads which float about in it when the bottle is moved. Tourne bacteria attack the fixed acids, sugar, glycerine★ and, particularly, the tartric acid of a wine, so that its fixed acidity★ is reduced and its volatile acidity★ increased. The bacterial activity also releases carbon dioxide, which pushes out the staves at the bottom of the barrel and makes the wine froth as it is drawn out.

The disease can be prevented, and even in the initial stages halted, by dosing the wine with sulphur dioxide★ and tannin★, by racking★ it frequently with accompanying doses of sulphur dioxide, and by pasteurisation★.

traminer An Alsatian vine known elsewhere as Savagnin Blanc (or Rosé), one of the principal noble★ varieties of the Jura★. It derives its name from a village in the Italian Tyrol called Termeno, which was known as Traminer when it belonged to Austria. Its wine is never acid – sometimes even quite sweet – and has a pleasant aroma. It is a full-bodied, smooth, generous wine, with a very flowery taste and bouquet in which the flavours of rose and jasmine are the most distinct. Traminer is grown chiefly in the Rhine valley, the Italian Tyrol and in California. The best Traminers are called Gewürztraminers.

tuilé *Rouge tuilé*, or brick-red, is a colour often acquired by old wines whose constituent elements have become oxidised, and as such is a useful gauge of quality. The colour is normal, however, in Rancio★ wines.

Tunisia Wine production fell considerably following a phylloxera★ attack around 1936 which destroyed a large portion of the vineyards. Consumption in the country is minimal as the Moslem population do not drink alcoholic beverages. Although the table wines are fairly ordinary, except for some agreeable rosés, the vins de liqueur are remarkable, especially the Muscats. Made from the Muscats of Alexandria, Frontignan and Terracina, they contain a minimum of 17°

alcohol and at least 70 g of sugar per litre. These fragrant, powerful, fine Muscats are produced east of Bizerte between Ras-el-Djebel and Porto-Farina, and on the east coast in two other areas, between Kelibia and Menzel-Temin and between Beni-Aichoum and Beni-Khair.

Turkey Turkey produces very little wine – only 5% of the total grape harvest is vinified. Most of the crop is sold as fresh eating grapes, and a quarter is kept back to be dried and sold as raisins. Turkish vineyards are few and far between, and none of them is really big. They are grouped chiefly in the regions of Pergamum, Aydin-Tire-Izmir (which produces the best wine), Ankara, Gaziantep, Malatya, Kayseri, Konya and Niğde. In fact, Turkish wines are generally quite good: whether red or white, they are dry and pleasant – Buzbağ, Doluca, Kavaklidere, Marmara and Trakya are all good examples. Izmir is an excellent white wine, quite light and fruity, and should be drunk chilled. Sweet, Muscat-based wines like Miskit, on the other hand, are markedly less good than other Turkish wines.

Tursan A vineyard in the Sud-Ouest★ region whose origins go back to well before the fifteenth century, when it was considered the heart of the basco-béarnais *pays des vignes*. Its VDQS★ wines, which are mostly white, are produced on the hillsides of about forty communes in the Landes department, notably around Geaune and Aire-sur-Adour. A local variety called Baroque makes up 90% of Tursan's vines. Vinified in the co-operative at Geaune, the wines are improving all the time and are steadily increasing in popularity. They are crisp, smooth and very dry, and have a pronounced character of their own.

Tursan also makes red and rosé wines, although not in large quantities (less than 1000 hl out of a total of 8000 hl of VDQS wines annually). Like Madiran★ wines, these are made from Tannat grapes, which produce strongly-coloured, full-bodied wine with a high tannin content. As in Madiran, Tannat is combined with a certain quantity of Fer★ and Cabernet Franc★ grapes; the proportion of Cabernet Franc in the vineyards is being increased every year, as it suits Tannat particularly well.

U

Ukraine According to figures published in 1959, the republic has 379,000 ha of land under vine, which makes it the largest viticultural region in the Soviet Union. It produces 1,600,000 hl of wine a year. At first viticulture was practised mainly in the Dnieper, Boug and Dniester valleys, but around 1800 it started to spread out into the Steppes. At present, there are three main viticultural regions in the Ukraine: the subcarpathian region on the Hungarian border, which has Muk-hachevo as its centre; the coastal region around Kherson, Odessa and Nikolaievsk; and most important of all, the Crimea, which specialises in large-scale production of sparkling wine – its annual output is twelve million bottles! There is a particularly well-equipped plant for the mass-production of this wine at the village of Massandra, near Yalta. The Crimea also produces dessert wines: Portvein, an imitation port, and various Muscats (Massandra and Zolota Balka).

USA When one considers wine production in the United States, California★ immediately comes to mind. Indeed, Californian vineyards are the most important and alone produce 80% of wine consumed. Nevertheless, there are a number of other wine-growing areas which, though less well known, account for about 14% of production (the rest is imported). These areas include, to the east, the states of New York★ and Ohio★ and to the west, on the Pacific coast, those of Washington★ and Oregon.

USSR According to figures published in 1964, there are 1,046,000 ha of vineyards in the Soviet Union, producing 9,800,000 hl of wine a year. They are mostly in the southern regions, and are planted mainly with Chasselas, Cabernet-Sauvignon, Pinot Gris, Riesling, Isabelle and Concorde grapes. In the extreme east of the Soviet Union there is also a variety of grape created by the naturalist Michurin which can withstand a temperature of −40°C (unfortunately, however, it is not immune to phylloxera★). The main Soviet viticultural regions are now, as in the past, Georgia★, whose wines have always been much admired, Moldavia★, which supplies a third of all Soviet wines, the Ukraine★,

Vinicultural co-operative in the Crimea. Phot. Novosti.

Vineyards on the banks of the Black Sea. Phot. Novosti.

Usakhe-Lauri No. 21, Kindzmareuli No. 22 and Ojaleshi No. 24. The Ukraine produces two wines of this type called 'Château Eyquem' and 'Barsac'.

There are several types of 'sweet' wine. Muscats are a speciality of the Crimea and of the viticultural complex at Massandra. Their alcohol content is from 12–16° and their sugar content varies from 20–30%. They are left to mature from two to four years before being delivered to retailers. The best are Krasnyi Kamen ('red stone') and Tavrida (made from Muscat Noir). There are also wines called 'Tokay', again produced mostly in the Crimea, made in the villages of Ai-Danil and Magarach. Some sweet wines are also made in Central Asia. 'Cahors' wines, which in the USSR are liqueur wines, are matured for at least three years before they are sold. The best known are the Shemakha of Azerbaijan, the Artashat of Armenia and the Yuzhno-berezhnyi of the Crimea, all of which have an alcoholic strength of 16° and a proportion of 18–20% sugar. The 'Cahors' of Uzbekistan is both stronger (17°) and sweeter (25% sugar) than these. Kiurdamir, made in Azerbaijan, has a velvety texture and a curious taste of chocolate. This category could also include sweet wines like the Crimean Pinot Gris, an amber-coloured wine (23% sugar and 13°), and the Georgian Salkhino No. 17, a dark, coffee-coloured wine with 30% sugar. Central Asian wines always have a high sugar content; the best are Iasman Salyk and Ter Bash from Turkmenistan, and Shirini from Tadzhikistan.

The 'fortified' wines have a strength of up to 20°, and are imitations of the famous liqueur wines of Spain, Portugal and Italy. Among the port-type wines, the best red ones are the Crimean Livadia and Massandra, and the best whites, the Crimean Yuzhnoberezhnyi and Surozh, the Armenian Aigeshat, the Georgian Kardanakhi No. 14, and Akstafa from Azerbaijan. The best 'sherry' is made in Armenia in the Ashtarak region. It is not unlike real sherry, having a deep golden colour, a fine and fruity bouquet and a slightly nutty flavour. The best 'Marsala' is produced in Turkmenistan. It slightly resembles Madeira and has an alcoholic strength of 18–19°. Soviet Madeira is mostly produced in the Crimea and Georgia – the Georgian Anaga No. 16 is tolerably good.

where almost all the sparkling wine is produced (in the Crimea) and Azerbaijan★, which has a long viticultural tradition. The RSFSR★ and Armenia★ also have vineyards of considerable importance.

In general, Russian wines are not helped by the continent's latitude and climate, particularly the white wines which tend to lack freshness. Those of Hungary★, Romania★ and Bulgaria★ are of distinctly superior quality. The USSR puts a lot of effort into the production of sparkling wines, which it calls, quite simply, 'Champagne'. This wine is in fact a passable imitation of Champagne, and can be very pleasant. In Moscow, Leningrad and other big cities there are special basement wine-shops where one can buy and drink it at leisure.

The Soviet Union also has a very wide and varied range of extremely pleasant dessert wines, which could provide serious competition if they were ever exported on the world market. These wines, of which there are a great number, can be divided into three categories: 'semi-sweet', 'sweet' and 'fortified'. The 'semi-sweet' wines have an alcohol content of less than 15°. The best are made in Georgia and have a distinctive aroma. Some are white, like Chkhaveri No. 1 and Tvishi No. 19, others are red, such as Khvachkara No. 20,

Valdepeñas An important viticultural centre in central Spain, situated south of Madrid near the city of Ciudad Real in the old province of New Castille, which was the home of Don Quixote de la Mancha. Although its name means 'valley of stones', the area is more like a large plain than a valley, and the soil, although arid, is not in fact particularly stony.

The extensive vineyards produce a very pleasant, pale, light-bodied red wine that is drunk young, particularly in Madrid, as a *vino corriente*, or vin ordinaire. It is cheap and usually served in carafes. The white wine is golden-yellow, full-bodied, fairly rough and much less agreeable. Until recently, Valdepeñas wines were rarely bottled or exported, and could only be sampled in Madrid.

Valpolicella An excellent red wine of northern Italy made from the same grape varieties as Bardolino★. Valpolicella is produced north-west of Verona on five communes: Negrar, Funane, Marano, San Pietro Incariano and Sant' Ambrogio. Ordinary Valpolicella is drunk in carafe in the first year.

The better wine, Valpolicella Superior, is bottled after eighteen months in cask, but should generally be drunk before the fifth year. It is a lively, fruity, velvety, light wine and, although rather full-bodied, possesses much finesse.

Valtellina A viticultural region in northern Italy★ near the Swiss border whose red wines are among the best of the country. The best are produced on five small mountainous slopes east of the town of Sondrio: Sassella, Grumello, Inferno, Grigioni and Fracia. The wines of this region are usually sold under their proper name, not under the appellation Valtellina. They are made from the famous Nebbiolo grape, called locally Chiavennasca, and is the grape from which the good reds of Piemonte are made.

The wines of Valtellina have a lot of personality. They are dark purple in colour – in fact, almost black – and are powerful and vigorous. They should not be drunk young as their beautiful qualities only develop after several years in bottle. A special wine of the area, called Spurzat, is transformed into a dessert wine reaching about 15 to 16° alcohol after it has aged a long time in bottle. It is marrowy and round with a colour bordering on orange.

velvety A velvety wine imparts a sensation of smoothness and softness to the palate because of its low acid content and fairly high level of glycerine★.

vendange The vendange, or grape-harvest, is a crucial time in the vineyard. After a year spent tending the vines, the vigneron finally gathers his grapes, which is the first stage of wine production. Thanks to the INAO★ and the Institut Technique du Vin (see control of maturation), the vigneron no longer has the burden of deciding when to start his harvest. The best compromise between the ripening times of different vine varieties, in regions where several varieties are combined to make a particular wine (in the Midi and Bordeaux areas, for example), is also calculated. The date of the harvest depends on the type of wine required. For dry wines the grapes are picked before they are fully ripe in order to preserve a pleasant touch of acidity. Sweet wines, on

the other hand, are made from overripe grapes that may have been attacked by pourriture noble★.

The main problem nowadays is labour, of which there is sometimes a disastrous shortage, and it is becoming more serious every year. There are special grape-picking machines in use in California, but they necessitate a rigorous pruning of the vines and, in any case, are not suitable for European vines or vineyards.

After the grapes have been picked they have to be brought back from the vineyards as quickly as possible to avoid oxidisation, and with the utmost gentleness to avoid damaging the grapes. This can pose problems for the vignerons, especially when the vineyards are on steep slopes – in the Valais region of Switzerland, for instance, they sometimes have to use cable-cars to bring the grapes down. Various kinds of receptacles are used to carry the grapes: tubs, baskets, hods, buckets, bags and wheelbarrows. Iron is always avoided, owing to the danger of casse ferrique★, and the materials used are the traditional wickerwork, wood and modern plastic.

véraison A word used in the south of France for the last phase of a grape's development. At the *véraison* stage the grape has reached its maximum weight and volume but is not yet completely ripe; its sugar content begins to increase and its acidity decreases. In the period between *véraison* and full maturity the outside of the grape hardly changes at all, which used to make it extremely difficult to judge the right time to start the harvest. Nowadays, the local representative from the INAO★ or Institut Technique du Vin (see control of maturation) makes this much easier for the vignerons by deciding, and officially announcing, the best date for the harvest for each area.

Villaudric This VDQS★ wine made in the Sud-Ouest★ region has a distinct resemblance to Fronton★. It is produced in fairly small quantities by the communes of Villaudric, Bouloc, Villemur, Fronton, Villematier and Villeneuve-les-Bouloc.

vin chaud 'Hot wine', a preparation which the French make in winter as a tonic for sufferers from colds and flu. It is made by gently heating sugar, cinnamon, one or two cloves and slivers of orange or lemon peel with a little water for seven to ten minutes. A bottle of table wine (Bordeaux, if possible) is added, and the mixture is brought to a fast boil. If the wine's alcohol content is sufficiently high, one can set the rising fumes alight. The concoction is ready when cool enough to drink.

vin de primeur The wine of the year, the new wine which generally appears after 15th December of the same year as the vendange.

Only certain wines can be offered so early in their youth, and have a corresponding freshness: Muscadet, Gros-Plant, Zwicker and Edelzwicker, Sylvaner, Gaillac, Beaujolais (but not the Beaujolais crus), Beaujolais-Villages, Mâcon Blanc and Rosé and the café wines.

vin de sucre A concoction that hardly deserves the name of wine. This artificial beverage was manufactured without using a single grape, mainly around 1903. The perpetrators of the fraud made a mixture of water, sugar and tartric acid to which, after fermentation, they added tannin and colouring matter. The Aimargues commune (which was by no means an exception) in the canton of Nîmes used nearly 450,000 kg of sugar for this purpose during September and October 1903. These deplorable operations were continued until 1907, when the honest vignerons started to stage violent demonstrations. The battle, fought mainly in the Languedoc, finally resulted in a law being passed in July 1907 prohibiting the 'watering' of wines. A decree in the same year also laid down the first legal definition for wine.

Another effect of this battle was to make the vignerons realise that they would have to band together to protect their produce. As a result, they formed the profession's first organised body, the *Confédération Générale des Vignerons*.

vinegar, wine Wine vinegar, which has been known since ancient times, owes a great deal to the work of Louis Pasteur, who established its production methods. For culinary purposes it is infinitely preferable to ordinary malt vinegar. Its preparation is based on the light, acid wines that used to be produced in great quantities in the region around Orléans in France, and it is now in fact one of that city's best-known products. The wine is poured into 230-litre oak casks, which are only half-full so that enough air can circulate. Every week ten litres of vinegar are siphoned off and replaced with the same quantity of wine. Care must be taken not to drown the *mère du vinaigre*, or vinegar 'culture', formed by *Mycoderma aceti*★ bacteria, which need

oxygen to survive. The vinegar has a distinctive flavour and contains the free organic acids of wine (malic, tartric and succinic).

Vinho verde The famous 'green wine' of Portugal. The name does not refer to its colour – there are both red and white vinhos verdes – but to its distinctive 'young' taste. About seven times as much red is produced as white, out of a total annual production of three million hl. The wines are made in the north of the country between Minho and the Douro in the districts of Moncao, Lima, Braga, Basto, Amarante and Penafiel. Each of these areas has its own traditional combination of grapes, but the most common varieties are the red ones: Vinhao, Borracal, Espadeiro and Azal Tinto. There are a great many different white varieties, the main ones being Azal blanco and Dourado.

Vinho verdes have been known for

many hundreds of years, and their production was subject to rigorous control as long ago as the eighteenth century. Today, their preparation is governed by strict regulations which affect the unusual methods of cultivation. The vines are grown on trellises supported by *enforcados*, which are usually living stems of chestnut or oak. They reach a height of anything from 1·5–5 m, and are never grown in vineyards as such but around the edges of fields, along the sides of paths and roads, and on

Véraison: the state of a grape at the moment it begins to ripen. Phot. M.

odd corners of unused farmland. The *enforcados* are pruned at the same time as the vines so that they do not deprive them of any sunlight. The wine can only be called vinho verde if it is made from vines grown by these methods.

The vinification procedures are unusual, too. Properties of the natural yeasts peculiar to the region cause a large amount of malic acid to be left in the wine after fermentation. This later provokes an intense malo-lactic fermentation★ which gives the wine its agreeable and characteristic sparkle. It is bottled early, around February or March. The wine is extremely refreshing, slightly effervescent, not very alcoholic and quite sharp. The white wines are bright and light-bodied, and are a perfect accompaniment to hors d'oeuvres and fish, besides being marvellously thirst-quenching. The red wines are more full-bodied and have a lovely bright colour, not unlike Beaujolais, and go extremely well with red meats.

vino santo   A golden, very sweet, Italian dessert wine produced mainly in Tuscany, sometimes in Trentino and on the Greek island of Santorini. Various vines are used, but the most usual is Trebbiano. The grapes undergo supermaturation, either on the vine or in the chais★, in order to produce very concentrated musts with a high sugar content.

Vintage cave at Ferreirinha, Portugal. Phot. Cuisset.

vinous, vinosity   Rich in alcohol. It may seem superfluous to call a wine vinous, but it does have a real meaning in the sense that such a wine has a definite character, with a pronounced 'winy' flavour and bouquet.

vins délimités de qualité supérieure (VDQS)   These letters or words are a guarantee of quality and describe regional wines made according to strict regulations which apply to the area of production, vines grown, alcoholic strength and maximum yield per hectare. Such wines are of excellent quality, and have been stringently checked and controlled by the INAO★ and the *Service de la Répression des Fraudes* (see repression of frauds). The vine-growers' unions themselves decide which wines should qualify for the label, and this is conferred only when their recommendations have been judged by an impartial commmission. The wines are always clearly labelled either with the words in full or simply with the initials VDQS.

vins fins de la Côte de Nuits   Certain communes lying north and south of the line of grands crus are permitted under certain conditions to sell some of their wines as 'Vins fins de la Côte de Nuits'. They are Fixin, Brochon, Prissey, Comblanchien and Corgoloin. The official appellation 'Vins fins . . .' has recently been shortened to 'Cote-de-Nuits-Villages'.

vintage   The year of vinification helps the gourmet★ to choose his wine. Certain years of distinction linger in the memory of oenophiles – years such as 1921, 1929, 1947 and 1949 (see table in appendix). Some specialists have observed that these are normally odd-numbered years. This seems true when considering 1943, 1945, 1953, 1955, 1957, 1959 and 1961, but the even years of 1942, 1950, 1952 and 1962 are also considered great. Within a ten-year period, three to five excellent years usually occur and one exceptional.

Sometimes wine-lovers tend to put too much weight on the year, forgetting that some years are relatively unheralded until the wines have matured, and years following famous ones are sometimes automatically overlooked. Wines coming after a mediocre year may be overestimated and not live up to their promise. In buying for a cellar it is best to follow this advice: 'Buy the petit cru in the great years and the grand cru in the lesser years'.

Vintage port A Portuguese wine made in special years and bottled without being blended after two or three years in wood. Some vintage years have been 1921, 1924, 1927, 1934, 1947, 1950, 1955, 1960, 1964 and 1970. Usually not more than 10% of that year's harvest is reserved for vintage port.

After bottling, port must age slowly for at least ten years, during which time it acquires a special aroma and the bottle becomes encrusted with a white sediment. A special official label on the bottle guarantees the authenticity of the vintage. Port was a great British favourite in the nineteenth century.

The corkscrew is not used in opening port. Instead, special pincers are heated over a flame and used to slice the neck off. In this way no mustiness from the cork has a chance to mix with the wine, which can sometimes happen with the corkscrew method. After the ceremony of opening the bottle the wine is decanted so that it may aerate and be separated from its sediment.

virile A 'virile' wine is the opposite of a feminine★ one. It is powerful, vigorous and has great strength and character. Madiran★, Châteauneuf-de-Pape★ and the wines of the Côte de Nuits★ are all typical, virile red wines, while Pouilly-Fuissé is a typical white one.

Volnay Documentary evidence dates Volnay's great reputation back to 1250, and it has been called 'the most pleasing wine in all France'. Produced in the Côte de Beaune★, Volnay wines have great finesse, delicacy and rare distinction. They are well balanced, supple and light, and their aroma is fleetingly reminiscent of violets. They are the finest wines of the Côte de Beaune, just as Musignys are for their part the finest of the Côte de Nuits. Volnay only makes red wines. The best climats are les Caillerets, En Champans, Chevret, les Angles and Fremiets. (See Index.)

voltigeurs These are small particles of solid matter suspended in the wine which 'fly about' when the wine is moved or poured. They are composed of potassium bitartrate crystals, dead yeasts and solidified colouring matter★. Their existence usually has to be tolerated, unless too obtrusive. Absolute clarity in a wine is often obtained only at the expense of flavour.

Vosne-Romanée Despite its relatively low output, this is possibly the most outstanding viticultural commune in France. It produces incomparable red Burgundies whose names are synonymous with quality and distinction: Romanée-Conti, Richebourg, Romanée, la Tâche,

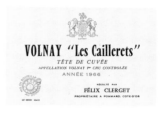

General view of Volnay.
Phot. Aarons-L.S.P.

Romanée-Saint-Vivant, Echezeaux and Grands-Echezeaux, seven of the most celebrated wines of Burgundy. They have brilliant colouring, a pronounced and subtle bouquet and exceptional smoothness and finesse.

Also worthy of mention are the following appellations: la Grande-Rue, les Suchots, Aus Malconsorts and les Beaux-Monts (which are always preceded by the name Vosne-Romanée). These all possess, though with less dazzling perfection than the seven mentioned above, the great characteristics of Vosne-Romanée wines, i.e. elegance, equilibrium and finesse of bouquet. (See Index.)

Vougeot Renowned for its world-famous cru Clos-de-Vougeot, this commune in Burgundy is also known on account of its picturesque castle, which is owned by the *Confrérie des Chevaliers du Tastevin*★ and used for their meetings.

Clos-de-Vougeot is a powerful, well-balanced wine which ages extremely well. Connoisseurs consider it one of the very best Côte d'Or wines. Vougeot also produces an excellent white wine, Clos-Blanc-de-Vougeot.

Vouvray Mounted like a precious jewel on the right bank of the Loire, Vouvray lies with its deep cellars cut into the chalk (sometimes hidden behind cave-like dwellings) and its valleys draped with vines. The vineyard comprises eight communes: Vouvray, Rochecorbon, Vernou, Sainte-Radegonde, Noizay, Chançay, Reugny and part of Parçay-Meslay.

The wines of Vouvray have been exported to Holland and Belgium for a long time, where they are enriched with must from Spain whose fermentation has been arrested with sulphur dioxide★. Then, following a secret recipe, fermentation begins again and sweet, highly alcoholic wines are produced.

Vouvray became a favourite on good

Vougeot: Chevaliers du Tastevin. Phot. Serraillier-Rapho.

258

French tables after phylloxera★ as the vine made a quick recovery.

Vouvray is made from the grape called Pineau de la Loire and takes on a different taste depending on the year, the aspect of the vineyard and the vinification method. Sometimes it is dry, light and lively, or full-bodied and powerful; at other times it is marrowy, fragrant and sweet and sometimes it tickles the nose and sparkles in the glass. It always has an amiable elegance and an exquisite freshness.

Still Vouvray must have 11° minimum alcohol. When young it is dry or semi-dry and gives great satisfaction, but reveals its splendour when kept for a few years. The 'heady' Vouvrays are made in great years although a cask of it can always be found, even in mediocre years.

Vouvray always keeps its freshness and fruitiness and is one of those astonishing wines which seems to have discovered the secret of eternal youth. Vigorous and solid, this golden, topaz-tinted wine has an extraordinary blend of aroma and taste reminiscent of acacia, fresh grapes, quince and almond.

Vouvray has a natural tendency to sparkle – a quality which is utilised in making semi-sparkling or sparkling wines, which must reach 9·5° before the second fermentation in bottle. Delicately fruity, supple and fragrant, they have a light sparkle which is produced by the natural sugar remaining in the wine after the first fermentation. This is enriched by cane sugar added as in the Champagne method★. Although prepared with a larger dose of sugar than that for the crackling or semi-sparkling wines, it is not an imitation Champagne. They are an attractive golden colour, finely perfumed, which preserve all the personality and grace of a still wine.

The sparkling wines of Vouvray, unlike other sparkling wines, improve with age and keep for a long time.

Aerial view of Vouvray.
Phot. Lauros-Beaujard.

W-Z

Washington   A wine-producing state in the extreme north-west of the USA★, bordered by Canada and the Pacific. The coastal region is relatively cold and damp and does not produce any outstanding wine. Further inland, however, the eastern part of the state has a continental climate and long, very hot summers. This region produces large quantities of strongly fortified liqueur★ wine and also, in the irrigated vineyards around Yakimo, some good table wines which are made from Sylvaner, Riesling, Pinot Noir, Pinot Blanc, Carignan, Concorde and Delaware vines (the last two being American varieties).

Y

Y   A dry wine produced by Château d'Yquem★ which is a good deal less expensive than the sumptuous sweet white wine made by the same château.

yeasts   One-celled micro-organisms responsible for turning grape juice into wine through the process of alcoholic fermentation★. The yeasts exist naturally on the skin of the grape or are trapped there by the bloom★. Thus alcoholic fermentation is often spontaneous and the role of the vigneron consists of observing the yeasts at work and making sure they have a favourable atmosphere.

There are several families of yeasts which work in different ways during the course of fermentation. Some can work at a low temperature, but a good fermentation point is between 25 and 28°C, which explains why it is necessary to reheat or cool the must depending on the climate.

The yeasts are slowly killed by the alcohol produced during the course of fermentation and their activity comes to a halt when the alcohol level reaches 15°.

This characteristic is utilised in the mutage★ by alcohol of vins doux naturels.

The role of the yeast is not wholly confined to converting sugar into alcohol. The yeasts also attack other substances and create amino acids, glycerine, ethers and aldehydes. These elements give each wine its special character and aroma. For example, a special species of yeast gives vins de flor their particular taste.

YEASTS (SELECTED)   Yeast cultures are sold under the name of famous viticultural areas, e.g. Burgundy, Beaujolais, Champagne, which are thought to give the particular characteristics of the wines of these regions. However, in reality, each grape variety and patch of soil has a complex mixture of yeasts in unknown proportions which there is no known way of calculating or reproducing.

If wines treated with the aforementioned yeasts seem to have the characteristics of the said wines during the first few weeks, these qualities tend to diminish rapidly. It is better to assure a good

fermentation with a good cuve base. The selected yeasts are best used in the case of defective white grapes which, after the necessary addition of sulphur dioxide★, need the added yeasts to ensure that fermentation begins and is maintained.

young This adjective takes on a different sense depending on the wine to which it is applied. If the wine is capable of maturing, it is called young or very young when it has not unfolded its qualities. If the wine has reached a certain age and is still lively and fruity it is also said to be young.

Certain wines should be drunk young as

and some rare Chiantis. A young wine is not a vin de primeur★.

Yquem (Château-d') Words can hardly do justice to this magnificent wine of Sauternes★, the most famous sweet white wine in the world. The estate belongs to the Lur-Saluces family, who have supervised production of the wine for over two centuries. Château d'Yquem has a rich golden colour, a delicately fragrant aroma and an incomparable smoothness. Its quality is never less than perfect. In poor years the wine is simply sold under a regional appellation, i.e. Sauternes.

Château d'Yquem and its vineyards. Phot. M.

they acquire their personality and qualities very quickly and will not develop any further. It is therefore futile, even harmful, to conserve these wines for a long period.

The following wines should be drunk (generally) at around three and certainly before five years: all rosés, the dry whites of the Loire and Alsace, the white Burgundies, except the great appellations, the white Bordeaux, except the liquoreux and the Graves of good years, and the majority of white wines, with some exceptions. Red wines of good appellation should be conserved, except for some poor years. Nearly all the other reds can be drunk young, except in exceptional years, as well as Italian wines except the great reds from the Nebbiolo (Barolo, Gattinara, Barbaresco)

Yugoslavia The vine is found in all parts of this country, which is at the same latitude as Italy. Although total production is around six million litres, the wines never exceed the vin de pays★ level as far as quality is concerned. The following six republics contain important viticultural areas.

Serbia has vineyards in the Danube and Morava valleys, on the slopes of the Vojvodine and in the south. The Danube valley produces the Fruška Gora, an agreeable white wine, a table wine around Smederevo called the Smederevska and a dessert wine, the Smederevska Malaga. The Morava valley produces a white wine called Sicévacko around Negotin and Bagren, and Zupsko, a white or very fine rosé which is a speciality of Alexandrovac.

Ružica is made in the Danube valley as an agreeable rosé and in Morava as a red. Finally, Vojvodine near Subotica on the Hungarian frontier produces the Rizling (Riesling) of Kraljev Berg.

Dalmatia produces two fruity wines around Mostar: the red Blatina and the full-bodied, dry, white Zilavka. It is also known for Prošek, a sweet, alcoholic red or white dessert wine, and Ružica, a rosé.

Slovenian viticulture used to be famous but is quickly dying out. The remaining vineyards are found in Istrie in the Drave valley where Bizelj and Cirček are produced for local consumption. Four wines are produced around Lutomer: Lutomer Riesling, Sylvanac, Traminac and Moslavac.

Macedonian vineyards are found throughout this republic, including the forest areas, and it is becoming an important viticultural area. The wines fit somewhere between those of the Mediterranean and Central European areas. The red wines are made from several grapes of which the Serbian Prokupac is considered the national variety. It gives a rich, fleshy wine. The white wines are made from Zilavartea and Smerderevka grapes, the latter producing a quality wine in the Smederevo zone of Serbia. Macedonia also produces rosés and dessert wines.

Montenegro vines are cultivated on the hills and valleys of the Adriatic Coast in this mountainous country.

Croatia devotes only 5% of its area to viticulture. The best wines are found in Dalmatia and in the Save valley around Brod, Daruvar, Moslavina and Zagreb. The charming, slightly tart wines of the Save valley include Daruvar, Ivan Zelina and Okić-Plješivica. The Bermet and Karlovački Rizling are made around Karlovac.

Z

Zwicker A white Alsatian wine made from a blend of the must of different grapes, including noble★ varieties. The base is generally the Chasselas to which the Sylvaner is often added. The fact that it is a blended wine does not make the Zwicker a mediocre one, as the local viticultural syndicates demand certain standards of quality.

The Zwicker is a beautiful carafe wine, supple, light and easily drunk, but it lacks great character.

THE VINEYARDS OF FRANCE

Outstanding vineyards

Secondary vineyards

Northern limit
of viticulture

CHAMPAGNE
C. DE MOSELLE
Aÿ Verzy
Épernay
Vertus
Barr
Thomery
GÂTINAIS
Bar AUBE
Ribeauvillé
ALSACE
LOIRE
ANJOU Vouvray
Chablis
Saumur TOURAINE Sancerre Pouilly
Muscadet
BURGUNDY
Beaune
Arbois
POITOU
St-Pourçain
Mâcon
JURA
AUVERGNE Beaujolais
Chanturgue
Seyssel
SAVOIE
CHARENTES
Apremont GRAISIVAUDAN
BORDELAIS
St-Émilion
CÔTES DU RHÔNE L'Hermitage
Monbazillac Die
Sauternes
Moissac
CORSICA
GARONNE Gaillac Châteauneuf-du-Pape
ARMAGNAC LANGUEDOC PROVENCE
BÉARN
Sartène Jurançon Béziers
Limoux
ROUSSILLON
Banyuls

0   100   200
km

BORDEAUX WINES

Classification of the crus of the Médoc

This is the official classification which dates from 1855. The wines are listed in each category, not in alphabetical or geographical order but according to merit. This classification has been the object of much criticism. Some wish to preserve it as it is, while others would change it completely. A third group favour a two-tier system in which the old classification would be treated as a historical souvenir and a new, flexible hierarchy would be created to exist parallel with the old one. This new classification could be examined each year and wines would move up or down depending on their quality that year. Wines would have a chance of promotion, a move which would have benefited Mouton-Rothschild which was only recently reclassified as a premier cru under the present system, a position it shares with Lafite-Rothschild, Margaux and Latour.

CHATEAUX	COMMUNES		
Premiers crus		*Deuxièmes crus*	
		Rausan-Ségla	Margaux
Lafite-Rothschild	Pauillac	Rauzan-Gassies	Margaux
Margaux	Margaux	Léoville-Las-Cases	Saint-Julien
Latour	Pauillac	Léoville-Poyferré	Saint-Julien
Mouton-Rothschild	Paulliac	Léoville-Barton	Saint-Julien
Haut-Brion	Pessac, Graves	Durfort-Vivens	Margaux

CHATEAUX	COMMUNES
Gruaud-Larose	Saint-Julien
Lascombes	Margaux
Brane-Cantenac	Cantenac
Pichon-Longueville (Baron)	Pauillac
Pichon-Longueville (Comtesse-de-Lalande-)	Pauillac
Ducru-Beaucaillou	Saint-Julien
Cos-d'Estournel	Saint-Estèphe
Montrose	Saint-Estèphe

Troisièmes crus

Kirwan	Cantenac
Issan	Cantenac
Lagrange	Saint-Julien
Langoa	Saint-Julien
Giscours	Labarde
Malescot-Saint-Exupéry	Margaux
Cantenac-Brown	Cantenac
Boyd-Cantenac	Margaux
Palmer	Cantenac
La Lagune	Ludon
Desmirail	Margaux
Calon-Ségur	Saint-Estèphe
Ferrière	Margaux
Marquis-d'Alesme-Becker	Margaux

Quatrièmes crus

Saint-Pierre-Sevaistre	Saint-Julien
Saint-Pierre-Bontemps	Saint-Julien
Talbot	Saint-Julien

Branaire-Ducru	Saint-Julien
Duhart-Milon	Pauillac
Pouget	Cantenac
La Tour-Carnet	Saint-Laurent
Rochet	Saint-Estèphe
Beychevelle	Saint-Julien
Le Prieuré	Cantenac
Marquis-de-Terme	Margaux

Cinquièmes crus

Pontet-Canet	Pauillac
Batailley	Pauillac
Haut-Batailley	Pauillac
Grand-Puy-Lacoste	Pauillac
Grand-Puy-Ducasse	Pauillac
Lynch-Bages	Pauillac
Lynch-Moussas	Pauillac
Dauzac	Labarde
Mouton-Baron-Philippe (called Mouton-d'Armailhacq since 1956)	Pauillac
Le Tertre	Arsac
Haut-Bages-Libéral	Pauillac
Pédesclaux	Pauillac
Belgrave	Saint-Laurent
Camensac	Saint-Laurent
Cos-Labory	Saint-Estèphe
Clerc-Milon	Pauillac
Croizet-Bages	Pauillac
Cantemerle	Macau

Classification of the crus of Sauternes and Barsac

This official classification dates from 1855 (see classification of 1855).

Grand Premier cru

Yquem	Sauternes

Premiers crus

La Tour-Blanche	Bommes
Lafaurie-Peyraguey	Bommes
Clos Haut-Peyraguey	Bommes
Rayne-Vigneau	Bommes
Suduiraut	Preignac
Coutet	Barsac
Climens	Barsac
Guiraud	Sauternes
Rieussec	Fargues
Rabaud-Sigalas	Bommes
Rabaud-Promis	Bommes

Deuxièmes crus

Myrat	Barsac
Doisy-Dubroca	Barsac
Doisy-Daëne	Barsac
Doisy-Védrines	Barsac
Arche	Sauternes
Arche-Lafaurie	Sauternes
Filhot	Sauternes
Broustet	Barsac
Nairac	Barsac
Caillou	Barsac
Suau	Barsac
De-Malle	Preignac
Romer-Lafon	Fargues
Lamothe-Bergey	Sauternes
Lamothe-Espagnet	Sauternes

Classification of the crus of Saint-Emilion

A century passed after the classification of 1855 before the wines of Saint-Emilion were ranked. After consultation with producers and the consent of the Institut National des Appellations d'Origine, the decree of 7th October, 1954 established the following classification for the crus based on their quality and reputation:

Saint-Emilion; Saint-Emilion Grand Cru; Saint-Emilion Grand Cru classé; Saint-Emilion Premier Grand Cru classé.

Although Château Ausone and Château Cheval-Blanc were classified 'Premier Grand Cru classé' they are considered as a special category.

CHATEAUX	CHATEAUX
Premiers Grands Crus classés	
A	
Ausone	Cheval-Blanc

B	
Beauséjour	Figeac
Beauséjour-Fagouet	La Gaffelière-Naudes
Bélair	Magdelaine
Canon	Pavie
Clos Fourtet	Trottevieille

Grands Crus classés

L'Angélus	Canon-la-Gaffelière
L'Arrosée	Cap-de-Mourlin
Balestard-la-Tonnelle	La Carte
Bellevue	Chapelle-Madeleine
Bergat	Le Châtelet
Cadet-Bon	Chauvin
Cadet-Piola	Clos des Jacobins
Clos la Madeleine	Lamarzelle
Clos Saint-Martin	Larmande
La Clotte	Laroze
La Cluzière	Lasserre
Corbin	Mauvezin
Corbin-Michotte	Moulin-du-Cadet
La Couspaude	Pavie-Decesse
Coutet	Pavie-Macquin

Le Couvent	Pavillon-Cadet
Croque-Michotte	Petit-Faurie-de-Souchard
Curé-Bon	Petit-Faurie-de-Soutard
La Dominique	Le Prieuré
Fonplégade	Ripeau
Fonroque	Sansonnet
Franc-Mayne	Saint-Georges-Côte-Pavie
Grand-Barrail-la-Marzelle-Figeac	Soutard
Grand-Corbin-d'Espagne	Tertre-Daugay
Grand-Corbin-Pécresse	La Tour-du-Pin-Figeac
Grand-Mayne	La Tour-Figeac
Grand-Pontet	Trimoulet
Grandes-Murailles	Trois-Moulins
Guadet-Saint-Julien	Troplong-Mondot
Jean-Faure	Villemaurine
Larcis-Ducasse	Yon-Figeac

Classification of Graves

The châteaux of Graves were ignored in the classification of 1855, except for Château Haut-Brion, which was ranked as a premier cru in company with the Médocs. In 1953 the Institut National des Appellations d'Origine officially classified the crus of Graves. This was confirmed by the Order of 16th February, 1959.

Premier Cru classified in 1855

Château Haut-Brion (Pessac)

Crus classified in 1959

CHATEAUX	COMMUNES
White Graves	
Carbonnieux	Léognan
Domaine de Chevalier	Léognan
Couhins	Villenave-d'Ornon
Olivier	Léognan
Laville-Haut-Brion	Talence
Bouscaut	Cadaujac
Latour-Martillac	Martillac
Malartic-Lagravière	Léognan

Red Graves	
La Mission-Haut-Brion	Talence
Haut-Bailly	Léognan
Domaine de Chevalier	Léognan
Carbonnieux	Léognan
Malartic-Lagravière	Léognan
Latour-Martillac	Martillac
Latour-Haut-Brion	Talence
Smith-Haut-Lafitte	Martillac
Olivier	Léognan
Bouscaut	Cadaujac
Fieuzal	Léognan
Pape-Clément	Pessac

Classification of the crus of Pomerol

No official classification of the wines of Pomerol exists. However, Château Pétrus is traditionally ranked first and the principal châteaux are more or less classified in the following order :

Premiers Grands crus

Château Pétrus	Ch. Gazin
Ch. Certan	Ch. Petit-Village
Vieux-Château-Certan	Ch. Trotanoy
Ch. la Conseillante	Ch. l'Evangile
Ch. Lafleur	Ch. la Fleur-Pétrus

Premiers crus

Dom. de l'Église	Ch. la Pointe
Ch. la Croix-de-Gay	Ch. Gombaude-Guillot
Ch. la Grave-Trigant-de-Boisset	Ch. Guillot
Clos l'Église	Ch. l'Église-Clinet
Ch. Latour-Pomerol	Ch. le Gay
Ch. Beauregard	Ch. la Grange
Ch. Certan-Marzelle	Ch. la Vraye-Croix-de-Gay
Ch. Clinet	Ch. Rouget
Ch. Nénin	

Deuxièmes Premiers crus

Ch. la Commanderie	Clos du Clocher

Ch. la Croix-Saint-Georges	Ch. Lacabane
Ch. la Croix	Ch. Moulinet
Ch. Plince	Clos René
Ch. de Salles	Dom. Haut-Tropchaud
Ch. Bourgneuf	Ch. Pignon-de-Gay
Ch. le Caillou	Clos Beauregard
Ch. l'Enclos	Dom. de Haut-Pignon
Enclos du Presbytère	Ch. Cantereau
Ch. Gratte-Cap	Ch. Mazeyres
Dom. de Tropchaud	Ch. Taillefer
Ch. la Violette	Ch. du Chêne-Liège
Ch. Lafleur-du-Gazin	

Deuxièmes crus

Ch. Bel-Air	Ch. Haut-Maillet
Ch. la Croix-Taillefer	Ch. Couprie
Ch. Ferrand	Ch. Franc-Maillet
Dom. de Mazeyres	Ch. Thibaud-Maillet
Enclos du Haut-Mazeyres	Ch. Hautes-Rouzes
Clos des Templiers	

CLIMATS OF BURGUNDY

It is not possible to rank the vineyards of Burgundy with such precision as those of Bordeaux. On the Côte-d'Or and at Chablis most of the vineyards are divided among a number of owners (more than sixty proprietors, for example, have a share of the famous Clos de Vougeot!). Well before the modern system of Appellations d'Origine Contrôlées an authoritative and exhaustive listing and classification of the crus was published in 1861 by the 'Comité d'Agriculture de l'Arrondissement de Beaune'.

The following list is inevitably incomplete. There are 419 climats recognised in the Côte de Nuits and twice as many in the Côte de Beaune! Although not official, the list mentions most of the 'climats' which the wine-lover is likely to encounter in more or less the order accepted by the majority of experts.

COMMUNES	CLIMATS
Côte de Nuits	
Fixin	Clos de la Perrière
	Les Hervelets
	Clos du Chapitre
	Les Arvelets
	Clos Napoléon
Gevrey-Chambertin	CHAMBERTIN
	CHAMBERTIN-CLOS DE BÈZE
	Charmes – Chambertin
	and Mazoyères – Chambertin
	Chapelle
	Griotte
	Latricières
	Mazis
	Ruchottes
	Clos Saint-Jacques
	Les Véroilles
	Aux Combottes
	Cazetiers
	Combe-aux-Moines
	Estournelles
	Lavaut
Morey-Saint-Denis	BONNES-MARES (a part)
	Clos de Tart
	Clos de la Roche
	Clos Saint-Denis
	Clos des Lambrays
Chambolle-Musigny	MUSIGNY
	BONNES-MARES (a part)
	Les Amoureuses
	Les Charmes
	Les Baudes
	Les Cras
	Derrière-la-Grange
	Les Fuées
Vougeot	CLOS DE VOUGEOT
	Le Clos Blanc-de-Vougeot
	Les Petits-Vougeots
Vosne-Romanée	ROMANÉE-CONTI
(and Flagey-Échezeaux)	RICHEBOURG
	LA TÂCHE
	ROMANÉE-SAINT-VIVANT
	ROMANÉE
	GRANDS-ÉCHEZEAUX

ÉCHEZEAUX	
Les Malconsorts	
Les Beaux-Monts	
Les Perdrix	
Clos de la Maréchale	
Clos des Argillières	
Clos des Corvées	
Clos des Forêts	
Les Argilats	
Côte de Beaune	
Aloxe-Corton	
(Ladoix and parts of	
Pernand-Vergelesses)	CORTON
	CORTON-CHARLEMAGNE
	CORTON-BRESSANDES
	CORTON-CLOS DU ROI
	Les Maréchaudes
	En Pauland
	Les Valozières
	Les Chaillots
	Les Perrières
	Les Meix
	Les Chaumes
	La Vigne-au-Saint
	Les Languettes
	Les Grèves
	Les Fiètres
	Les Fournières
	Les Renardes
Pernand-Vergelesses	
	Ile des Vergelesses
Savigny-lès-Beaune	Aux Vergelesses
	Les Marconnets
	La Dominode
	Les Jarrons
	Les Lavières
	Les Gaudichots
	Les Suchots
	La Grande-Rue
	Aux Brûlées
	Les Reignots
	Clos des Réas
Nuits-Saint-Georges	
(and Prémeaux)	Les Saint-Georges
	Les Vaucrains
	Les Pruliers

	Les Cailles
	Les Porets
	La Perrière
	Les Thorey
	Les Murgers
	Les Boudots
	Les Cras
	La Richemone
	Les Didiers
Beaune	Grèves
	Fèves
	Clos des Mouches
	Les Bressandes
	Marconnets
	Clos du Roi
	Champimonts
	Les Avaux
	Les Cras
	Clos de la Mousse
	Aigrots
	Les Cent-Vignes
	Les Theurons
	Les Sizies
	Toussaints
Pommard	Rugiens
	Épenots
	Rugiens-Hauts
	Petits-Épenots
	Clos Blanc
	Les Pézerolles
	Clos de la Commaraine
	Les Arvelets
	Les Boucherottes
	Les Argillières
	Les Charmots
	La Chanière
	Les Saussiles
	Les Chaponières
	Clos Micot
	Les Chanlins-Bas
	La Platière
	Les Fremiers
	Les Bertins
	Les Croix-Noires
	Les Poutures
	Les Combes-Dessus
	Clos du Verger
Volnay	CAILLERETS

266

	CHAMPANS
	Les Angles
	Clos des Ducs
	Fremiets
	Chevret
	Les Mitans
	Clos des Chênes
	Les Santenots
	Les Brouillards
	En l'Ormeau
	Carelle-sous-la-Chapelle
	Pointe-d'Angles
	Ronceret
	Bousse-d'Or
	En Verseuil
Meursault	PERRIÈRES
	GENEVRIÈRES
	CHARMES
	La Pièce-sous-le-Bois
	Les Santenots
	Le Poruzot
	Goutte-d'Or
	Les Bouchères
	Les Petures
	Les Cras
	La Jennelotte
	Sous-le-Dos-d'Ane
Puligny-Montrachet	
	MONTRACHET (a part)
	CHEVALIER-MONTRACHET
	BÂTARD MONTRACHET
	(a part)
	BIENVENUES-BÂTARD- MONTRACHET
	Les Combettes
	Les Pucelles
	Les Folatières
	Les Chalumeaux
	Le Cailleret
	Clavoillon
	Champ-Canet
	La Garenne
	Sous-le-Puits
	Hameau-de-Blagny
	Les Referts
	Les Levrons
Chassagne-Montrachet	
	MONTRACHET (a part)
	BÂTARD-MONTRACHET

	(a part)
	CRIOTS-BÂTARD-MONTRACHET
	Les Ruchottes
	Cailleret
	Morgeot
	Les Chenevottes
	La Boudriotte
	Les Macherelles
	Les Vergers
	Clos Saint-Jean
	La Maltroie
	La Romanée
Santenay	Les Gravières
	La Comme
	Clos de Tavanne
	Beauregard
	Beaurepaire
	La Maladière
	Le Passe-Temps

Côte Chalonnaise

Mercurey	Clos du Roi
	Les Voyens
	Les Fourneaux
	Les Montaigus
	Les Combins
	Clos Marcilly
Givry	Clos Saint-Pierre
	Clos Saint-Paul
	Clos Salomon
	Clos du Cellier-aux-Moines
Rully	Margotey
	Grésigny
	Mont-Palais
	Les Pierres
	Vauvry
	La Renarde

Chablis

Chablis Grand Cru	Vaudésir
	Les Clos
	Grenouilles
	Valmur
	Blanchots
	Preuses
	Bougros
Chablis Premier Cru	
	Monts-de-Milieu

Montée-de-Tonnerre
Chapelot
Vaulorent
Vaucoupin
Côte de Fontenay
Fourchaume
Les Forêts
Butteaux
Montmain
Vaillon
Sechet
Chatain
Beugnon
Melinots
Côte de Léchet
Les Lys
Beauroy
Troeme
Vosgros
Vogiros

Chablis and Petit Chablis
To merit the appellation, the wines must come from the twenty following communes: Chablis, Beine, Béru, La Chapelle-Vaupelteigne, Chemilly-sur-Serein, Chichée, Courgis, Fleys, Fontenay, Fyé, Ligny-le-Châtel, Lignorelles, Maligny, Milly, Poilly, Poinchy, Préhy, Rameau, Villy and Viviers.

Beaujolais

The wines from the thirty-five following communes are entitled to the appellation Beaujolais-Villages: Arbuissonnas, Beaujeu, Blacé, Cercié, Chanes, La Chapelle-de-Guinchay, Charentay, Chénas, Chiroubles, Durette, Émeringes, Fleurie, Juillé, Juliénas, Lancié, Lantigné, Leynes, Montmélas-Saint-Sorlin, Odénas, Le Perréon, Pruzilly, Quincié, Regnié, Rivolet, Romanèche-Thorins, Saint-Amour-Bellevue, Saint-Étienne-des-Oullières, Saint-Étienne-la-Varenne, Saint-Julien-en-Montmélas, Saint-Lager, Saint-Symphorien-d'Ancelles, Saint-Vérand, Salles, Vaux-en-Beaujolais, Villié-Morgon.

VINS DÉLIMITÉS DE QUALITÉ SUPÉRIEURE (VDQS)

R: red wine   **r**: rosé wine   **W**: white wine

	types	department of production
LANGUEDOC AND ROUSSILLON		
Corbières	R r W	Aude
Corbières supérieures	R r W	Aude
Corbières du Roussillon	R r W	Pyrénées-Orient.
Minervois	R r W	Hérault
Roussillon-dels-Aspres	R r W	Pyrénées-Orient.
Picpoul-de-Pinet	W	Hérault
Coteaux du Languedoc	R r	Hérault, Aude
Coteaux de la Méjanelle	R W	Hérault
Saint-Saturnin	R r	Hérault
Montpeyroux	R r	Hérault
Coteaux de Saint-Christol	R r	Hérault
Quatourze	R r W	Aude
La Clape	R r W	Aude
Saint-Drézery	R	Hérault
Saint-Chinian	R	Hérault
Faugères	R W	Hérault
Cabrières	r	Hérault
Coteaux de Vérargues	R r	Hérault
Pic-Saint-Loup	R r W	Hérault
Saint-Georges-d'Orques	R	Hérault
LOIRE		
Gros-Plant du pays nantais	W	Loire-Atlantique
Coteaux d'Ancenis	R r W	Loire-Atlantique
Mont-près-Chambord-Cour-Cheverny	W	Loir-et-Cher
Vins de l'Orléanais	R r W	Loiret
Coteaux du Giennois or Côtes de Gien	R r W	Loiret
Châteaumeillant	R r	Cher, Indre
Saint-Pourçain-sur-Sioule	R r W	Allier
Vins d'Auvergne Côtes d'Auvergne	R r W	Puy-de-Dôme
LORRAINE		
Vins de la Moselle	R r W	Moselle
Côtes de Toul	R r W	Meurthe-et-Moselle
LYONNAIS		
Vins du Lyonnais	R r W	Rhône
Vins de Renaison-Côte roannaise	R r	Loire
Côtes du Forez	R r	Loire
PROVENCE AND CORSICA		
Côtes de Provence	R r W	Var, Bouches-du-Rhône
Coteaux d'Aix-en-Provence	R r W	Bouches-du-Rhône

	types	department of production
Coteaux des Baux	R r W	Bouches-du-Rhône
Coteaux de Pierrevert	R r W	Basses-Alpes
Sartène	R r W	Corsica
RHÔNE		
Châtillon-en-Diois	R r W	Drôme
Haut-Comtat	R r	Drôme
Coteaux du Tricastin	R r W	Drôme
Côtes du Ventoux	R r W	Vaucluse
Côtes du Luberon	R r W	Vaucluse
Côtes du Vivarais	R r W	Ardèche
Costières-du-Gard	R W	Gard
SAVOIE-BUGEY		
Vin de Savoie	R r W	Savoie, Haute-Savoie, Isère
Vin de Savoie + name of cru	R r W	Savoie, Haute-Savoie, Isère
Roussette	W	Savoie, Haute-Savoie, Isère
Mousseux de Savoie or Vin de Savoie mousseux	W	Savoie, Haute-Savoie, Isère
Vins du Bugey	R r W	Ain
Roussette du Bugey	W	Ain
SUD-OUEST		
Côtes du Buzet	R W	Lot-et-Garonne
Côtes du Marmandais	R W	Lot-et-Garonne
Vins de Tursan	R r W	Landes
Cahors	R	Lot
Vins de Béarn	R r W	Pyrénées-Atlant.
Rosé de Béarn	r	Hautes-Pyrénées
Rousselet de Béarn	W	Pyrénées-Atlant.
Irouléguy	R r W	Pyrénées-Atlant.
Fronton or Côtes de Fronton	R r W	Haute-Garonne, Tarn-et-Garonne
Villaudric	R W	Haute-Garonne
Lavilledieu	R W	Haute-Garonne, Tarn-et-Garonne
Vins d'Entraygues and du Fel	R r W	Aveyron
Estaing	R r W	Aveyron
Marcillac	R r	Aveyron

LIST OF FRENCH APPELLATIONS D'ORIGINE CONTRÔLÉES (AOC)

R: red wine   **W**: white wine   **r**: rosé wine

ALSACE

	W	R	r
Vin d'Alsace	W	R	r
Vin d'Alsace followed by the name of the grape	W	R	r
Vin d'Alsace Zwicker	W		
Vin d'Alsace Edelzwicker	W		
Vin d'Alsace followed by the name of several grapes	W	R	r
Vin d'Alsace Grand Vin or Grand Vin d'Alsace	W	R	r
Vin d'Alsace Grand Cru	W	R	r
Vin d'Alsace followed by the name of the commune of origin	W	R	r

BORDEAUX

	W	R	r
Barsac	W		
Blaye or Blayais	W		r
Bordeaux	W	R	
Bordeaux clairet or Bordeaux rosé			r
Bordeaux Côtes de Castillon		R	
Bordeaux Haut-Benauge	W		
Bordeaux supérieur	W	R	
Bordeaux supérieur clairet or Bordeaux supérieur rosé			r
Bordeaux supérieur Côtes de Castillon		R	
Bordeaux mousseux	W		r
Bourg, or Bourgeais, or Côtes de Bourg	W	R	
Cérons	W		
Côtes de Blaye	W		
Côtes de Bordeaux-Saint-Macaire	W		
Côtes de Fronsac		R	
Côtes de Canon-Fronsac, or Canon-Fronsac		R	
Entre-deux-Mers	W		
Graves	W	R	
Graves supérieurs	W		
Graves de Vayres	W	R	
Haut Médoc		R	
Lalande-de-Pomerol		R	
Listrac		R	
Loupiac	W		
Lussac-Saint-Émilion		R	
Margaux		R	
Médoc		R	
Montagne-Saint-Émilion		R	
Moulis or Moulis-en-Médoc		R	
Néac		R	
Parsac-Saint-Émilion		R	
Pauillac		R	
Pomerol		R	
Premières Côtes de Blaye	W	R	
Premières Côtes de Bordeaux	W	R	
Puisseguin-Saint-Émilion		R	
Sables-Saint-Émilion		R	
Sainte-Croix-du-Mont	W		
Saint-Émilion		R	
Saint-Émilion Grand Cru		R	
Saint-Émilion Grand Cru classé		R	
Saint-Émilion Premier Grand Cru classé		R	
Saint-Estèphe		R	
Sainte-Foy-Bordeaux	W	R	
Saint-Georges-Saint-Émilion		R	
Saint-Julien		R	
Sauternes	W		

BURGUNDY

	W	R	r
Aloxe-Corton	W	R	
Auxey-Duresses	W	R	
Bâtard-Montrachet	W		
Beaujolais	W	R	r
Beaujolais supérieur	W	R	r
Beaujolais-Villages	W	R	r
Beaune	W	R	
Bienvenues-Bâtard-Montrachet	W		
Blagny, or Meursault-Blagny	W	R	
Bonnes-Mares		R	
Bourgogne	W	R	
Bourgogne clairet or Bourgogne rosé			r
Bourgogne Marsannay		R	r
Bourgogne Hautes Côtes de Beaune	W	R	
Bourgogne rosé (or clairet) Hautes Côtes de Beaune			r
Bourgogne Hautes Côtes de Nuits	W	R	r
Bourgogne Passe-tous-grains		R	r
Bourgogne aligoté	W		
Bourgogne ordinaire or Bourgogne grand ordinaire	W	R	
Bourgogne ordinaire or Bourgogne grand ordinaire rosé (or clairet)			r
Bourgogne mousseux	W	R	r
Brouilly		R	
Chablis	W		
Petit-Chablis	W		
Chablis Grand Cru	W		
Chablis Premier Cru	W		
Chambertin		R	
Chambertin-Clos de Bèze		R	
Chambolle-Musigny		R	
Chapelle-Chambertin		R	
Charmes-Chambertin, or Mazoyères-Chambertin		R	
Chassagne-Montrachet	W	R	
Cheilly-lès-Maranges	W	R	
Chénas		R	
Chevalier-Montrachet	W		
Chiroubles		R	
Chorey-lès-Beaune	W	R	
Clos de la Roche		R	
Clos Saint-Denis		R	
Clos de Vougeot		R	

	W	R	r
Clos de Tart		R	
Corton	W	R	
Corton-Charlemagne	W		
Côte de Beaune	W	R	
Côte de Beaune-Villages		R	
Côte de Brouilly		R	
Criots-Bâtard-Montrachet	W		
Dezize-lès-Maranges	W	R	
Échezeaux		R	
Fixin	W	R	
Fleurie		R	
Gevrey-Chambertin		R	
Givry	W	R	
Grands-Échezeaux		R	
Griotte-Chambertin		R	
Juliénas		R	
Ladoix	W	R	
Latricières-Chambertin		R	
Mâcon	W	R	r
Mâcon supérieur	W	R	r
Mâcon-Villages	W		
Mazis-Chambertin		R	
Mercurey	W	R	
Meursault	W	R	
Montagny	W		
Monthélie	W	R	
Montrachet	W		
Morey-Saint-Denis	W	R	
Morgon		R	
Moulin-à-Vent		R	
Musigny	W	R	
Nuits, or Nuits-Saint-Georges	W	R	
Vin fin de la Côte de Nuits, or Côte de Nuits-Villages	W	R	
Pernand-Vergelesses	W	R	
Pommard		R	
Pouilly-Fuissé	W		
Pouilly-Loché	W		
Pouilly-Vinzelles	W		
Puligny-Montrachet	W	R	
Richebourg		R	
Romanée		R	
Romanée-Conti		R	
Romanée-Saint-Vivant		R	
Ruchottes-Chambertin		R	
Rully	W	R	
Saint-Amour		R	
Saint-Aubin	W	R	
Saint-Romain	W	R	
Sampigny-lès-Maranges	W	R	
Santenay	W	R	
Savigny, or Savigny-lès-Beaune	W	R	
La Tâche		R	
Volnay		R	
Vosne-Romanée		R	
Vougeot	W	R	

CHAMPAGNE

	W	R	r
Champagne			
Champagne rosé			
Rosé des Riceys			r
Vin nature de la Champagne (appellation not 'contrôlée')	W	R	r

CÔTES DU RHÔNE

	W	R	r
Château-Grillet	W		
Châteauneuf-du-Pape	W	R	
Clairette de Die	W, tranquille and mousseux		
Condrieu	W		
Cornas		R	
Côtes du Rhône	W	R	r
Côtes du Rhône (appellation followed by the names of the following communes: Rochegude, Saint-Maurice-sur-Eygues, Vinsobres, Cairanne, Gigondas, Rasteau, Roaix, Séguret, Vacqueyras, Valréas, Visan, Laudun)	W	R	r
Côtes du Rhône-Chusclan			r
Côte-Rôtie		R	
Crozes-Hermitage	W	R	
Ermitage, or Hermitage	W	R, vin de paille	
Lirac	W	R	r
Muscat de Beaumes-de-Venise	W		
Rasteau	W	R	r
Saint-Joseph	W	R	
Saint-Peray	W		
Saint-Peray mousseux	W		
Tavel			r

JURA

	W	R	r
Arbois	W	R	r, vin de paille, vin jaune, vin mousseux
Château-Chalon			vin jaune
Côtes du Jura	W	R	r, vin jaune, vin de paille, vin mousseux
L'Étoile	W, vin jaune, vin de paille, vin mousseux		

LANGUEDOC

	W	R	r
Blanquette de Limoux	W, mousseux		
Clairette de Bellegarde	W		
Clairette du Languedoc	W		
Fitou		R	
Muscat de Frontignan or Frontignan, or Vin de Frontignan	W		
Muscat de Lunel	W		
Muscat de Mireval	W		
Muscat de Saint-Jean-de-Minervois	W		

LOIRE

a) *Nivernais and Berry*

	W	R	r
Blanc fumé de Pouilly, or Pouilly fumé	W		
Menetou-Salon	W	R	r
Pouilly-sur-Loire	W		
Quincy	W		
Reuilly	W	R	r
Sancerre	W	R	r

b) *Touraine*

	W	R	r
Bourgueil		R	r
Chinon	W	R	r
Coteaux du Loir	W	R	r
Jasnières	W		
Montlouis	W		
Montlouis mousseux	W		
Montlouis pétillant	W		
Saint-Nicolas-de-Bourgueil		R	r
Touraine	W	R	r
Touraine-Amboise	W	R	r
Touraine-Azay-le-Rideau	W		

	W	R	r
Touraine-Mesland	W	R	r
Touraine mousseux	W	R	r
Touraine pétillant	W	R	r
Vouvray	W		
Vouvray mousseux	W		
Vouvray pétillant	W		

c) *Anjou*

	W	R	r
Anjou	W	R	
Anjou mousseux	W		r
Anjou pétillant	W		
Anjou-Coteaux de la Loire	W		
Bonnezeaux	W		
Cabernet d'Anjou			r
Cabernet de Saumur			r
Coteaux de l'Aubance	W		
Coteaux du Layon	W		
Coteaux du Layon + name of the commune of origin	W		
Coteaux de Saumur	W		
Quarts-de-Chaume	W		
Rosé d'Anjou			r
Rosé d'Anjou pétillant			r
Savennières	W		
Savennières-Coulée-de-Serrant	W		
Savennières-Roches-aux-Moines	W		
Saumur	W	R	

d) *Pays nantais*

	W	R	r
Muscadet	W		
Muscadet des Coteaux de la Loire	W		
Muscadet de Sèvre et Maine	W		

PROVENCE AND CORSICA

	W	R	r
Bandol or vin de Bandol	W	R	r
Bellet or vin de Bellet	W	R	r
Cassis	W	R	r
Palette	W	R	r
Propriano	W	R	r

ROUSSILLON

	W	R	r
Banyuls	W	R	r, Rancio
Banyuls Grand Cru		R	
Maury		R	
Côte d'Agly	W	R	r, Rancio
Rivesaltes	W	R	r, Rancio
Muscat de Rivesaltes		R	
Côtes de Haut-Roussillon	W	R	r, Rancio
Grand-Roussillon	W	R	r, Rancio

SAVOIE

	W	R	r
Crépy	W		
Seyssel	W		
Seyssel mousseux	W		

SUD-OUEST

	W	R	r
Bergerac		R	r
Bergerac sec	W		
Côtes de Bergerac		R	
Côtes de Bergerac moelleux	W		
Côtes de Duras	W	R	
Côtes de Montravel	W		
Gaillac	W		
Gaillac mousseux	W		
Gaillac Premières Côtes	W		
Gaillac doux	W		
Haut-Montravel	W		
Jurançon	W		
Madiran		R	
Monbazillac	W		
Montravel	W		
Pacherenc-du-Vic-Bihl	W		
Pécharmant		R	
Rosette	W		

THE GOOD VINTAGES AND THE GREAT VINTAGES OF THE PRINCIPAL WINES

The good years are in roman, the great years in bold italic

ALSACE
1900	1911	1915	1918	1919	1920	1921	1923	1926
1928	***1929***	***1934***	1935	1937	1942	1943	***1945***	1947
1949	1953	***1959***	***1961***	1964	***1966***	***1967***	1969	***1970***
1971	***1973***	1974						

ANJOU AND TOURAINE
1900	1921	1928	1933	1934	1937	1943	1944	1945
1946	1947	1948	***1949***	1950	1952	1953	1954	***1955***
1957	1958	***1959***	1960	1961	1962	1964	1966	***1969***
1970	1971	1974						

WHITE BORDEAUX
1900	1904	1906	1914	1916	1919	***1921***	1924	1926
1928	***1929***	1934	***1937***	1942	***1943***	***1945***	***1947***	1948
1949	1950	1952	1953	***1955***	1957	1959	***1961***	***1962***
1966	***1967***	1969	1970	1971				

RED BORDEAUX
1900	1904	1906	1914	1916	***1920***	1921	***1924***	1926
1928	***1929***	***1934***	1940	1942	***1943***	***1945***	***1947***	1948
1949	1950	***1953***	***1955***	1959	1960	***1961***	***1962***	***1964***
1966	1967	1969	***1970***	1971	1973	1974		

WHITE BURGUNDIES
1904	1911	1915	1921	1923	1928	***1929***	1933	1934
1937	1942	1943	1945	1948	1950	1952	1953	***1955***
1957	1959	1961	1962	1964	1966	1967	***1969***	***1970***
1971	1973							

RED BURGUNDIES
1904	1906	1911	***1915***	1921	***1923***	1926	***1928***	***1929***
1933	1934	***1937***	1938	***1942***	1943	1945	***1947***	1948
1949	1952	1953	***1955***	1957	***1959***	***1961***	1962	***1964***
1966	1967	***1969***	1970	1971	1972			

CHAMPAGNE
1904	1906	***1911***	1914	1917	1919	1920	***1921***	1923
1926	***1928***	1929	1933	1934	1937	1942	1943	1945
1947	***1953***	1955	1959	1961	***1964***	***1966***	1969	1971

CÔTES DU RHÔNE
1904	1923	1926	***1929***	***1933***	1934	1942	1943	***1945***
1947	***1949***	1950	***1952***	***1954***	***1955***	***1957***	1959	1960
1961	1962	1964	1966	***1967***	***1969***	1970	1971